HYPNOTHERAPY and HYPNOANALYSIS

HYPNOTHERAPY
and
HYPNOANALYSIS

Daniel P. Brown
The Cambridge Hospital

Erika Fromm
The University of Chicago

LEA LAWRENCE ERLBAUM ASSOCIATES, PUBLISHERS
1986   Hillsdale, New Jersey   London

Lawrence Erlbaum Associates, Inc., Publishers
365 Broadway
Hillsdale, New Jersey 07642

Library of Congress Cataloging-in-Publication Data

Brown, Daniel P., 1948-
   Hypnotherapy & hypnoanalysis.

   Bibliography: p.
   Includes indexes.
      1. Hypnotism.   2. Hypnotism — Therapeutic use.
3. Psychotherapy.   I. Fromm, Erika.   II. Title.
III. Title: Hypnotherapy and hypnoanalysis.
RC495.B76   1986   616.89′162   86-19736
ISBN 0-89859-783-8

Printed in the United States of America
10   9   8   7   6

Table of Contents

II: CLINICAL HYPNOSIS

List of Figures

List of Tables

Acknowledgments

A work like this could not have been written without the hard work of many people who assisted us at various stages of the process. We are grateful to our research assistants, Michael Dysart and Stephanie Morgan, who did an enormous amount of work collecting the many hypnosis and hypnotherapy papers reviewed in this book. Lisa Lombard, Mary Hallowitz, Betty Johnson, Lisa Lombard, and Stephen Kahn were of considerable help in critically reading the manuscript in its near-final stages, making two indices, and, along with Michael Greenstone, proofreading. We are especially grateful to Sarah Skinner for preparing the various drafts of the manuscript on the word processor. Her dedication, insightful editorial comments, critical judgment, and conscientious diligence helped produce good drafts. We are also especially grateful to Estelle Keren, who faithfully tackled the tedious task of putting the extensive references on the word processor and checking, and rechecking, them for accuracy. In addition we want to thank Marushka Glissen for help in this task of checking the reference list against the original published works. Our thanks also go to Eleanor Starke Kobrin for her consistently reliable editing and for expediting publication. Last, we want to express our deepest appreciation and gratitude to our families and friends for their patience and tolerance while we were so deeply immersed in writing this book.

Foreword

This book by seasoned practitioners of clinical hypnosis should be welcomed by all who are already using hypnosis in their clinical practice, as well as by graduate students. Their searches for and summarizations of the variety of methods available have been thorough, and the voice of experience shows in their recommendations for practice. For those not entirely familiar with the possibilities offered by hypnosis, the many detailed accounts of what actually is done will serve as an invitation to obtain training in the use of hypnosis. Indeed, the experiences reported here will provide a head start on accumulating the kinds of hands-on knowledge that otherwise would require years of practice with patients in all their variety.

Scientific hypnosis has made great advances particularly since World War II, both as part of basic psychological science concerned with the understanding of brain, mind, and personality and as a professional skill in which knowledge of hypnosis is used to serve human welfare by enhancing the quality of life for those who have the good fortune to benefit from hypnotherapy and the related practice of hypnoanalysis.

The reader is brought abreast of these developments through the arrangement of the chapters into two sections of the book, with the first four chapters explaining the basics of hypnosis as an altered state of consciousness interpreted theoretically from several points of view. The exposition moves ahead to the therapeutic relationship in the first chapter, but returns then in the next chapters of this first section to treat such basic issues as the depth of hypnosis and the alterations within hypnosis as perceived by the hypnotized person. The next two chapters deal with the art of hypnotizing and the most widely used induction and deepening techniques. One without wide acquaintance with hypnotic lore may well be surprised by the variety of approaches that are available to match the preferences, abilities, and needs of the subject or patient. By the end of this section the authors have introduced the reader to the major aspects of hypnosis and how hypnotic procedures are carried out. In the five chapters of the second section, the reader learns about selecting patients for hypnotic treatment (because it is not appropriate for all who come), how to plan the treatment, and what techniques are available in therapeutic practice, and, in the final chapter, finds a full-length case history of hypnoanalysis.

Because hypnosis *per se* is not psychotherapy, the authors wisely distinguish various ways in which hypnosis can be used in therapies based on different perspectives. The authors make important distinctions among three perspectives on the use of hypnosis in therapy. Briefer hypnotherapy includes two of these: the first described as *hypnobehavioral* perspective, the second as *dynamic hypnotherapy*, or psychoanalytically oriented psychotherapy. The third is *hypnoanalysis*.

The hypnobehavioral therapy is appropriate to some of the simpler conditions in which symptom relief restores the patient's ability to cope, without the therapist's delving into such issues as the emotionalized transference between patient and therapist.*

Dynamic hypnotherapy uses hypnosis in the context of brief psychotherapy as practiced by psychoanalytically oriented psychotherapists and requires that the therapist be sensitive to transference. Here, though, working through the transference may not be essential as it is in hypnoanalysis, the other perspective considered.

Hypnoanalysis is the utilization of hypnosis in connection with the long-term treatment that is usually associated with psychoanalysis. It may use hypnosis as an uncovering technique, taking advantage of the hypnotic condition to supplement the more typical free association technique of psychoanalysis; or it may use hypnosis to advantage as it facilitates ego strengthening in cases of character problems or maladaptive human relationships. Here working through the transference becomes essential to provide the corrective emotional experience upon which therapeutic success depends.

The orientations of dynamic hypnotherapy and hypnoanalysis — central to this book — are avowedly based on contemporary psychoanalytic theory, and the practitioner must understand and be able to use approaches essential to these therapies, independent of hypnosis. That is,

---

*Therapy using the hypnobehavioral perspective is treated in detail in another volume by the authors, on *Hypnosis and Behavioral Medicine* (1986).

hypnosis is an adjuvant, often a highly favorable one, but not always to be recommended. The theoretical background not only includes classical psychoanalysis but shows the influence of many psychoanalytic thinkers since Freud, such as influences deriving from Franz Alexander and Thomas French, the later ego psychology within psychoanalysis of Heinz Hartmann, Anna Freud, and Erik Erikson, and the emphasis on narcissism by Heinz Kohut — to mention but a few of the many cited.

It comes as no surprise that the thorough documentation is shared between the references citing many workers in the field of hypnosis whose work is directly relevant and those who are writing in the context of psychoanalytic theory and practice with little or no mention of hypnosis. The originality of the authors rests in the manner by which they integrate psychoanalytic understanding with the advantages in treatment that hypnosis provides for those already committed to psychoanalytic psychology. The old taboo of psychoanalysis against hypnotic therapy, a taboo initiated by Freud when he turned from hypnosis to free association, has of course been broken from time to time by his followers. In this book we find an able case made for the advantages of integrating hypnosis and psychoanalysis in clinical practice.

Those already committed to therapies based on psychoanalytic assumptions will be prepared to assimilate the new teaching most readily, but at the same time there is much wisdom in this book to appeal to the practicing clinician who is uncommitted to psychoanalytic theory.

Ernest R. Hilgard
Stanford University

Preface

This book was written in response to the needs of many professionals who have sought training in clinical hypnosis. We have tried to fold into a single volume a comprehensive review of the scientific understanding of hypnosis, above all, a detailed account of the typical hypnotic procedures with emphasis on the wording of suggestions, and a rationale for and illustration of hypnotherapy and hypnoanalysis that is well grounded in clinical theory and research. We have included in the book what we have found to be most useful from the many workshops on clinical hypnosis we have taught to professionals over many years.

This book represents 15 years of collaboration, which began while Dr. Brown was a graduate teaching and research assistant to Dr. Fromm, a relationship that was to evolve into a mutually enriching and rewarding colleagueship. It is the outcome of many joint teaching efforts, collaborative research projects on hypnosis and self hypnosis, and numerous discussions of our clinical hypnosis cases over the years. The teaching curriculum that served as the basis for this book was originally devised by Dr. Fromm for her courses at The University of Chicago, The Society for Clinical and Experimental Hypnosis, and elsewhere. This curriculum was modified and refined through clinical observation by Dr. Brown on the various applications of hypnosis to a large number of patients representing a wide range of presenting problems in a diverse patient population at The Cambridge Hospital/Harvard Medical School and in a group private practice of hypnotherapy.

While the book represents all that we have learned from each other over these years, it also represents all that we have learned from others.

No work is written in a vacuum. We have tried to build upon the modern scientific understanding of hypnosis and our understanding of classical and contemporary psychoanalytic thinking. In certain new areas of special application of hypnotherapy, notably the treatment of psychotic and borderline patients and the treatment of post-traumatic stress, we are indebted to our colleagues Elgan Baker, Ph.D. and Sarah Haley, L.I.S.W. We are thankful not only to our teachers and colleagues but especially to our many patients and students, from whom we have learned so much. There has been no greater joy for either of us than to watch a patient use hypnosis to discover coping resources and gain mastery over symptoms, or to watch clinical students and professionals discover the phenomena of hypnosis, assimilate hypnosis into clinical practice, and then grow to become seasoned hypnotherapists. In this respect we hope that this work will serve a new generation of clinical students and their patients.

Basics of Hypnosis

1
The Domain of Hypnosis

WHAT IS HYPNOSIS?

Hypnosis is a special state of consciousness in which certain normal human capabilities are heightened while others fade into the background. About 90% of the population has some ability to enter a hypnotic state. Hypnosis can be combined with any type of therapy: supportive types, behavior modification, dynamic therapy, and others. When combined with dynamic types of therapy, that is, psychoanalytic methods, it is called dynamic hypnotherapy or hypnoanalysis; when combined with other therapies, it is called hypnotherapy. Hypnosis itself is not a therapy, although the relaxation that accompanies it can be beneficial.

The historical roots of hypnotherapy reach back to tribal rites and the ancient practices of witch doctors. Its scientific history begins at the end of the 18th century, with Mesmer. For detailed discussion of the history of hypnosis and hypnotherapy, the reader is referred to Fromm and Shor (1979, pp. 15–43), Weitzenhoffer (1957) and Hull (1933).

Hypnosis as an Altered State of Consciousness

It is generally accepted now that hypnosis is best understood as an altered state of consciousness. Ludwig (1966), who coined the term "altered state of consciousness" (ASC), defined such states as follows:

> . . . any mental state(s), induced by various physiological, psychological, or pharmacological maneuvers or agents, which can be recognized subjectively by the individual himself (or by an objective observer of the individual) as representing sufficient deviation in subjective experience or psychological functioning from certain general norms for that individual during alert, waking consciousness. (p. 225)

Ludwig thus defined an altered state according to subjective experience and altered psychological functioning. Such states can be produced by alteration in sensory input or motor activity, altered alertness, or altered physiology (Ludwig, 1966). In an altered state, one's perception of and interaction with the external environment are different from those in the waking state, and the individual is more deeply absorbed in internal experience. In his classic works on altered states of consciousness, Tart (1969, 1975) essentially adopted Ludwig's definition for ASCs, but more carefully defined the relationship between attention and changes in psychological functioning characteristic of ASCs. According to Tart, a discrete state of consciousness is defined as a "unique, dynamic pattern or configuration of psychological structures" (1975, p. 5). Each discrete state of consciousness is a stable pattern. It takes a certain energy and application of attention to disrupt this stable pattern and to produce a new quasi-stable state, that is, an altered state of consciousness. Attention is especially important in the production of altered states.

Hypnosis meets the criteria for an altered state of consciousness as set forth by Ludwig and Tart. The altered state of hypnosis—the trance state—has been described both theoretically and experientially (Ås, 1967; Ås & Ostvold, 1968; Field & Palmer, 1969; Fromm, 1977a; Fromm et al., 1981; Gill & Brenman, 1959; E. R. Hilgard, 1973, J. R. Hilgard, 1970; Orne, 1959; Shor, 1959) along the dimension of absorption in an unusual experience, the fading of awareness of one's surroundings, and alterations in perception and in cognition.

Hypnosis and Attention

Hypnosis is the skillful use of attention to affect the phenomena characteristic of hypnotic experience and behavior. There have been surprisingly few studies on attention in hypnosis and its central role in hypnosis has only recently been appreciated. Yet, for the clinician, attention plays a critical role in the induction, deepening, and utilization of hypnosis. The task of the clinician is to capitalize on the capacity of some patients to attend selectively to certain stimuli, or to teach patients who are poor attenders better selective attention by means of hypnotic instruction. In either good or poor attenders, the clinician must attempt to enhance attentional skill.

Some have subjectively defined the careful focusing of attention as the ability to narrow attention to a small range of preoccupations (Leuba, 1960), that is, to the suggestions given by the hypnotist and to the development of a "special orientation" to these suggestions (Shor, 1962); others have defined it as a condition of intense concentration on the task at hand (Ås, 1962a). Because attention during the ordinary waking state is usually unfocused, "total attention" enhances the salience of whatever is being attended to at the suggestion of the hypnotist. Such a careful focus may result in unusual perceptual effects (Orne, 1977). Although, in general, responsiveness to cues from the environment decreases (Shor, 1959), there is some reason to believe that careful focus may improve the efficiency of whatever perceptual information is *attended* to. For example, more susceptible subjects show a faster rate of information processing than do less susceptible ones (Ingram, Saccuzzo, McNeill, & McDonald, 1979), and focusing attention has been shown to improve the rate of information processing in nonhypnotic subjects (Beck & Ambler, 1973; Kahneman, 1973).

Related to the careful focus of attention is the ability to resist distraction by internal and external stimuli. Obliviousness to distracting stimuli is commonly reported by hypnotic subjects (Field & Palmer, 1969). More readily hypnotizable subjects seem to have an easier time shutting out distractions caused by both internal and external stimuli; are less distracted by internal intrusions (thoughts or daydreams) when concentrating (Van Nuys, 1973); and are more resistant to distraction by external visual and auditory stimuli when being vigilant (Fehr & Stern, 1967; Graham, 1970; Mitchell, 1976). Hypnosis involves the ability to shut out distractions, although subjects are not usually aware of exactly how they do this (Ås, 1962a). They may become so absorbed in their experience that they don't even think about the need to shut out distractions, even though they are doing it.

Whereas skill in focusing attention and the related ability to resist distraction are essential for the induction of hypnosis, certain additional attention skills are important in determining the quality of the subsequent hypnotic experience. There are at least two types of attentional skills tapped during hypnosis (Fromm et al., 1981; Krippner & Bindler, 1974). One is increased selective focus of attention, usually involving effortful concentration, during which attention is focused on a limited range of stimuli; all other stimuli are considered distractions. The other attentional skill is increased expansiveness of attention, usually associated with effortless receptivity to the contents of the stream of consciousness. During hypnosis, attention may become diffuse (Hilgard, 1965) or expansive (Fromm, 1979). Expansive attention means being aware of a wide range of contents floating by in the stream of consciousness. Depending on the nature of the instructions, the clinician can enhance either selectively focused or expansive-receptive attention, or both alternately. Expansive-receptive attention is more useful in gaining access to internal experience, that is to imagery, memories, and feelings (Bowers & Bowers, 1972; Fromm, 1977; Fromm et al., 1981). Selective attention is more useful in the cognitive strategies needed for solving problems and altering symptoms and behaviors during hypnosis. Inasmuch as both are important dimensions of hypnotherapy, hypnotic instructions should include both aspects of attention.

Attention is so important in hypnosis because it contributes to alteration of both the content and the structure of the experience. Careful selective attention increases salience of the stimuli at hand. Expansive receptivity to whatever occurs in the stream of consciousness opens access to feelings and memories that are usually outside of awareness. Continued application of some forms of attentional skill may destabilize waking consciousness to the extent that a new quasi-stable state, an altered state of consciousness, or a trance state, unfolds (Tart, 1975).

Hypnosis and Relaxation

Hypnosis is usually associated with relaxation. Most hypnotic inductions contain simple, direct suggestions for relaxation, for example, "You are becoming more and more relaxed." Some hypnotic inductions utilize elaborate and detailed protocols to produce a profound state of deep relaxation. The most common of these contain suggestions for alternately tensing and relaxing the major muscle groups in the body (Jacobson, 1938). Another includes suggestions for imagining waves of relaxation throughout the body, carrying relaxation to each area and pushing out tension. Relaxation of the body pertains to the subjective sense of the overall musculature's becoming less tense. During the induction, the person may report some shift in bodily awareness, as if the body were settling into itself.

Suggestions for maintaining an unstrained, tranquil state of mind during induction and deepening often accompany suggestions for deep bodily relaxation. Relaxation of the mind pertains to the subjective sense of mental tranquility. The stream of consciousness no longer manifests itself as a constantly changing and confusing process (James, 1961), but unfolds in an orderly way wherein distinct contents—thoughts, images, body sensations, memories and feelings—appear in a clearly recognizable way. The content may also seem to unfold at a slower rate than in the waking state. The relaxed person might feel a deep inner calm. His or her attitude may be uninvolved but interested, as the contents of the stream of consciousness unfold.

The subjective sense of deep relaxation does not necessarily mean physiological relaxation (Shor, 1979). Hypnosis does not always produce the physiological effect Benson (1975) has called the "relaxation response." Physiological relaxation engenders a decrease in muscle tonus, a slowing of the respiration rate, an increase in skin resistance, increased brain wave synchrony and coherence, and various cardiovascular and metabolic changes. If the hypnotist carefully constructs the induction in a particular way, it is certainly possible to produce the subjective sense of deep relaxation along with a physiological state of relaxation (Edmonston, 1977). But whether or not such a physiological state occurs depends on a number of variables, not the least of which are the individual characteristics of the hypnotized subject and the wording of the suggestions by the hypnotist. A large number of studies on the physiology of hypnosis have been done. The results have been contradictory and thus inconclusive (Sarbin & Slagle, 1979). No reliable physiological concomitants of trance have so far been found. Slight changes in the wording of hypnotic suggestions can influence these physiological variables. Words and phrases like "relaxed," "drowsy," "focus on the breath," "focus your attention" may have unique physiological concomitants. Combining such wordings in a single induction may result in considerable confounding of variables and confuse the physiological picture.

Hypnosis also is commonly associated with change in arousal relative to the waking state. Throughout history, hypnosis has been viewed as a state related to sleep. Many hypnotists suggest sleepiness or drowsiness in their inductions. Hypnotized people often—but not always—spontaneously report feeling drowsy following a hypnotic induction. It is possible, however, to induce an active-alert (Bányai & Hilgard, 1976) or a hyperalert (Gibbons, 1979) state of trance. How? Once again, it depends on the way suggestions are worded. It seems that the human organism is capable of both hypo- and hyperaroused states (Fischer, 1971). Hypnosis can relax or arouse, depending on the wording of the hypnotic induction and the expectations of the subject.

Altered Perception During Trance

In the normal waking state, we actively maintain an orientation to the reality around us. At times, however, our reality orientation is preconscious, not fully conscious. For example, a person driving a car on a two-lane highway may at times be aware of the solid or broken line dividing the two lanes. At other times, the driver may be totally unaware of it or even of the road. Why, then, does he not go off the road? Because he has a stable internal frame of reference to orient himself to the road, even when he does not minutely and carefully attend to external cues. This framework is called the "generalized reality orientation (GRO)" (Shor, 1959). The GRO is a cognitive schema in the background of awareness that allows us to go "beyond the information given" (Brunner, 1973) at any moment of perception so as to maintain our orientation to reality.

The GRO is not maintained, however, in sleep and during hypnosis. Good hypnotic subjects are able to relinquish their GRO. During trance, one's perception of reality is altered. Hypnotized people usually report less awareness of, or responsiveness to, the immediate surroundings. They may register external sounds but find them less distracting, or they may fail consciously to "hear" sounds that otherwise would be distracting, like a jet plane flying overhead or an ashtray crashing to the floor. If their eyes are open, they may see nothing but a small object placed right in front of them or may report being detached from the surroundings or less concerned with the changing events around them than they would be in the waking state. They are likely to be less attentive to peripheral details of external visual and auditory stimuli (Graham & Evans, 1977; Smyth & Lowy, 1983). In deep states of trance, most subjects are oblivious of their surroundings. They are, instead, preoccupied with or absorbed in their own imagery and in the content of the given suggestions. The imagery and the content of suggestions given become an encompassing reality to the person in trance.

In deep states of trance, inhibition of higher cognitive interpretations of sensory processes can occur, with or without suggestion, in the form of sensory changes, visual, auditory, olfactory, and gustatory hallucinations, and analgesia. Suggested hallucinations, which occur only in deeply hypnotized subjects, illustrate some of the perceptual alterations possible during trance. Some subjects are capable of positive hallucinations, in which they construct percepts for which there are no external stimuli. For example, with open eyes, a subject may hallucinate a cat lying on a chair across the room. The chair really stands there; the cat is a product of the imagination. Expectation effects may play some role in the subject's hypnotic hallucinations, but hypnotic hallucinations cannot be entirely reduced to expectation effects. Genuinely hallucinating hypnotic subjects are consistent in their description of the hallucinated phenomena, whereas nonhypnotizable people, asked to simulate trance and positive hallucinations, alter their description according to the context. For example, genuinely hallucinating subjects see the seat of the hallucinated chair *through* the body of the hallucinated cat they see sprawling on it. Genuinely hallucinating subjects also behave differently from simulators; they shy away from sitting on the chair when asked, or they first shoo away the imagined cat. Simulators do not—they just sit down (Bowers & Gilmore, 1969; Orne, 1959).

Hypnotically produced visual hallucinations like the cat are experienced by hypnotic subjects convincingly and as real and vivid as actual percepts seen in the waking state (Orne, 1959; Sheehan & McConkey, 1982). It is clear that hallucinating individuals do not objectively "see" anything as a result of new external stimuli, yet they interpret available information as if they were "seeing" additional stimuli. People in the normal waking state possess a reality monitor by which they distinguish external sensory percepts (i.e., "real" percepts) from internal imagery. During trance, this reality monitor becomes inhibited for hallucinating persons, so that imagined phenomena like the cat are interpreted as external percepts (Kunzendorf, 1980).

The mechanisms by which negative hallucinations operate also involve inhibition. A common example of a negative hallucination is hypnotic deafness, in which the hypnotized person fails to hear real sounds consciously. Hypnotic deafness is different from organic deafness: hypnotically deaf subjects react to loud tones with increased muscle potentials; organically deaf patients do not (Malmö, Boat, & Raginsky, 1954a). Hypnotic deafness seems to involve an inhibition of the *conscious experience* of the sound while preconsciously or unconsciously the sensory information is still registered.

Hypnotically produced analgesia is related to negative hallucinations. Certain hypnotized subjects can be made to feel no pain or to feel only numbness in the presence of stimuli that in the waking state would be painful. They register the sensory component of the pain and respond to it physiologically, yet do not consciously experience these sensations as pain. In a review of the many experimental studies of pain and hypnosis, E. R. Hilgard (1969) interprets the findings as an inhibition of the cognitive interpretation of the sensation of pain.

A consistent picture emerges from many studies, a picture that discloses an underlying mechanism perhaps common to all perceptual alterations accompanying hypnosis—positive hallucinations, negative hallucinations, and analgesia. The trance state is characterized by a general inhibition of the reality-oriented thinking by which sensory data are interpreted in the waking state. This results in unusual perceptual effects— internal imagery can be experienced as real percepts (positive hallucinations), and external, objective, real percepts may not be consciously registered (negative hallucinations). Whereas visual hallucinations are seldom useful in clinical situations, other perceptual alterations definitely are useful, notably, the fading of the generalized reality orientation and analgesia. Even though few persons manifest hypnotic hallucinations, when they do, it is experientially genuine. Therefore, such distortions in perception characterize something of the "essence" of hypnosis (Orne, 1959).

The Organization of Experience in the Trance State: Time Distortion and Timelessness

In trance, information is processed in ways different from those in the waking state. Less information is processed per unit of time than in ordinary waking consciousness. Hypnotized subjects take in less from the external surroundings because of the fading of the GRO. They are aware only of the voice of the hypnotist and what the hypnotist suggests they should pay attention to. Suggestions are repeated often. The information a hypnotized person processes is both reduced and redundant (Bowers & Brenneman, 1979).

One consequence of the reduction in the amount of information processed is greater efficiency of what is processed. More deeply hypnotizable subjects process information at a faster rate than less deeply hypnotizable subjects (Ingram et al., 1979). Objectively, hypnotized subjects are able to process this reduced information load with greater accuracy and greater attentional skill. Subjectively, what is attended to is the focus of intense interest, so that phenomena are experienced in a new way.

The subjective sense of time is related to the amount of information processed per unit of time (Ornstein, 1970). Since the amount of information processed is considerably altered in hypnosis, it is not surprising that the ordinary sense of time is easily altered in trance. Hypnotized subjects are less accurate than waking people in their estimation of time spans. Subjects may either underestimate or overestimate the duration of the trance state (Schwartz, 1978), though the tendency is to underestimate it by as much as 40% (Bowers & Brenneman, 1979). Because hypnotized subjects lack their usual sense of temporal duration, they are more likely to anchor their time sense to external sources, for example, the suggestions of the hypnotist. They readily respond to a hypnotist's suggestions for time distortion, for instance, to speed up or slow down time. A suggestion may be given in trance, say, that a few minutes of clock time be experienced as if a few hours had passed, or vice versa (Cooper & Erickson, 1959; Kraus, Katzell, & Krauss, 1974; Weitzenhoffer, 1964; Zimbardo, Marshall, & Maslach, 1971; Zimbardo, Marshall, White, & Maslach, 1973).

More important for our understanding of the structure of the hypnotic state, hypnosis affects not only the amount of information processed but also its organization. In ordinary waking consciousness, information typically is processed in a sequential manner and ordered chronologically. Such organization gives us a sense of experiential history. In hypnosis, information is processed differently; it is not processed in a sequential, chronological manner (Schwartz, 1978). The very organization of events is different. Studies on posthypnotic suggestion have shed light on the organization of experience in hypnosis. Hypnotizable subjects may be given a posthypnotic suggestion for amnesia. Upon waking, responsive subjects report little or no recall of the tasks undertaken in hypnosis until they are given the cue to terminate the amnesia. They are then able to recall the tasks, but the order of recall is usually incorrect: the subjects recall the sequence of hypnotic tasks in a disorganized manner. In contrast, while awake, subjects usually recall what they did in a session in the temporal sequence in which they experienced the events. Some researchers have interpreted the disordered recall characteristic of posthypnotic amnesia as a suspension of ordinary sequential information processing during amnesia (Kihlstrom, 1978); others have interpreted it in terms of expectation effects (Spanos, Radtke-Bodorik, & Stam, 1980). Whereas some (Kihlstrom, 1978) believe disordered recall is characteristic of hypnosis only where amnesia is suggested, others believe it illustrates a more general decrease in sequential processing, that is, a dimension of the hypnotic trance itself (Schwartz, 1978). Consistent with the latter interpretation are reports of increased randomization of the hypnotic experience. People in the waking state are usually unable to generate random numbers when asked to give numbers from one to ten randomly. Most people have a natural tendency to structure the numbers into some pattern. Highly hypnotizable subjects, however, generate numbers in a more random fashion (Graham & Evans, 1977).

The trance state involves a partial inhibition of the ordinary cognitive structures involved in information processing—in this case, those contributing to the usual sense of time and the sequencing of events in ordinary experience. The distinctions between past and present experience may not apply during trance. This may help us understand the frequent reports of hypnotized patients that vivid memories occur as if they were happening in the present. Because of the lack of sequential organization of the trance experience, Freud's claim that the unconscious is timeless may be more applicable to hypnosis than has been realized.

Dissociation

Another dimension of the trance state is dissociation. In dissociation an aspect of the experience is kept out of conscious awareness. According to Janet (1925), dissociation occurs when certain pathological contents of consciousness are completely split off from the conscious personality and operate independently. They become available only in trance. In E. R. Hilgard's (1974, 1977) reformulation of the concept of dissociation, dissociation is seen as an extension of normal cognitive functioning. During ordinary consciousness, information is processed by a hierarchy of cognitive operations and controls on a number of different levels. Ordinarily these operations are integrated. During hypnosis, the integration of the levels of processing and cognitive controls diminishes. As a result, certain aspects of experience are no longer available to consciousness. Dissociation is part of many hypnotic experiences. For example, a person in trance may experience automatic writing: His hand writes, but he is not aware of it and has no conscious knowledge of the content of the writing.

In an experiment involving hypnotic analgesia and automatic writing Hilgard (1977) has shown, however, that subjects are still capable of gaining access to the aspects that are dissociated from awareness during hypnosis. Waking subjects report a linear increase in the subjective experience of intensity of pain while immersing their hand in ice water. During hypnotic analgesia, subjects do not report any increase in pain intensity; consciously they are experiencing no pain. However, they still register the sensations physiologically. Subjects can be aware of the increasingly intense sensory input by means of a "hidden observer." While in trance, they can gain access to the physiological registration of pain usually dissociated from experience if the hypnotic situation is set in a certain way. The subjects can be told that the hand will represent the part that may still be aware of the pain on some level. The hypnotized subjects orally report no conscious experience of pain, but they automatically write down numbers representing a linear increase in pain intensity. Although the pain is dissociated from conscious experience, this hidden observer can be used to demonstrate awareness of painful physical sensations. The same can be done with otherwise unavailable painful emotions.

Trance Logic or Tolerance for Incongruity

Another dimension of the trance state is trance logic (Orne, 1959), or tolerance for incongruity (Sheehan & McConkey, 1982). Orne (1959), who originally coined the term, believed trance logic to be a characteristic of deep trance and illustrative of something of the "essence" of hypnosis. He defined trance logic as follows: "It refers to the ability of the S to mix freely his perceptions derived from reality with those that stem from his imagination and are perceived as hallucinations. These perceptions are fused in a manner that ignores everyday logic" (p. 118).

Trance logic involves two simultaneous levels of perception: the accurate registration of reality and interpretation of this reality through rational thinking, and an imaginal experience suggested by the hypnotist that is in contrast with the perceived reality. In trance, the subject is able to tolerate what from the perspective of normal waking consciousness would be incongruous perceptions or logically inconsistent ideas. In each instance of trance logic, the hypnotized subject fails to experience a contradiction, even when confronted with it. From the perspective of the altered information processing that is characteristic of hypnosis, there is no contradiction. A good example of trance logic is the double hallucination. The subject is given a suggestion to hallucinate a person in one location (e.g., sitting in a chair to the right) while the person is in reality somewhere else (e.g., sitting in a chair to the left). Subjects who manifest genuine trance logic perceive the real person and the hallucinated person simultaneously in both places without experiencing any incongruity. Another example of trance logic pertains to the transparency of a hallucination. The subject may perceive the caning of the real chair *through* the body of the hallucinated person.

Perceived Involuntarism

Another dimension of hypnosis is known as involuntarism, which we are renaming here "perceived involuntarism." Hypnotized people often seem to respond passively; they appear to respond to suggestions without volition, in what is known as the "classic suggestion effect" (Weitzenhoffer, 1974). During hypnosis normal, purposeful behavior becomes inhibited, while at the same time a new condition of perceived involuntarism is established. Nevertheless, hypnotic behavior is goal directed (White, 1941), actively and voluntarily directed by the subject (though the subject is not consciously aware of his decision making and voluntarism). This paradoxical combination of subjectively sensed involuntarism and goal-directed enactment constitutes what is known as involuntarism in hypnosis.

In an arm levitation, for example, hypnotized people typically experience the arm as lifting by itself (according to the hypnotist's suggestions), yet it is their own capacities for focused attention and imaginative involvement that cause the arm to rise. Involuntarism contributes to "effortless involvement" (Bowers, 1982) or "non-analytic attending" (Spanos, Stam, Rivers, & Radtke, 1980) during hypnosis, which is similar to the passive volition required during biofeedback training (Green, Green, & Walters, 1970). Nevertheless, hypnotic behavior is goal directed in that hypnotized persons preconsciously utilize various cognitive strategies, as well as imaginative involvement, to realize the hypnotic suggestions (Spanos, 1982; Spanos, Rivers, & Ross, 1977). But such strategies usually operate outside the subject's awareness. To the subject, it seems as if the arm lifts involuntarily when suggestions for arm levitation are given or as if the hypnotist were making the arm lift. Thus, hypnotized people often feel compliant toward the hypnotist and go along with the hypnotist's suggestions, while failing to realize their own (voluntary) contribution to making the suggestions work.

Clinically, perceived involuntarism is a mixed blessing. Intensifying involuntarism in the patient is a way of bypassing the purposeful planning and habitual frames of reference characteristic of normal waking consciousness and deepening the trance experience. However, if the subjective sense of involuntarism is too strong, the patient cannot come to believe that he can learn to cope with his problems. The clinician frequently must remind the patient that all hypnotic experiences are produced by the patient's own capacities of absorption and imagination. The hypnotherapist should not exploit the situation in favor of his own narcissistic needs for grandiosity and power. Perceived self-efficacy is a crucial ingredient in any form of therapeutic change (Bandura, 1977).

The Content of the Stream of Consciousness During Trance

The hypnotically altered state is associated with certain categories of content in the stream of consciousness: imagery, thoughts, memories, emotions, and bodily sensations. Extensive clinical observations of patients during trance (Gill & Brenman, 1959) and the detailed reports of subjects in experiments on self-hypnosis (Fromm et al., 1981) have elucidated the ways in which the content of the stream of consciousness typically manifests itself in trance. Changes in thinking from reality-oriented, sequential, logical thinking (secondary process thinking, which employs mainly the mode of inner language) to preverbal, pictorial, fantasy-full thinking in imagery (primary process thinking) is characteristic of the trance state. Reasoning and critical thinking are to a great extent suspended in hypnosis, and in their place appears much more dreamlike fantasy.

Here are some examples of the content of the stream of consciousness in trance:

Imagery. "I was swinging high on a swing in a dress that swirled around. I would fly out of the swing and twirl into the cloud. The cloud turned out to be a rain cloud, and I fell into the sea. A shark came by, and I held on to its fin. It brought me deep into the sea. At the bottom of the sea, an old, old turtle took me on its back. We swam through the sea. He brought me to a beautiful island. There I and the turtle lay in the sand in the sun. I decided to stay for a while. Then I became a turtle. . . ."

Memory. "(Such vivid memories . . . I haven't thought of these things in years.) I remembered as a child going down the wooden steps to the beach, to avoid the poison ivy, running on the sand, picking sea shells smeared with clay . . . then jumping in the water. I could see the wave ripples in the sand . . . clumps of water grass and brownish-speckled fish. I had such a good feeling. Then I was sitting with the family under a maple tree in front of Uncle Abe's little house. Later I climbed up to my 'branch' in the tree, eating something and looking down at the grownups sitting on Grandpa's homemade log furniture, eating cookies, drinking tea, and talking a kind of Russian Yiddish with a little German and English thrown in."

Change of Body Image. "I decided to fly and centred on becoming a condor. My nose became my beak; I preened my feathers and quivered my arms as wings. Soon I was sailing above some mountains, tense-winged, and flapping every once in a while."

Compared with some other altered states, notably meditation, in which there is little thinking (Brown, Forte, Rich, & Epstein, 1982–83), hypnosis is a highly cognitive process. In self-hypnosis, subjects use primary process cognition actively to invent and create the hypnotic experience, and secondary process thinking to plan self-suggestions and to develop strategies to help themselves go into trance or into deeper stages of trance. In heterohypnosis, of course, subjects use a good deal of their own imaginative thinking, too, that is, imagery that has not been suggested by the hypnotist or that amplifies the images offered by the hypnotist. And they develop strategies and plans for responding to the hypnotist's suggestions (Spanos, 1982; Sheehan & McConkey, 1982); that is, they also use secondary process thought. The subject actively engages in thought processes throughout most of the hypnotic experience. However, he thinks quite differently from the way in which he thinks in waking consciousness, namely, with much more primary than secondary process (Fromm, 1979). Trance is characterized by a considerable increase in the quantity and quality of imagery. Spontaneous imagery readily occurs and is usually experienced in greater detail and with greater vividness than in the waking state (Fromm et al., 1981; Lombard, Kahn, & Fromm, in press).

In addition, memory changes characterize trance. During trance, one is able to gain access to memories not readily available in the waking state, particularly emotionally relevant forgotten or repressed personal memories (Fromm, 1970). Age regression, either spontaneous or suggested, is also characteristic of hypnosis. It does not occur in other altered states (Brown et al., 1982–83). There also is a greater range of affect available in trance than in the waking state. A variety of specific emotions, some unavailable in normal, waking consciousness, are likely to erupt in hypnosis. Emotions are often of great intensity. The hypnotized person may also experience a variety of bodily sensations in trance: numbness, tingling, muscle twitches, pounding of the heart, and the like. Distortion of the body image, for example, changes in its size and shape, or changes in attitudes about one's body, are typically reported (Schneck, 1966a).

These various changes in the ordinary content of the stream of consciousness have important clinical implications. Hypnotized people have access to bodily sensations, emotions, memories, and fantasies that are usually beyond their grasp in waking consciousness. They also tend to think about such experiences in new ways while hypnotized. These factors contribute to the efficacy of hypnosis as an uncovering and an integrative method of therapy.

THE SPECIAL HYPNOTIC RELATIONSHIP

A third dimension of hypnosis is interpersonal relationship. A number of special qualities of this relationship are not fully apparent in initial experiences with hypnosis, especially when the subject is hypnotized in the laboratory for experimental research only. If subjects have hypnotic experiences in the laboratory with more than one experimenter, the interpersonal relationship in general and certainly the hypnotic transference are minimized.

Repeated hypnotic experience with the same hypnotist, however, particularly in a clinical situation, soon leads to a state in which a special relationship emerges. Because the trance state affords greater accessibility to one's internal world, vivid fantasies, personally meaningful memories, and intense emotions spontaneously emerge and increasingly color the interaction. With a sensitive and respectful therapist, they lead to trust and respect, on which a strong therapeutic alliance is built. These repeated experiences with trance also intensify the transference. Due to the greater availability of vivid fantasies, personally meaningful memories, and intense emotions, a special transference relationship develops in which the personal qualities of both the patient and the hypnotist and their respective unconscious fantasies more clearly influence the manifest interaction.

The Effects of Hypnosis

Hypnotic Role.   Hypnosis is a relationship in which people tend to take on a special role (Sarbin & Coe, 1972; Shor, 1962). From cultural stereotypes, most patients have a general view of how a hypnotized person would or "should" act. During hypnosis, particularly during early sessions, patients strive to assume their conception of this role and to act hypnotized. The role of the hypnotized person is further modified by the patient's perception of the hypnotist's tacit cues and explicit suggestions during the induction. For example, a patient who thinks that the hypnotic role involves passive compliance may try to take such a part during hypnosis, as an actor tries to develop a role when acting. A well-developed hypnotic role is more convincing to both the subject and hypnotist, just as a well-developed role in acting is more convincing to the actor and the audience.

Some actors are more talented than others in developing a role. Similarly, some hypnotic subjects are more able than others to develop the hypnotic role during trance. Sarbin and Coe (1972) have studied in detail the factors that contribute to better role development in hypnosis. Good role development depends on an accurate conception of the hypnotic role, as well as on the ability to read the hypnotist's cues to how the role is to be played. Skillful use of attention and imaginative involvement are important in developing the hypnotic role and carrying it out smoothly. The patient's role is easier to adopt, too, when it is congruent with some aspect of his self-image. In addition, the patient needs to be sensitive to the consequences of good and poor role performance and to use such feedback to refine the role. Those who lack these elements of role development experience hypnosis in a way that is unconvincing to themselves and to an observer and in which suggestions are carried out in an erratic, ambivalent, or idiosyncratic manner, not smoothly as defined by the hypnotic situation. For example, in carrying out an arm levitation, patients with poor hypnotic role development will lift the wrong arm, do it in a way contrary to the suggestions, or struggle with it in some other way.

Hypnosis requires not only the performance of a particular role as a hypnotized person, but also a certain depth of participation in this role. Hypnotic role taking is not simply compliant, "as if," behavior. The deeply hypnotized person has integrated the role at a level that involves participation of the total organism, both psychologically and physiologically (Sarbin & Coe, 1972), responds to the role at a nonconscious level (Shor, 1962, 1979), and believes in the role with some degree of conviction.

Communicative Influence.   One feature of the special hypnotic relationship pertains to the type of communication that becomes possible. Whether or not one subscribes to Sarbin and Coe's (1972) theory of hypnosis, hypnosis is certainly a form of communication in which therapeutic change can be maximized. Erickson and his students (Erickson & Rossi, 1979) are perhaps best known for their studies of hypnosis as a form of communicative influence. Erickson was especially interested in naturalistic observation and indirect forms of suggestion. From his observations, he articulated the subtle ways in which social influence is at work in most ongoing communication. Erickson insisted that hypnotists train themselves to become aware of these communicative influences so that they can utilize them in the service of therapeutic change. Much of Erickson's contribution centered on indirect forms of communication, especially the manipulation of ordinary and paradoxical forms of speech. Hypnotherapy is an interaction in which these subtle communicative influences are accentuated for the purpose of altering symptomatic behavior. When the hypnotist is present, the patient is receptive to hypnotic suggestions and may accept them uncritically (Reyher & Pottinger, 1976).

The Here-and-Now Strong Interpersonal Relationship

During hypnosis, a person gains entry to his inner world. The more experience with hypnosis, the wider the access to this inner world of strange body sensations, memories of significant life events, vivid visual images, and elaborate fantasies. These idiosyncratic and often deeply personal fantasies, memories, and emotions color the interaction between the person in trance and the hypnotist: the patient in trance may be surprised or made anxious by their spontaneous, very personal nature; the beginning hypnotist may feel similarly. The relationship may be very intense, and both the person in trance and the hypnotist must learn to become comfortable with this emotional intensity and depth of intimacy.

The Hypnotherapy Relationship

The Therapeutic Alliance in Hypnosis.   If the hypnotist is skillful in inducing hypnosis and offers a series of successful experiences without challenge so that the patient will gain greater confidence in his own abilities, then trust builds in the relationship. Trust grows if the hypnotherapist fosters an atmosphere in which much of the experience emerges from the patient's own inner resources (Eisen & Fromm, 1983) rather than from a preconception imposed by the hypnotist. The hypnotist should be sensitive to the needs of the patient in trance and respect the patient's inner resources. The patient in trance has greater access to his inner world than he does in the waking state, and is likely to disclose deeply personal aspects of this private world to the hypnotist. He is less well defended than in the waking state or before the level of trust has been established through ongoing work, and may more readily share his spontaneous memories, fantasies, and emotions. This sharing creates a certain depth of intimacy in the hypnotherapeutic relationship. The increasing trust and intimacy contribute to a strong therapeutic alliance, but only when the hypnotic interaction is handled with care.

The Special Hypnotic Transference.   For the clinician, the most important aspect of the special hypnotic relationship is the special hypnotic transference. During repeated hypnosis experiences with the same person, as in the clinical setting, a transference develops in which the patient's infantile patterns of object relationships are reestablished with the hypnotherapist (Smith, 1984). The transferential qualities that emerge are evident throughout the clinical material, especially in the patient's descriptions of the hypnosis and the hypnotherapist, and also in the way in which the patient becomes predisposed to respond to the intent of the hypnotist (Sheehan, 1980). The patient is disclosing elements of unconscious fantasies about hypnosis and the hypnotherapist. The hypnotherapist may be seen as warm and nurturant, or hostile and domineering, or competitive. Gill and Brenman (1959) conducted extensive psychoanalytic studies of hypnotic patients and hypnotherapists to discover the unconscious meanings hypnosis had for both parties. Gill and Brenman view hypnosis as a complex interaction between the unconscious fantasies of two people. Most often, the patient's hypnotic fantasies are related to passive, infantile wishes that the hypnotist would take over for the patient, and to wishes to participate in the magical power of the hypnotist. These are the most common themes, but not the only ones. The clinically sensitive hypnotherapist will try to identify the individual patterns of transference for each patient.

Kubie and Margolin (1944) and Gill and Brenman (1959) have attempted to show how the hypnotist's induction fosters transference regression. According to Gill and Brenman, the induction procedure disrupts the normal level of adjustment in relationships and leads to regression. The hypnotist's purposeful limiting of the bodily actions and sensory input, as well as the control of the communication, tips the balance of ordinary relationships in favor of gratification of infantile wishes. Kubie and Margolin believe that the induction recreates the sensorimotor state of the infant with respect to the outside world, through restriction of sensorimotor input and narrowing of communication with the world to communication with the hypnotist, perceived as a parentlike figure. With the relinquishment of the generalized reality orientation, the hypnotized patient becomes more dependent on the hypnotist for negotiation with the external world. The style with which the hypnotist approaches the induction may further stir up a particular form of transference, especially if the hypnotist is domineering or very nurturant in his approach. As Ferenczi (1965) wrote:

> The hypnotist with an imposing exterior, who works by frightening and startling, has certainly a great similarity to the picture impressed on the child of the stern, all-powerful father, to believe in, to obey, to imitate whom, is the highest ambition of every child. And the gentle stroking hand, the pleasant monotonous words that talk him/her to sleep: are they not a reimpression of scenes that may have been enacted many hundred times at the child's bed by a tender mother singing lullabies or telling fairy tales? (p. 177)

Although the hypnotic induction itself may be a "parameter of the therapy" (Eissler, 1958) weighting the transference in a particular direction, the transference is nevertheless likely to unfold according to the salient and repetitive patterns of the patient's object relations unless the hypnotherapist's style is so skewed toward being either domineering or nurturant that it interferes with the natural unfolding of the transference.

It must be emphasized that the transference manifestations during hypnotherapy, although no different in content from those observed in non-hypnotic psychoanalysis and psychoanalytic psychotherapy, are different in their manner of occurrence. In psychoanalysis it often takes many months for the transference to unfold with full intensity and with clear manifestations. The same intensity and clarity of transference manifestations can occur in hypnosis in the initial sessions. Full-blown transference manifestations occur very rapidly, often immediately after induction. The sudden onset of intense and clear transference manifestations seems to be related to the state of trance. The free access to intense feelings and memories that the trance affords in the context of the hypnotherapeutic relationship leads to more intense transference manifestations. These manifestations fluctuate rapidly both during single hypnotic sessions and over many sessions (Gill & Brenman, 1959). Because of the sudden onset of these intense and clear transference manifestations during the hypnotic induction, Kline (1955) has referred to hypnosis as being characterized by a special hypnotic transference. In nonhypnotic psychotherapy, transference unfolds more slowly.

The Realistic Perception of the Therapist as a Person.   Transference feelings in hypnotherapy are extremely strong and develop rapidly, but not every emotion the patient feels for (or against) the therapist is unrealistic and reflective of transference. The patient also, to some degree, has a here-and-now relationship with the hypnotist. Besides transferring onto the therapist his own conflicting feelings towards important figures in his childhood, the patient also sees his therapist as the person he really is: a person who cares for him (or does not care for him), a person who genuinely wants to help him (or, on the other hand, one who is more interested in money than in his patients). Thus, the patient also has reality-based emotional reactions to the hypnotherapist.

This means that the hypnotherapist must expect the patient at times to give him a very honest and sharp evaluation of his own personality or motives. Sometimes he will hear favorable things that are true about him, and sometimes unfavorable ones, equally true. Not all that transpires in hypnotherapy and hypnoanalysis is due to transference (or countertransference). To have a warm, caring, but nonseductive person available with whom the adult patient, *here and now,* can form a mature, real relationship is paramount in therapy. It helps the patient to feel that the therapist really empathizes with his suffering and wants him to become better so he can fulfill his potential and live a happier life.

Because intense emotions often arise quickly in hypnosis, in contrast to their slower unfolding in nonhypnotic psychotherapy, the therapist must be able to make the hypnotherapy a container for intense affective experience. He must be able to do this without the advantage of the preparatory understanding of such affective states gained through watching the material slowly unfold, as in nonhypnotic psychotherapy. Although this may be a mixed blessing, the very intensity can quicken the pace of the therapy. The suggestive nature of hypnotherapy allows the hypnotherapist to structure the experience. Because of the greater availability of symbolic material in trance, the hypnotherapist can also ask for the meaning of intense affective states directly, through dreams and imagery or through free association, and thereby offset the lack of preparatory understanding of these highly affect-laden states. The skillful hypnotherapist is able to turn the very intensity of the process to clinical advantage.

A clear understanding of all the dimensions of the hypnotic relationship is vital for the clinician who wishes to learn hypnosis. Yet, many experienced clinicians who begin to learn hypnosis become fascinated with the hypnotic state, the trance. In their attempts to understand its unusual features—the perceptual changes, dissociation, perceived involuntarism, and nonsequentiality—they suspend their clinical experience. It is very important to remember that the hypnotherapy relationship falls within the traditional doctor–patient relationship. The same ground rules apply—respect for the patient, professional neutrality, consistency of approach, and a real desire to help the suffering patient to grow and learn to cope.

EXPECTATION AND SUGGESTIBILITY

It is generally known that expectation effects, which are manifest in the openness of the patient to the experience and the anticipation of a favorable outcome, are very important in successful clinical outcomes. Hypnosis is certainly no exception. Studies on the placebo effect have also contributed to an understanding of patients' anticipation of whether or not a treatment like hypnotherapy will be successful. There are various kinds of expectation effects having to do with attitude, motivation, and efficacy beliefs (Barber & Calverley, 1962, 1963). Closely related to these expectations, either to the hypnotic experience in particular or to the overall therapeutic context in general, is the issue of suggestibility. Whereas expectation effects pertain to receptivity of the patient toward hypnotherapy, suggestibility pertains to responsiveness to the interventions made by the hypnotherapist. The clinician must always keep in mind how expectation and suggestibility contribute to the overall effectiveness of the treatment. The sensitive clinician will attempt to establish just the right atmosphere to capitalize on expectation effects and suggestibility and thereby maximize receptivity to the healing process (Erickson & Rossi, 1979).

Expectation Effects

The patient's initial attitude about and motivation toward hypnosis is extremely important. Motivation is the willingness to have the experience. The patient who anticipates disliking hypnosis because of fear or lack of interest will not be as receptive as the patient who expects the experience to be interesting and enjoyable. Even more important are the patient's efficacy expectations of the experience. The social behaviorist Bandura (1977) has defined efficacy expectations as "the conviction that one can successfully execute the behavior required to produce the outcome" (p. 193). He believes efficacy expectations are central to all forms of therapeutic change. These various expectation effects contribute to the overall hypnotic effect (Barber & Calverley, 1962). One's belief in being capable of hypnotic experience is an important determinant of the outcome. In the clinical situation, patients who believe, or who through successful initial experiences with hypnosis are led to believe, in their ability to be hypnotized and to use hypnosis to alter their symptoms are more likely to have a favorable outcome. With pessimistic patients, one task of the clinician is to alter their beliefs about hypnosis and the ability to change in therapy. Frank (1962) has shown that for waking state therapies, altering beliefs and assumptions about the symptoms, as well as one's ability to effect change in these symptoms (Bandura, 1977), can influence the therapy in a positive way. The same is true for hypnotherapy.

Responsiveness to hypnosis depends in part on the tasks set by the hypnotist; the manner in which these tasks are communicated also affects the attitudes, motivation, and expectations of the hypnotic subject. To demonstrate the important contribution expectation effects make to hypnosis, Barber and his associates (Barber & Calverley, 1962, 1963) constructed a series of experiments in which attitudes, motivation, and expectations were manipulated. Groups were compared on their performance on such tasks as ideomotor phenomena (e.g., arm stiffness) and hypnotic hallucinations. In one group, a formal hypnotic induction was given; in the other, expectations were manipulated, but no formal hypnotic induction was given. Motivation was also manipulated in a similar manner. Nonhypnotized subjects were told that everyone was capable of experiencing arm stiffness or hallucinations and that previous subjects as well as the experimenters could do so. After such purposeful attempts to alter attitudes, motivation, and expectations, control subjects who were not given a formal hypnotic induction performed as well as those given a formal hypnotic induction. From such experiments Barber has deduced that when people are motivated and expect a favorable outcome, it is possible to produce most, but not all, of the effects of hypnosis, even without a formal hypnotic induction.

Suggestibility

Just how important suggestibility—the responsiveness of a person to the communications of another—is to hypnosis has long been a matter of controversy. Many have viewed hypnosis as a condition of "heightened suggestibility" (Weitzenhoffer, 1957); others have questioned the extent to which suggestibility during hypnosis is different from suggestibility in the waking state (Evans, 1967). Hypnotized people are indeed suggestible, but so are many people while they are awake (witness the effects of advertising). People who are very suggestible in their everyday waking life are also likely to be suggestible when they are hypnotized. Conversely, people who are not very suggestible in waking life may not be more suggestible during hypnosis. Nevertheless, hypnosis cannot be reduced to being merely suggestibility (Hilgard & Tart, 1966).

Whereas expectation effects and suggestibility contribute to a substantial portion of the total effect of hypnotic responsiveness, it is clear that hypnosis involves something more. The formal induction of hypnosis produces an altered state of consciousness, a state in which cognition and perception are altered in fundamental ways (Frankel, 1976; Fromm, 1977; Orne, 1977). This altered state is not accounted for by expectation effects and suggestibility alone. Fisher's (1954) classic experiment on posthypnotic suggestion, later modified and replicated by Orne, Sheehan and Evans, (1968) has convincingly demonstrated that hypnosis entails something more than expectation effects. Orne and his colleagues used one group of highly hypnotizable subjects and another group who were on the lowest end of the continuum of hypnotic susceptibility (nonhypnotizable). The nonhypnotizable subjects were told to simulate hypnotic responsiveness in a manner that would be convincing to, and thereby fool, the hypnotic experimenters. The hypnotist/experimenters proceeded to hypnotize both the hypnotizable and the simulating subjects without knowing who fell into which group. All subjects were then given the posthypnotic suggestion (with amnesia for that suggestion) that for the next 48 hours they would scratch whenever they heard the word "experiment." In Orne's experiment the simulators stopped scratching when led to believe the experiment was over; the hypnotizable subjects continued to scratch "for the next 48 hours." Although expectation effects may have contributed to the posthypnotic scratching of both groups, the experiment was designed in such a way as to distinguish between expectation and genuine hypnotic effects. Simulators respond only to contextual or task demands. In addition, hypnotizable subjects respond to internal cues, following the hypnotic suggestion in a literal manner.

SUMMARY AND CLINICAL IMPLICATIONS

Figure 1.1 summarizes our current knowledge of the domain of hypnosis. Hypnosis involves an altered state, a special relationship, and expectation effects. It is difficult to assess just what portion of the domain of hypnosis is attributable to the altered state, to the special relationship, or to expectation effects it involves. The portion each contributes to the total effect of hypnosis probably varies with each patient. The skilled clinician will take all these effects into consideration in his approach to and induction of hypnosis in the patient. For those patients highly responsive to hypnosis, the clinician can directly capitalize on the special features of the hypnotic state, the trance, with less need to adopt special parameters designed to alter expectations and cultivate the special hypnotic relationship. For patients moderately responsive to hypnosis, a negative attitude, low motivation, or doubt about their ability to be hypnotized may interfere with the manifestation of hypnotic potential. Even though we assume that hypnotic ability is a quasi-stable trait, its manifestation may be less than optimal when expectation is poor. In such instances, special attempts to alter expectation may have to be made, along with continuous utilization of the special hypnotic relationship in a permissive manner, as a means to gain access to the unique characteristics of the hypnotic state. For the least responsive patients, hypnosis may simply not be indicated. If for certain reasons hypnosis is deemed desirable for them, the clinician needs to maximize the therapeutic effects of expectation and waking sug-gestibility as well as to adopt special parameters to facilitate the special hypnotic relationship, while not expecting much contribution from the special characteristics of the hypnotic state.

The Domain of Hypnosis

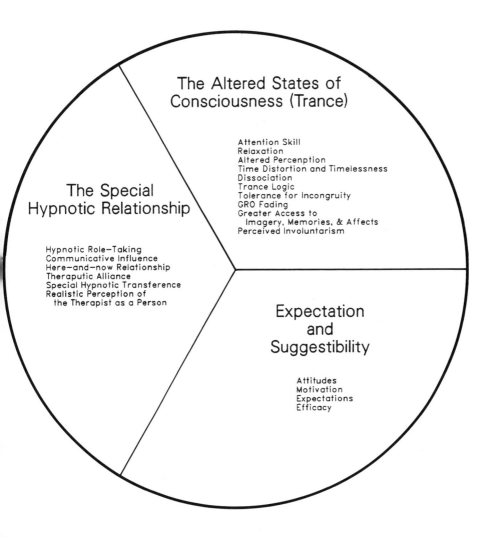

The Altered States of Consciousness (Trance)

Attention Skill
Relaxation
Altered Percenption
Time Distortion and Timelessness
Dissociation
Trance Logic
Tolerance for Incongruity
GRO Fading
Greater Access to
  Imagery, Memories, & Affects
Perceived Involuntarism

The Special Hypnotic Relationship

Hypnotic Role—Taking
Communicative Influence
Here—and—now Relationship
Theraputic Alliance
Special Hypnotic Transference
Realistic Perception of
  the Therapist as a Person

Expectation and Suggestibility

Attitudes
Motivation
Expectations
Efficacy

FIG. 1.1.   The Domain of Hypnosis

2 Hypnotic Depth: Behavioral and Experiential Aspects

How do we know when a patient is hypnotized? How do we know how deeply the patient is hypnotized? The answers to these questions vary, depending on the perspective taken.

The degree to which people become hypnotized is commonly referred to as hypnotic depth, or responsiveness. Hilgard defines hypnotic responsiveness as "the ability to become hypnotized, to have the experiences characteristic of the hypnotized person, and to exhibit the kinds of behavior associated with it [hypnosis]" (p. 67).

Hypnotic depth may be viewed objectively as a behavioral response to hypnotic induction and hypnotic suggestions; for example, arm levitation or moving hands together. Or it may be viewed subjectively in terms of the sense of how deep into the *experience* of hypnosis a person feels he is going at any given time. Unfortunately, observable, objective behavior indicative of depth and subjectively felt depth do not always coincide. It is possible for a hypnotized person to feel deeply hypnotized and intensely absorbed in the hypnotic experience while failing to respond behaviorally to simple ideomotor suggestions. On the other hand, sometimes a subject very successfully performs a series of tasks of hypnotic *behaviors,* but after coming out of trance doubts he has been hypnotized. Although for some hypnotized persons, depth may manifest itself in a more behavioral way and for others in a more experiential way, hypnotic responsiveness involves both a strong behavioral and a strong experiential response, at least for highly hypnotizable people.

When hypnotic responsiveness, or depth, is defined behaviorally—as an observable response to hypnotic suggestions, such as arm levitation—it is the *degree of hypnotizability or susceptibility* that is measured objectively. When hypnotic responsiveness or depth is defined by subjective reports—the subjective sense of being absorbed in the experience or being in an altered state of consciousness—*depth is measured by means of the subjective experience.* Our position, like that of E. R. Hilgard (1965), is that assessment of depth involves both behavioral and experiential viewpoints.

The sensitive clinician both observes how the patient responds and encourages the patient to verbalize the experience of hypnosis. It is important to do this with all patients, but especially so when a discrepancy between observable behavior and subjective experience is suspected.

HYPNOTIC DEPTH AS BEHAVIORAL RESPONSE: ASSESSMENT OF HYPNOTIC SUSCEPTIBILITY

The Distribution of Hypnotic Susceptibility

One of the most powerful preconceptions of patients seeking hypnotherapy is that the hypnotist has special powers. This magical expectation has been transmitted through cultural stereotypes about hypnosis since Mesmer's (1774) claims about the magnetic powers of the hypnotist. Today the expectation of and fascination with the supposed powers of the hypnotist persist, especially in the popularity of stage hypnotists.

These deeply ingrained cultural stereotypes are entirely contrary to the findings of an extensive and sophisticated tradition of research into the nature of hypnosis. Initial responsiveness to hypnosis is due much less to the skills of the hypnotist than to the subject's susceptibility to hypnosis. The skill of the hypnotist is certainly important and becomes even more important as the hypnotic relationship develops over time, but the depth reached in the initial encounters between the naive patient and the hypnotherapist more likely reflects the degree to which the patient manifests hypnotic ability, and, only to a lesser degree, the capabilities of the hypnotist.

Innumerable research studies, especially those with the Stanford Hypnotic Susceptibility Scales (Weitzenhoffer & Hilgard, 1959, 1962) and the Stanford Profile Scales of Hypnotic Susceptibility (Weitzenhoffer & Hilgard, 1963), have made it very clear that there are vast individual differences in behavioral response to hypnosis. Hypnotizability can be viewed as a quasi-stable trait, a trait some people have more of than do other people. Like any personality trait, hypnotizability is a relatively enduring characteristic, which presumably exists independently of whether the person has been hypnotized. However, as with many traits, the degree to which this enduring characteristic is manifest varies with the situation. Expectation, motivation, attitude, anxiety, mood, and rapport with the hypnotist—all exert their influence. To get an estimate of enduring hypnotic ability while minimizing the effects of these other variables, scientists have attempted to restrict the investigation of hypnosis to responsiveness in a neutral laboratory setting with standard hypnotic procedures and a hypnotist unknown to the subject. This situation is, of course, very different from the clinical setting, but it does shed light on the degree of hypnotic ability, which is more enduring and less context bound.

Very sophisticated standardized scales have been devised at the Stanford Hypnosis Laboratory and elsewhere to measure hypnotic susceptibility. The most commonly used are the Stanford Hypnotic Susceptibility Scales, Forms A and C, and a modified version of the Form A, the Harvard Group Scale of Hypnotic Susceptibility. A straightforward way of knowing whether a person is hypnotizable is to hypnotize him and assess the responsiveness in terms of his behavior. Each of these standard scales contains a trance induction and suggestions for 12 hypnotic tasks to be performed. The performance can be observed and objectively scored, for example, eye closure or arm drop. The degree of hypnotic ability is indicated by the number of tasks a person performs in response to the 12 hypnotic suggestions, which are worded and reworded in various ways. On the Stanford scales, only *observable* hypnotic behaviors, not subjective experiences, are scored. The experiential dimension, so important to the clinician, is not taken into account in the laboratory. Nevertheless, despite these limitations or biases in perspective, the standard scales have greatly contributed to our understanding of initial individual differences in behavioral responsiveness to hypnosis.

General hypnotic ability varies across subjects. Hilgard (1965) has been able to show that it is bimodally distributed. In Fig. 2.1, the lower mode describes those subjects whose hypnotic susceptibility is in the low and

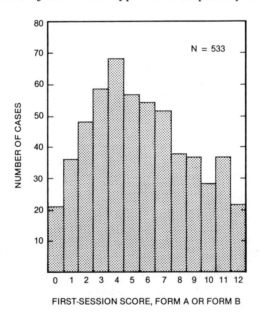

FIG. 2.1.   Distribution of First-Session Scores, Stanford Hypnotic Susceptibility Scale, Form A or Form B.

TABLE 2.1
Revised Norms for Initital Induction of Hypnosis

General level	Raw scores	Number of cases	Percent of cases	Centile equivalent	Standard score[a]
Very high	12	21 ⎫ 56	4 ⎫ 11	98	71
	11	35 ⎭	7 ⎭	93	65
High	10	28 ⎫	5 ⎫	87	61
	9	35 ⎬ 100	7 ⎬ 19	81	59
	8	37 ⎭	7 ⎭	74	57
Medium	7	47 ⎫	9	66	54
	6	50 ⎬ 151	9 28	57	52
	5	54 ⎭	10	48	49
Low	4	67 ⎫	13 ⎫	36	47
	3	57 ⎪	10 ⎪	25	43
	2	47 ⎬ 226	9 ⎬ 42	15	40
	1	34 ⎪	6 ⎪	7	35
	0	21 ⎭	4 ⎭	2	30
		$N = $ 533	100		

Mean = 5.62
SD   = 3.27

[a] Mean = 50, SD = 10.
From: Hilgard (1965), p. 215. Reprinted by permission.

moderate ranges. Considered alone, these people roughly fit a normal distribution curve; the highest clustering is around a score of about 4 out of 12 points. They respond best to simple, direct suggestions, especially when asked to effect changes in motor experience and performance, and to fantasize. The higher mode describes only those subjects who are highly hypnotizable—they have a special talent for hypnosis. In addition to being more responsive to motor items and fantasy suggestions, they also produce the more unusual cognitive and perceptual distortions historically associated with hypnosis.

Table 2.1 shows the norms for initial responsiveness to hypnosis using the standard scales. About 8% of the general population make up the highly susceptible group. The rest of the population varies from low to moderate/high susceptibility. About 2% of the general population is nonhypnotizable, for reasons as yet unknown.

Only moderate susceptibility is needed for most clinical situations. This means that about 60% of all people are initially responsive enough to hypnosis to warrant consideration for hypnotherapy based on susceptibility alone. Of these 60%, 8% are highly responsive. Most of the quick, and lasting, improvements through hypnotherapy are achieved with these highly susceptible patients. With them, one can argue, the gain perhaps can be attributed to hypnosis alone. For the great majority of the population, special parameters usually need to be introduced to maximize expectation of gain and motivation, to develop a helpful transference relationship, and to improve susceptibility through learning so that therapeutic change can occur. In the great majority of all hypnotherapy and hypnoanalysis cases, the therapeutic gain is likely due to the meaning the hypnotic situation has for the patient (i.e., the expectations and the interpersonal relationship with the hypnotherapist) more than to the effects of the hypnotic state itself.

Specific Hypnotic Abilities

There is great variability among both moderately and highly susceptible persons in the types of hypnotic suggestions to which they are most responsive. There appears to be within the domain of hypnosis a number of "specialty areas" within which people manifest differing degrees of talent. Two persons may be equally talented in music, one with the violin, one with percussion instruments. Likewise, two persons may be equally susceptible to hypnosis, but they may be talented in different specialty areas of hypnotic ability, one in imagery and the other in unusual motor effects.

In addition to developing unidimensional standard scales to assess general hypnotic susceptibility, the researchers at the Stanford Hypnosis Laboratory also developed scales to tap a number of specialty areas within the general domain of hypnotic susceptibility: the graded difficulty scale (the Stanford Hypnotic Susceptibility Scale, Form C; Weitzenhoffer & Hilgard, 1962) and the multidimensional scales of various specialty areas (the Stanford Profile Scales of Hypnotic Susceptibility, Forms I & II; Weitzenhoffer & Hilgard, 1963). According to extensive research with all of these scales, the different specialty areas within the general domain of hypnosis are both conceptually clear and empirically supported by factor analysis. These areas are: (a) ideomotor phenomena; (b) cognitive effects (imagery, dreams, hypermnesias, and age regression); (c) persistent effects (posthypnotic suggestions and amnesia); (d) alterations in meaning; (e) denials of reality (negative hallucinations and analgesias); (f) construction of a new reality (positive hallucinations and hyperesthesias). A person susceptible to hypnosis may demonstrate strengths in one or several of these areas while being less responsive in other areas. In clinical as well as in experimental hypnosis, it is important to assess each area of hypnotic ability. The hypnotherapist who knows the strengths and weaknesses of his patient's hypnotic responsiveness can direct his suggestions for induction and deepening to those areas in which the patient has abilities and avoid those in which he is likely to fail.

Ideomotor Phenomena. Ideomotor Phenomena are unusual alterations in motor functioning caused by ideational processes (thinking and
imagination) in hypnosis. For example, a man may think his arm is stiff
and rigid. Such thinking may cause even a poorly hypnotizable subject
actually to experience arm rigidity and be unable to bend the arm; or he
may utilize imagery, imagining the arm in a splint and then experiencing
the stiffness and the arm rigidity. Or a subject might think her hand and
arm are light and buoyant, so light and buoyant that the arm simply floats
up off the table; or she can imagine her arm to be supported by helium
balloons that allow the arm to float up. In each case, thinking about or
imagining the desired effect produces the actual behavioral response in the
motor system. Other examples include imagining the fingers of both hands
to be stuck together so they cannot be separated; imagining an outstretched arm to be so heavy it cannot be held up; imagining the eyelids to
be so heavy that they sink down and close; or imagining magnets between
outstretched hands so that the hands are pulled towards each other.

There seem to be two different types of ideomotor phenomena. The first
involves ideation to bring about a certain motor response, for example, eye
closure, hand lowering, arm levitating. In this type, the hypnotist encourages the subject to experience visual motor effects by thinking about them
intensely or by imagining them vividly. The second type involves ideation
to inhibit motor responses, for instance, finger lock, eye catalepsy, arm
immobilization. In the latter type, the hypnotist first gives a suggestion
inhibiting a motor response and then repeatedly challenges the subject to
break the motor inhibition. He might say, "Your eyelids are *sooo* heavy,
you cannot possibly open your eyes. You won't be able to." After repeating
this a number of times, he says, "Try to open your eyes, *try!* You won't be
able to do so," and the hypnotically responsive person is actually unable
to open his eyes.

Cognitive Effects. A second special area of hypnotic talent is cognitive
effects. For the majority of hypnotizable subjects, hypnotic responsiveness may facilitate access to the content of one's inner world considerably, especially access to imagery and dreams, emotions, and personal
memories. While hypnotized, some people experience a great increase in
the quantity and quality of their imagery (J. R. Hilgard, 1974; Fromm et
al., 1981; Lombard et al., in press). Imagery is more vivid in hypnosis, and
it may have much greater detail than in the waking state. Sometimes more
sensory modalities are involved in the hypnotic imagery. Often spontaneous, unbidden imagery emerges. Hypnotized people may also actively
create and structure their imagery into elaborate daydreams (Fromm &
Hurt, 1980).

To those who manifest hypnotic talent in this specialty area, it is also possible to suggest dreaming a dream somewhat like the dreams one dreams at night. Although the psychophysiology of hypnotic dreams is not like that of nocturnal dreaming, it is more like that in the hypnagogic state (Domhoff, 1964)—in exceptionally hypnotizable patients the structure and content of hypnotic dreams are like those of nocturnal dreams. In less hypnotizable patients, the structure and content resemble daydreams (Barrett, 1979). Dreaming during hypnosis can be a means to gain access to unconscious wishes.

Another aspect of the cognitive area pertains to memory. Many people readily experience a heightening of memory in hypnosis—hypermnesia, the recovery of memories not available through the normal search and retrieval processes of the waking state. The truth of the popular notion that hypnosis greatly improves learning and memory depends on the type of learning and memory in question. There are two kinds of memory: (a) memory for semantic material, such as schoolwork; (b) memory for the personally meaningful, emotion-laden events of one's own life. Hypnosis does not directly improve recall of semantic, intentionally learned material (e.g., nonsense syllables), unless the material is personally meaningful and recalled in its original context (DePiano & Salzberg, 1981; Hagedorn, 1970). Hypnosis can, however, improve semantic memory indirectly; hypnotic focusing of attention may improve encoding of semantic material. Hypnotic desensitization may also remove anxiety, which might otherwise inhibit recall of the material. *Direct recall* of such semantic material is not especially improved through hypnosis, except under special conditions. Enthusiastic claims of hypnotic learning of languages, for example, are unfounded. On the other hand, hypnosis does directly improve the recall of personally meaningful and, often, intensely emotional events from earlier times in one's life. On awakening, the patient may be surprised by the intensity of the hitherto unconscious emotional memories and the persistent impact they have had on his life.

Some people, though fewer in numbers, also have talent for the experience of age regression. Age regression is somewhat different from hypermnesia. It is more than becoming aware of forgotten memories; it is a partial reinstatement of earlier modes of functioning and behavior. Some have viewed age regression as a temporary ablation of adult modes of functioning (Fromm, 1970; Spiegel, Shor, & Fishman, 1945) or the temporary forgetting of adult experience (LeCron, 1948). The age-regressed person more or less returns to the functioning of a child of the suggested age, even including the physiological aspects. For instance, age regression to infancy can sometimes yield infant reflexes, such as the plantar, the sucking, or the grasping reflex (Gidro-Frank & Bowersbuch, 1948; Raikov, 1980, 1982; True & Stephenson, 1951).

Another aspect of age regression is affect regression. During age regression people often experience strong affects and manifest emotional development, wishes, and fantasies characteristic of a child of the age to which they are regressed (Nash, Johnson, & Tipton, 1979). There is a revivification of certain meaningful experiences of the suggested age, and a return to the quality of object relationships characteristic of it (Nash et al., 1979). There also is a similar cognitive/perceptual regression. Adults age-regressed to certain developmental periods of childhood produce cognitive and perceptual responses roughly equivalent to those of these periods (Reiff & Scheerer, 1959). An adult subject, age-regressed to, for example, age 5 and then given Piaget's (1950) perceptual/cognitive test of the Hollow Tube, would produce the childlike, not the adult response. Age-regressed adults may recover a primary childhood language no longer available to them (Fromm, 1970; Sheehan & McConkey, 1982).

Age regression, however, is not an exact reinstatement of the cognitive/perceptual functioning and experiencing of childhood. Age-regressed hypnotic subjects tend to act more childlike than real children and often overplay the situation (Sheehan & McConkey, 1982). They also respond at somewhat higher developmental levels than the suggested age (Crasilneck & Michael, 1957; Fellows & Creamer, 1978; Sarbin, 1950; Spiegel, Shor, & Fishman, 1945). Hypnotic age regression is a *partial* return to the general level of functioning and the type of experience of the suggested childhood age (Reiff & Scheerer, 1959). It is often only a partial return because age-regressed subjects also more or less effectively try to create the regressed experience they think the hypnotist wants them to relive. During any age regression, even with highly hypnotizable subjects, fluctuations between genuine and role-playing elements are typical (Greenleaf, 1969). Sometimes age-regressed subjects report the dual experience of being the child of the suggested age and being the observing adult (Laurence & Perry, 1981). Even though age regression is a mixed experience, the genuineness of at least some elements of hypnotic age regression cannot be denied, and its clinical implications are great.

Persistent Effects: Posthypnotic Suggestions and Posthypnotic Amnesia.

Another specialty area of hypnotic talent lies in the ability to carry out faithfully and persistently in the waking state, after the trance has been terminated, suggestions received during trance. Many laboratory suggestions for posthypnotic effects involve simple persistent behavior, for example, on cue, to scratch, stretch, or cough. Clinical posthypnotic suggestions may involve more complex behaviors, such as to do self-hypnotic practice upon noticing the onset of symptoms. Posthypnotic suggestions may also involve cognitive alterations that facilitate the further unfolding of the clinical experience after the termination of the trance.

Patients can be told that their understanding of a problem will become more and more clear over time after they awaken from trance and leave the office.

It is also possible to produce amnesia for the experiences of trance, or posthypnotic amnesia. In posthypnotic amnesia, what has been experienced in hypnosis is temporarily repressed after termination of the trance. About 30% of the population can produce posthypnotic amnesia (Evans & Kihlstrom, 1973). For example, if 12 hypnotic tasks are given during a trance session, the final suggestion may be that on awakening the person "temporarily forget" all 12 experiences until hearing the signal, "Now you can remember everything." Persons talented in posthypnotic amnesia are unable to recall, upon awakening, more than 3 of the 12 trance suggestions (Hilgard, 1965) and often complain that their memory is clouded or fogged over. Unlike people asked to simulate hypnosis, they seem to have no conscious access to the memories (Bowers, 1966). In contrast to the experience of real amnesia patients, in whom amnesia is of long duration, hypnotically induced amnesia is reversible at any time when the patient is given the prearranged signal.

Alterations in Meaning.   Still another specialty area of hypnosis is the ability to manifest significant changes in the meaning or interpretation of ordinary experience. Some hypnotizable persons are capable of unusual cognitive alterations, such as changes in the meaning of words, thoughts, fantasies, or beliefs about experiences.

It is possible hypnotically to suggest failure in understanding familiar experiences. A hypnotist may give a posthypnotic suggestion that, after awakening, the subject will no longer know what the word "flower" means. Posthypnotically, on hearing this hitherto familiar word and until the posthypnotic suggestion has been revoked, the subject responds as if hearing a foreign word with which he is completely unfamiliar.

Of course, while experiments like this need to be done in laboratories, it is not good practice to take away from a patient—even temporarily—any skill or knowledge he possesses, not even a single word. After all, the patient should learn in hypnosis that he can do *more* than he always thought he could do, not less. And he certainly should not feel overwhelmed by the therapist.

Therefore, posthypnotic suggestions should be used only to help the patient cope with symptoms or to facilitate an understanding of incomprehensible experiences. The hypnotherapist may give a posthypnotic suggestion that the meaning of fantasies, dreams, or other experiences uncovered in hypnotherapy will become more and more clear over time as the patient is ready to understand them. Hypnotizable patients with talent in producing cognitive alterations arrive at quicker and more penetrating insights than other patients.

One can also alter beliefs for those patients who manifest this special ability for cognitive alteration. The hypnotist may directly suggest alterations in the way a patient views his symptoms and maladaptive behaviors. Erickson and his colleagues (Erickson & Rossi, 1979) have conducted extensive clinical investigations emphasizing how hypnosis can be used to help a patient "reframe" beliefs about symptoms and thereby alleviate the symptom. Hypnosis can also be used to alter beliefs in the opposite direction, to produce mental or physical symptoms. In order to study psychopathology, hypnotists (Erickson, 1939) have given belief-altering suggestions to induce neurotic conflicts in certain otherwise healthy hypnotizable subjects so that neurotic symptoms result. Psychophysiological symptoms such as warts can be produced in a similar manner (Barber, 1961).

Changes in the sense of self can be produced in some people. Stage hypnotists often capitalize on this ability, by suggesting, say, that a man be a ballet dancer, whereupon the man may dance about the stage and later, upon awakening, feel embarrassed in front of his family and friends. Clinicians more respectful of hypnotizable people with talent for alterations in the self system may hypnotically evoke a patient's ideal self and give posthypnotic suggestions that the patient over time become as much like the ideal self as realistic possibilities allow.

Alterations of affect also can be produced with hypnosis. Affect is the way in which a person enhances or amplifies the meaning of certain aspects of ordinary experience (Tomkins, 1962–63). Some hypnotizable subjects are capable of manifesting significant alterations in affective experience. It is possible for such people to evoke specific affects, for example, to make a neutral statement seem hilarious, as in the Stanford Profile Scales (Weitzenhoffer & Hilgard, 1963), or to evoke a strong affect like anxiety for the purpose of clinical investigation (Watkins, 1971). The clinician may also suggest an increase in the intensity of affects spontaneously emerging in the hypnotherapy session or suggest a decrease in their intensity through relaxation. Working with affect in this way can improve the efficacy of hypnotherapy for those patients who have an ability for affective alterations through hypnosis.

Perceived Alterations of Reality.   One of the more unusual talents of some hypnotic subjects is the ability to produce perceptual distortions— positive and negative hallucinations, hyperesthesias, and analgesias. Fewer than half of all subjects can produce hallucinations (Hilgard, 1965). To evoke a positive hallucination—a percept for which there is no real stimulus—the hypnotist might suggest that a fly is buzzing around the subject's head and will soon land on his face. The subject may be told that he can relieve the irritation by brushing away the fly. Some subjects feel a mild irritation or an itch. Others scratch but do not experience the fly. Still others actually claim to "hear" or "see" a fly. Subjects respond with a variety of tactile, auditory, and visual effects ranging from the imagined to the genuinely hallucinated. Or the hypnotist might suggest that the subject open his eyes in trance. Many hypnotic subjects can be taught to maintain the level of trance after opening their eyes. They then may be told to look straight ahead, where they will see a chair on which a friend is sitting. (In reality no one is sitting on the chair.) Some people genuinely hallucinate a person on the chair. They may describe his features, expression, and the way he is dressed. They typically see the whole chair, even those parts of the chair that should be hidden by the body of the hallucinated person sitting on it.

Fewer than 25% of subjects (Hilgard, 1965) are capable of producing negative hallucinations; they do not consciously perceive objects or events for which real stimuli are presented. A subject may be told that one of the hands of his watch is missing. After opening his eyes, he may be unable to tell the time. Another subject may be told that a chair in front of her will no longer be there. An interesting variation on this theme is to place a real book on the chair and then suggest only that the subject will "no longer see the chair." Hypnotizable subjects often take suggestions literally and thus will fail to see the chair but will still see the book. The subject is likely to give some rationalization for why the book is seen now in mid-air, no longer supported by the chair. In other cases, suggestions may also be given for hypnotic deafness. Hypnotizable subjects with the talent for negative hallucinations fail to exhibit a startle response to sudden, unexpected loud noises.

Some subjects are capable of significant alterations in pain and temperature sensation, hyperesthesia or analgesia. Hyperesthesias are enhanced bodily sensations. For instance, a hypnotist might suggest that a pencil held in the hand is a hot metal rod. Subjects capable of such hallucinations may drop the pencil, or, if they do not, they may produce a burn. Analgesia is a reduction in pain sensation. Hypnotic suggestions can be given for, say, numbness in a limb. Subjects may still feel something but will not consciously experience the sensations as painful when they are subjected to painful stimulation produced by cold, pressure, ischemia, or shock. Clinically, suggestions for alleviation of pain have proven to be a very effective means of pain control for those hypnotizable subjects who have special talent in analgesic effects.

Personality and Hypnotic Susceptibility

If hypnotizability is a trait more characteristic of some people than of others, the question arises, what sort of personality traits contribute to one's being more hypnotizable? Are there characteristics of highly hypnotizable people that distinguish them from other people? In search of answers to these seemingly straightforward questions, scientists enthusiastically initiated a great number of studies in the attempt to correlate hypnotic susceptibility with a wide range of single personality traits by using available personality inventories. After much energy was expended, few reliable correlations were discovered. Few, if any, single personality traits appear to correlate with hypnotic susceptibility. Those that were discovered could not be replicated. A second wave of research began to focus on several personality variables in interaction (Bowers, 1971). Some statistically significant findings emerged. For example, emotional warmth correlates with hypnotic susceptibility, but only in low-anxious, not high-anxious, people (Rosenhan, 1969). Creativity correlates with hypnotic susceptibility, but only in women (Bowers & Bowers, 1972; Bowers & van der Meulen, 1970). The answers to the questions about the correlation between personality traits and hypnotizability turned out to be very complex.

More recent studies have identified a cluster of traits that correlate significantly with hypnotic susceptibility. The first, derived originally from studies on meditation, is the ability to resist distraction (Van Nuys, 1973). The second, stemming from the results of J. R. Hilgard's (1970, 1979) analyses of careful posthypnotic interviews, is the capacity for imaginative involvement. The third, derived from a personality test constructed by Tellegen and Atkinson (1974), is absorption. Tellegen and Atkinson isolated this trait, which reliably correlates with hypnotic susceptibility. They define absorption as "full commitment of available perceptual, motoric, imaginative, and ideational resources to a unified representation of the attentional object" (p. 274). Examples of absorptive experience include imagining something so vividly that it holds one's attention the way a good movie does, or being so fascinated by the sound of a voice that it is easy to go on listening to it. This finding is exciting because absorption is one of the very few clearly identifiable traits that correlate with hypnotic susceptibility. There is, however, no reason to believe that absorption is specific to hypnosis. It may be a nonspecific factor related to the ability to experience a number of altered states of consciousness—relaxation, meditation, reverie, and hypnosis.

Another area of promise is imagery and fantasy. Vivid imagery correlates with hypnotic susceptibility and, like absorption, it correlates with other altered states as well (Sutcliffe, Perry, & Sheehan, 1970; J. R. Hilgard, 1970, 1979). Highly susceptible subjects are usually good imagers, yet there are many good imagers who are not especially hypnotizable. Daydreaming does not correlate highly with hypnotic susceptibility, but actively created, goal-directed fantasy, especially fantasy evoked in response to external events or the suggestion of others, does (Bowers, 1976; Spanos, 1971). In sum, traits can be identified that correlate with hypnotizability in the areas that directly tap dimensions of hypnosis: attention skill (absorption, resistance to distraction, and state and interpersonal dimensions, such as emergent imagery and the suggestions of others.

Is there any correlation between psychopathological diagnosis and hypnotic susceptibility? The cultural stereotype inherited from the Victorian era is that hysterics are highly hypnotizable. Actually, there is only a low positive, but not significant, correlation between hysteria and hypnotic susceptibility (Barber, 1964). Another stereotype that has long existed is that schizophrenics are not hypnotizable. A series of studies using standard scales with schizophrenics have clearly shown that hypnotizability in schizophrenics follows pretty much the same distribution curve as in normative populations: most schizophrenics are moderately hypnotizable, some are highly hypnotizable, and some are barely hypnotizable (see review in Lavoie & Sabourin, 1980). The only finding relating psychopathology to hypnotic susceptibility is that phobic symptomatology correlates significantly with hypnotic susceptibility (Frankel & Orne, 1976). Frankel (1976) explains that phobic patients often experience spontaneous trance-like behaviors associated with their symptomatology. The motivation for these trance-like experiences may be defensive; nevertheless, these experienced probably resemble hypnotic phenomena.

Except for imaginativeness (Hilgard, 1970, 1979) and the ability to become deeply absorbed (Tellegen & Atkinson, 1974), no personality traits or combination of them have been found that correlate highly with hypnotic susceptibility. But certain kinds of life experiences do. Ås (1962b), Shor (1960), and Bowers (1976) have independently found that unusual experiences in waking life reliably correlate with hypnotic susceptibility. People who report spontaneous mystical experiences or lapses into altered states of consciousness usually are more hypnotizable than others. It does not seem to matter how many or how few unusual experiences a person has had; what seems to matter is the intensity of the experience.

Stability and Intentional Modification of Susceptibility.   How stable and enduring is hypnotizability over time? If hypnotic susceptibility in college students is measured with standard scales over successive days, the correlations of the scores are about $r = .90$, which means that over a short span of time susceptibility as measured by similar tests remains quite constant (Hilgard, 1965). When the college students were tested with the same hypnosis scales 10 years later, after they had entered a different phase of life, the correlations in the scores were $r = .60$ (Morgan, Johnson, & Hilgard, 1974). In other words, susceptibility also manifests some degree of long-term stability in adults. The degree of hypnotic susceptibility in adults is reasonably fixed under normal life circumstances. Can susceptibility, then, be intentionally modified? The question is especially important to the clinician who may desire to improve hypnotic responsiveness in his patients.

There are several ways to modify hypnotic susceptibility. The first entails profound but unstable modifications. Experiences with other altered states of consciousness—especially those in which the structure and experience of the state are drastically discontinuous with the structure and experience of normal, waking consciousness—affect susceptibility in significant ways. Experiences with sensory isolation, as well as with hallucinogenic drugs, produce radical alterations in cognition and perception. Following such experiences, hypnotic susceptibility may increase up to 5 out of 12 points on standard scales. Unfortunately, these significant increases in susceptibility are seldom maintained beyond a few weeks following the experience with the major altered state (Sanders & Reyher, 1969; Sjoberg & Hollister, 1965). People who use EMG biofeedback to reduce muscle tension may also increase susceptibility to hypnosis up to 5 points. These changes may last longer, although how long they last is unclear (London, Hart, & Leibovitz, 1968; Wickramasekera, 1973). The mechanisms that produce profound but unstable alterations in hypnotizability may not be the same as those that cause alterations of consciousness in biofeedback, in sensory isolation, and under hallucinogenic drugs. Nevertheless, in these major altered states, people may gain experience with cognitive and perceptual alterations analogous to those naturally experienced by hypnotically highly susceptible people. Once such alterations are experienced, these people may learn how to manifest similar perceptual alterations in response to hypnotic suggestions. In the case of autonomic learning with biofeedback, people learn to achieve voluntary control over random muscle activity and thereby reduce internal noise, which in turn may enhance absorption and attentional focus, important ingredients of hypnotic susceptibility.

There are other ways to bring about modest but stable modifications in hypnotic susceptibility. Stable gains of 2 to 3 points out of 12 points on the standard scales have been reported following participation in personal growth and encounter groups. Presumably, these group experiences are based on trust and encourage greater openness to inner experience as well as disclosure to others (Roberts & Tellegen, 1973; Tart, 1970a). When special efforts are made to motivate a person or to convey the notion that hypnosis is a very desirable and pleasurable experience, hypnotizability improves too (Barber & Calverley, 1963). When information is provided to help the subject understand what hypnosis is like, hypnotizability also improves (Diamond, 1974; Reilley, Parisher, Carona, & Dobrovolsky, 1980). In addition, it improves when individuals are slowly led to believe that they can be hypnotized and can successfully respond to a wide range of suggestions, that is, when self-efficacy is fostered (Kidder, 1972). The use of behavior modification methods to reinforce successful hypnotic responses also improves hypnotizability to some degree (Sachs & Anderson, 1967; Stolar, 1975). Steady and frequent practice of hypnosis or related attentional practices, like meditation, produces enduring gains of two to three points (Cooper, Banford, Shubat, & Tart, 1967; Reilly et al., 1980).

There is a third possibility for bringing about profound but stable modifications in hypnotizability. Clinicians have long reported great gains or losses in hypnotizability when working with patients over a long time (Erickson, 1965; Gill & Brenman, 1959). Neither the gains nor the losses have yet been fully substantiated in the laboratory. Neither are likely due to hypnotizability alone. They may be caused by changes in the patient's expectations, changes in the object relationship between patient and therapist, resistances, transferences, or the patient's reaction to countertransference phenomena in the therapist.

In a series of experiments by Sachs and his associates (Kinney & Sachs, 1974; Sachs, 1971; Sachs & Anderson, 1967), an attempt was made to show that susceptibility can be lastingly improved up to 4 to 6 points. The key to success was through individualizing the hypnotic experiences. They developed a series of exercises with graded difficulty for all suggestions the subject failed to respond to successfully within each specialty area of hypnosis. The subjects learned to become successful in areas of hypnotic ability where they had previously been unresponsive.

While, overall, hypnotic susceptibility is fairly stable during adult life, the clinician who thoughtfully attempts to enhance the patient's motivation and desire for hypnosis as well as his self-efficacy may aid the patient to manifest his full, natural hypnotic ability. Practice may further improve susceptibility. Without the introduction of special parameters, the clinician should not expect great gains in patients' hypnotizability. There seems to be a plateau in the modification of hypnotizability (Bowers, 1976). Under most conditions, low to moderately hypnotizable patients are unlikely to become highly susceptible. Yet, when care is taken to positively reinforce those areas in which the patient is more talented in following hypnotic suggestions, and when exercises graded in difficulty are introduced slowly in order to teach the patient to respond in areas where he may be less responsive, hypnotic ability may improve in a significant and enduring way. Such tedious hypnotic training is usually unnecessary because only a moderate degree of hypnotizability is necessary for most therapeutic work. Yet, if there are special areas in which a patient is less responsive but which the clinician wishes to enhance as part of the clinical work (e.g., the ability to follow posthypnotic suggestions, the production of hypnotic dreams, or analgesic effects), it can be done.

Hypnosis and the Life Cycle

Until very recently, hypnotic susceptibility was considered to be stable from adolescence throughout the life span. On the basis of the little research that had been done on children's hypnotizability before 1960, children, particularly young children, were thought to be unhypnotizable or poorly hypnotizable. Inasmuch as imagery plays so great a role in hypnosis, and small children are usually much more imaginative than adults, these results were questioned and, indeed, were found to be wrong. The error was due to the fact that hypnotizability scales standardized on college students (adolescents and young adults) had been used to test for the hypnotizability of young children. When the wording and content were revised to be more appropriate to children, it was found that children are at least as hypnotizable as adults. Specifically, results (London, 1962; Morgan & Hilgard, 1973; Morgan & Hilgard, 1978–1979) showed hypnotizability to be quite high in the 1-to-4-year and 5-to-8-year range and to reach its peak between the ages of 9 and 12 years. It then drops off, stabilizes from adolescence through adulthood, and drops off again at midlife. There are no clear data yet on susceptibility beyond midlife.

Thus, if susceptibility is viewed over the course of the entire life cycle, a complicated pattern emerges: children's hypnotizability is higher than that of adults; latency and preadolescent children's hypnotizability is higher than that of adolescents and higher than that of preschool children (who cannot concentrate their attention for a long enough time); and hypnotic responsiveness does not remain on a plateau throughout adulthood. The degree of hypnotic responsiveness of adolescents and adults is likely to be less than what they exhibited when they were 9–12 years old. It is during late latency (ages 9–10) that hypnotizability is at its peak.

Another question, much more easily answered, is: Why do most people in our Western culture lose the higher susceptibility characteristic of childhood by the time they reach adolescence and adulthood, whereas people in some other cultures, for example, the Balinese, do not lose it? In

Bali, most adults are highly hypnotizable. Hypnotic susceptibility is a potential that children in all cultures seem to have; yet, in Western cultures, by the time a person reaches adolescence, some is lost permanently because we do not support, nourish, and practice this talent as other, more primitive societies do.

The acquisition of hypnotic susceptibility is much like the acquisition of many other abilities in childhood. There may be a critical period in which the innate potential for susceptibility needs environmental reinforcement in order to manifest itself fully. Presumably, if those elements which contribute to hypnotic susceptibility are reinforced during the critical period prior to adolescence, there will be less dropoff and stronger preservation of hypnotic potential into adult life; if it is not reinforced, there will be more dropoff, less preservation. Once susceptibility has diminished beyond the critical period, it is difficult to recover the full potential.

A number of developmental factors affect the extent of retained hypnotizability in adulthood. Among these are the belief systems of the culture in which a person lives and specific activities within the family system. Within the wider cultural environment, belief systems can be important determinants of hypnotic susceptibility, especially if the belief system legitimates the altered states of consciousness. Examples could be drawn from many of the so-called primitive cultures that utilize group rituals (Eliade, 1958), such as seasonal or life transition rites, and certainly from those subcultural groups within more complex cultures that practice trance and possession states (Bourguignion, 1973). Complex modern societies, on the other hand, may have a negative attitude towards hypnosis and thereby discourage the development of hypnotic susceptibility. Increased secularization of the society has discouraged widespread participation in religious rituals, exceptions being small subcultural groups like the charismatic Christians and countercultural cults (Zaretsky & Leone, 1974). Until recently, drugs and alcohol provided the main access to experiences of altered states of consciousness in secular society. Of late, stress reduction methods (progressive relaxation, imaginal techniques, meditation, and sensorily restricted environments) have become popular through employee assistance and behavioral medicine programs.

Another discouragement to hypnotic susceptibility is the educational system. Children are taught that daydreaming in the classroom is bad. Reality-oriented achievement, rather than fantasy involvement, is strongly encouraged.

On the other hand, within the family system, certain interests and activities engaged in during the critical period by child and parents together tend to positively reinforce hypnotic susceptibility in contradiction to the negative attitude transmitted by the wider Western culture. Some of these interests and activities are directly modeled by parents or enjoyed by parents and child together. Some are discovered by the child to compensate for deficiencies in the parent–child relationship. In either case, certain interests and activities may increase the likelihood of retaining high hypnotic susceptibility into adulthood. J. R. Hilgard (1970) has conducted extensive research to determine which childhood activities reinforce hypnotic susceptibility. There are many, and they vary across children: appreciation of the sensory delights of nature, for example, enjoyment of a brightly colored sunset or the sound of a babbling brook; reading imaginative literature or intensely watching a play or movie and strongly identifying with the characters; acting and losing oneself in a role; absorption in daydreams and active imagination and greatly diminished concern with the surroundings; adventure, for example, mountain climbing, spelunking; participation in skilled individual sports that require disciplined concentration such as skiing; being so absorbed in play or work that generalized reality orientation fades into the background of one's awareness; and punishment by parents, which may cause the child to create a substitute reality in fantasy. Some activities limit susceptibility: competitive sports, which emphasize winning and scanning reality to assess the position of other players; and scientific thinking, which usually emphasizes reality orientation and secondary process thinking.

There may be multiple pathways to hypnotic susceptibility, all of which seem to entail what J. R. Hilgard calls "imaginative involvement" to the point of increased absorption and decreased reality orientation. If the wider cultural system provided sanction, more people in our culture would be hypnotizable. Without such general sanctions, it is difficult for most people to manifest the full potential of hypnotic susceptibility in this culture, except for the approximately 8% of children who discover one or several imaginative involvements and engage in these frequently throughout a critical period of childhood. These children are utilizing an ability that reinforces hypnotic susceptibility and predicts higher hypnotic susceptibility in adulthood.

EXPERIENTIAL DEPTH

There are ways by which a person subjectively knows he is in trance, but these do not always manifest themselves in observable behavior. The depth experienced by the hypnotic subject (how deep a person *feels* to be in trance) can be described only by the subject. Evaluation of experiential depth (Shor, 1979) differs from evaluation of behavioral depth in several important respects. Evaluation of behavioral depth is based on objective signs the examiner can observe; experiential depth pertains to the subject's own sense of having entered an altered state of consciousness qualitatively different from ordinary waking consciousness. The subject may describe a state in which he no longer is aware of his actual physical surroundings or a state in which he, without conscious volition or deliberation, allows things to happen by themselves. A patient may experience strong transference feelings. He may feel relaxed or be aware of more vivid imagery (both quantitatively and qualitatively) than he ordinarily would be in the waking state. He may also be attentively engrossed in the moment-to-moment experience and become aware of fanciful primary process ideation or forgotten, emotionally charged memories (Shor, 1979). Patients often report variations in that state of consciousnes during sessions (Ludwig, 1966; Tart, 1979). For good hypnotic subjects, trance has a unique configuration of attentional, cognitive, perceptual and emotional functioning. People in deep trance usually know they are in trance. They are able to judge their state, and the experiences within this state, as fundamentally different from normal waking consciousness. Having entered a "discrete state of consciousness" (Tart, 1975), people in trance are able to sense further changes and fluctuations in their own experience. When reporting their experience of the altered state, they often mention temporary variations in their experiential depth within this altered state of consciousness over the duration of the trance.

What kinds of temporal changes in depth do people notice? On entering trance, they usually have an initial sense of depth that is predictive of the type of experiences they will have in trance (Tart, 1970b). Medium and deeply hypnotizable subjects also are likely to report a number of fluctuations in depth in a single session (Tart, 1979, for heterohypnosis; Fromm et al, 1981, for self-hypnosis) and over a number of sessions (Fromm et al., 1981). Subjects who are only lightly hypnotizable, of course, will not have much fluctuation in depth. The sense of being deeper in trance often varies with the particular hypnotic suggestion given, usually in reaction to how well the person is able to respond to the suggestion (Laurence & Perry, 1981; Tart, 1979). Sometimes hypnotized subjects, temporarily left to their own devices to explore the trance, experience minor and major variations in depth according to the type of experience they have, or they may lapse into very deep states. On the other hand, some patients sometimes suddenly come out of trance, either on account of external distraction or because they have come close to some unconscious material they are not ready to deal with yet. They are defending themselves against its coming into awareness by getting out of hypnosis.

Especially when relying on subjective reports, it is important to establish criteria for judging the depth of trance at any given moment. Teaching hypnotized people standard self-report scales is one way. On these scales, viewed along a continuum, hypnotized subjects are asked to judge the depth of their trance and quantify it according to some scale. A number of such scales have been used. The original scale (LeCron, 1953) required subjects to assess the degree of depth using a 100-point scale. Others (Field, 1966; Hilgard & Tart, 1966; O'Connell, 1964, Shor, 1979; Tart, 1963; Tart, 1966) have used 40-point, 4-point, and 10-point scales (see Table 2.1). With the help of these scales, it has become possible to study experiential fluctuations in a single trance session and to begin to understand when and why these fluctuations occur. On Tart's (1963) North Carolina Scale, subjects are asked to report a number spontaneously, that is, to let the appropriate number quickly enter their mind when the word "state" is called out to them. On most of these scales, subjects are also asked to evaluate depth according to some vague, subjective criterion—awake versus deep, or light versus deep. None use carefully defined experiential anchor points, simply because we do not yet know a great deal about the kinds of experiences people in trance have in common.

It is clear that when asked for state reports, hypnotized people report changes in the subjective sense of depth during a single session; it is less clear how they know they are lighter or deeper at any given moment. What experiential criteria do they use? How do they go about deciding when they are deeper, when lighter?

The problem is that not all hypnotized people judge depth in the same way. When they are asked what sort of changes make them report different numbers on the self-report scales, they give a wide variety of answers. The criteria for assessing experiential depth are highly individual (Tart, 1979). For example, Tart interviewed 34 subjects about their experiential criteria of depth and found they reported no fewer than 56 criteria. The problem of making sense of experiential depth, then, is due mainly to the great variability of trance experiences.

Nevertheless, while the variability is great, it is possible to gain some understanding of how people in trance typically judge their experiential depth at given moments. A unidimensional approach involves a search for a single, main criterion by which to assess experiential depth. There is some reason to believe that people evaluate the depth of their trance experience according to momentary fluctuations in the intensity of their attentional focus. We speculate that they might report being deeper at those moments when they are more absorbed in the experience (Tellegen & Atkinson, 1974), show intense involvement with a limited range of preoccupations (Shor, 1960), or are high in imaginative involvement (Hilgard, 1970). All three of these depth criteria refer to the feeling of being more absorbed in the experience.

The other approach, a multidimensional one, has been to search for a number of important criteria by which to assess experiential depth. For example, Tart (1979) believes there are two main criteria by which people assess their own depth:

1. People feel deeper if they find themselves responsive to suggestions. If they are capable of responding well to a given suggestion, they give higher state reports; if they do not respond well, they give lower state reports. Furthermore, since most people expect some suggestions to be considerably harder (e.g., dreams, amnesias, hallucinations) than others (e.g., the arm drop), they typically consider themselves to be much deeper if they accomplish what in their judgment is difficult (Tart, 1979). In other words, people judge depth according to success or failure in accomplishing particular hypnotic phenomena.

2. People feel deeper, the more they believe their consciousness has been altered. Through retrospective interviewing about trance experiences, Tart (1979) identified a number of ways people used to judge changes in their state: the extent to which they felt drowsy, the degree of relaxation, the degree to which the generalized reality orientation (GRO) faded, the extent to which their body image changed, and the feeling of compulsion to respond or go along with suggestions.

Field and Palmer (1969) similarly used empirical methods to discover changes in experience that correspond to depth. They created 300 questionnaire items about typical hypnotic experiences to find out which experiences hypnotized people use to judge their depth. Three categories emerged: unawareness of the body and the surroundings, compulsion, and discontinuity with waking consciousness. Fromm et al. (1981) created two other questionnaires for subjects who practiced self-hypnosis over a number of weeks. Two types of experiential dimensions emerged; (a) four structural dimensions—concentrative and expansive attention, absorption, fading of the GRO, and the subjective feeling of depth; and (b) a great variety of content dimensions, such as vividness of imagery, hypermnesias, and age regressions. Results indicate a definite correlation among absorption, attentional states, and vividness of imagery. Shor (1979) interviewed subjects immediately after a heterohypnotic experience and then rated them for depth according to eight experiential dimensions: the fading of the GRO, nonconscious involvement, archaic involvement, drowsiness, relaxation, vividness of imagery, absorption, and access to the unconscious. According to Shor, only the first three can be clearly related to depth.

There is considerable consistency in the categories of experience expected in all of these studies. While people use a great variety of means to assess momentary changes in depth, they tend to use the same dimensions. If we pool the data from all these studies, about a dozen criteria emerge. People know they are deeper by the following subjective criteria:

1. How relaxed they are.
2. How drowsy they are.

3. How well they respond to a given suggestion they know is difficult.
4. How absorbed they are in the experience.
5. How much their generalized reality orientation has faded.
6. How discontinuous the trance seems to be from the waking state of consciousness.
7. How vivid their imagery is.
8. How much they feel compelled to go along with the experience.
9. How much the hypnotic relationship evokes earlier patterns of object relationships (i.e., transference feelings).
10. How much access they have to their unconscious.
11. How totally and nonconsciously they become involved in the hypnotic role.
11. How skillfully they deploy their attention in either a selective or expansive manner.

SUMMARY AND CLINICAL IMPLICATIONS

Table 2.2 summarizes our current knowledge on hypnotic depth as viewed from both behavioral and experiential perspectives. Viewed behaviorally, hypnotizability refers to observable behaviors in response to the hypnotist's suggestions. It can be characterized unidimensionally as a general ability (hypnotizability), or multidimensionally as a series of specific hypnotic talents in various areas (e.g., ideomotor phenomena, cognitive alterations, etc.). Viewed phenomenologically, experiential depth refers to the subjective sense of being in an altered state of consciousness. Again, experiential depth can be either unidimensional, as an altered state in which depth is characterized by degrees of absorption, or multidimensional, in terms of numerous criteria (degree of relaxation, degree of fading of generalized reality orientation, access to the unconscious, vividness of imagery, etc.).

TABLE 2.2
Judging Hypnotic Depth

Behavioral Perspective		Phenomenological Perspective	
		one of the following:	*at least several of the following:*
(unidimensional)	*(multidimensional)*		
general hynotizability	specific hypnotic talents	degree of involvement with a limited range of preoccupations	relaxation
	ideomotor phenomena		drowsiness
	cognitive effects	imaginative involvement	responsiveness to a difficult suggestion
	posthypnotic suggestions & amnesias		absorption
	alterations in meaning		fading of the GRO
	negative hallucinations & analgesias		discontinuity with waking state
	positive hallucinations & hyperesthesias		vivid primary as well as secondary process imagery
			changes in body image
			compulsion
			unawareness, compulsion
			transference feelings
			nonconscious involvement
			archaic involvement
			heightened ego receptivity
			focused as well as expansive attention
			access to the unconscious

3 Learning How to Hypnotize

STYLES OF HYPNOTIC SUGGESTION

There are three distinct styles of hypnotic suggestion: directive, permissive, and Ericksonian. Each represents a certain "philosophy of life," a different view of the hypnotist's involvement, the nature of the hypnotic communication, the patient's role as a recipient of this communication, and the nature of the response expected. These differences are summarized in Table 3.1. It is beyond the scope of this book to trace the evolution of these three very different styles of hypnosis. Suffice it to say that each style is clinically useful in its own right, though often for very different clinical situations.

Directive Style

Historically, the directive style was the first to emerge. Its roots go back to Anton Mesmer's charismatic healings and to Bernheim's (1889) theory of suggestibility. In directive hypnosis, the hypnotist adopts an authoritarian stance toward the patient and by means of direct suggestions tells him what he must do. The patient is likely to view the hypnotist as a prestigious and highly credible source of communication. The transference toward the hypnotist is often intense. The hypnotist takes on the qualities of a magically powerful parental figure, especially if he is at all charismatic or intentionally exploits the parental role. Particularly when the hypnotist is authoritarian, there is a discrepancy in the distribution of power between him and the patient, with the hypnotist an active and forceful source of communication and the patient a passive, often submissive, recipient of the suggestions. The patient, expected to listen attentively and comply with the suggestions, is able to respond because he is suggestible. Directive hypnotists equate hypnotic trance with suggestibility. Suggestibility is a complex attribute, a function of many factors, hypnotic susceptibility and social persuasability being noteworthy among them. Because the hypnotist adopts the stance of the credible, authoritative communicator, directive hypnosis in some ways is similar to nonhypnotic persuasive communication, a field that has been extensively investigated

TABLE 3.1
Styles of Hypnotic Suggestion

	Directive	Permissive	Ericksonian
CHARACTERISTICS OF THE HYPNOTIST			
View of hypnotist	Authoritative highly credible, persuasive source	Facilitative	Authoritative/facilitative
Use of transference	Often exploited	Integration of naturally unfolding transference	Often exploited
CHARACTERISTICS OF HYPNOTIC SUBJECT			
View of trance	Hypersuggestibility and persuasion	Hypnotizability (limited to subgroup of overall population)	Everyday trance (entire population)
Mode of action	Passivity	Ego activity/receptivity	Perceptual readiness to understand embedded message
THE HYPNOTIC COMMUNICATION			
Nature of the suggestion	Direct, specific suggestions	Open-ended, permissive, ego-strengthening, and coping suggestions	Nonspecific (e.g. stories, metaphors, jokes, binds, and utilization)
Style of delivery	Commanding (with repetition)	Offering possibilities	Indirect (disguised and embedded suggestions)
THE NATURE OF THE RESPONSE			
Response style	Uncritical acceptance	Development of coping and mastery	Development of new meaning
Attribution of change		Self efficacy and coping	Altered frames of reference and beliefs

by social psychologists (e.g., Insko, 1967). However, while directive hypnosis certainly entails a very high degree of social persuasion, it also entails something more, something specific to the hypnotic condition.

The message given by the directive hypnotist is usually unambiguous and specific. Suggestions pertain to circumscribed symptoms and behaviors. They are unidimensional in selectively eliciting only one type of response and leaving little doubt about the response desired. Opposing response possibilities are inhibited (Jones, 1923). The suggestions typically address salient symptoms and behaviors, which the subject or patient can readily identify. Such suggestions are directed at the patient's inner wish to relinquish the symptom or behavior in question and in this sense are designed to enable the patient to justify to himself the therapeutic change. Hence, the directive style is most effective when the suggestions are congruent with the patient's own values and expectations for change.

Directive suggestions are couched in a way that explicitly tells the patient what to do. They are delivered in a firm, sometimes dictatorial, manner, with or without attempting to challenge the patient. Verbal exchange between patient and hypnotherapist is not encouraged. The hypnotist simply delivers the command. Then the suggestion is repeated, often with little variation according to Braid's (1843) principle of monoideism. Moreover, the suggestions are sometimes designed to elicit a certain optimal level of affect, either enhancing feelings of relief or arousing fear, believed to be necessary for therapeutic change. For a feeling of relief, the hypnotist may say, *When I count to 10, your symptom will go away* . . . or *When you awaken, you will no longer have* ———. The suggestion is repeated a number of times. Or, to arouse fear, the hypnotist might, for example, tell a patient to stop smoking by appealing to the health hazards of smoking.

The directive style of hypnosis can produce dramatic and quick responses. Some patients respond to this form of communication with uncritical acceptance. Their subjective experience of the response is involuntary, and they attribute the effects totally to the hypnotherapist (as if the curative work were done solely by the hypnotist). However, the directive style does not work for everyone. Simply telling a subject to follow a suggestion quickly or telling a patient that his symptoms will go away works for some, but for most people it is ineffective. In our estimation, a strictly directive style of hypnosis is useful for less than 10% of the population. It is effective for patients who meet the criteria of moderate to high hypnotizability and presuadability. The latter is a characteristic of the intellectually unsophisticated person and of the person who has an external locus of control.

Permissive Style

The permissive style derived from modern research on hypnosis. From this research it became increasingly clear that hypnosis is an ability, a talent of the *subject* collaborating with the hypnotist. The results of this research necessitated a change in the view of the respective roles of hypnotist and subject. In permissive hypnosis, the hypnotist plays a facilitating role, not an authoritative one. The hypnotist is viewed as skilled in establishing a context where the subject can explore his hypnotic ability. The hypnotist and the patient are nearly equal collaborators in the exploration. Although transference to the hypnotist occurs, it is not exploited but is allowed to unfold naturally.

Permissive hypnosis emphasizes hypnotizability and ego receptivity[1] (Deikman, 1971; Fromm, 1979). The patient is believed to enter an altered state of consciousness after formal trance induction has been used. During trance, the patient is expected to become receptive to the events in his stream of consciousness, report these to the hypnotist, and display the behaviors intended by the suggestions. The emphasis is placed on the patient's discovery of his inner resources in effecting the response or the patient's discovery of coping strategies and solutions to problems, and on the development of self-efficacy as the patient discovers the capacity to respond effectively.

The suggestions given by the hypnotist using a permissive style can be nonspecific or specific, depending on the intended effect. Often open ended and projective, they address the patient's inner resources, which potentially can be mobilized around the behaviors and symptoms and are not necessarily directed at only salient behaviors and symptoms. Suggestions are also tailored to the patient's unique resources, especially imagery and coping strategies, and idiosyncratic response style. Thus, permissive suggestions should be highly congruent with the patient's own attitudes and values regarding hypnotic response or therapeutic change. Although suggestions to enhance feelings of immediate relief of anxiety are not used very frequently in permissive hypnosis, ego-strengthening suggestions are (Hartland, 1965). The patient is specifically told that he will feel more confident and assured as the response to the suggestion occurs.

Permissive suggestions are delivered quite differently from directive

---

[1] The word "ego" is used throughout this book in the psychoanalytic sense, not in the common usage sense of "selfishness." In the psychoanalytic conception, the ego is that conglomeration of functions dealing with the outside world and which, within the personality, moderates between the demands of the drives and those of the superego (the conscience). These functions comprise perception, motility, cognition, imagery and fantasy, attention, memory, talents, defenses, integrative and coping mechanisms, and the unconscious as well as the conscious decision-making processes.

suggestions. They are suggestive, not dictatorial; they merely offer possibilities for the patient to explore. They are unidimensional, that is, they are worded to elicit responses along a particular line of inner exploration. They are repeated, often in different ways. Permissive suggestions are a two-way form of communication, which encourages dialogue between patient and hypnotist. The hypnotist continually asks for feedback from the patient, monitors the patient's responses, and modifies the suggestions as necessary.

The permissive style is very popular today and is used exclusively by many hypnotists. Since World War II—in accordance with our democratic *Weltanschauung* and distaste for authoritarianism, and influenced by the newer clinical research on hypnosis—the majority of hypnotherapists in the United States have utilized the permissive style. Hypnotherapeutic results may not be as dramatic as those gained by directive hypnosis, but they may be more permanent. Clinically, permissive hypnosis is applicable to a wider range of patients, and the clinical outcome is directly associated with such factors as hypnotizability, self-efficacy, and the quality of the interaction between hypnotist and patient. It is the style the authors use in nearly all cases.

Ericksonian Style

Out of his considerable experience with hypnosis, Milton Erickson devised new methods particularly suited to the difficult client, the client with intractable symptoms, or the difficult-to-hypnotize client. An innovative view of hypnosis was borne of these methods. In Ericksonian hypnosis, the hypnotist is informal and conversational. At the same time, the hypnotist is seen as a healer. There is, then, some discrepancy in the distribution of power between patient and hypnotist, the degree of the discrepancy more or less depending on the particular hypnotist. Formal, ritualized trance inductions are seldom used. Suggestions are embedded within ordinary conversation. The Ericksonian hypnotist employs indirect communication to activate a process of unconscious search within the patient.

As in permissive hypnosis, Ericksonian suggestions tap the subject's own inner resources; but, unlike permissive hypnosis, the emphasis is placed much more on unconscious response possibilities than on coping strategies. The goal of Ericksonian suggestions is to bring about a reorganization of the patient's inner life, specifically changing the beliefs about his illness.

Ericksonians view trance very differently from permissive hypnotists. Permissive hypnotists view trance as an altered state, a state which people are more or less able to enter, depending on their hypnotizability. (Hilgard and Weitzenhoffer [Hilgard, 1965; Weitzenhoffer & Hilgard, 1959, 1962,

1963, 1967] have shown that hypnotizability is a talent or trait people possess in varying degrees. It is distributed in the population according to a bimodal bell-shaped curve. Ericksonians, however, view trance as an everyday event experienced by everyone. They consider momentary lapses in awareness and reverie states to be trance manifestations. Using this liberal interpretation of trance, Ericksonians believe that *all* people are hypnotizable (by the method best suited to each). The patient's role is a matter not so much of entering an altered state as of being in a state of perceptual readiness. The patient must vigilantly scan the hypnotist's complex, disguised, and often multidimensional communication and be able to make sense out of the message in accordance with his own inner resources, belief systems, and response possibilities. Skill has less to do with hypnotizability than with the subject's ability to interpret the hypnotist's disguised and often cryptic communication.

Ericksonian suggestions are delivered in a manner so strikingly different from either directive or permissive suggestions that Ericksonian hypnosis is quite unlike conventional hypnosis. The communications are nonspecific, indirect, ambiguous—often disguised. Suggestions may be interspersed within ordinary conversation. Certain key phrases may be embedded or implicit in anecdotes, stories, analogies, metaphors, juxtaposition of opposites, puns, jokes, and binds. All represent styles of suggestion with many levels of meaning. These devices are intended to disrupt the patient's habitual belief systems and frames of reference and invite the patient to search for new response possibilities. Because Ericksonian hypnotists make use of confusion and surprise in their suggestions, it is possible to "hypnotize" a person in the Ericksonian way without his knowledge.

The subject is expected to listen passively to the hypnotist's words. Exchange between patient and hypnotist is encouraged, however. One of Erickson's significant contributions is the utilization approach, in which the hypnotist utilizes the aspects of the subject's immediate experience as the medium from which to develop suggestions and to lead the patient to new possibilities that lie within himself.

There is a certain amount of guesswork in Ericksonian hypnosis. The hypnotist simply assumes that his stories and metaphors are relevant to the patient; the patient, in turn, must find in them something relevant to his concerns. Consequently, the congruency between the hypnotist's message and the patient's values and beliefs may at times be low.

Since the death of Erickson in 1980, Ericksonian hypnosis has become increasingly popular. There are many hypnotists today who use Ericksonian hypnosis exclusively with a great variety of patients. Ericksonian hypnosis has thus become somewhat divorced from its original context. Ericksonian suggestions were originally advanced and specialized techniques developed for the difficult-to-hypnotize and difficult patient. It is especially difficult to evaluate the outcome when such indirect methods are used indiscriminately for all kinds of patients, especially where more straightforward hypnotic procedures are available for the majority of hypnotherapy patients.

Each style discussed here is clinically useful. None is useful for all patients. Selection of a hypnotic style is taken up in chapter 6. Because the permissive style is useful for most people (the directive and Ericksonian styles being suitable only for specialized patient populations), the remainder of this chapter is devoted to the permissive style.

THE ART OF HYPNOTIZING

Setting

The hypnotist should protect the hypnotic patient from environmental distractions as much as possible. Hypnotherapy is best conducted in a quiet office. The level of noise in the surroundings should be at a minimum. Soundproof rooms or white noise generators are advisable. Unexpected sounds may disturb the trance. The therapist also must be careful to arrange the situation so that the session is not disrupted by knocks at the door or telephone calls.

If, in spite of precautions taken, external distractions occur, the hypnotist must be flexible enough to work with them constructively. The sounds of a plane, siren, or telephone are potential distractions. Whether or not the sound is disruptive depends to a large extent on the hypnotist's skill in incorporating it into the ongoing plan of suggestions. The hypnotist might give a general suggestion: "Although you hear outside sounds, you will find that you will be less and less bothered by them; and as you see that you are becoming less and less bothered, it will indicate to you how deeply hypnotized you are becoming." The hypnotist might also tailor the suggestion specifically to the distracting sound: "As you hear the sound of _____ fading more and more into the background, you will go deeper and deeper into trance." Thus, the distracting sound can be folded into the flow of the hypnotic experience.

Trance becomes possible when the patient's normal intake of sensory information from and behavioral engagement with the environment is inhibited (Gill & Brenman, 1959). The lighting of the room should be kept relatively dim to reduce the intake of visual stimuli, but not so dark that it is difficult to observe the patient. It is advisable to ask the patient how much light he feels comfortable with before proceeding.

Having the patient sit or lie down comfortably limits bodily activity. It makes little difference what type of furniture is used. Some prefer a couch;

others, a reclining chair; others, an upright chair. Whatever the choice, the chair must be comfortable enough so that the patient easily can sit in it for an hour.

The positioning of the chairs is more important than the type of chair used. It is best to place the hypnotherapist's and the patient's chairs close together at an angle of about 90°. The chairs are placed close to each other so the therapist can hear the patient. (It is likely that the patient will talk much more softly while in trance than when awake.) They are placed at a right angle, not face to face, in order to convey symbolically that the interaction between patient and therapist involves mutual exchange, not confrontation. Certain countertransference motives may underlie placing the chairs face to face: Using the old-fashioned Mesmerian techniques of staring into the patient's eyes and staring him down expresses the hypnotherapist's unconscious desire to overpower the patient. If a male hypnotist places the chairs in a facing position so close together that he has to wedge his legs between the spread-out legs of a female patient, it is likely due to a seductive or intrusive wish of his. At least some of the nonverbal aspects of these countertransference reactions can be minimized by placing the chairs at right angles. The therapist is not in a position that would obstruct the patient's field of vision if, for example, an eye fixation is used as an induction. And the patient who sometimes feels a bit embarrassed need not face the therapist. However, if he wants to, he can turn his face towards the hypnotist. The therapist is seated close enough to observe the patient's nonverbal behavior and hear the patient's description of the trance experience. He is also close enough to utilize touch, when indicated.

Set

The purpose of an hypnotic interview in a session prior to starting hypnotherapy is to establish a positive mental set towards hypnosis and to prepare the patient for the new experience. The preparation begins by determining the patient's initial motivation for, attitudes about, and expectations of hypnosis. The patient is asked, "Why do you want to use hypnosis?" An attempt is also made to ascertain the patient's attitude about hypnosis. Does the patient view the hypnotic state as a desirable experience, or is he fearful of it? What is the nature of these fears? What does the patient expect will happen in hypnosis? Does he think he will be able to be hypnotized? With this initial inquiry the therapist tries to identify possible problem areas: low motivation, fears of hypnosis, and unrealistic positive or negative expectations regarding the efficacy of hypnosis. These problem areas are addressed directly with the patient in the prehypnotic interview.

It is also a good idea to ascertain the patient's view of trance, which stems from a number of sources: cultural stereotypes, information about hypnosis gleaned through the media, literature, and myth, and sometimes from actual experiences with hypnosis (previous professional hypnotherapy, stage hypnosis, unsupervised experimentation with hypnosis with friends). The image of trance is determined by asking the patient, "What do you imagine it is like to be hypnotized?" or "What do you imagine being in trance is like?" Some patients answer the question by saying they can't know because they haven't yet been hypnotized. The therapist agrees, adding, "Yes, but you must have *some* idea of what it is like. You've no doubt heard something about hypnosis." Most patients are able, with a little prodding, to respond adequately.

The patient's idea of trance is useful in several ways. The a priori image of the trance is related to the ease or difficulty with which the patient initially goes into trance, as well as to the course of the treatment (McCord, 1961). Conflict-free images of trance are associated with ease of entering trance and indicate a symptomatic approach to hypnotherapy; conflict-laden images of trance are usually,but not always, associated with difficulty in entering trance and indicate the need for a dynamic approach to hypnotherapy. (More is said about this in chapter 6.) The information on the image of trance also may be helpful in tailoring the initial hypnotic experience for the patient. Verbatim descriptions of the patient's image of trance can be incorporated into the initial hypnotic suggestions. If, for example, the patient imagines trance to be "like a fog . . . you don't know what's going on around you," the hypnotist may suggest that hypnosis is, among other things, like being in a fog. In this manner the hypnotist ensures that the initial experience is congruent with the patient's own conception of hypnosis, provided, of course, that the image of trance is not too inaccurate or too fear-laden.

The discussion that ensues after the inquiry is designed to provide the patient with accurate information about hypnosis. The social psychologists Leventhal and Everhart (1979) have convincingly demonstrated that anticipation of a new experience is usually accompanied by symptoms of distress when concepts about the experience are discrepant with the experience itself. When accurate information is provided to reduce that discrepancy, the symptoms of distress are alleviated (Johnson, 1973; Leventhal & Everhart, 1979). The same level of reasoning applies to hypnosis. If the patient's misconceptions and fears about hypnosis are not cleared up beforehand, initial hypnotic experiences can be very distressing. Leventhal's findings point up the value of providing the patient with accurate information about hypnosis beforehand, thereby decreasing the likelihood of distress during the initial hypnotic experience. Therefore, regardless of whether or not the patient is able to verbalize fears about hypnosis, as a matter of course we explain the nature of hypnosis to the patient before the first induction.

We explain that hypnosis is an altered state of consciousness, neither a state of sleep nor an unconscious state, but rather a state in which the patient will still be conscious, alert, and quite attentive. It is a state in which one can bring into awareness material from the unconscious: unconscious thoughts, feelings, memories. We also explain that hypnosis is a condition of careful attentiveness and point out to patients that most people are not carefully attentive in the normal waking state. It is difficult to fix attention for any length of time without becoming distracted; there are significant gaps in awareness when one is lost in reverie. We tell patients that during hypnosis, in contrast to the waking state, attention will be more focused so that the patient can experience interesting events and have new experiences. We also ask our patients to develop an attitude of receptivity, *not* to try to *make* the experiences happen, but to *let things happen as they happen.*

We tell them that the experiences, however, are fully under their control; we will not make them do things they would not feel comfortable doing while awake. We remind them that the role of the hypnotherapist is to help them discover and explore their own inner experience, not to impose an experience on them. Some patients worry about remembering the experience. We tell them that they are likely to recall the details of the experience as they would recall any experience in the waking state. If they find the experience especially interesting, they are likely to recall more of it; if it is too conflict laden to face, they will remember it only when they are ready to do so. Finally, we reassure them that there is little danger of harmful effects when hypnosis is conducted in the manner previously explained. Above all, we try to emphasize that hypnosis is an exploration of the patient's *own* experience; the hypnotist's function is to provide the context for this exploration and to facilitate it.

Alleviating fears through the kind of information provided in the prehypnotic discussion is the first step. Absence of fear is not the same as a positive set, however. It is also necessary to activate and cultivate a positive mental set in the patient's initial hypnotic experience and to build this positive set over the succession of hypnotic experiences. The therapist must convey an attitude of acceptance and positive anticipation toward the hypnotic experience. This can be done by intentionally incorporating certain phrases into the hypnotic suggestions: "You are looking forward to . . ."; "You are pleased to see _____ happening" (or "beginning to happen").

Most patients are doubtful and skeptical during the initial hypnotic experience. Some carry on a running critical commentary, even while successfully responding to the suggestions. The patient must be encouraged to suspend logical and critical thinking in favor of genuine openness to the experience. The therapist may reframe the doubt. He may say, for example, "You may find yourself wondering about [instead of doubting] the experience as it happens, and this will help convince you of what can happen for you in hypnosis." The therapist may also give suggestions contrary to the doubt: "No matter what happens, you will find the experience interesting and will be more and more open to it."

Focusing Attention During Hypnosis

Skill in paying attention underlies all hypnotic experience. Seen in this light, suggestions are merely the items to which the patient attends. The hypnotist's function is to enable the patient to pay careful attention and to strengthen attentional skills. Therefore, it is very important for the hypnotist to incorporate into the wording of the hypnotic suggestions ways of training attention. Sometimes the hypnotist explicitly tells the patient to fix attention by using such phrases as "Focus your attention on _____," "Notice carefully," or "As you become aware of _____." Because the hypnotist wishes the patient to attend carefully to his suggestions, patients are sometimes explicitly told to "listen carefully to what I am about to tell you." The goal is to get the patient to exercise selective attention so as to be able to focus on one thing while dismissing everything else as potential distractions. The hypnotist's words serve as a reminder of what to focus and keep attention on. Without this input by the hypnotist, the patient is more likely to become distracted by irrelevant thoughts and reveries.

The hypnotist structures the experience so that the patient learns to pay more attention to his internal experience and less attention to external stimuli. The hypnotist chooses words that will increase the patient's state of receptivity: "You are becoming more interested in the things which are going on inside of you . . . " or "You are fascinated by the thoughts and feelings that just seem to come up in your mind." The patient is introduced to the idea that he may discover things that normally are outside his awareness—bodily sensations, thoughts, memories, images, fantasy productions, feelings. The hypnotist can introduce this idea by saying, "Perhaps you will find that you are more open to letting things come up in your mind that are usually below the threshold of awareness" or "You may discover a lot of interesting things about yourself as we proceed." The hypnotist wants to evoke curiosity in his patient. And as the patient becomes more fascinated with his inner experience, he is less likely to be concerned with external events. The hypnotist might explicity encourage the fading of the generalized reality orientation (Shor, 1959) by saying, "You will become so interested in _____ that you won't even notice what's going on around you." The hypnotist should structure the patient's attention by purposeful wording of the suggestions.

Observing the Patient's Response

Just as the hypnotist has to pay careful attention to the wording of suggestions, he also must carefully observe the patient's behavioral response to suggestions. The therapist should not let his own generalized reality orientation fade, but must be vigilantly attentive to even the slightest changes in the patient's nonverbal behavior.

Changes in posture often reveal the status of the hypnotic alliance. The hypnotherapist must note, for example, whether the patient in the chair leans toward or away from him. Sudden shifts in posture and excessive restlessness may be associated with discomfort about the trance induction. Changes in muscle tone may be associated with the patient's level of comfort or discomfort. The hypnotist observes just how relaxed the patient is or is not. He should also be alert to spontaneous motor occurrences during trance, for example, eye fluttering and blinking, spontaneous catalepsies, bodily rigidity or passivity, or looseness and relaxation.

One of the most important observations to be made is of facial expression. An extensive literature now exists substantiating the relationship between specific patterns of facial muscles and emotional expression. The activity of facial muscles is a valid indicator of emotional response, and reliable observations of facial emotional expressions can be made (Izard, 1977). The hypnotist who learns to become sensitive to subtle changes in the facial responses of the patient during trance can pick up valuable cues about emotional responses to the trance experience, such as anxiety, sadness, anger, and the like. Changes in the rhythm of breathing, though more subtle than facial expression, also reveal ongoing changes in the emotional response of the patient and in his hypnotic depth. With depth and relaxation, breathing becomes slower and more regular.

For rapport to be built, the patient needs to feel that the hypnotist is carefully attuned to his ongoing experience. The hypnotherapist may explicitly show his attunement by incorporating observations into the ongoing hypnotic suggestions. For example, if the therapist observes an important change in the patient, he may mention this change with a suggestion: "There, you notice now that your eyes are fluttering, your breathing is getting heavier." Not only does the hypnotist thus demonstrate awareness of the patient's experience, but he also conveys that such changes are not unusual and can even be expected. Furthermore, the hypnotist may utilize these immediate changes in the service of the hypnotic induction. He can, for example, reframe eye fluttering as a step in trance induction: "There, you notice that your eyes are fluttering. This means that the eyes want to close, and soon they will close, and you will experience what it is like to be in trance." Of course even though these changes can be observed (and incorporated into the ongoing induction), it is not always possible to know their meaning from observation alone. Nonverbal responses in trance are often idiosyncratic. Therefore, the therapist may have to ask the patient what the behavior means: For example, he may say, "Is something bothering you right now?"

Establishing Communication

In the permissive style of hypnosis, the hypnotherapist takes care to establish the right atmosphere of communication with the patient, one that will foster a genuine dialogue—active, reciprocal, and open ended. The beginning hypnotherapist often mistakenly views hypnosis as a condition in which the hypnotist talks *to* or *at* the passive recipient of the hypnotic suggestions and fails to involve the hypnotic patient enough in the construction of the ongoing experience. They feel totally responsible, taking it upon themselves to create each suggestion down to the subtlest detail. In so doing, they discourage the hypnotic patient's participation. An extreme example of this tendency is the beginning hypnotist who "guides" the patient through a fantasy that is entirely the hypnotist's own, not the patient's. The patient is supposed to listen to the hypnotist's fantasy and experience it as it is suggested. Another example of failure to obtain the patient's participation is the use of touch without first announcing it. Such an approach to suggestion represents directive, not permissive, hypnosis. In the truly permissive approach, the therapist would say: *Now, with your permission, I'm about to lift your arm up, like this."*

The hypnotherapist encourages the patient to become ego-involved, not only in the hypnotic experience itself but also in its creation, because greater ego involvement means greater learning (Allport, 1937). Much better therapy can be done when the patient is an active agent, one of two people constructing the ongoing events of hypnosis. This involvement can be fostered by the hypnotist's suggesting explicitly not that the patient have a particular kind of experience, but rather that the patient describe his own experience, whatever it may be. For example: "Perhaps you wouldn't mind describing what you are experiencing" or "As _____ happens, you will be able to describe it to me." Such suggestions for description are interspersed throughout the entire hypnotic protocol.

The hypnotic patient thus learns to communicate actively not only the salient but also the subtle changes in the ongoing hypnotic experience. The immediate feedback on the suggestions allows the therapist to become more attuned to the patient's needs at any given moment, and to adapt to these needs by making modifications and corrections in the wording of suggestions. The ongoing dyadic interchange becomes more and more reciprocal, the hypnotist adapting suggestings according to the feedback from the patient, and the patient continuing to provide feedback on responses to subsequent suggestions. When a working dialogue is established, the hypnotic patient will tell the hypnotist more or less everything he needs to know about what to observe, how to word suggestions, and what direction to take with the suggestions.

The Wording of Suggestions

It is extremely important to word every hypnotic suggestion very precisely. How the hypnotist words suggestions structures the hypnotic experience for the patient and the way suggestions are worded can have a strong influence on the nature of the unfolding experience. Sloppily worded suggestions or technical errors are likely to produce unintended, and often unexpected, effects. If the mistakes in wording are inconsequential, the resultant changes in the patient's experience may go unnoticed, producing benign, albeit interesting, changes in the patient's hypnotic experience; other errors are harmful.

Hypnotized patients understand and respond to suggestions literally. Failure to account for this literalness can have untoward effects. As an example of the failure to take literalness seriously, consider the beginning hypnotist who attempted to induce trance by means of a coin drop. The hypnotist suggested that the subject's hand would slowly turn over and drop the coin. Immediately thereafter, the subject would enter a deep state of trance. The hypnotist kept repeating to the subject that the hand would slowly turn. Fifteen minutes passed, and the hand had not yet turned to the point of dropping the coin. The supervisor then recommended that the hypnotist tell the subject that his hand would turn more quickly. The hand immediately turned over, and the subject experienced trance. The hypnotist was surprised at the immediacy of the response. He might mistakenly have concluded that the subject had not responded to the initial suggestion. In fact, the subject had responded quite literally to the suggestion that the hand turn "slowly." Once the hypnotist modified the suggestion, the subject responded equally well to the suggestion that the hand turn quickly.

Beginning hypnotists are seldom confident of their ability to hypnotize. Their doubts are often conveyed in the wording of their suggestions. It is a good idea to avoid using words like "can," "might," or "perhaps" in suggestions. To produce an arm levitation, for example, do not say, "Your arm *might* be getting lighter" or "*perhaps* the arm is getting lighter." Be definitive and certain in the wording of the suggestion; use words like "is" or "will." Say, for example, "The arm *is* getting lighter" or "The arm *will* get lighter." It is likewise important to avoid questions that convey doubt, such as "Is your arm light?" As a rule of thumb, wherever possible, use imperative over interrogative sentences, make questions into gentle requests: "*allow* the arm to become light, and as it becomes light, it *will* move in a way that we both can see."

Posing a question too quickly often reveals the hypnotist's lack of confidence that the effect will happen. The confident hypnotist believes the patient will respond to the suggestion in due time. Therefore, many suggestions are worded in the future tense. The hypnotist may say, "*soon* the arm will lift." Or, if addressing a question to the patient, "Have you *begun to* notice the lightness in the arm *yet*?" Words and phrases such as "soon," "yet," "becoming," "beginning to happen" are part of the standard repertoire of the hypnotist. Sometimes the hypnotist may wish to build anticipation in the patient by saying, "The arm is *about to* lift up." By using the near-future orientation, the hypnotist conveys certainty that the patient will have the experience and that it is simply a matter of time before the effect is produced.

Sometimes the hypnotist uses what may be called graded suggestions, i.e. suggestions whose effects occur gradually over a short or a long span of time. The double comparative is one device commonly used to create graded suggestions. The hypnotist may say, "The arm is getting light*er* and light*er*" or "It is happening *more and more*." Reference to the passage of time is another way to compose a graded suggestion. The hypnotist may say, "The lightness is *gradually* spreading"; "*As time passes,* you will feel the lightness"; or "*At first* the lightness is subtle, *but then* you will be able to feel it more distinctly."

In the permissive style of hypnosis, the hypnotist must be careful to word suggestions in a permissive, not an authoritarian, manner. One can be permissive and at the same time be definite. Being certain and authori*tative* is not the same as being commanding and authori*tarian*. Of course, the hypnotist does not want to be too authoritative. The role of the hypnotist is to facilitate the unfolding of the patient's inner experience, not to get the patient to respond to the hypnotist's agenda. In giving suggestions, it is best to avoid saying, "I . . . ." Beginning hypnotists frequently use the phrase, "I want you to . . . ." Try to avoid saying, "I want you to let your arm feel light." Try, instead, to use the phrase, "*You will* notice" or "*You will* now find . . . ." Say, for example, "*You will* now discover a lightness in your arm." The permissive hypnotist also introduces suggestions with phrases such as "With your permission . . . " or "Perhaps you wouldn't mind noticing that . . . ," and follows the suggestion with phrases like "Allow yourself . . . " or "Let it happen."

The best suggestions are given in a manner that enables both hypnotist and patient to explore the patient's inner experience during trance. One way is to phrase suggestions in a neutral and open-ended manner. The more specific the suggestions, the less freedom the patient has in responding; the less specific, the more possibilities are opened up. For example, the patient may imagine walking along a road in a forest. A closed suggestion would be, "You will soon see an animal on that road, and it will be a deer." An open-ended suggestion would be, "You will soon see somebody or something along that road, and when you see it, you will describe what you see." Sometimes the hypnotist may be more specific in order to structure the experience around clinical goals: "You will see something along that road that will somehow relate to the problem you have been concerned with." In each case, the hypnotist has purposely refrained from specifying what the patient will experience, while definitively suggesting that the patient will experience *something*. The hypnotist can both provide structure and facilitate the spontaneous unfolding of the patient's inner experience. Another way to make neutral suggestions is to give a patient a number of choices or suggest a number of possibilities: "Perhaps you will notice [x]" or "Perhaps it will be [y] or [z] along that road."

In permissive hypnosis, the hypnotist does not so much create as amplify the experience that is unfolding. Therefore, the hypnotist carefully addresses the patient's immediate experience by saying such things as "You now notice" or "You can see" or "Notice the sensations" or (in a fantasy scene), "Look carefully, and you can see _____." Sometimes it is advisable to amplify the experience intentionally by the wording of suggestions, especially when encountering bodily sensations and feelings. The hypnotist may say, for example, "As you experience the sensations [or feelings], you soon will notice that the feeling becomes more intense."

Similarly, with fantasy productions, suggestions are given to enhance engagement with the imagery that presents itself rather than to create the imagery for the patient. If a patient imagines himself, for example, swimming under water, the patient may be told to "swim around and see what is there around you." The hypnotist would not suggest what is around the patient in the water; it must come from the patient's own productions. The hypnotist may, however, enhance what the patient produces. If, for example, the patient subsequently reports a form swimming far off in the water, the hypnotist may say, "You may wish to go toward that form, see what it is, and see what happens."

Skill in hypnotizing frequently requires saying the same thing in many different ways. The hypnotist seldom gives a suggestion only once; it is repeated a number of times, with brief pauses between reiterations. Each time the suggestion is worded slightly differently; the hypnotist tries to select different ways of saying the same thing, for example, "drowsy," "sleepy," or "relaxed." Such multiple repetitions may be likened to a musical score with numerous variations on a single theme. The purpose of varied repetition is to enhance the likelihood of a positive response to the suggestion. Weitzenhoffer (1957) explains that multiple repetitions of a suggestion progressively sensitize the patient to respond. He believes that each repetition produces a minute response. Multiple repetitions cause an accumulation of subtle responses, culminating in a behavioral response that can be observed by the hypnotist. In this sense, multiple repetition contributes to a learning effect, while variation in the repetition minimizes habituation and allows the hypnotized individual to "work through" the suggestion to the point of response (Weitzenhoffer, 1957, p. 219). Weitzenhoffer calls the learning effect a "homoactive effect" because the elicitation of a series of submaximal responses through repetition increases the probability of the same response in each successive repetition.

Another way of intentionally facilitating the learning process is by "chaining." The hypnotist chains suggestions together by explicitly linking one suggestion to another. The hypnotist says, "As [x] happens, you will find that [y] happens, and as [y] occurs, [z] will happen." The hypnotist may say, for example, "As you notice the lightness in your arm $[x_1]$, your arm will begin to lift $[x_2]$, your eyes will close $[y_1]$, and you will begin to feel more and more relaxed $[z_1]$ . . . and as your arm lifts higher and higher $[x_3]$, you will become even more relaxed $[z_2]$," and so on. In this way the hypnotist is able to integrate a series of suggestions into a continuous experience, with the likelihood that a positive response to one suggestion will lead to a positive response to the next, and so forth.

The Structure of an Hypnotic Suggestion

Each response to an hypnotic suggestion in a way involves a learning process. Each unit of the hypnotist's suggestive language constitutes a stimulus to which the patient may or may not respond. A single item—for example, a suggestion for arm levitation—can be broken down into a sequence of microsuggestions intended to produce a sequence of subtle events within the patient, which culminate in a full behavioral response to the suggestion. For an understanding of exactly how the hypnotist facilitates the full response to the suggestion, the sequence of his suggestive verbal communications can be examined in detail. The language of suggestion has its own structure, and, in this sense, it is possible to speak of the structure of a single hypnotic suggestion. Although the hypnotist has a great variety of suggestions from which to choose, the underlying structure of each of these suggestions is often quite similar. Learning to hypnotize is like learning a language; once the student grasps the syntax, novel and unfamiliar linguistic forms are readily assimilated, and new linguistic forms can be generated. Similarly, once the beginning hypnotist grasps the basic structure of hypnotic suggestion, he will realize the common elements across a great variety of suggestions and can create new possibilities.

The structure of each hypnotic suggestion can be broken down into a series of microsuggestions given in sequence. We identify these operations here in general and illustrate them with the particular example of an arm levitation.

1. *Focusing attention.* Each suggestion begins with instructions to focus attention. If the hypnotic patient is unaware of the hypnotist's suggestions, there can be no response. To increase the response potential, the hypnotist explicitly introduces the suggestion with some reference to paying attention. The hypnotist may say, "Now *focus your attention on* the fingers of your right hand."

2. *Observing immediate experience.* To increase the patient's awareness of immediate experience, the hypnotist continues with "And *you will begin to notice the sensations* in the fingers and hand and can describe them to me." Note that the hypnotist here simply suggests that the patient become aware of whatever is happening; he is not attempting to make something happen.

3. *Observing something new in the experience/leading the subject.* The hypnotist next suggests something new to the patient and tries to establish a set in which the patient expects to encounter additional new experiences: "And soon you *will begin [set] to notice other sensations.* In fact, you will begin to notice a lightness in the fingers and hand." The hypnotist can ensure that the patient actually has the experience by adding, "*Have you noticed* the lightness yet?" or "Tell me *how far* up the fingers you experience the lightness *at this point.*" If the patient fails to respond, the hypnotist adds, "At first the experience of lightness is subtle, but soon you will experience it more distinctly . . . Have you *noticed* it *yet in this subtle way?*" If the answer is yes, the patient has responded to something that was introduced by the hypnotist. Technically, the patient has made a response to an outside suggestion.

4. *Setting the overall goal of the suggestion.* Next, the hypnotist introduces the total behavioral response he hopes the patient will make. The goal is introduced as something that will happen in the near future, but not immediately: "*At some point soon* the lightness will increase so that your entire hand and arm will want to lift up, and *it will lift up and float up off the arm of the chair.*"

5. *Repetition and variation.* Next, the hypnotist returns to the suggestion introduced in step 3 and repeats it in various ways to increasingly sensitize the patient to learn to respond. The hypnotist puts the suggestion

in a progressive spatial and temporal framework: "The lightness is *increasing more and more*. It is *spreading* to the fingers . . . Now the entire hand is light . . . The arm is becoming light now . . . ." The hypnotist varies the wording: "The hand is light and buoyant . . . very light . . . as if it is floating."

6. *Enhancing dissociation and involuntarism.* At some point in the sequence, the hypnotist changes the language in subtle ways to enlarge the dissociative and involuntary nature of the trance experience. The hypnotist begins to say, "*The* hand [dissociation] is getting lighter" instead of saying "*Your* hand is getting lighter." The hypnotist may also say, "The lightness is spreading *in its own way*" or "The hand is beginning to lift *all by itself* [involuntarism].

7. *Enhancing the anticipation of a positive response.* As the patient progressively responds to the hypnotist's sequence of suggestions, the hypnotist introduces a reminder that the total behavior response will soon come. The hypnotist does this to heighten the sense of anticipation and to focus the patient's attention on the emerging behavioral response, the goal of the suggestive sequence. The hypnotist says, "There, the hand and arm *are about to* lift up . . . they are *just beginning to* lift up now."

8. *Adjusting the rate of response.* If the patient responds too slowly (or too quickly) to all or part of a given suggestion, somewhere in the sequence of suggestions the hypnotist can speed up the response or slow it down. "The lightness spreads more quickly now" or "The hand and arm will lift up very soon"; or "The hand and arm will move more slowly now."

9. *Focusing on a positive response.* The hypnotist closes the sequence of suggestions with a comment on the behavioral response: "There, it's happening now" or "There, you're experiencing _____" or "Notice the effects . . . notice what it is like as you experience _____" or "You can see that _____ is happening." The hypnotist may comment, "The arm is lifting up now"—the patient's self-efficacy is reinforced when he knows that the response is being produced.

The structure underlying most induction and deepening techniques follows the sequence just outlined. A variety of suggestions for induction and deepening is presented in the next chapter. Once the hypnotist learns this structure, it is easier to utilize aspects of the patient's immediate experience and generate new plans for suggestions based on that experience.

Attunement to the Patient

Much of hypnosis remains a private, internal experience for the subject. Hypnotized patients are less inclined to talk than are waking people. The hypnotist is forced to rely on nonverbal cues for much of his understanding of the patient's experience. Thus, the need for the hypnotist to carefully observe and become attuned to the patient's facial expressions and body movements is more urgent than in many other types of interactions. One of the most difficult things for beginners to learn is how to become attuned to the hypnotized patient.

Attunement is poor when the hypnotist's plan for carrying out suggestions is different from what the hypnotized patient actually experiences in response to these suggestions and the hypnotist does not become aware of this discrepancy. This happens when the hypnotist is blind to spontaneous changes in the patient's behavior, such as changes in breathing or increases in body tension, or when the hypnotist dismisses clinically relevant idiosyncratic responses that are incongruent with the suggestions he has given and their expected responses. Attunement requires flexibility, as the hypnotist must continually monitor both the ongoing plan for the suggestions and the patient's ongoing responses and modify suggestions to match them more closely with the patient's emergent experience.

In permissive hypnosis, the hypnotist keeps in phase with the patient by utilizing whatever comes up in the patient's immediate experience and manifest behavior. If, for example, the patient begins the hour by talking about driving to therapy, the hypnotist might incorporate the comment into an induction. The patient can be told to imagine himself driving along a road and to see something along that road that will pertain to his problem. After the induction of trance, the patient's spontaneous experiences can be utilized in the hypnotherapy part of the session. If, for example, the patient complains of having a dry mouth, it would be insensitive of the hypnotist to ignore the comment and just continue the planned suggestions. The hypnotist can, instead, suggest that the patient hallucinate a refreshing drink (symptom relief) or can otherwise explore the meaning of the symptom through hypnoprojective techniques (dynamic exploration). In Erickson's (1959) utilization approach, too, the hypnotherapist also aims to assimilate all salient changes in the patient's immediate behavior and experience into the plan of suggestions.

One of the most common manifestations of being out of phase with the hypnotized patient is poor pacing of suggestions. Hypnotized patients have their own individual rates of response. Extremely passive patients respond very slowly. Highly motivated or highly hypnotizable patients sometimes respond very quickly. The hypnotist must be flexible enough to adjust the pacing of suggestions to the natural rate of response of the patient. Beginning hypnotherapists often fail to make the adjustment. If, for example, a patient responds to a suggestion for heaviness of the eyelids by closing the eyes quickly, a novice hypnotist might continue to suggest heaviness of the eyes as if the patient had not responded. Or, with a patient who typically responds to suggestions slowly, the novice may prematurely discontinue the suggestion and think of it as a failure.

In clinical work it is advisable to avoid challenge suggestions (except in the case of symptom challenge). Challenge suggestions can hamper the smooth flow of therapy. It is not necessary, for example, to challenge the patient to open his eyes after eye catalepsy suggestions. The challenge serves no real purpose, except perhaps to demonstrate the hypnotist's power over the patient, in which case it signifies a countertransference problem. If the patient fails to meet the challenge, he may come to believe he cannot be hypnotized and to think that he won't succeed in resolving his problems in hypnotherapy.

In giving a sequence of suggestions, it is advisable to use the termination of the preceding suggestion as the preparation for the next one. Beginning hypnotists always have difficulty making smooth transitions from one suggestion to the next. The beginning hypnotist is likely, for example, to tell the patient who responds successfully to an arm levitation to end simply by lowering the arm. The more experienced hypnotist is likely to utilize the arm-lowering event in the service of the ongoing plan of suggestions: "And as the arm floats down, you will get even more relaxed" or "At the moment you feel the arm touch your lap, you will go into an even deeper state of trance."

According to Shor (1962), the depth of the hypnotic experience can be viewed algfg three separate dimensions: trance, nonconscious involvement, and archaic involvement. Not all patients respond equally well along the various dimensions. For most, the hypnotic experience lacks "balance" along these three dimensions. For example, subjects who manifest trance more weakly than they do the other dimensions of hypnosis still experience hypnotic phenomena; but they are likely to complain of being acutely aware of themselves, of the events in the surroundings, or of the passage of time throughout the hypnotic experience. They are unable to relinquish self-critical monitoring of the unfolding experience or monitoring of the external environment. Subjects who manifest nonconscious involvement more weakly than they do the other dimensions complain that the hypnotic experience is too much under their conscious, deliberate control. They often respond to the hypnotist's suggestions in a voluntary or an idiosyncratic manner, for example, by raising the arm voluntarily rather than letting it happen in response to a suggestion for an arm levitation. Still others manifest weak archaic involvement (transference). They fail to have a strong emotional reaction to the hypnotist and in some instances do not form a special hypnotic relationship. While they may find hypnotic phenomena interesting, they do not have a strong enough emotional reaction to the hypnotherapist to sustain interest in hypnosis beyond the first or second experience.

The hypnotist must be aware of the specific routes along which patients enter trance. He must be able to correct the imbalances in the patient's hypnotic experience by utilizing suggestions specifically designed to emphasize those dimensions in which hypnotic experience is weakest. If the patient complains of interference from the external surroundings, the hypnotist adds suggestions that help the patient to deepen the experience. For instance, if the patient complains about the distracting noise of typing going on next door, the hypnotist may suggest that the patient is walking in the woods, seeing and hearing a redheaded woodpecker peck on a tree. Alternatively, the hypnotist may build into the overall plan of suggestions comments like, "Although you may remain aware of the surroundings, you will be less and less concerned with what is going on around you" or "The room is fading as if it were in a fog, and the noises you may have heard seem to become more and more like a barely audible buzz in the background." The patient who complains of too much conscious control or gives an idiosyncratic response can be told in various ways to "Let go," "Allow . . . to happen what may be happening by itself," or "Soon your own way of doing it will come to you, and you will then . . . ." It is more difficult to devise specific suggestions to correct weak archaic involvement. Such a failure is indicative of a type of resistance to the formation of the hypnotic relationship and is best handled through interpretation in the waking state prior to restarting hypnotic work.

Beginning hypnotists often fail to adjust to the aspects of the altered state of consciousness that become apparent as the patient enters a deep state of hypnosis. Consider an example taken from an introductory training workshop. Both the hypnotist and the subject were having their first exposure to hypnosis. Upon being hypnotized, the subject had a spontaneous age regression and found herself sitting in a classroom in grammar school. She was in considerable distress as she struggled with her "takeaways" (subtractions). The hypnotist talked with the subject as if to an adult, because he did not believe the subject's experience could be like that of a latency-age child. It was later learned that the subject was very highly hypnotizable. She easily lapsed into spontaneous age regressions, manifested trance logic, and experienced a variety of hallucinatory phenomena. In this experience she "hallucinated" the classroom and "saw" the room and other classmates even while her eyes were open. She also manifested a form of trance logic: although in reality she sat in a chair hypnotized, she experienced herself as standing at a blackboard in front of the class. The hypnotist failed to perceive the genuineness of the regression, the intensity of her affect, the positive hallucination, and the trance logic. The supervisor observing the situation suggested that the hypnotist, an experienced child psychologist, approach the hypnotized subject as if she were a child. The hypnotist changed his manner of approach. He learned to view the experience and make suggestions according to the perspective of the patient's altered state of consciousness, not the ordinary waking state. Accepting that as a child the patient really did not know how to do "take-aways," he presented her with an (hallucinated) arithmetic book and asked her to stand up and work out the problem on the blackboard. He patiently tutored her to the point of providing her with an emotionally corrective experience before terminating the trance.

Even the experienced hypnotist will not always be carefully atuned to the hypnotized subject. During induction and deepening, the unfolding hypnotic experience is characterized by many internal changes that are not communicated to the hypnotist. The hypnotist simply cannot know everything the patient experiences. Subtle empathic failures are characteristic of the interaction between the hypnotist and the patient. Technical errors inevitably will also occur occasionally. As failures in being atuned to the hypnotized individual cannot entirely be circumvented, it is good practice to admit mistakes and technical errors whenever possible. If the hypnotist recognizes making a mistake in the wording of a suggestion while giving it, he can simply correct the wording. If the mistaken wording is recognized after the suggestion has been given, the hypnotist should simply admit the mistake and give a countersuggestion. Admitting mistakes and making corrections is a way of conveying to the patient a willingness to strive continually to understand the patient's hypnotic experience and act in the patient's best interest. This is true for mistakes made in induction and deepening as well as for blunders made in hypnotherapy and hypnoanalysis.

Adjusting to the Responses to Suggestions

It is good practice to positively reinforce each successful behavioral reponse to a suggestion with comments like "That's fine" or "That's very good." In permissive hypnosis, the emphasis is placed not only on the behavioral response itself but on the patient's own sense of accomplishment. As soon as the patient begins to show a response, the hypnotist may comment, "There, now you can see for yourself what you are beginning to experience" or ". . . what is happening" or ". . . what you are able to do." These comments are intended to help the patient realize that he is capable of entering and deepening the hypnotic state. After the patient makes a successful response, the hypnotist may add, "You are pleased to discover that you are able to do ＿＿＿＿＿＿＿" or "A feeling of pride develops in you as you are able to do these things." Such suggestions enhance the patient's sense of self-efficacy in the hypnotic experience.

When the patient fails to respond, the hypnotist must adjust the suggestions accordingly. Patients who fail to respond because they are poorly hypnotizable may, nevertheless, have a need to see themselves as being hypnotized. When the patient is not capable of entering a hypnotic trance, the hypnotist can still utilize the meaning of the hypnotic situation

(Gruenewald, 1982). Of course, the hypnotist should not communicate to the patient that he has failed to be hypnotized. Without debating whether the patient was or was not hypnotized, the hypnotist can simply proceed with relaxation training and (waking) imagery suggestions, to which even poorly hypnotizable patients are likely to respond.

Even patients who are hypnotizable may fail to respond to specific suggestions. The reasons for failure are many: lack of hypnotic ability in specific areas within the overall domain of hypnosis, technical errors on the part of the hypnotist, emergence of conflicts associated with the specific suggestions, and so forth. The hypnotist should try to find out the exact reason for the failure. Giving suggestions designed to tap the full range of specific hypnotic abilities in the initial hypnotic sessions should provide the hypnotist with an understanding of weak and strong areas within the domain of the patient's hypnotic responsiveness. Specific suggestions can be designed to make such an assessment. For example, a patient may report, "I don't see anything," after the suggestion that he will imagine watching a television program about some problem he is experiencing. It may not be clear from the patient's response whether the failure is due to the operation of the patient's defenses and, therefore, is associated with the conflict or simply due to a lack of talent in experiencing visual imagery. If the hypnotist has previously utilized neutral imagery suggestions and found the patient responsive to them, the hypnotist can conclude that the current failure to respond is due to the operation of defenses, not to a failure in imagery. If the hypnotist has not previously utilized imagery suggestions, he might first ask the patient to visualize a television set and describe the way it is visualized before asking the patient to visualize a program. If the patient describes the television set but not the program, the hypnotist can be reasonably sure that the failure is defensive in nature. The hypnotist, of course, also must determine whether the failure is due to a technical error in his own wording rather than to a conflict in the patient.

It is good practice to ask the patient about the failed suggestion. If the patient does not respond to a suggestion after a reasonable amount of time has elapsed, the hypnotist can simply say, "Notice what you are experiencing, and you will be able to describe your experience to me." He can also say, "Do you need more time, or is there some difficulty?" On the basis of the patient's response, the hypnotist tries to determine whether the patient has been confused by a technical mistake the hypnotist made or is struggling with some inner conflict precipitated by the suggestion. The hypnotist may have conveyed hesitation or doubt in giving the suggestion, or he may have worded the suggestion in a confusing and contradictory manner. If so, the hypnotist tries to establish an atmosphere wherein the patient can freely give the hypnotist feedback on the nature of the experience which has resulted, and make corrections accordingly. If the patient has embellished the suggestion in some idiosyncratic way, the suggestion can be modified. For instance, if after a suggestion for coin drop the patient fails to turn the hand over because the hand "is too heavy," the hypnotist simply adjusts the subsequent suggestions to the patient's experience. He might say, "Fine, and as the hand gets heavier and heavier, your eyes will close and . . . ." Whether a technical error by the hypnotist or the patient's idiosyncratic embellishment caused the failure, the adjustment in wording often results in a successful response. If the failure to respond is due to conflict, it becomes an opportunity for clinical exploration.

The rule in managing failed responses is to communicate to the patient that there is no such thing as a failure. Sometimes the hypnotist conveys this through an attitude adopted toward the failure. The hypnotist says to the patient, "That's fine," as if to convey no expectation of a response other than what the patient did, and simply goes on to something else. Sometimes the failure can be reframed as a positive response. To the patient complaining that his had is "too heavy" to turn, the hypnotist may say, "Yes, and that heaviness is one of the things you may notice as you experience a deeper state of trance . . . notice now how the sense of heaviness increases not only in your hand and arm but throughout your entire body as you go deeper and deeper. . . ." Whereas minimizing the failure and simply going on to something else may be indicated, it is sometimes best to stay with the suggestion until it becomes a positive experience for the patient.

A suggestion can also be broken down into hierarchical steps. For example, an arm levitation that at first does not work can be reframed first into lightness of the fingers; then, in addition, lightness of the hand, lightness of the arm up to the elbow; and, finally, arm levitation itself. The suggestion for arm levitation is then repeated as a graded series of suggestions within the same session or across a series of sessions, with the expectation that a positive response could mean something less than total arm levitation along a continuum of response possibilities. Supplemental suggestions can be given for the patient to search for inner resources that might help develop a full, positive response: "As I count from one to five, a thought, an image, or a feeling will come into your mind about something that will help you to experience your arm lifting up," or "You will find something to make it easier for you to have your arm lift." Both hypnotist and patient are often pleasantly surprised when an image occurs that enables each to modify the suggestion and help bring about a successful response.

The hypnotist must also adjust his comments to the speed of the patient's response to suggestion, which can vary widely from patient to patient. Some patients respond extremely slowly, although they do respond successfully if given enough time. For them, the hypnotist can incorporate suggestions for speed into the overall plan of suggestion: "It is beginning to happen more quickly." Other patients respond so quickly that they complete the full behavioral response before the hypnotist has finished the suggestion. For them, the hypnotist learns to state the goal of the suggestion or the intended response very early in the overall plan of the suggestion.

Sometimes patients have strong emotional reactions that may or may not be directly related to the suggestions given. The hypnotist must adapt to these often intense, spontaneous emotional reactions, neither denying them by trying to carry out the original plan of suggestion nor attempting to minimize them with suggestions for relaxation. The good clinician uses the spontaneous emergence of the patient's affective states as an opportunity for therapeutic exploration, both in and out of trance.

The Overall Plan of the Hypnotic Session

Each hypnotic session can be divided into four phases: induction, deepening, trance exploration, and termination. The hypnotist develops an overall plan of the hypnotic session by choosing tasks for each phase and arranging the suggestions for the task in a sequence.

Induction. In any session, the very first task and the suggestions connected with it constitute the "induction"; subsequent ones serve the "deepening" process. Tasks particularly fitted for induction purposes are: coin drop, eye fixation, waves of relaxation, and arm levitation. Hypnosis should be induced slowly the first few times: about 15 minutes for the induction phase (not including deepening) of the first hypnotic experience and considerably less time in subsequent sessions. Naive subjects need time to relinquish their hold on ordinary waking experience and discover an alternate mode of functioning characteristic of the trance state. When the induction proceeds slowly within the context of good communication between the hypnotist and the patient, anxiety and doubts about the unfolding experience can be addressed as they occur.

Deepening. The series of suggestions right after induction is designed to deepen the experience (e.g., stairs, elevator, counting, breathing, imagery of lying on a lovely beach, or direct suggestions for deepening). It takes a good deal of time for most patients new to hypnosis to establish the trance state and to recognize it, as it is something different from the waking state (Tart, 1975).

Exploration.   After trance has been deepened enough and stabilized, the patient is given the chance to explore the phenomena of trance. In the initial hypnotic sessions the sequence of suggestions is chosen to familiarize the patient with the range of experiences possible in trance. The hypnotist chooses suggestions that cut across a wide range of specific hypnotic abilities and arranges these tasks into a sequence from easier to more difficult. In subsequent hypnotherapy sessions, after trance has been deepened and stabilized, the sequence of suggestions designed for the exploration of the patient's problems and conflicts are given.

Termination.   Hypnosis is a "regression in the service of the ego" (Fromm, 1979; Gill & Brenman, 1959; Kris 1936/1952), a temporary regression to earlier forms of thinking and feeling. Termination of a trance means a return to reality. When bringing the patient back from the hypnotic to the waking state, the hypnotherapist must respect the patient's regressive needs and the altered state and allow him to take a little time for the process of returning to reality and maturity.

It is poor practice to tell a patient that he will awaken when the hypnotherapist snaps his fingers. On the other hand, counting slowly backwards from ten to one allows the patient time to anticipate the changes as he returns to normal consciousness and to make the necessary adjustment. Most patients awaken without any difficulty. Some patients manifest an aura effect for a few minutes; they appear to remain in trance in a way and return to normal consciousness a bit more slowly.

Although patients often fear not being able to come out of trance, one seldom comes across a patient who fails to awaken. Even if a patient refuses to awaken, there is little to be alarmed. The reason for the failure to follow the awakening suggestion is probably more a matter of the patient's secondary gain than of technical error by the hypnotist. The ability to awaken from trance has been shown in the laboratory to be under the subject's voluntary control; and when left alone most experimental subjects awaken themselves spontaneously (Orne & Evans, 1966). If the hour has terminated and the patient fails to awaken, he can be told that he can remain in trance if he wishes to do so but must go and sit in the waiting room because the hypnotist now has to attend to other things. The patient is told to bring himself to the full waking state when he is ready to leave the waiting room. Most patients awaken before returning to the waiting room; a few remain in trance a bit longer in the waiting room. No patient continues in trance for long once the secondary gain has been removed.

Though the patient's refusal to come out of hypnosis may represent a challenge ("I, the patient, dare you, the hypnotherapist, to get me out of hypnosis!", or "I can dominate you, reduce you to impotence, make you uncomfortable, embarrass you, make you afraid"), the hypnotherapist should under no circumstances react as if the patient's refusal to come out of trance were a challenge to him, and he should not get into a power struggle with the patient.

Under all circumstances, even with normal termination, it is important that the hypnotic state be fully terminated and that the patient regain normal contact with reality before he leaves the office. Always permit a few minutes at the end of each hypnotic session for interaction in the conscious, waking state.

After the initial hypnotic experience, many patients express doubts about having been hypnotized. They can then be reminded of successful responses to suggestions. Some patients still complain of not having been hypnotized, even while admitting successful responses to all suggestions. Here it is likely that the expectations about hypnosis and the initial image of trance were unlike the actual experience. In the posthypnotic discussion the hypnotist tries to identify and modify these usually unrealistic expectations and fantasies about what hypnosis really is.

4 The Most Widely Used Induction and Deepening Techniques

Every hypnotherapeutic session has four phases: the induction of the hypnotic state, the deepening of the hypnotic state, its utilization (the part devoted to hypnotherapy), and the termination of the hypnotic state. In this chapter we discuss induction, deepening, and termination.

A wise hypnotherapist frequently says in induction and deepening procedures: "With your permission . . . " or "If you want to involve yourself even deeper . . . " or " . . . at your own rate." For instance, when the patient sees himself standing on an imaginary escalator in the Escalator Technique (described later), the hypnotherapist can say: "If you want to go deeper, the escalator will take you down into a much deeper state at your own rate." This shows the patient that the hypnotherapist is not going to overwhelm the patient but, rather, respects the patient's desires, needs, personal timing and style.

BASIC INDUCTION AND DEEPENING TECHNIQUES

The Chevreul Pendulum

The Chevreul Pendulum (Easton & Shor, 1975) can be used both as a sort of hypnotizability test—really a quick but not fully reliable estimate of hypnotizability—and as an induction technique.

> The patient is seated at a 90° angle beside a table or desk with his elbow resting on the table and his forearm and hand sticking up into the air near-perpendicularly. The patient holds between the tip of his thumb and index finger the end of a long, thin string on which a shiny or bright-colored object hangs about ½ inch from the surface of the table. He is asked to fixate his gaze on the shiny object and watch what it is

doing. We usually put an 8½" × 11" white sheet on the table under the pendulum, for contrast, to make it easier to watch the movements of the pendulum. One or two overhead lights are placed slightly to the side of the patient to create interesting shadows of the pendulum on the paper.

[1] *Focusing attention*

The patient is told to [1] *fixate on the shiny object* and watch what the pendulum, or its shadows, will do. As it is practically impossible to hold the hand totally still in a near-upright position, the pendulum will almost immediately start to move. The hypnotist simply [2] *comments on the direction of the movement as if that were intended.* If it moves from the patient's left to the right, the hypnotherapist says to the patient, "Look how the pendulum (or the shadow) moves from left to right, left, right," describing for some 30 seconds, or perhaps a minute, exactly what the pendulum is doing.

[2] *Observing immediate experience*

Then the hypnotist begins to [3] *suggest where the pendulum will go next.* His comments now go beyond simple description of how it is moving as of that moment. He suggests a wider and wider movement in the same direction: "And now the arc through which it is moving is [4] *getting wider and wider . . .* [5] *wider and wider* . . . as the pendulum moves in a line from *left to right . . . left to right . . . left . . . right, left, right, left,* right." If the patient follows this suggestion, [6] *the therapist suggests a new movement,* e.g., that the arc now will get smaller and smaller again. When this has happened, he suggests that now [6] *the direction of the pendulum swing will change and the pendulum will go "back and forth . . .* and back and fourth . . . and back and forth. . . . It is [7] *as if the pendulum has a mind of its own".* . . . After this has occurred, he may suggest that the pendulum

[3] *Leading the subject*

[4] *Testing of ego receptivity by means of ideomotor phenomenon;*
[5] *Repetition and variation;* [6] *Therapist one step ahead of patient*

[7] *Involuntarism*

8 *Dissociation*

9 *Setting the overall goal*

10 *Enhancing anticipation of a positive set;*
11 *Chaining*
12 *Focusing on a positive response*
13 *Encouraging active participation*

will now describe an ellipse for a while and then a more widening, or narrowing, circle. Eventually he may suggest, 8 *"The arm* is now getting so tired that *it will want* to sink to the table."* (In order for dissociation to occur, the hypnotist must carefully avoid saying "your arm.") He goes on to 9 *set the goal of the suggestions: "At the very moment you hear the pendulum hit the table, you will find yourself sinking into a much deeper state of hypnosis.* This state will become 10 *even* deeper as the arm *is beginning to fall now . . .*11 *it's starting to float* down to the table now. There, *as the forearm touches the table,* your eyes close . . . and you go into a deep, deep, and 12 *thoroughly enjoyable trance,* deeper than you ever imagined you could go. . . . 13 *Notice what this state is like for you. . . ."*

If the Chevreul Pendulum—or any other induction technique—does not work, the therapist must not let the patient become disappointed or feel like a failure. He can simply say, "That's fine," and go on to another induction procedure. Or he can expand the width of the arc's amplitude and ask the patient what he experienced after he corrected it.

Eye Closure

The Chevreul Pendulum is an induction method that requires open eyes for most of the procedure. Only towards the very end, when the pendulum comes to rest or the arm sinks down, can the therapist suggest that the patient's eyes will close too. Another induction procedure, which leads to early eye closure, enables the patient to fulfill one of the basic preconditions of the hypnotic state—sensory deprivation. Sensory deprivation helps to increase fantasy and absorption in the altered state of hypnosis. When the eyes are closed, all visual stimuli coming from the outside world are automatically cut off. Eye closure, next to Progressive Relaxation, is the most widely used induction technique.

The therapist has on or near the ceiling of his office, or hanging down from the ceiling, but in any case high above the eye level of the patient, an interesting or shining object that can serve as the fixation point: a small, artistic mobile, a colorful dot high on the wall, or a thumbtack stuck into the ceiling. He asks the patient to fixate his eyes on this object—or to select a fixation point of his own choice high up in the room[1]—and to stare at it. Then the therapist says to the patient:

[1] *Focusing attention*	[1] *"Continue to stare at the object* of your choice
[8] *Dissociation*	and focus all your attention on it. [8] *The* eyelids
[7] *Involuntarism*	will get *so* heavy that *they* [7] *will want to close by*
	themselves. You can let them close whenever the
[9] *Setting the overall*	eyelids *want to close,* [9] *and when they close, you*
goal	*will find yourself in a deep state of trance. . . ."*

When the patient's eyelids begin to flutter or blink, as they usually do after a short while, the therapist builds that into his patter:

[2] *Observing*	[2] *"You may already have noticed* that your
immediate	eyelids have become so tired that they have
experience;	started to flutter [7] *all by themselves.* . . . There,
[7] *Involuntarism;*	it just happens. It is so hard to keep[8] *them*
[8] *Repetition of*	open. . . . You do not need to keep [8] *them* open
dissociation	any longer. . . . The eyelids will just close when
[10] *Anticipation of a*	they are ready to close. [10] *Beginning to close*
positive response;	*tightly now,* very tightly closed. [12] *You'll be*
[12] *Focusing on a*	*interested to discover what the experience of*
positive response	*hypnosis is like as the eyelids close."*

The hypnotherapist may also say to the patient:

	"As you are staring at the object, the thought
[14] *Adjusting the rate*	comes to your mind, [14] *How soon will it be that*
of response	*my eyes will close?* . . . Will I *achieve* this state
	quickly . . . or will it take me a bit longer before
[15] *Establishing a*	I achieve this state? . . . [15] *You are looking*
positive set	*forward* to achieving this state . . . because it is
	a comfortable, pleasurable, deeply relaxed
	state. . . . Think to yourself: 'With each breath I
	take, I will come closer and closer to this nice,
	glowing, enjoyable state. I will feel so good. . . .'
[16] *Permissive*	You can go into this state in [16] *your own unique*
hypnosis	*way . . . in the way that is most comfortable to*
	you."

---

[1] The fixation point must be above eye level, making it necessary for the eyes to open wide, which is tiring and makes the patient want to let the eyelids close.

Progressive Relaxation

Eye closure works particularly well as an induction when combined with the Progressive Relaxation Technique or its variation (Jacobson, 1938), waves of relaxation. The therapist gives the patient the following patter:

"Make yourself as comfortable as you can in your chair [or on the couch] . . . Let your head sink back on the pillow . . . let your arms and hands lie loosely on the arms of the chair [or at your side] . . . and look at the object up there

[16] *Permissiveness* — that [16] *you have chosen to stare at. . . .* Keep

[1] *Focusing attention* — [1] *listening carefully to my voice* as you attentively focus on the spot. [2] *Notice what that*

[2] *Observing immediate experience;* — *spot looks like.* You [7] *don't need to do anything* or not do anything. . . . *Just let things happen,*

[7] *Involuntarism* — and keep listening to my voice as it goes on.

[2] *Observing something new: alteration of perception;* — [2] *"Pretty soon you will notice* that the object you are staring at *is changing* a bit. . . . Perhaps it is radiating or becoming somewhat nebulous. . . . Just enjoy that and keep staring at it. . . . [2] *And*

[2] *Observing something new: waves of relaxation* — *you will find that from the top of your head . . . where I am going to touch it now [therapist puts his hand on the patient's head lightly for a moment] . . . wave after wave of relaxation will roll into you. . . . The waves will roll into your forehead . . . making the muscles in your forehead relax. . . . They will roll into and through your brain, making your thoughts and*

[5] *Repetition and variation* — *your feelings so relaxed. . . .* [5] *Relaxed and drowsy. . . . Drowsy and relaxed.* And perhaps

[9] *Setting the overall goal* — the idea comes into your head that [9] *pretty soon you will enter that warm, glowing, comfortable state that we call hypnosis.* . . . Should you get sleepy, that will be all right, too. [7] *Just let*

[7] *Involuntarism* — *happen whatever happens* as you keep staring at the object for a while. . . . There will come a time that your eyelids will feel *so* heavy that they will [7] *want* to close . . . so tired that they will want to fall closed all by themselves. When

[16] *Permissiveness* — this happens, [16] *you don't need to keep them*

open any longer. You can just let them close. Let your eyelids fall closed, let them fall closed. . . . Let yourself relax completely. Let every muscle in your body relax. [17] *Imagine* that from the top of your head, where I touched it before, *wave after wave of heavy, drowsy, comfortable sleepiness* is rolling into you.

[17] *Imaginative involvement and bodily sensations*

[10] *Anticipation of positive response*

[10] *Perhaps you can feel* the warm, glowing sensation of this drowsy heaviness as it is radiating through your body from the spot, making you feel increasingly happy and comfortable. . . . The wave is spreading through your head . . . relaxing your thoughts and feelings . . . now it rolls down into the muscles of your face, rolling into your cheeks, and up into your head again and down into your neck.

[12] *Focusing on a positive response*

[12] *You can actually feel* the muscles relaxing. The first wave of relaxation pours down into your shoulders now . . . spreads into your upper arms, filling them with heaviness, spreading . . . and pushing ahead of itself any tension that you may have felt.

"The wave of relaxation is coming down from your neck now like [17] two big brooms that sweep out into your shoulders . . . sweeping ahead of themselves any tension that you may have felt today. They sweep the tension down into your upper arms . . . and from there down into your lower arms . . . and from there you can see and feel them sweep the tension out into your hands, and from there into your fingers . . . out into the air and far away from you. Watch it, how it floats away from you . . . away . . . away. You feel so good all over, comfortable, floating in a nice, comfortable, warm, dark space, drifting, drifting and drifting. . . . You get more and more drowsy, more and more sleepy, . . . you can relax and see how easy and comfortable it feels . . . how much more you would like to go into a very, very deep state of sleep. . . . And now other

[17] *Imagery*

[7] *Involuntarism*

waves of relaxation, each wave [7] *comes by itself*

now . . . they ripple down your back, and go deep into your chest. . . . With every breath you take, [4]*you allow yourself* to go deeper and deeper, deeper and deeper. Notice how the waves of relaxation move along with the movement of your breath. With each breath the waves are carried effortlessly along, moving to all parts of your body. You go deeper and deeper in that altered state that we call hypnosis. . . .

[4]*Ego receptivity*

[10]*And you are looking forward to* going even deeper than you are now, even deeper, as the first waves of relaxation, always starting from the top of your head where I have touched it, continue to roll down over you. . . . The waves of relaxation roll down into your pelvis and from there down into your upper legs, again sweeping ahead of themselves any tension that may have been left. They sweep it down like big brooms, sweep it down from your upper legs into your lower legs, from your lower legs into your ankles . . . from your ankles into your feet. . . . And if there was any tension left, you can just let it seep from your ankles and feet into the hassock on which your feet are resting. Watch it go down quickly through the hassock, and from there into the floor, and from there to the outside wall, all the way down, till it comes to the yard and flows outside, deep into the earth far away from you." If the patient is not relaxed yet, say, "You may notice some parts of your body have become more relaxed than others. . . . [18]*What do you notice?*" [Patient responds.] "Good . . . you will also notice the waves are more distinct in some areas of your body than others" (patient responds again) ". . . good . . . now, notice where the waves are so distinct . . . soon these waves will move more clearly into those areas of your body which are not yet completely relaxed. [18]*Have they started moving there yet?*" [Patient responds.] "Good. Now they will continue to move. . . . When your body is [12]*completely*

[10]*Enhancing anticipation of a positive response*

[18]*Establishing communication*

[12]*Focusing on a*

positive response   relaxed, you will be able to tell me by having your head fall forward." The therapist waits, then says, *"There, now you are completely relaxed."*

If after 5 or 10 minutes the Eye Closure Technique does not lead to the patient's involuntarily shutting his eyes, the hypnotist simply says, "You can just close your eyes now," and the patient will do it voluntarily.

The Clenched Fist Technique

This is a very simple relaxation technique invented by Calvert Stein (1963).

The patient is asked to extend one of his arms in front of himself. The hypnotist says: "Close your [name nondominant hand, right or left]

[17] *Imagery*   hand and make a fist. . . . [17] *Imagine that your body is a pitcher and your* [name nondominant] *arm a spout.* . . . Make a fist with your

[18] *Ideomotor action and relaxation*   [nondominant] hand . . . [18] *let your body bend over to that side* . . . and now let all the tension or that feeling that is too strong . . . flow into *that* hand . . . and as the feeling flows into the hand, the fist will become tighter and tighter. It becomes very tight. [Pause. Therapist keeps silent for a moment to give that process a chance to occur.] . . . And now you can open your fist, slowly, and let as much of the tension

[16] *Permissive hypnosis*   [or anger or fear, etc.] [16] *as you want to get rid of* flow out into the air . . . pooff, away from you. . . ." At the same time, he tells the patient

[11] *Chaining (as "x," then "y")*   that [11] *as the tension streams away from him* (x), the *patient will go deeper and deeper* (y), deeper and deeper into trance.

Because beginners learning to induce hypnosis usually feel insecure about how to word their patter, the instructions for the Chevreul Pendulum, Eye Closure, and Progressive Relaxation are here detailed at length. After a while, each hypnotherapist develops his own way of wording these and other instructions.

Coin Drop

Coin drop is an induction method that can be done while the patient's eyes are either open or closed. The hypnotist says to the patient:

[1] *Focusing attention*

[8] *Dissociation ("the" hand, not "your" hand);* [17] *Imagery;* [2] *Observing something new;* [7] *Involuntarism*

[5] *Repetition*

[20] *Observation of spontaneous movements*

[21] *Giving patient collaborative role;* [14] *Adjusting the rate of response;* [9,11] *Setting the overall goal; Chaining;* [10] *Enhancing anticipation of a positive response;* [12] *Focusing on a positive response*

[1] "Close your eyes [optional]. Here is a coin. I will put it into your hand. Make a fist around it and [1] *concentrate all your attention on your sensations in* [8] *the hand.* Now stretch out your arm at shoulder height and [17] *imagine that the coin is in a little balloon.* From the warmth of the hand the [2] *balloon will expand* so that [7] *it will force the fist open and force the fingers apart.* Perhaps you can already imagine *the balloon* swelling in the hand, trying to force *the fist* open. As the balloon is [5] *getting warmer and warmer, swelling and swelling more,* the fingers of the hand will open. There, notice how the fingers are moving now. The fingers [20] *open by themselves.* I am going to stroke the hand now, and, as I do so, the blood is rushing into the hand, making the hand become warmer and warmer (hypnotist strokes hand slowly and rhythmically a few times, each time starting a few inches above the wrist). At the same time, you may wish to count from 1 to 15. [21] *By the time you have come to 15 . . .* [14] *or before that . . .* the fingers will be open so far that the coin will drop. [9,11] *When you hear it drop* to the floor . . . or feel it drop on your leg or lap, *you will go down suddenly into a deep, deep, deep trance.* The coin is [10] *about to drop now"* [coin drops]. "There, [12] *notice what this state is like for you, and you'll be able to describe what it is like. . . ."*

Whether the hypnotist ties the "set" of the patient's going into a deeper trance to the patient's hearing or feeling the coin drop depends on the physical situation. If the fist is stretched out above a wooden floor, the patient can hear the coin drop. If the room is carpeted, the therapist should position the hand so that the coin will drop into the patient's lap.

In a variation of the Coin Drop Technique, the therapist asks the patient to stretch out his arm with the open palm facing upward and then places the coin on the ball of the hand near the edge of the palm and tells the patient that the hand and arm will roll inward and over by themselves. Because it is uncomfortable to have the arm stretched out in front with the palm of the hand upward, this movement occurs quite naturally. As the hand rolls inward and over, the coin slips from the hand to the floor or the lap naturally (if the patient is not sweating), at which point most patients close their eyes and go into trance. The patient may also be encouraged to count up to 15 by himself—usually he does it silently—because that gives him some control about whether he wants to go into trance quickly or slowly. Or the hypnotist counts aloud.

Counting Techniques and Breathing Techniques for Induction and Deepening

Counting can be used in many different ways to help the patient go into trance or to deepen the trance. It is used in the staircase technique in combination with imagery and sensory phenomena, but it can also be used alone, as a method of attention concentration. For instance, some hypnotists just suggest that the patient count backward from 50 to 1, or count backward by threes from 100, or count the cycle of his breaths. In addition, it can be suggested that with every breath he takes, he will go into deeper and deeper trance. The patient, obviously, can not resist the breathing part of the suggestion. Tying the suggestion to something natural, inevitable, and nonfrightening facilitates the deepening of the trance. Shor and Easton (1973) asked their subjects to count their breaths from 1 to 150 and used counting breaths as an induction for self-hypnosis. This can be combined with visualization in which the patient breathes in light and relaxation or breathes out darkness and tension with each breath. Many clinicians ask their patients to count backwards silently by threes while listening to the hypnotist's patter. That requires concentrated attention (for the subtraction) and at the same time free-floating attention to what the hypnotist says. In our researches (Fromm, 1977; Fromm et al., 1981; Fromm, Skinner, Lombard, & Kahn, in preparation), we find more and more that a combination of concentrated and expansive attention or a quick alternation between them characterizes the hypnotic state. Counting backwards by threes while listening to the hypnotist's patter is a difficult task, requiring so much attention that other thoughts, such as negative suggestions the patient might give himself about not being able to go into trance, are kept out.

Ideomotor Phenomena

Ideomotor phenomena are movements—or the inhibition of natural movements—both of which the patient involuntarily produces in reaction to a thought or an image. In heterohypnosis the thought in the patient's mind is stimulated by a direct or indirect suggestion the hypnotist gives; in self-hypnosis it is due to a self-suggestion. In contrast to hypnotic imagery, which is a purely subjective phenomenon, ideomotor phenomena are objectively observable by the hypnotist or other outside observers.

Magnets.   The therapist gives the following instructions to the patient:

[22, 19] *Indirect Suggestion of Ideomotor Action*

[7, 27] *Involuntarism and Giving Patient Main Role in the Collaboration*

"Stretch out your arms in front of you, palms facing each other . . . about a foot apart from each other. . . . Now let's imagine . . . that there is a small but very powerful [22, 19] *magnet* in the palm of your right hand . . . fastened with a strap around the back of your hand . . . that holds it securely in your palm. . . . The north pole of this magnet is turned toward the palm of your right hand. . . . And in your left hand . . . in the same way . . . another, equally strong magnet is fastened. The south pole of that magnet in your left hand . . . is turned toward the north pole of the magnet . . . in your right hand. . . . [7, 27] *Watch . . . what happens.*"

The therapist then remains silent. For most patients the hands will slowly move toward each other until they touch. Often one can see an amused expression spreading over the patient's face, indicating that the patient enjoys observing that something has happened "by itself," something he has not voluntarily done, and that what has happened is not dangerous, does not overwhelm him, can be fun to experience. Simulation, that is, voluntary motion, can be easily detected by the therapist. It is a much faster, smoother bringing together of the hands.

The patient who succeeds in these hypnotic tasks has reacted to the therapist's talking about magnets and opposite poles with the conscious or preconsious thought that magnets with opposite poles turned toward each other attract each other, which leads to the motor execution of this idea in trance.

When the patient's hands have touched, the therapist can say: "Now I am going to turn the magnet in your right hand around so that its south pole is facing the south pole of the magnet you have in your left hand. Watch what happens now."

Again he sits silently, and watches whether the hands separate and move away from each other.

This induction technique works well with most patients. While by itself it seldom helps the patient to go into more than a light trance, it has several advantages over other induction techniques:

1. It shows the patient that *his* own thoughts or images influence his actions. The therapist has not directly suggested that the hands will attract each other. He simply has set the patient to thinking about the laws of magnetism; and as the patient thought about the fact that opposite magnetic poles attract each other, his hands moved toward each other. The technique can be used easily to explain to the patient that our own unconscious and preconscious thoughts can influence our behavior. This hypnotic item, and many other ideomotor phenomena, can be used to show the patient, for instance, that unconscious ego-dystonic and repressed thoughts underlie tics and muscular paralyses and that the neurotic symptom always represents an unacceptable thought or wish and the defenses against it.
2. The experience of the magnets establishes hypnosis in the mind of the patient as a cognitive process and a genuine ideomotor phenomenon, that is, one in which ideation significantly affects the motor system.
3. It shows the patient that he can set himself apart from himself, that he can dissociate the observer within himself from that part of his personality that experiences or acts: He smiled as he observed what was happening.
4. It establishes hypnosis in his mind as something intriguing, something in which things happen, something that is not dangerous or frightening.
5. It fosters self-efficacy. Patients realize that they are capable of using the powers of their own imagination.

The Magnet Technique works best when the patient has his eyes closed. When the eyes are open, he can counteract any small movement immediately and probably will counteract it because he would feel more embarrassed than surprised and intrigued.

The Chiasson Technique.   The Chiasson (1973) Induction Technique is started with the eyes open. Toward its end the patient may be told that his eyelids have now become so heavy that they want to close. In this technique the patient is asked to stretch out one arm horizontally in front of himself and to put the hand into a near 90° position to the arm, with the back of the hand facing himself. The forefingers are held close together vertically and the patient is asked to "allow" the hand to move slowly toward his face. (When the hand is held in this position, the fingers separate naturally and involuntarily.) He is told that as his hand comes closer to his face and as the spaces between the fingers widen, he is going to go deeper and deeper into trance and that as the hand or the fingers touch his face, he will suddenly go into a deep, deep, deep trance.

Arm Levitation.   The patient is asked to settle comfortably in a chair with one arm lying on the arm rest of the chair or on a low table next to him. This technique can be administered with open or with closed eyes. The hypnotist says:

[1] *Focusing Attention*   [1] *"Please pay special attention* now to your hand and arm. *Something interesting and strange is going to happen to them.* Look at your hand." [It is not necessary to say this if the patient has his eyes closed.] "Pay close attention to your hand. . . As you pay close attention to your hand, [2] *you will become aware of things you may not be aware of ordinarily. . . .* [34] *You become aware of how warm or cold your hand is, of little muscles in your hand and arm that twitch ever so slightly . . .* And now, [17] *perhaps you would like to imagine . . . that I am fastening a string around your wrist."* [Therapist's fingers *traces a line over the patient's wrist.*] "Fastened to the other end of the string . . . over there on the ground . . . lies a balloon that is not yet blown up. . . . It is kind of wrinkled. . . . [13] *Can you see it yet?"* [Patient responds.] "It is lying there on the ground. That's right. [17] *What color is it?"* [Patient names the color he sees. Let's say "red."] "That's right. It is kind of a dull, dark red. The balloon *isn't yet blown up* and is all wrinkled and dark. . . . [9] *but soon it will be blown up, and it will lift up. . . .* And now imagine the balloon is being filled with helium. The helium is being pumped into it. [17] *You can hear the hissing.* And you know how light, how very light helium is. As the skin of the balloon

[2] *Observing immediate experience; helping patient become aware of sensory phenomena usually below the threshold of awareness;* [34] *Observing something new/ leading;* [17] *Tactile imagery;* [13] *Encouraging dialogue;* [17] *Visual imagery*

[9] *Setting the goal*

[17] *Auditory imagery*

[17] *Visual Imagery*

[17] *Tactile imagery*
[10] *Focusing on a positive response;*
[8] *Dissociation;*
[14] *Ideomotor Phenomenon;*
[15] *Establishing a Set*

[16] *Permissive (nonauthoritarian) suggestion;* [9] *Setting the overall goal*

expands, [17] *it becomes shinier and the color becomes brighter.* You can see the balloon lift off the ground and rise, rise higher and higher, higher and higher. . . . [17] *The string around your wrist becomes taut. . . .* [10] *Watch what happens to* [8] *the arm"* (in most cases the hand and arm will lift). [14] *"Yes . . . it is pulling the arm and hand up. . . .* [8] *The arm and hand are lifting . . .* higher and higher. [15] *Pretty soon the hand is going to touch your face. Neither you nor I know* whether it will touch your face at the chin or at the forehead or at the nose. [16,9] *When the hand touches your face, you are going to fall into a deep trance, very deep,* suddenly. . . . The balloon is rising, higher and higher, and now the wind is catching it way up in the air." [The hypnotist must now suggest that the wind blows from a direction that will make it possible for the hand indeed to touch the face.] "It is blowing the balloon toward your left side and slightly behind you, left and behind you . . . and the hand is coming closer and closer to your head . . . closer and closer to your head. You

[10] *Enhancing anticipation of a positive response*

[1] *Focusing on a positive response;*
[23] *Utilizing lowering the arm in the service of deepening*

know that [10] *when the hand touches your head, you are falling into a trance,* a much deeper trance than you ever have been in before." After the hand has touched the face, the hypnotist says: [1] *"There. . . . That's good . . . deep . . . deep . . . deep. . . .* [23] *As your hand and arm sink down to your lap, you will go even deeper, even deeper."* [The hypnotist touches the wrist of the patient as if cutting a string.] If the arm does not lift after about five minutes, the hypnotist ties one or more additional imaginary ballons to the elbow.

The only limit to the variations of this—and other—induction and deepening techniques is the extent of the hypnotist's own imagination. One of the variations would be to tell the patient that he is lying in a bathtub, arms on the bottom of the bathtub next to his body, and that now the arms feel as if they were light as cork, and he can feel that they are bobbing up to the surface of the water, like a cork in water.

In another variation of the Arm Levitation Technique, the hypnotist says:

[7] *Highlighting patient's awareness of involuntary processes involving*

[7] *"You will become aware now that your hand is being drawn to your face as if by a magnet. . . .* When the hand reaches your face . . . you will go down into an even deeper relaxed and thoroughly enjoyable state. . . . You look forward to it as a distinct achievement . . .

[4] *Ego receptivity and leaving some initiative to patient*

[4] *allowing yourself* to get a new psychological experience . . . a complete relaxation. . . . You feel a glowing sensation. . . . You enjoy involving yourself in this process. . . . As you wish, you can go deeper and deeper."

Arm Catalepsy. Arm Catalepsy can be used for testing whether a patient is in a medium or deep trance. After the arm has levitated and the hand has touched the face, the hypnotist says nothing about its coming down. In the deeply or medium-to-deeply hypnotized patient, the hand remains at the face, or if the arm has been raised above the head, it remains in an upright position for any length of time, even an hour or longer, apparently effortlessly. The patient usually even becomes unaware that his arm is raised high into the air and without support.

He is also not aware of the pain this position causes him. Before the patient returns to the waking state, the hypnotherapist therefore must counteract pain by moving the patient's arm into a comfortable position and by suggesting that there will be no pain after the patient has awakened.

Arm Drop. This is the counterpart of Arm Levitation. The patient is asked to stretch out his arm and hand in front of him, horizontally, and the hypnotist says:

[22] *Indirect Form of Suggestion*

[22] *"I am going to put a big, empty aluminum pail over your wrist now"* (hypnotist touches wrist) *". . . and slowly pour in a pint of water . . . and another pint of water . . . and another . . . and another. . . . And now imagine a quart of water being poured in . . .* and the pail is getting heavier and heavier . . . heavier and

[11] *Chaining*

heavier. [11] *As the pail is getting heavier and heavier, you are going into a deeper and deeper state of trance . . .* deeper and deeper . . . deeper and deeper."

The Arm Drop Technique—and most of the other techniques we have already discussed—can be a type of indirect suggestion if the words "As the pail gets heavier, your arm will drop and you will go into a deeper and deeper state of trance" are left out. No *direct* suggestion, then, has been given to the patient that he should go deeper. But it is implied indirectly, through the weight increase of the pail being filled.

Fatigue and the law of gravity (as well as imagery) play a role in the Arm Drop Technique. It is tiring to hold up an arm on which one experiences the pull of a heavy pail.[2]

Imaging Methods

One of the characteristics of hypnosis is that imagery is greatly increased. The patient or subject in hypnosis is highly receptive to the imagery the hypnotist suggests; he easily goes along with images the hypnotist invokes. And in self-hypnosis there is an abundance of images that rise into the patient's awareness from his own unconscious and preconscious. Even in heterohypnosis, while the hypnotist is spinning out induction or deepening fantasies for the patient, the patient simultaneously may have other images or fantasies arise from within himself. The hypnotist also may move back and forth between the patient's imagery and his own, leading the patient into deeper trance along pathways some of which the patient himself is creating and therefore is more willing to follow. This decreases his resistance to trance and often is very joyful.

The use of imagery and fantasy involves one of the more sophisticated approaches to hypnosis. The patient is asked to imagine a scene and progressively to "dwell within it." The fantasy becomes the experienced reality of the moment. The more pleasurable the fantasy, the better the induction.

Especially potent in inducing hypnotic trance are those fantasies involv-

---

[2] We have often used the Arm Drop Method as an informal diagnostic test for obsessive-compulsive neurosis. Whereas in normal subjects, or in patients who are not obsessive-compulsives, the arm will ordinarily just sink slowly, the obsessive-compulsive, who is plagued by constant doubts, will characteristically let the outstretched arm sink down an inch or two and then quickly pull it up to the starting position, then let it sink a bit again, and again pull it up into the position in which it was first. This is due to cognitive processes going on in his mind, and represents the compulsive's typical "doing and undoing." The arm sinks down a bit, then he wonders, "Does the hypnotist want me to let that arm go down? No, he doesn't—he wants to see whether I can keep up my arm, even though it is getting heavier and heavier . . . no, perhaps he wants to see whether my arm will go down." Back and forth, *ad infinitum*.

We are not proposing the Arm Drop as a scientific test for compulsion neurosis. But it is an interesting phenomenon for the therapist to watch and can help him understand the dynamics underlying obsessive-compulsive behavior.

ing sensory elements and the fantasies that appeal to immature, regressive cravings. Skin eroticism ontogenetically precedes genital eroticism. Thus, when the hypnotist pictures for the patient a deep, shaggy, long-piled carpet on which the patient is lying, the soothing touch of a soft, grassy slope on which the patient is reclining, or the smooth, velvety sensation about his body when he is imagining himself floating on a cloud, or when the hypnotherapist talks about a soft, warm space with the most beautiful feelings of comfort and peace and the patient's feeling rocked to and fro as in his mother's arms, the hypnotist is evoking tactile-erotic fantasies reminiscent of the maternal touch in early childhood and encourages a hypnotic regression in the service of the ego[3] (Kris, 1936/1952).

In the initiation of such fantasies, the pictorial, descriptive powers of the hypnotist must be fully utilized. The more of the patient's sensory channels the hypnotherapist can involve (visual imagery, tactile, auditory, gustatory, olfactory, and proprioceptive imagery), the better he can help the patient to go into deeper stages of trance. Vivid descriptions, attention to minute details within the images, and the hypnotist's willingness to modify the fantasy he is producing according to the patient's direction—all enhance the induction and deepening processes. The patient must be given enough time to become involved in the fantasy and the patient must imagine himself participating in the fantasy, not simply looking on. Moreover, it is important to amplify the emotional quality the subject or patient experiences as he participates in the fantasy.

We have mentioned imagery as a factor in some of the induction and deepening procedures described. We think it is of such overreaching importance that we build it into the patter of nearly all our induction and deepening procedures.

The Staircase Technique.   This induction and deepening technique is an imagery technique. In order to produce better imagery, especially better visual imagery, voluntary or hypnotically induced eye closure should precede the staircase induction. If the eyes are open, reality awareness interferes.

The hypnotherapist says to the patient:

[35] *Direct suggestion*   [35] I will now count from 1 to 20. With each
                               number you hear, you will go down into a
                               deeper and deeper state of trance."

This is a direct suggestion, somewhat crude. It works with good hypnotic subjects. But it lacks finesse. Disrespectful hypnotists will not even

---

[3] In a regression in the service of the ego, the healthy person regresses for a limited time to developmentally earlier modes of thinking and functioning in order to gain enough strength to go ahead again, faster.

give the subject time to enter the hypnotic state and will count only to 3, or to 5; or, worse, they will say, "When I snap my fingers, you will go into a deep state of trance."

Most hypnotists refine the Counting Method by adding imagery and sensory material to it. One of the most common variations is the staircase image:

[17]*Imagery*
[25]*Hypnotist establishes himself as protector and helper;*
[18]*Establishing communication*
[26]*Involving various sensory modes*

"Perhaps you would like to [17]*imagine that you are at the top of a beautiful staircase* and [25]*I am standing right next to you.* The staircase is covered by a rich, luxurious carpet. [18]*Notice what color the carpet is and describe it to me.*" [Patient responds.] "That's right; it is [red or blue]. . . . You are standing with bare feet on that carpet. As you stand there, you can [26]*feel your feet sink into the soft richness of this warm [red] carpet.* And as you look down the staircase, which has 20 steps, you can [26]*see the color* of the carpet getting deeper and deeper, deeper and more vibrant. At the right side of the staircase, there is a [27]*solid bannister. What is it like?*" [Patient responds.] "Yes, it is a smooth marble [or solid oak wood] bannister. [28]*Many hands have glided down it before yours.* As you are standing there on the top step, [10]*the idea may come up in your mind* that you might want just tentatively to move your right bare foot to that part of the staircase close to the bannister that has not been covered by a rich, deep, velvety carpet. What is it like?" [Patient responds.] "That's right; it's [marble or wooden]. Move your foot over and[26]*feel* the [coolness of the marble or hardness of the wood] *under your toes,* and then bring the foot back again to the lovely softness of the velvety carpet. [29]*As you go down the stairs, I will go down with you,* step by step, and I will count the steps. [13]*Perhaps you would also like to count them with me.* Hold on to the bannister with your right hand, and step down to the second step. [9]*As you go farther and farther down, you will be able to go deeper and deeper into trance, deeper and deeper*

[27]*Symbolically telling patient it is safe to go down into hypnosis;* [28]*Open-ended suggestion;* [10]*Enhancing anticipation of a positive response*

[29]*Building a positive relationship*
[13]*Encouraging patient's active involvement*
[9]*Setting the overall goal*

[5] *Repetition and variation*

[22] *Indirect Suggestion to go deeper*

[30] *"Set"*

[9] *Reinforcing the overall goal of the staircase*

[16] *Permissive style of suggestion*

[12] *Focusing on a positive response*

[10] *Enhancing anticipation of a positive response*

relaxed, [5] *deeper and more deeply relaxed and sleepy and drowsy.* Now let's step down to the third step. Farther and farther down, deeper and deeper asleep. As you continue to the fourth . . . and fifth step, you may notice that [22] *the color of the carpet is becoming even deeper, deeper* and *deeper,* a more *restful* color . . . 6 . . . 7. . . [30] *with every breath you take, you go deeper and deeper, deeper and deeper asleep.* . . . It feels so good to let your feet sink into the thick pile of the carpet . . . as you go down the stairs. Going into this wonderful, relaxed, deep, drowsy and sleepy, sleepy and drowsy state . . . 8 . . . deep, deep, deep relaxation . . . 9 . . . deeper and deeper. . . . You may notice that the staircase begins to spiral down to the left, counterclockwise. And you begin going around as you go down . . . 10 . . . 11 . . . down and around . . . deeper and deeper . . . 12 . . . 13 . . . 14 . . . very comfortable . . . very drowsy. . . . [9] *Soon you will reach the bottom of the staircase . . . At the bottom of the staircase there is a very private room, a private space of your own.* . . . You can already see the threshold at the bottom of the stairs, the threshold that leads into this [16] *private space of your own, a very deep, a very comfortable place.* . . . At the count of 20, you will have reached the bottom. [12] *You will step over the threshold, and at that moment you will go into an even much deeper state of trance than you have ever been in before* . . . 15 . . . 16. . . . You are going deeper and deeper, deeper and deeper and [10] *are looking forward to going* into a deeper state than you have ever been in before. Deeper and deeper, around and down . . . down and around . . . 17 . . . closer and closer to the bottom of the staircase to a very special room, a very private place that is very deeply relaxed and comfortable. [10] *You will feel so comfortable there that you will want to continue to remain in*

this deep state . . . 18 . . . 19 . . . and . . . 20!
[13] *Encouraging active*   *. . . Deep, deep, deep, deep."* [The final number
participation and   must be spoken with emphasis.] *"There,*
communication   [13] *notice what it is like for you."*

The Elevator and the Escalator Techniques.   Variations of the Staircase Technique are the Elevator and the Escalator Techniques. In the
Elevator Technique it is suggested to the patient that he is inside an
elevator that can take him down into a deeper and deeper hypnotic state or
up into a lighter and lighter state. He can see the numbers of the floors
light up above the elevator door going from 20 to 1 or 1 to 20. [With
patients fearful of "going down," the hypnotist may suggest that the
numbers go up from 1 to 20 and that the patient gets into higher and higher
states of altered hypnotic awareness.] Depending on whether the patient
likes to have control or likes to have things happen to him, he can either be
told or not be told that he has the control of the elevator in his hand.

In the Escalator Technique, counting or numbers are not used. The
patient is told that he is going to step onto an escalator that will transport
him into trance smoothly. Or the hypnotist suggests that the patient has
the control stick for the escalator in his hand. If he pulls the stick close to
himself very fast, he will go into a deep trance fast. If he pulls it slowly, he
will go into trance slowly. The advantage of this technique is that it
symbolically conveys to the patient: You have control of the hypnosis in
your own hands. Patients can also learn to experiment going up the
elevator into a lighter state of trance and down the elevator into a deeper
state of trance until they find the level of trance most comfortable for
them, which they can indicate with an ideomotor finger signal.

The Boat Technique

[17] *Imagery and*   The hypnotist suggests to the patient that he
regression in the   [17] *sees himself lying in a gently rocking boat,*
service of the ego   drifting down a placidly flowing river. He either
describes to the patient various kinds of restful
scenes or interesting, absorbing events, the
patient sees on the banks of the river as he drifts
by or, better, has the patient describe in detail
what he sees. Again, the more imagery and the
more sensory channels are involved (*seeing*
[26] *Involving various*   *people picnicking on the bank of the* [26] *river,*
sensory modes   *smelling the pungent odor coming from their*
barbecue, hearing them talk or call to each
other, seeing them folkdance and perhaps

participating in their dance, etc.), the better. The gently rocking boat that the hypnotist suggests is, of course, an allusion to the cradle, the famous nursery rhyme "Row, Row, Row Your Boat," and being rocked in one's mother's arms. These allusions aid the deepening process; they are symbols of the regression in the service of the ego.

The Beach Fantasy.   The hypnotist suggests that the patient sees and feels himself lying in the sunshine on a beautiful beach. Palm trees sway gently in the wind. He suggestively asks the patient whether he can hear the surf rolling up, see the whitecaps on the water, smell the salty air, and hear the surf pounding against some rocks not far away. He asks the patient to pick up a handful of dry sand and let it run through his fingers. The beauty and peacefulness of the scenery are emphasized. To assist the regression in the service of the ego that is characteristic of the hypnotic state, he can also conjure up a boat that picks up the patient, floats him along the shore line, gently rocking him. Again, this procedure represents the use of imagery involving many different sensory modalities.

As with all induction and deepening techniques, the hypnotist should talk to the patient in a gentle, calming, rhythmical fashion. Ordinarily, the patient's breathing slows down as he goes down into trance. The hypnotist should tie the rhythm of his speech to the patient's breathing.

The Cloud Fantasy.   The Cloud Fantasy is another form of guided imagery that makes use of people's natural tendency to regress temporarily in the service of the ego. It also *promotes* this adaptive regression. The hypnotherapist evokes the picture of a nice, warm summer day and a grassy mountaintop on which the patient is lying, staring up into the blue sky. Then the hypnotist says to the patient:

[17] *Imagery that aids regression*

"Now something strange and beautiful is going to happen. See, a big, white, fluffy cloud is drifting into your field of vision. It is [17] *nice and fluffy. Like a warm blanket, fluffy and cozy like the blanket you had when you were a baby.* As the sun's rays fall on it, it may look pink, or light blue, or yellow, or perhaps any other color. What color is it to you? [Patient responds.] Now the cloud is coming down towards you, towards you . . . and it is enveloping you warmly, cozily and snugly, [17] *lifting you up, turning you around . . . and around* . . . and around in the blue sky, so you can look down onto the earth over your left shoulder, and then straight down, and then over your right shoulder, and then look up into the sky again. Around and around as on a merry-go-round. And you are floating along now. [18] *Tell me, what is the floating like for you?* [Patient responds.] Floating, floating in the sky, floating higher and lower, lower and higher. . . . Soon you will float off to some special place. . . . Neither you nor I know yet where you are floating to, but you are floating along toward that special place. . . . When you are there, you will indicate it to me. That is, the index finger will lift up." When the finger lifts, the therapist says, "Now, where are you?"

[17] *Disorientational imagery to aid regression*

[18] *Encouraging communication*

The therapist also can let the patient float in that cloud to a particular place that was important to the patient in childhood or to any special place that the patient wants to explore. Thus, the hypnotist can use the cloud fantasy just for deepening purposes, for uncovering purposes, or even for finding out where the therapy is going to go in the future and how fast it will go.

Other Fantasy Inductions

Strolling Through a Museum or Listening to an Imaginary Concert.   If the patient is interested in art or music, the therapist can, as one of the deepening procedures, describe the patient strolling through a beautiful museum, walking from picture to picture and enjoying the stroll through the museum so much that he forgets about his worries and takes deep enjoyment in his museum stroll. The therapist describes a few pictures first and then lets the patient tell him what he sees. Or the therapist may suggest that the patient is at a concert, hearing some beautiful music. He may let the patient describe what he hears and what feelings the music arouses in him. We have had a couple of patients, survivors of the Holocaust in Nazi concentration camps, who had frequently imagined—in a sort of self-hypnotic state—that they were walking through a museum looking at their favorite pictures, or at a philharmonic concert listening to fine music.

In these ways they could emotionally escape the horror of the concentration camp from time to time for a little while and gain the inner strength to endure it.

Watching an Exciting Sunrise.   It has been an historical tradition to induce or deepen trance by emphasizing that the hypnotized person is getting tired and sleepy. The habit stems from the time when hypnosis was conceived of as being similar to or a form of sleep. Hypnosis certainly is a relaxed, altered state of consciousness. But while it can be compared to sleep, it can also be conceived of and experienced as a state of hyperemperia (Gibbons, 1979), a state of heightened sensory experience and excitation. Gibbons has developed a number of induction and deepening techniques that stress hyperemperia. Among them is a beach scene in which the patient lies on the beach during the night, looking up at the sky and the stars; after a while dawn arises, and the patient watches a glorious and exciting sunrise.

An Induction and Deepening Technique for Children.   Sometimes. particularly in child hypnotherapy, the hypnotist suggests that by entering hypnosis the patient will experience increased self-efficacy. For instance, a frequently used method in pedodontics is to ask the child in the dental chair to close his eyes, to picture a TV screen, and to imagine that he is watching "Mighty Mouse"—that small creature who is always successful in overpowering the great giant, lion, or other symbolic representations of parent-figures. The little patient's fantasy wish-life is stimulated in order to divert his attention and help him hypnotically to concentrate it on an exciting, wishful fantasy. The pain from the dentist's drill can then be ignored.

In the initiation of such fantasy, the pictorial descriptive powers of the hypnotherapist must be fully utilized. Vivid description, attention to minute details within the imagery, allowing time for the patient's involvement, and the willingness to modify the fantasy as directed by the patient—all enhance the induction or deepening process.

The Deep Sea Technique.   Another imagery technique for deepening trance, one we have recently developed, is the Deep Sea Technique. For this technique, we have modified a fascinating description of a scientific deep sea diving report by Beebe (1954). When we use it, we want symbolically to convey to the patient that the exploration of one's own unconscious (the deep sea) can be a fascinating, safe, and intrinsically rewarding experience. Here is the full text of the Descent into the Deep Sea:

[17] *Fostering*
imaginative

[17] *"Imagine* that we are going on a deep sea
exploring trip . . . down in the warm waters off

involvement
[31] *Evoking curiosity*

[27] *Symbolically*
stressing safety

the Florida Keys. We have come to Key Largo, where a group of young deep sea [31] *explorers is preparing a trip in an enclosed capsule into the depth of the ocean.* The [27] capsule can be lowered from a ship on a steel cable. It can safely make descents of thousands of feet down into the ocean. Imagine a metal sphere with four portholes of [27] *thick plate glass.* Two or three people can wriggle inside the capsule . . . and sit in it, and observe. They are supplied with [27] *oxygen lines and a telephone line to the boat on the surface.*

"Imagine yourself for several days watching the young ocean divers on the beach in Key Largo, preparing the capsule for their next trip. They have fitted it out with food and with a number of scientific instruments. You have made friends with them, and several of them have invited you to join them on their trip soon to see the wondrous sights of the deep sea. You have accepted the invitation and are intrigued, delighted, and curious. . . .

[26] *Involvement of*
various sensory
modalities in
imagery
[27] *Symbolically*
indicating to patient
that therapist has
expertise in helping
patients explore their
unconscious safely

"Imagine yourself and the deep sea explorers standing on the deck of the ship that will take you out to sea. You are going out to sea now. You [26] *see* the long, low swell of the sea and [26] *hear* the waves rolling in on this calm, sunny, beautiful, warm spring day. . . . You can [26] *feel* a light breeze on your face. . . . Now imagine [27] *yourself and two of the explorers—who have descended deep into the ocean many a time before*—wriggling into one of the capsules lying on the deck. . . . Its [27] *portholes are being screwed tight so that no water can penetrate.* . . . [27] *Strong cranes* swing out your capsule over the side of the ship. . . . You can [26] *hear it splash,* and descend beneath the surface of the water. Notice the sudden shift from the golden yellow light above the water to a turquoise green all around you. You [26] *see the foam and bubbles* from the splash. Look upwards. . . . You see the strong steel cable from which your capsule is being lowered down close to the ship's side. Now you are being lowered 100 feet. [1] *Notice* what it feels like to dangle there for a while. Peer up; you can see the watery ceiling crinkling . . . and slowly lifting and settling . . . while here and there . . . pinned to this ceiling . . . are tufts of seaweed. . . . [1] *Notice* small dots moving just below the weed . . . and you try . . . successfully . . . to [1] *focus* a pair of binoculars that one of the explorers has handed to you on these moving dots. You have no trouble recognizing a flying fish . . . trailing its half-spread wings as it swims. You can [26] *feel the capsule revolving slightly,* and the bottom of the ship's hull comes into view. It is encrusted with coral and shells. . . . Great streamers of plant and animal life float from it. . . . [32] *There is something unreal* . . . and at the same time rather amusing about an upward view of the slowly rolling bottom of an unanchored boat . . . whose deck a few minutes before had seemed so solid and staunch.

"The people on the deck of the boat phone down to tell you that the sun keeps blazing over the ocean, the surface is unusually quiet, and conditions are ideal for going down further.

"You are being lowered further. . . . The green of the water fades imperceptibly as you go further down, and at 200 feet it is impossible to say whether the water is greenish blue or bluish green. You make your eyes focus in mid-water and see a lovely colony of jellyfish drift past . . . gracefully floating in the deep water. . . . They are beautiful. They sweep slowly along . . . alive and in constant motion.

"Two hundred feet lower, a deep sea fish looks in on you. . . . Two deep sea turtles go by. Several silvery squid balance for a moment in front of your porthole . . . then shoot past.

[1] *Focusing attention and active involvement*

[26] *Involvement of various sensory modalities in imagery*

[32] *Fostering GRO fading*

"Slowly, steadily, you are lowered farther, deeper . . . and deeper. . . . At 500 feet a pair of funny looking fish, shaped like lanterns, peer at the capsule, unafraid.

"At 600 feet the color of the sea appears to you to be a [27] *dark, luminous blue. The sun has not given up; it penetrates deep into the sea and creates a shimmering* in the water all around you. Open your eyes and look at the swarm of chunky, big-eyed fish swimming in front of your porthole. Open your eyes for a moment and see them clearly. They pass by . . . they wheel and return. And then a lobster and some crabs. And then . . . suddenly . . . you see something to which you can give no name: It is a network of luminosity, delicate . . . with large meshes . . . all aglow and in motion . . . waving slowly as it drifts. Then a long eel snakes by [and so on].

[27] *Deep sea symbolizes patient's unconscious*

"At 1000 feet the sun is gone . . . it is dark . . . all color has gone . . . and you have to flash an electric light beam into what has been jet black for two billion years. You can see a large black fish, wide-mouthed, with a pale, lemon-colored light on a slender tentacle. His teeth glow dully. And some other fish that look like silvery, transparent willow leaves twisting and tumbling.

"At 1200 feet a loose, open school of shrimps and shellfish bob about. The explorers tell you that their [27] *shedded empty shells form most of the sea bottom in this area.*

[27] *Symbolic reference to patient's defenses and character armor as perhaps no longer needed and disposable*

"And still farther down you go. The deeper you go, the more fish and other creatures you see from which some light emanates. . . . A cheek-light or a light on a tentacle . . . or on the tail fin. Make a careful count and notice that there are never fewer than 10 lights—pale yellow and bluish—in sight at any one time.

"You are becoming aware now that the farther you have been going down toward the bottom of the ocean, the more relaxed you have become.

[32] *Fostering GRO fading*

[4] *Suggesting ego receptivity and expansive attention*

[32] *You are less and less concerned with the upper world.* You feel a restful, quiet, and happy removal from it . . . while [4] *you plunge into new strangenesses . . . and unpredictably beautiful sights continually open up to you. Your attention is relaxed . . .* very relaxed.

"And you keep on going down . . . 2,100 feet . . . 2,200 feet . . . 2,300 . . . 2,400. At 2,500, your capsule gently settles down on the ocean floor. You can feel it settle. It is very, very quiet now.

"A fish . . . with long, almost continuous vertical fins, swims into the beam of your light. A big eye . . . small mouth. . . . The skin is brownish, smooth. You swing around a few degrees, bringing the fish into the center of your

[33] *Giving a gratifying experience*

light beam. . . . [33] *And then you see its real beauty:* Along the side of its body are five unbelievably beautiful lines of light . . . a straight one in the middle . . . with two curved ones above and below. Each line is composed of a series of little pale yellow lights . . . and every one of these lights is surrounded by a circle of very small, but intensely purple, glowing dots.

"The fish turns slowly, and . . . shows you its

[39] *Posthypnotic suggestion*

other side also. Look at it again. [39] *It will live in your memory as one of the lovelist things you have ever seen.*"

When the Descent into the Deep Sea technique is used in hypnoanalysis for uncovering purposes rather than for deepening the trance, the patient, of course, is not given images. Rather, the patient is frequently asked to notice and to communicate to the hypnoanalyst what he sees and feels during his descent.

In connection with the Deep Sea Technique, here are some examples the hypnotherapist can use to estimate the patient's depth of trance. The first three are done while the patient is still in trance; the last two are posthypnotic suggestions (i.e., they are given while the patient is still in trance but are to be realized after he has awakened).

"Now you are settled comfortably at the bottom of the ocean in your watertight observation

	chamber. You are becoming aware now of a strange and delightful feeling of weightlessness.
[35] *Limb levitation*	[35] *Your arms and perhaps your legs want to float up into the air . . .* they are weightless. See what it feels like. And become aware of the great silence around you. . . Look out of your
[36] *Negative auditory hallucination*	window again . . . see the many fish floating by, silently. [36] *A heavy metal object strikes the outside of your capsule, but you don't hear a sound. . . . "*

The hypnotist drops a heavy object to the floor noisily (if the patient has his eyes open, this must be done outside his field of vision) and watches for any startle effect. If there is none, the patient has a negative hallucination; that is, he has not perceived the noise, has hallucinated it away. This is possible only in deep trance, not in the medium and light states.

The hypnotist also may test for positive hallucinations and the ability to follow posthypnotic suggestions:

[37] *Positive auditory hallucination*	[37] *"Now you will hear a great, roaring, overwhelming noise,* like the noise the waves of the ocean make when they are whipped by a furious, high gale against a rocky coast. . . . The roar will become so overwhelming that you will
[38] *Coping and Mastery*	want to stop it. [38] *You can do that* by touching your hand to the back of your head. As soon as you do, the overwhelming noise will stop."

Positive hallucinations also can be done successfully in deep trance. The hypnotist watches to see if the patient touches the back of his head, even furtively. The suggestion about stopping the furious, overwhelmingly loud noise is worded to give the patient the idea that in hypnosis he can learn to gain mastery.

The next is a posthypnotic suggestion of heaviness and analgesia.

	While you are still resting comfortably on the bottom of the ocean in your capsule, the other explorers tell you about a number of sensations and experiences you will have [39] *right after you*
[39] *Posthypnotic suggestion*	*have come up to the surface again.* They themselves have made this descent into the deep sea many times already, and each and every single time they have had these experiences.

'You will have them, too,' they say, 'everyone does.' [39] *But you will forget that anyone told you about them.* Suddenly . . . to your own surprise . . . these perceptions, sensations, and feelings will come up very vividly after you are back on the surface . . . [39] *and each time one of them does come up, your head will nod gravely three times.*

"Right after you have come up, fully awake, a full, numb, heavy feeling will be spreading from your toes backwards through your feet . . . your heels . . . upwards through your feet . . . your heels . . . upwards through your ankles and your lower legs. Your feet will feel *soooo* heavy for 2 minutes, as if they were made of lead. They will feel numb, totally numb. If someone touches your leg or your foot, you won't feel it. However, after 10 minutes, the wave of heaviness and numbness will recede . . . and your legs and feet will feel normal again."

The hypnotist then dehypnotizes the patient and watches for the three nods of the head after he has tapped the patient's foot to test the patient's ability to follow posthypnotic suggestions.

Posthypnotic suggestions can be followed successfully even if the patient was in no more than a medium trance. They are valuable aids in hypnotherapy (see chapter 6).

A Confusion Technique: Fractionation

Fractionation is a method that helps the patient to go into deep trance very quickly. It is a confusion technique and thus is, in our opinion, to a certain degree disrespectful of the altered state and of the patient too. That is, rather than leading the patient gently into a deeper trance, it overwhelms him and forces him to flee into deep trance. On the other hand, it saves the patient valuable time in his therapy hours, time that need not be wasted with lengthy induction and deepening techniques.

The Fractionation Method is based on hypnotic and posthypnotic suggestion. Therefore, the first time it is employed, the patient must be at least in a medium hypnotic trance if the posthypnotic suggestion is to take effect. At all later times it can be used as an induction technique that gets the patient into deep trance within minutes, and no further deepening is required.

The first time, the therapist says to the patient:

³⁹ *Posthypnotic*
suggestion

[39] Whenever a hypnotist of your choice touches you on your right shoulder like this [hypnotist puts gentle pressure on the patient's right shoulder], you will go down into a very, *very* deep state of hypnotic trance. And whenever a hypnotist of your choice touches you on the left shoulder [hypnotist gives two quick taps to the patient's left shoulder], you will wake up. This will not happen when someone else touches or slaps you on your shoulder.

Without necessarily saying anything further, the hypnotist presses and taps the patient's shoulders rhythmically and alternatingly for roughly two minutes. *It is important that these alternate touches be done without pause*—the pressing of the right shoulder having the duration of a dotted quarter note (a beat and a half), the light taps on the left shoulder that of an eighth note (half a beat) followed by a quarter note (one beat), as shown in Fig. 4.1. The pressing and taps should be repeated for about two minutes. The final touch must be on the shoulder used for deepening. It should be firm, and longer than the others. Concurrent with the final touch, the patient must be given a *very specific* hypnotic task, for example, arm levitation, so that he will not lighten his trance anticipating that he will again be awakened by the therapist. What happens most of the time with the Fractionation Method is that the patient becomes so confused about and irritated with the quick alternation of going into trance and waking up that after a while he flees into a deep state of trance, shutting off the therapist's alternate suggestion to wake up. When a suggestion for a specific hypnotic task is used to punctuate the final touch for deepening, the subject interprets the suggestion as the first unambiguous communication from the hypnotist since the fractionation began, and responds readily. Fractionation increases the probability of a positive response to subsequent specific, unambiguous suggestions.

When fractionation is used for the first time, it is important that the patient understand that he will not go into trance when someone other than the hypnotist of his choice touches him on the right shoulder. This precaution must be taken for two reasons: (a) frequently when people meet each other, one gives the other a friendly touch or slap on the shoulder; (b) fractionation is an authoritarian technique, and the hypnotherapist should not overwhelm the patient and force him to go into trance if for any reason the patient on a particular day does not wish to do so. Hence, the suggestion is worded as "when *a hypnotist of your choice*

FIG. 4.1.   Rhythm for Fractionation Method

touches you . . . ," telling the patient that even with this method, he will go into deep trance only if he (consciously or unconsciously) chooses to do so on that particular day and with his own therapist. It demonstrates that the hypnotherapist respects the patient's wishes and integrity.

Milton H. Erickson (Erickson, 1964c) invented Confusion Techniques and used them with great virtuosity. The reader who would like to employ other Confusion and Surprise Techniques is referred to Erickson's work.

Idiosyncratic Meanings of Hypnotic Induction and Deepening Procedures

Many beginning hypnotherapists think of hypnosis as a state entered by the patient in reaction to certain phrases or cues provided by the hypnotist. They often frantically try to memorize the "words" they have heard their teachers use for induction or deepening, oblivious to the fact that it is the *meaning of the interpersonal interaction* at least as much as the stimulus value of certain cues or words that causes the hypnotic response.

The meaning or inner significance with which the patient endows the hypnotist's communications sometimes can be very idiosyncratic. For instance, to close one's eyes may mean: (a) to one person, that he is at rest; (b) to another, that he is given the freedom to imagine or even to pretend; (c) to another, that he is to ignore the outer world; (d) to still another, that something will be put over on him, something over which he has no control; (e) and to still another, to die.

To relax in a chair or on a couch may mean to some patients the relinquishment of vigilance and defenses. To be receptive to another's suggestion may signify becoming submissive or dependent. To some this is distasteful. To others it is enjoyable, relieving them of accountability for their fantasies and actions and thus allowing them to feel free of guilt. In their minds, their fantasies and actions are the hypnotist's responsibility; he is to blame for what transpires. Such people sink rapidly into deep trance. On the other hand, a person who has devoted his life to the struggle for independence may conceive of hypnosis as submission. Submission to him constitutes a real threat, and induction becomes a signal for a battle of wills. Naturally, he will resist hypnosis. The resistance must be handled tactfully and must be analyzed by the therapist and patient together.

Not infrequently, patients conceive of hypnosis as an erotic fantasy experience or a symbolic seduction. This can be felt as such a pleasurable sensation that the patient spontaneously responds to the induction. Or he may be so afraid of seduction that he is hard to hypnotize. The hypnotist must reassure the patient that he will protect him against acting out his desires and fears.

The same suggestion given by different hypnotists may be felt or interpreted differently by the same patient, for instance, if Hypnotist A is viewed as a helper and Hypnotist B as an exploiter.

In fact, the same patient may react to a standardized procedure differently from time to time because of a change in his real-life situation, mood, or his transference feelings. When he is in a positive transference, he sees the same hypnotherapist quite differently from when he is in a negative transference.

Sometimes the patient can tell us what his conscious fears, wishes, fantasies about the hypnotic state or the hypnotic relationship are; why he resists induction or deepening; why he sinks into it deeply or quickly. Frequently these feelings, fears, and wishes are unconscious or unverbalized. Usually they are a combination of fears and wishes, communicated nonverbally through facial expressions, posture, slight movements, gestures. The patient may even express one feeling while communicating the opposite nonverbally.

The hypnotist must always observe his patients minutely and try to understand all the mixed feelings the patients have and may express nonverbally.

The therapist must understand, respect, and take into account the patient's personal idiosyncrasies. He must gain the trust and confidence of the patient. He must protect him, not shame him, not arouse guilt, not take advantage of his vulnerabilities. He must respect the patient's integrity. He must also bring into focus the patient's unconscious conflicts, interpret as much as the patient can tolerate at a time, and slowly bring more and more into consciousness. He must help the patient to grow and to cope with life.

The psychodynamic situation in the hypnotic relationship varies from patient to patient, from hypnotist to hypnotist, and within a given hypnotist-patient dyad. Induction and deepening procedures, therefore, should never be applied mechanically. The hypnotherapist always must watch his patient carefully, sensitizing himself to his patient's needs, fears, idiosyncrasies, and his individual, preferred way of regression in the service of the ego.

STATE REPORTING

Tart invented two self-report scales of hypnotic depth by means of which subjects can report the hypnotic depth they are in at any given moment: the NCS, or North Carolina Scale (1963), and the ENCS, or Extended North Carolina Scale (1979, pp. 587–590). We use the ENCS. Both are very simple procedures. Subjects or patients are told that whenever the hypnotist says "state," a number between 1 and 40 (or between 1 and 100) will flash in the subject's mind, indicating the depth of trance he is in at that time. It may come up as a visual image such as a scale with an indicator that comes to rest at the particular number, as the picture of a number the patient sees, or as a number he hears. On the 40–point ENCS, zero indicates the waking state; 1 to 12, light hypnosis; 13 to 29, a medium hypnotic state; and 30 and higher, a deep hypnotic state. Some subjects give numbers above 40. Many hypnotherapists prefer to use the scale with numbers ranging from 0 to 100. On a scale from 0 to 100, the patient is told, zero means "awake"; 1–19, "lightly hypnotized" or "relaxed"; 20–59, "moderately hypnotized"; 60–89, "deeply hypnotized"; and 90–100, "the deepest you can imagine."

The scale is reliable (Sossi, Kahn, & Fromm, in press), easily administered, and especially useful in self-hypnosis (Fromm et al., 1981) and in clinical situations. During the therapy hour the patient can be asked many times for self-reports on his hypnotic depth, which show the therapist the fluctuations in depth of trance.

The ENCS is the same as the NCS, but subjects or patients are told that there really is no "top" to the ENCS scale and they can go much deeper than what has been defined as "40."

TERMINATION OF TRANCE

Termination of trance is always done with very simple techniques—a counting technique or a direct suggestion. When using the counting technique, the hypnotherapist says to the patient: "Now I am going to count you back from 10 to 1 (or from 20 to 1). By the count of 5 your eyes will open; by the count of 1 you will be fully awake." In an animated voice, the hypnotist then counts backwards from 10 to 1 (or from 20 to 1) and watches carefully whether the patient opens his eyes at the count of five. If he does not, the therapist lingers a bit on number 5 until the eyes have opened, or repeats that number two or three times. If the staircase was used as a deepening technique, the hypnotist might suggest that the patient see or feel himself walking up that staircase while the therapist counts him back from one step to the next. The hypnotist can also suggest the patient count himself back to wakefulness.

Using a direct—but permissive—suggestion technique, the hypnotherapist says: "And now it is time to return to the waking state. When you are ready to wake up, your eyes will open by themselves." It seldom takes more than a minute or two for the patient to wake himself up.

We routinely add to the wording of either procedure that the patient will bring back with himself from the trance only those memories, feelings, images and thoughts that, deep within himself, he knows he can face in the waking state.

Clinical Hypnosis

5 Treatment Planning with Hypnosis

THE CLINICAL EFFICACY OF HYPNOSIS

In "Lines of Advance in Psycho-Analytic Therapy," Freud (1918/1955) said of hypnosis: "It is very probable, too, that the large-scale application of our therapy will compel us to alloy the pure gold of analysis freely with the copper of direct suggestion; and hypnotic influence, too, might find a place in it again, as it has in the treatment of war neuroses" (pp. 167–168). Compared with psychotherapy and perhaps also with psychoanalysis, hypnosis—at least permissive hypnosis, though not necessarily directive hypnosis—may be more "gold" than Freud was able to realize. In many cases it takes significantly less time to reach the same goals in hypno-analysis than it would take in psychoanalysis. Hypnosis increases the efficacy of treatment in most instances where the patient is at least moderately hypnotizable (Wadden & Anderton, 1982) and where the patient presents with relatively circumscribed symptoms (Beutler, 1979).

The clinical efficacy of hypnosis is attributable to its being such a powerful means of gaining access to symbolic processes, memories, and feelings, it enhances uncovering, an important dimension of dynamic psychotherapy. For example, it is possible in hypnotherapy to suggest that a patient dream about a specific symptom. The hypnotherapist need not wait for the clinical material to unfold slowly over a series of sessions in order to learn about the dynamics associated with this symptom, as is the case in psychotherapy. In hypnotherapy, the patient is likely to respond to the suggestion with a dream that reveals the dynamic meaning of the symptom, even while the patient attempts to conceal it.

Further, because hypnosis also produces cognitive and perceptual changes in some people (Frankel, 1976; Orne, 1977), and habitual frames of reference can be altered (Rossi & Erickson, 1979), it can contribute to changes in one's belief system, as Orne (1977) implied in his definition of hypnosis as "believed-in fantasy." Thus, hypnosis can contribute to the

---

[1] An earlier version of this section appeared in *Psychotherapy: Theory, Research and Practice*, 1980, *17*, 425–430, under the title, "Values in Hypnotherapy."

overall task of dynamic psychotherapy, namely, to helping the patient understand and then solve his conflict. It is also possible to give suggestions directly designed to enhance patients' insight into their problems. The hypnotist may say, for example, "The meaning will get more and more clear to you as you are ready to understand this."

Through posthypnotic suggestion, hypnosis can also influence the patient's behavior between therapy hours, allowing treatment effects to be carried beyond the therapy sessions to everyday life. For example, a typical problem in treating a phobic patient with desensitization therapy is whether or not the conditioned relaxation to imagined anxiety-provoking stimuli generalizes to real-life situations that provoke anxiety in the patient. When desensitization is combined with hypnosis, the patient can be given a posthypnotic suggestion to experience spontaneously the relaxation response whenever the anxiety-provoking situation is encountered.

Hypnosis is also a powerful way of altering maladaptive patterns of relationships, because of the intense transference relationship it entails. (Some psychoanalysts mistakenly believe that hypnosis is inferior to psychoanalysis because direct suggestions allegedly interfere with the spontaneous unfolding of the transference.) The criticism that an authoritarian hypnotherapist may evoke an intense parent transference reaction may have been justifiable in Freud's day, when authoritarian hypnosis was practiced, but it is certainly much less true today, when primarily permissive hypnosis is practiced. Hypnosis is also an adaptive regressive state (Fromm & Eisen, 1982; Fromm & Gardner, 1979; Gill & Brenman, 1959), in which earlier patterns of object relationships are reinstated (Nash, Johnson, & Tipton, 1979). The manifestation of these early patterns of object relations may occur dramatically during hypnosis. Even when less dramatic, these patterns are usually more clearly evident than in the waking state and are, therefore, more accessible to interpretation and working through.

GENERAL INDICATIONS AND CONTRAINDICATIONS

Some clinicians believe that hypnosis is useful for just about any clinical problem. In fact, some employ hypnotherapy exclusively in their clinical practice. Our position is that hypnosis is not indicated in all clinical situations. In each case, it is important to assess the patient's degree of hypnotizability, the nature of the symptom picture, and both the patient's and the therapist's motivation for using hypnosis. As a rule of thumb, though not without important exceptions, hypnotherapy is indicated for patients who are sufficiently motivated, are moderately to highly hypnotizable, and present with clearly circumscribed symptoms (in contrast to character pathology or major disturbances in capacity for relationship). The therapist should be guided by available clinical case studies and clinical outcome research in deciding whether or not to include hypnosis in the treatment plan for a particular patient.

General Indications

Susceptibility to Hypnosis. Hypnotherapy may be the treatment of choice for those patients who are moderately or highly hypnotizable, because hypnotizability is positively correlated with treatment outcome (Wadden & Anderton, 1982). About 10% of the population are highly hypnotizable and are likely to make quick and sometimes dramatic treatment gains when hypnosis is used. Most clinical work, however, can effectively be accomplished with patients who have only a medium level of hypnotizability, sometimes even with patients of low hypnotizability. About 60% of the population fall into the range of hypnotizability where hypnosis can be considered seriously as part of the treatment plan, provided other criteria are also met. Sometimes, however, hypnosis is appropriate even for less hypnotizable patients, for example, those highly motivated to use hypnosis, for whom the hypnotic situation has a special meaning that capitalizes on expectation effects, and for whom no other treatment is available, such as pharmacologically sensitive pain patients.

Type of Presenting Problem. From an extensive survey of the clinical literature on hypnosis, we have come to believe that hypnosis is more strongly indicated in the treatment of certain types of psychopathology than in others. In each of the areas for which we feel hypnosis can be usefully employed, either a good number of successful case studies have been reported or clinical outcome research has demonstrated the efficacy of hypnosis in the treatment. These areas are: the neuroses; psychophysiological disorders; behavioral and habit disorders; and maladaptive patterns of relationship.

Hypnosis is useful in the treatment of anxiety, phobic, conversion, and dissociative symptoms, but less useful in the treatment of obsessive-compulsive symptoms. It is also the treatment of choice for hypnotizable patients with a variety of psychophysiological disorders, provided the hypnotic treatment is integrated with the advances in behavioral medicine outlined in our book *Hypnosis and Behavioral Medicine* (Brown & Fromm, 1987). These disorders include pain, headache, respiratory disorders (especially asthma), cardiovascular disorders (especially hypertension), gastrointestinal disorders, skin disorders, and immune-related disorders (arthritic conditions and cancer). Hypnosis has yielded mixed results with habit and behavioral disorders (smoking, weight problems, sleep disorders, sexual dysfunction, and substance abuse) because outcome depends on the overall treatment approach in which hypnosis is embedded. The best outcomes occur when hypnosis is integrated with the established advances in behavioral modification—self-monitoring, intervention to alter motivation, stimulus control, behavioral regulation of symptoms, symptom discrimination, cognitive therapy, social support, and relapse prevention, as outlined in that book. The generally poor success rates of the past reflect less on the responsiveness of, for example, smoking and weight problems to hypnotherapy than on the uninformed way the treatment was conducted.

Some clinicians, particularly those working in clinics with diverse patient populations and problems, prefer to limit the use of hypnosis to cases where the patient meets the dual criteria of being sufficiently hypnotizable and presenting with relatively circumscribed symptoms. Patients with character problems and maladaptive patterns of relationships are likely to be assigned to long-term, nonhypnotic dynamic psychotherapy, where an emotionally corrective experience (Alexander & French, 1946) can be provided. In most clinics, hypnotherapy is limited more or less to brief interventions designed primarily to achieve symptom change. This preference for short-term hypnotherapy aimed at amelioration of symptoms may reflect trends in service delivery. In some clinical cases, however, hypnosis is also used as an adjunct to long-term therapy, especially where an ego-supportive uncovering approach to psychotherapy is indicated. Clinicians in private practice are more likely to use hypnotherapy and hypnoanalysis in the treatment of character problems and maladaptive patterns of relationships. In such treatment, the nature of the long-term psychotherapeutic relationship is emphasized. Working through the transference and adopting the stance that therapy should be an emotionally corrective experience for the patient are essential ingredients of the therapeutic relationship.

Hypnosis can also be useful in consultation, especially for long-term psychotherapy or psychoanalytic cases that have reached an impasse. A brief hypnotic uncovering approach can be employed for moving beyond the impasse by mobilizing and intensifying feelings in a very ideational patient, by uncovering material to which there has been resistance, and by identifying problems in the interaction between patient and therapist (unexplored transference and countertransference reactions, impairments in the therapeutic alliance, failures of empathy, etc.). Once the nature of the impasse has been identified, the material can be discussed by the hypnotherapist with the patient and the primary therapist, and referred back to the ongoing primary therapy to be worked through.

There are no well-established criteria for deciding whether to use psychotherapy alone, or hypnotherapy (psychotherapy combined with hypnosis). The decision depends in part on the patient's hypnotizability and in part on the therapist's preference of the treatment modality.

Contraindications

Low Susceptibility. The main contraindication to using hypnosis in treatment is lack of responsiveness to hypnosis. About 40% of the adult population manifests a sufficiently low level of hypnotic susceptibility to discourage the use of the hypnotic condition in therapy (Hilgard, 1965, p. 215; see Table 2.1, this volume).

Since the level of hypnotizability is related to treatment outcome in a variety of treatment situations (Wadden & Anderton, 1982), low susceptibility means that a trance state is unlikely to make much of a contribution to treatment outcome. Many would argue that since hypnotherapy is not going to contribute much beyond what may be available in nonhypnotic psychotherapy or in behavioral therapy with progressive relaxation, only those two types of therapy should be used with low hypnotizable patients. More conservative clinicians would rule out hypnosis from the treatment plan for less susceptible patients. Others, however, have taken the position that hypnosis may still benefit many low hypnotizable patients. Hypnosis does involve a considerable placebo effect and a special relationship irrespective of the degree of hypnotizability. Thus, low hypnotizable patients may have high expectations of benefit from the use of hypnosis (Barber & Calverley, 1964), or may manifest certain special talents in hypnosis only within a certain kind of hypnotic relationship (Sacerdote, 1982). A factor that may account for positive treatment gain in low hypnotizables is the special meaning of the hypnotic situation, not the condition of being in a hypnotic state (Gruenewald, 1982). Some hypnotists, then, are more willing than others to capitalize on the expectations even low hypnotizable patients have about the efficacy of hypnosis or on the specific hypnotic abilities likely to emerge in the context of a sensitive hypnotherapeutic relationship. These clinicians are more likely to use hypnotherapy, even if the patient is a poor hypnotic subject.

Still others, especially the Ericksonians, take issue with the whole concept of hypnotizability. Erickson devised special indirect hypnotic suggestions specifically for patients difficult to hypnotize or otherwise resistant to treatment. Some Ericksonians would claim that anyone is hypnotizable, provided the right hypnotic communication is used. From this more liberal perspective, hypnosis could be used for almost any patient.

Our own position recognizes the partial truth of each of these three perspectives. We recommend serious consideration of hypnosis with highly and moderately hypnotizable patients. We also recommend more judicious use of hypnosis with low hypnotizable patients if the particular case merits it. And in certain instances, an Ericksonian approach to hypnosis can be effective where other treatment approaches may not be. We do *not,* however, recommend the indiscriminant use of hypnosis with all patients simply because of a clinician's interest in it.

Low Motivation.   A second contraindication is low motivation for change. A patient may seek hypnotic treatment at the urge of others but may not really wish to change. A spouse may wish the patient to lose weight; a doctor may want the patient to stop smoking. Some patients use their symptoms for considerable secondary gain. For chronic pain patients, for example, litigation proceedings or disability benefits provide a strong incentive for maintaining the symptom. Low motivation is not necessarily a contraindication to hypnotherapy as long as the issue is addressed directly in the prehypnotic interview and in the initial hypnotic work. The issue of motivation, then, becomes the work of the hypnotherapy.

Hypnoprojective methods can be used to explore the systemic and the intrapsychic factors contributing to low motivation. Where motivation is seriously in question, it is advisable to contract for only a few (evaluation) sessions. At the end of these sessions (depending on how these sessions unfold), the patient and therapist will decide whether or not to proceed with hypnotherapy. The outcome of such evaluative work might include confrontation regarding secondary gain, recommendations for systemic interventions or lifestyle changes necessary before hypnotherapy can proceed, or payback contracts, as in the case of habit problems. Sometimes, however, low motivation is a manifestation of deep despair. Such patients do not seriously believe that *any* treatment can help them. The evaluative sessions may serve to uncover the specific roots of a given patient's despair. Some patients may begin to develop a sense of self-efficacy from being able to experience hypnosis (Frankel, 1976). They do well with hypnotherapy and are often very gratifying to work with. The rule of thumb is not to rule out hypnosis from a treatment plan because of initial low motivation, without first exploring the reasons for it. Continued low motivation will be evident after a few sessions and reliably serves as a contraindication.

CERTAIN KINDS OF PRESENTING PROBLEMS

Organic Brain Syndromes.   There are few areas of psychopathology where hypnosis can be readily ruled out as a treatment strategy. An obvious exception might be an organic brain syndrome with a manifest attentional disorder. Because hypnosis requires the ability to direct, focus, and sustain attention, and brain dysfunction makes attention deployment impossible, hypnosis cannot be used effectively. Such patients are highly distractable, and are unable to follow hypnotic suggestions for longer than brief moments. It is important to differentiate between those organic brain syndromes who have attentional deficits and those that do not. Hypnosis is not necessarily contraindicated for all organic brain syndromes. The few clinicians who have used hypnosis with organic brain syndromes have reported successes (Cedercreutz, Lahteenmaki, & Tullikoura, 1975; Ruth Illmer, personal communication, October, 1984).

Manic-Depressive Illness.   Another contraindication to hypnosis is manic-depressive illness. Few would contest that hypnosis, or for that matter any psychological intervention, is useless during a manic or a major depressive episode. However, hypnosis can be employed during remissions, although with great caution. The interpersonal difficulties of patients with manic-depressive illness make hypnotizing them technically complicated. Many manic-depressives show a tendency to form idealizing transferences, sometimes of psychotic proportions. They often seek magical identification with others they perceive as powerful and are extremely vulnerable to hurt and disappointment (Jacobson, 1971). The naive use of hypnosis with such people may all too readily play into their unrealistic expectations. The inevitable disillusionment in the hypnotherapy that follows is likely to lead to a negative therapeutic reaction, an irreparable rupture in the therapy relationship.

Caveats

There are a number of other areas in which hypnosis is generally contraindicated, but where it can be used if used with certain qualifications. Whether hypnosis is helpful or harmful depends on three factors: (a) the point at which hypnosis is introduced into the overall course of treatment, (b) the approach to the hypnotic treatment, and (c) whether or not special parameters are introduced to protect against harmful results. The five areas where hypnosis can be either useful or harmful, depending on the way it is used, are: compulsion neurosis, multiple personality, alcoholism and substance abuse, posttraumatic stress disorders, and in some psychotic and most borderline patients. Because of the potential dangers of using hypnosis with such patients, in these cases it should be employed only by a highly skilled expert, using the right approach at the right time. In the hands of hypnosis experts, some such patients make progress that is not possible in nonhypnotic therapy or that is possible only over many more years.

Obsessive-Compulsive Disorders.   As already noted, traditional dynamic hypnotherapy has not been especially effective with rigid obsessive-compulsive personalities, particularly when the trance state contributes to the patient's fear and uncertainty about the unknown and when hypnotic suggestions become part of a struggle for control. For such patients, hypnotherapy is usually contraindicated. However, we suggest that a permissive style of hypnotherapy, which encourages the patient's autonomy, along with a developmental approach designed to enhance affective awareness and tolerance, may be useful with obsessive-compulsive patients. It has not really been tried yet.

Multiple Personality.   Historically, hypnosis has been associated with the treatment of the multiple personality because the hypnotic state can be structured to explore dissociative phenomena. Hypnosis traditionally has been the treatment of choice for multiple personality because it is a means to gain access to the other personalities normally outside of the patient's conscious awareness and it can be used to integrate the split-off parts (Bowers et al., 1971; Braun, 1984; Prince, 1906; Thigpen & Cleckley, 1957; Watkins, 1984). But the hypnotic trance, itself a dissociative state, may exacerbate rather than correct splitting. And the therapist's fascination with the several personalities may give subtle cues to the patient that reinforce further splitting. A case that presents as two personalities may produce 20 or more as a result of hypnotherapy.

Some hypnotherapists feel hypnosis is contraindicated for the treatment of multiple personality because it is likely to contribute iatrogenically to multiple personalities (Gruenewald, 1984). Others (e.g., Braun, 1984; Prince, 1906; Thigpen & Cleckley, 1957; Watkins, 1984) feel it is the treatment of choice. In our opinion, hypnosis may be employed with some caution with the multiple personality syndrome, provided the clinician does not allow himself or others in the patient's environment to exploit or be drawn into the sensational dissociative aspects of the multiple personality; and provided the therapist adopts an approach designed to integrate the split self-representations into a cohesive inner representational world rather than attempting to tease out more and more split-off "personalities."

Alcoholism.   The conditions for using hypnosis with alcoholics are the same as those for employing nonhypnotic therapy with alcoholics. Many alcoholics have deficits in the ability to tolerate specific affects or to tolerate affect in general. Early in the course of alcoholism, the motivation for alcohol consumption is often the need to compensate for the failures in regulating affects (Khantzian, 1981; Krystal & Raskin, 1970). Dynamic psychotherapies, especially those that work with the transference, may be harmful to the alcoholic because they may stir up feelings in the transference that the alcoholic is not equipped to handle and that quickly may drive the alcoholic to drink even more than before. If the therapy fails to make the drinking behavior a central focus of the treatment, it may actually increase the drinking problem (Vaillant, 1981). Similarly, an uncovering approach in hypnotherapy with alcoholics may be harmful, especially if transference work is emphasized and drinking behavior is ignored. Hypnosis allows the alcoholic greater access to the feelings that are difficult to manage and creates an intense, special hypnotic relationship to the hypnotherapist, which may be equally difficult to handle. Because the alcoholic has little capacity to bear the emerging emotions, his urge to seek alcohol may become even stronger.

Hypnosis can be useful with alcoholics if it is designed to foster greater toleration of affects instead of uncovering the underlying dynamics. Hypnotically induced deep relaxation, posthypnotic suggestions designed to counter the urge to drink, and suggestions designed to increase the capacity to bear certain affects can be helpful in controlling the factors that contribute to the urge to drink. Whether or not to use hypnosis depends to a great extent on the course of the alcoholism. Although the initial motivation to drink may have been in part an attempt to regulate affects, the alcohol-related behavior takes on a life of its own at a certain point and must be treated as a disease in its own right (Jellinek, 1960). Thus, an affect-development approach to hypnotherapy may be useful for alcoholics at the earlier stages of the illness or sometimes in remission. But it is not necessarily useful in the later stages, when the alcoholic cannot stop and the therapeutic relationship is likely to drive him to drink even more.

Post-Traumatic Stress Disorders (PTSD). The area with the highest risk of hypnotic treatment failure is post-traumatic stress syndromes, which include: victims of incest, abuse, rape, assault, accidents, and natural disasters; survivors of the holocaust or political prison experience; and war neuroses. A major difficulty in treating such people by any kind of therapy is that they often present in a disguised form (Gelinas, 1983) after a symptom-free period (Niederland, 1968). After the initial intake evaluation, it is often not clear that the patient has a traumatic neurosis, nor is it necessarily clear even after initial hypnotic work has been done. However, in the early hypnotic sessions with these patients, vivid memories of the trauma often spontaneously emerge or threaten to emerge during trance induction, even where the induction is fairly nonclinical, as with the use of the standard scales. Both the patient and the therapist may be surprised by the intensity of the affect, by the emergence of symbolic derivatives of the trauma or memories of the trauma itself, or sometimes by the struggle over whether to enter trance. Many patients subsequently become fearful of hypnosis and come to view the hypnotic state as a return to the over-whelming traumatic experience, which they would rather deny, often for good reason. Since the traumatic material is likely to erupt too early without the support of a strong therapeutic alliance and without prepara-tion for coping with it, many of these patients drop out of hypnotic treatment.

The key to success is an assessment designed to identify early patients who have suffered—and often have repressed—severe traumata, and to formulate an hypnotic protocol designed to delay the emergence of the material or at least to titrate its emergence long enough to build a treat-ment alliance. Only then can the hypnotherapist attempt to help such patients develop adequate coping mechanisms that will enable them to tolerate the unbearable affects and to integrate the traumatic experiences into their overall identity and view of life. Because it can help to gain access to the traumatic experience as well as help integrate the experience into the overall meaning of the patient's life, hypnotherapy—often com-bined with adjunctive group therapy—is the treatment of choice for post-traumatic stress disorders (see chapter 9). But it must be handled skillfully and embedded within a comprehensive treatment plan, as outlined in chapter 8.

Psychotic and Borderline Conditions.   Traditionally, hypnotherapists have been warned not to use hypnosis with psychotic and borderline patients because, it was thought, such patients could not be hypnotized and hypnosis was ineffective with or harmful to such patients, possibly precipitating psychotic episodes (Abrams, 1964; Rosen, 1960). Recent investigations of the hypnotizability of schizophrenic patients have chal-lenged the first stereotype. It is now clear that at least some psychotic patients (about 20%) are reasonably hypnotizable. Whether hypnotherapy is effective or precipitates psychotic episodes depends on the particular hypnotherapeutic approach taken. A dynamic/uncovering approach is clearly contraindicated for some severely disturbed patients. It may pre-cipitate transient psychotic episodes for borderlines prone to such epi-sodes, and it may contribute to the schizophrenic's disordered thinking becoming more ego-syntonic.

However, set within a developmental framework, hypnosis can be used where there is a stable, ongoing therapeutic relationship with parameters designed to strengthen the patient's sense of control over the experience. The goal of such hypnotic interventions is what Gedo and Goldberg (1973) have called "structuralization." Dynamic interpretations of unconscious conflicts and genetic interpretations of the transference should be avoided. Hypnosis can enhance the patient's awareness of sensory and imaginal processes, which can be employed to develop and integrate the representational world (Baker, 1981; Fromm, 1984), to foster a more cohesive sense of identity (Bowers, 1961) and to enhance the experience of genuine affects and their tolerance (Brown, 1985) in schizophrenic and borderline patients.

EVALUATING WHETHER AND HOW TO USE HYPNOSIS WITH A PARTICULAR PATIENT

Prehypnotic Evaluation

The patient who comes for hypnotherapy is given the same kind of thorough diagnostic interview as a patient who is referred for psychotherapy or psychoanalysis: The good clinician, through skillful interviewing, obtains a thorough intake history from the patient, including information about the patient's developmental history, his relations to important figures in his childhood and adolescence (parents, siblings, caretakers, etc.), his relations to important figures in his adult life (wife, children, meaningful friendships, etc.), and his psychodynamics. The therapist evaluates these in the context of the patient's current life situation and formulates his diagnosis. The therapist not only must consider the patient's pathology in his diagnosis, he also must assess the patient's inner strengths and coping powers. In hypnosis, as in all other good therapies, not all difficulties can be treated in the same way. For instance, the hypnotic treatment of an hysterical neurosis with conversion symptoms is technically quite different from that of narcissism with hypochondriasis, which is very different from that of somatically caused physical pain. In the process of prehypnotic evaluation, psychodiagnostic testing, particularly projective tests such as the Rorschach and the TAT, can be used profitably.

Assessing Attitudes, Motivation, and Expectations

Patients come to hypnotherapy with certain attitudes, motivations, and expectations about hypnosis. Some are realistic, and some are unrealistic. All need to be evaluated by the hypnotherapist before he begins to treat the patient. This usually can be done by means of a few simple questions.

The patient's answer to the question, "How much would you like to be hypnotized?" reveals his attitude toward hypnosis. Does he conceive of hypnosis as an interesting new experience, one he thinks will be therapeutically helpful? Or is he afraid of it?

By asking the patient, "How much do you want to be hypnotized?", the therapist can find out how strong the patient's motivation is for entering hypnotherapy. And by posing the two questions, "Why do you want to be hypnotized?" and "How much do you think you will be able to be hypnotized?" the therapist can assess outcome expectations and self-efficacy expectations, respectively; that is, what the patient conceives of his own goal in hypnotherapy and how much he believes his own resources will enable him to reach this goal.

Determining Responsiveness to Hypnosis

When considering a hypnotherapy candidate, it is advisable to assess the degree to which the patient is hypnotizable. Although some clinicians maintain that *every* patient is hypnotizable (Erickson, 1954a; Schaefer & Hernandez, 1978) or that all patients can at least be trained to utilize hypnosis in therapy, the more accepted view is that hypnosis is useful primarily for those patients who are moderately or highly hypnotizable.

There is considerable controversy over how to assess hypnotizability. The controversy centers on whether standardized laboratory scales or nonstandardized clinical assessment procedures should be used.

Standardized Scales.   Until recently, most of the valid standardized instruments for measuring hypnotizability were designed for laboratory use. It is a matter of considerable debate just how well suited these standardized scales are for patients. Some clinicians (Frankel, 1982; Frankel et al., 1979; Hilgard & Hilgard, 1979) believe that the standardized scales, despite limitations, can be quite useful for patients in a clinical setting. From the perspective of clinical research, there is strong justification for applying these scales to the clinical assessment of hypnotizability. Measuring hypnotizability by means of these scales allows the clinician to evaluate the degree of a given patient's hypnotizability relative to well-established norms. Thus, the clinician is able to know which patients are and which are not able to enter the hypnotic condition and to select, for hypnotherapy as well as for clinical research, patients with the required hypnotic talent.

There are, of course, many problems involved in the use of laboratory scales in the clinical setting. Some clinicians (Gruenewald, 1982; Sacerdote, 1982) are opposed to their use and advocate instead more individualized, nonobjective clinical estimates of hypnotizability. The laboratory setting is different from the clinical setting, and laboratory scales, when used according to standards, must be given, or read, to all patients in exactly the same (verbatim) form. This stereotypes and impersonalizes the interaction between the hypnotherapist and patient and is likely to interfere with the establishment of rapport. In addition, because the standardized scales emphasize successful behavioral performance in response to hypnotic suggestions, patients may become discouraged when they do not perform well on various hypnotic tasks. Frankel (1982) admits that negative effects do result from use of laboratory scales in the clinical setting, but he believes their incidence has been overestimated.

We feel the greatest drawback of the laboratory scales is that they help very few patients develop the degree of encouragement required for clinical change. The scales fail to emphasize the development of self-efficacy, so critical to a successful treatment outcome. Another problem is that the more widely known standardized laboratory scales tap a restricted range of specific hypnotic abilities, and most of these are peripheral to the clinical situation. For example, the Stanford Hypnotic Susceptibility Scales, Form A (SHSS:A) (Weitzenhoffer & Hilgard, 1959) and the Harvard Group Scale of Hypnotic Susceptibility (HGSHS) (Shor & Orne, 1962), both widely used measures of hypnotizability, tap primarily ideomotor talent. They do not extensively tap imagery and other cognitive/perceptual, regressive, and affective phenomena more relevant to the clinical use of hypnosis.

Each clinician must make a choice between standardized scales and nonstandardized assessment procedures for assessing hypnotizability. Clinicians who wish to use the standardized scales can choose from a variety of scales. Those who wish *quick screening devices* may make a very brief assessment using *single-item scales*. There are several to choose from: one scale gauges hypnotizability by eye closure (Hull, 1933); another, by the rate of arm levitation (Hilgard, Crawford, & Wert, 1979). The advantage of such scales is the brevity of their administration (less than 10 minutes). But they cannot tap a range of specific hypnotic abilities, as each of these brief scales consists of only one item.

Hypnotherapists with clinical research interests who want to make a comprehensive and valid assessment are likely to choose the SHSS, Form A or B (Weitzenhoffer & Hilgard, 1959) or the HGSHS (Shor & Orne, 1962). The administration of the SHSS:A or B and the HGSHS requires one full hour for each. The HGSHS has the advantage of not having to be read verbatim to the patient; it is tape recorded. It is accompanied by self-scoring booklets. It is especially useful to clinical researchers who wish to assess hypnotizability in a large number of patients all at the same time. For example, hypnotherapist-researchers working in clinics or hospitals may wish to assess hypnotizability in a large patient population so as to select highly hypnotizable patients for hypnotherapy. Many patients can be scheduled to listen to the tape simultaneously, even as part of a routine assessment procedure. Although the Harvard Group Scale is one of the most convenient and cost-effective standardized scales, it is also limited in the range of specific hypnotic abilities tapped. Containing nine ide-omotor, two posthypnotic, and one hallucination item, it hardly covers the range of hypnotic abilities the clinician wishes to know about.

Clinicians who desire a standardized scale that taps a greater range of specific hypnotic abilities can choose from other scales. The Stanford C scale (SHSS:C) (Weitzenhoffer & Hilgard, 1962) may be used. This is a graded difficulty scale that taps ideomotor phenomena, age regression, dreams, positive and negative hallucinations in three sensory fields, and posthypnotic amnesia. But even the C scale is somewhat limited in the range of hypnotic abilities tapped and contains some items of less impor-tance to the clinician, notably the hallucination items. It is possible to substitute other items of equal difficulty for these without altering the normative value of the overall score. For example, the clinician might administer the C scale and substitute suggestions for automatic writing, analgesia, or evocation of affect for the original hallucination items (Hil-gard et al., 1979). As with the A or B scales, the C scale, or "tailored C," as Hilgard called it, must be read to each patient verbatim and is scored individually. The scale also contains challenge items, which, if failed, might undermine the patient's developing sense of self-efficacy.

There are two standardized scales designed specifically for clinicians. The quicker, but less reliable, clinical scale is the Hypnotic Induction Profile [(HIP) Spiegel & Spiegel, 1978]. This scale contains suggestions for rolling the eyes upwards, levitating an arm, and experiencing certain bodily sensations. The main advantage of the HIP is that it takes only 10 minutes to administer. The disadvantage is that the eye roll procedure is not a valid measure of hypnotizability (Sheehan, Latta, Regina, & Smith, 1979). Historically, the HIP was the first *clinical* hypnotizability scale. Because of the need for a standardized clinical scale, the HIP became very popular. It has remained popular, even though it contains an invalid assessment procedure. Since the remainder of the scale (arm levitation, sensory experience) is valid, those who wish to use the HIP may still do so, without the eye roll item. It is quick and easy to administer. The main disadvantage of using the HIP without the eye roll is that it approximates a single-item scale and thereby taps only a limited range of specific hypnotic abilities.

A much better and more reliable clinical scale is the Stanford Hypnotic Clinical Scale [SHCS] (Morgan & J. R. Hilgard, 1978/79). Its advantages over the more traditional standardized scales—SHSSs and the HGSHS—are that it takes less time to administer (20 minutes) and taps a reasonably wide range of specific hypnotic abilities, while preserving acceptable standards of validity and reliability. The SHCS contains a relaxation-induction and five different items: an ideomotor task, a dream, an age regression, a posthypnotic suggestion, and posthypnotic amnesia. Thus, it allows the clinician to assess a range of specific hypnotic talents directly relevant to the clinical situation. The main drawback to the scale is that it provides only a rough estimate of low, moderate, and high hypnotizability. But it is the best clinical scale we have at this time.

Clinical Assessment. Clinicians who are hesitant to introduce standardized laboratory scales into the clinical situation can design their own hypnotic procedures and tailor the suggestions to the individual patient. The main disadvantage of such idiosyncratic approaches to assessment of hypnotizability is that their results cannot be compared with the norms established with standardized scales. Nevertheless, although idiosyncratic assessment does not contribute to sound clinical research on hypnosis, it does have certain advantages for those more interested in clinical efficacy than in clinical research. Induction and deepening procedures can be designed in accordance with the patient's clinical needs. For example, a clinician may induce hypnosis with deep muscle relaxation for chronic pain patients, for whom muscle tension is known to exacerbate pain. In this testing situation, the clinician can also avoid suggestions that are bound to fail as test items because they touch upon the area of the patient's symptoms, such as using the elevator technique with a claustrophobic or telling an insomniac that he is getting drowsy and sleepy.

The wise clinician uses the prehypnotic interview to assess the patient's interests, hobbies, and daily activities. These often can be utilized directly in hypnosis to make the hypnotic experience personally meaningful. For example, a hypnotherapist was able to induce trance in a physicist by employing body heaviness and asking the physicist to imagine himself on a planet with a stronger gravitational field than earth. In an adolescent with a strong fascination for science fiction, he was able to induce trance quickly by asking the boy to imagine himself traveling in a space ship. The rapport between patient and therapist is greatly enhanced when care is taken to compose inductions that utilize the patient's interests and activities (Erickson, 1959). When such interests and activities are not clear from the prehypnotic interview, they often appear in spontaneous fantasy productions during the initial hypnotic sessions.

Suggestions can be carefully sequenced, from easiest to most difficult, to foster a sense of self-efficacy in the patient as he succeeds in "passing" item after item. For ideomotor suggestions, magnets are easier than an arm drop, and an arm drop is easier than arm levitation. Because magnets work well for the majority of patients, it is a good idea to start with this technique. Once patients draw their own conclusions about their ability to have a successful experience, they are likely to report a deeper state (Tart, 1979). A main goal of clinical assessment of hypnotizability is to have the patient conclude that he is capable of utilizing hypnosis in specific ways.

The clinician who employs a clinical assessment procedure can make the initial hypnotic experience much more interactive than is possible with the standardized laboratory scales. The patient can be encouraged not only to respond to the hypnotic suggestions but to describe his experience while responding. The therapist can then note the idiosyncratic way the patient responds to suggestions and can learn to tailor the wording of suggestions to the needs of the individual. Thus, by individualizing the initial induction and deepening procedures, the therapist is able to foster an atmosphere wherein the patient learns to be fully receptive to the experience, the therapist learns to be finely attuned to the patient's experience, and the expectations of the patient and the therapist become more congruent (Sacerdote, 1982).

In summary, a good clinical assessment procedure includes the following features:

1. A prehypnotic interview regarding the patient's interests and activities.
2. A prehypnotic assessment of the patient's expectations of hypnosis and hypnotherapy, especially the patient's notion of what it is like to be in an hypnotic trance.
3. Induction of hypnosis according to the information previously gathered about activities the patient finds relaxing. Suggestions for deepening might incorporate verbatim the patient's own descriptions of his image of trance.
4. A graded sequence of nonchallenge ideomotor suggestions from the least to most difficult (magnets, arm drop, arm levitation, respectively).
5. Explicit suggestions designed to improve communication between patient and hypnotist so each can learn from the other the best ways to proceed with the ongoing hypnotic experience.
6. A sequence of fantasy productions, at least some of which are projective: floating on a cloud to a special place (unspecified), an open-ended exploration of a path in a forest or a house with many rooms.
7. A vivid daydream or dream about hypnosis.
8. Simple posthypnotic suggestions, including suggestions to enter trance more quickly and easily in subsequent trance experiences.

The therapist should take care to ask the patient about his experience during or after each suggestion and should positively reinforce the patient's success. The most important consideration is the development of self-efficacy in the patient.

TREATMENT PLANNING WITH HYPNOSIS

Treatment Approaches in Hypnotherapy

There are at least four different approaches to the planning of hypnotherapy. Each has a different treatment goal and a unique set of hypnotherapy procedures and is based on a specific theoretical orientation. The duration of treatment also differs with each treatment plan. Table 5.1 lists the four types of hypnotherapy treatment plans.

Symptomatic hypnotherapy is brief hypnotherapy. The focus is on the presenting symptoms or habits, for instance, neurotic symptoms (anxiety, phobias, dissociative, conversion symptoms, etc.); psychophysiological symptoms (pain, asthmatic wheezing, high blood pressure, skin disorders, etc.); or habits (smoking, overeating). Symptomatic approaches use a variety of methods, including direct and indirect suggestion for alleviation, removal, transfer, or substitution of the symptom. Other methods employed in symptomatic hypnotherapy are hypnotic relaxation training, behavioral desensitization reinforced by hypnotic imagery conditioning and posthypnotic suggestion, behavioral self-monitoring combined with

TABLE 5.1
Treatment Approaches to Hypnotherapy

Presenting Problem	Theoretical Background for Treatment	Treatment	Duration
Neurotic and psychophysiological symptoms; habit disorders	Learning theory	Symptomatic	Brief
All kinds	Ego psychology	Supportive	Usually Brief/Long
Neurotic and Psychophysiological symptoms; post-traumatic stress; personality disorders	Psychoanalysis (Libido theory & Ego psychology)	Dynamic (Hypno-analysis)	Brief/Long
Borderline Pathology & Schizophrenia	Developmental Psychoanalysis (Object relations, Self psychology, Affect development theory)	Developmental (Hypno-analysis)	Long

hypnosis, and hypnotic psychophysiological control with or without bio-feedback. These approaches derive in part from learning theory. To use them effectively, the hypnotherapist must also understand the role of suggestion and imagery in facilitating therapeutic change.

Supportive ego-strengthening hypnotherapy (Hartland, 1965) can be either short- or long-term hypnotherapy. The goal of supportive hypnotherapy is to facilitate relaxation, foster self-efficacy and confidence, support and increase the patient's strengths and abilities to cope, and encourage the patient's autonomy. The methods usually involve direct or indirect suggestions for increased relaxation, increased confidence, strength, independence, or well-being. The underlying theory is derived from psychoanalytic ego psychology.

Dynamic hypnotherapy or hypnoanalysis may be brief but more often takes longer than symptomatic hypnotherapy. It goes more quickly into the patient's deep dynamics than psychoanalysis does. Like the psycho-analyst, the hypnoanalyst helps the patient to understand the latent symbolic meaning of his symptoms as unconscious wishes and defenses against them. But the hypnoanalyst uses hypnosis for uncovering unconscious conflicts and working them through in the transference situation. During hypnosis, when the unconscious can rise into awareness much more easily, the patient can be helped to make profound changes and a faster integration in personality structure than in psychoanalysis. Dynamic hypnotherapy utilizes a variety of hypnotherapeutic methods—imagery and fantasy, hypnotic dreaming, affect amplification, age regression and hypermnesia, the ideal self technique, and ego-strengthening posthypnotic suggestions. These methods are based on the dynamic theories of psychoanalysis (libido theory, ego psychology, the theory of object relations, and self psychology). (Hypnoanalysis is discussed extensively in chapters 7 and 9.)

Hypnotherapy of developmental deficits is long-term hypnotherapy set within the context of a stable therapeutic relationship, where internalization can take place. The focus is on assessment of developmental deficts in individual lines of development (in internal representations of self and others and in the affects connected with them) and developmental arrests in several of these lines. These arrests contribute to the psychopathology of schizophrenia and certain personality disorders (borderline, pathological narcissism). One of the authors (D. B.) has developed a variety of structural psychoanalytic interventions that utilize sensory awareness and imagery for building psychic structure. These approaches are based on several convergent current psychoanalytic theories: object relations theory, self psychology, and affect development theory. Dynamic hypnotherapy and developmental hypnotherapy are both forms of hypnoanalysis, whereas symptomatic and supportive hypnotherapy are not.

In planning treatment the clinician must choose among these four approaches. The choice is sometimes easy: In the treatment of the severely disturbed patient, the developmental approach to hypnotherapy is indicated, sometimes in combination with supportive hypnotherapy; with the depressed patient, supportive hypnotherapy is indicated; dynamic hypnotherapy is indicated for posttraumatic stress disorders and character problems with or without symptoms.

The choice of approach is more difficult when the patient presents with clear-cut symptoms, especially neurotic or psychophysiological symptoms and habit problems. Either symptomatic or dynamic hypnotherapy may be indicated. Many cases can be handled with briefer symptomatic hypnotherapeutic interventions, and it is not necessary to utilize the longer dynamic hypnotherapeutic approach. To do so may be more in the therapist's interest than the patient's. Unfortunately, our assessment procedures are not yet advanced enough for us to predict with certainty for which patients a symptomatic approach will be successful and for whom a dynamic hypnotherapeutic approach is indicated.

How, then, do we know when to use symptomatic and when to use dynamic hypnotherapy? In some instances, unconscious conflicts are so obvious in the presenting problem that dynamic hypnotherapy is clearly indicated. In most cases, however it is not so clear at the onset of treatment which approach would be the best for the patient. The clinician, nevertheless, must make his decision. The solution is to start routinely with a symptomatic approach. This approach might also include some dynamic assessment methods, such as dreaming, guided imagery, and projective imagery, in order to collect clinical material related to possible dynamic or systemic (family or work) conflicts associated with the symptoms. This material may or may not be used directly in the treatment. About 70% of cases can be treated with a straightforward symptomatic approach (5–15 sessions). The other 30% are destined for treatment failure if hypnotherapy is continued in a purely symptomatic manner. Only after a while can these cases be distinguished from those that can fully and quickly be treated with the symptomatic approach. Deeper conflicts and developmental arrests become obvious only as the treatment proceeds. Where such deep-seated emotional difficulties exist, symptomatic treatment tends to reach a plateau by the third to fifth session. When they do not, symptomatic treatment proceeds unimpeded toward symptom improvement. Starting with a symptomatic approach does not involve much loss of time. In the roughly 30% of cases where a switch to dynamic hypnotherapy is indicated, the clinician can easily make the transition.

Working With Symptoms

Behavioral and dynamic hypnotherapeutic approaches to symptom removal are often brief and are effective in many instances. The typical goal of working with symptoms in hypnotherapy is *symptom alleviation*. The hypnotherapist may use a variety of strategies to alleviate symptoms. With some hypnotizable patients, direct suggestions for symptom removal can be immediately and dramatically effective. With the greater majority of moderately hypnotizable patients, behavioral desensitization combined with hypnotic imagery conditioning can be successful (Clark & Jackson, 1983; Kroger & Fezler, 1976).

The unconscious meaning of the symptom can also be approached indirectly through metaphors, puns, jokes, and stories that address the underlying conflicts. Symptoms may even vanish without the patient's consciously realizing the meaning the symptom had for him (Erickson, 1964). Symbolic processes can be directly explored in hypnosis to discover the unconscious forces operating in the formation of symptoms. The symptom may abate as a result of insight into its meaning and resolution of the underlying conflicts in healthy, adaptive ways will usually then occur.

There are also situations in which the conflict that caused the symptom cannot be resolved but the therapist still wants to give the patient as much relief as possible. There may be reality constraints imposed on the therapy; for example, the patient may be unable to stay in treatment long enough for hypnoanalysis because of lack of time or money. Even when it is possible to continue therapy without such reality constraints, and the goal is explicitly symptom removal, the symptoms may persist or change form. The therapist must ask himself then whether he has failed to understand the meaning of the symptom in the total context of the patient's life. Or the patient may need the symptom to resolve some intrapsychic or family systems conflict that has not been adequately addressed in the therapy or that has been addressed but for which symptom formation is the best possible solution under the reality circumstances in which the patient has to live. Or the patient may have learned to derive considerable secondary gain from the symptoms.

In such instances, it is possible to work with the symptoms in other ways. An alternative goal is *symptom amelioration* rather than total symptom eradication. For example, a neurodermatitis patient may be asked to fantasize applying an imagined medicated salve to heal his skin disease. If it does not work, if the patient for some reason is unable to give up the symptom, and long-term dynamic hypnotherapy is not possible, the hypnotherapist may try to reduce the area of irritation to a small, less visible part of the body rather than try to cure the skin disease totally.

Another approach involves *symptom displacement*. The Clenched Fist technique (Stein, 1963) can be used with a patient suffering from bruxism. The patient can be given a posthypnotic suggestion that the fist or a finger will automatically contract at the moment tension would otherwise have increased in the jaw muscles during sleep. The muscle contraction of the hand or finger is less destructive physiologically than the teeth grinding. In another technique, *symptom substitution,* an innocuous symptom is substituted for a bothersome one by means of direct suggestion. The hypnotherapist may suggest a feeling of warmth to replace pain. Or he can suggest that a tinnitus patient hear pleasant music in place of ear ringing. It is also possible to utilize the symptom directly in the course of treatment.

Erickson (Erickson & Rossi, 1979, p. 78) tells of a dental patient who feared pain so much that he was unable to go into trance. The therapist suggested the patient concentrate on his left hand until the hand became hypersensitive to sensations. When the patient reported the hand to be painful, it was clear that he had become hypnotized, and subsequently he responded to analgesic suggestions for his mouth. The therapist utilized the patient's intense preoccupation with the symptom—fear of pain—to produce the trance necessary for its removal.

In certain instances, notably pain control, the therapist may use *symptom intensification,* suggesting an increase in pain at some point in trance. Once patients realize that they are able to increase the pain through their own imagery or thought, they more readily understand that they also can decrease their pain through their own inner resources. The skillful hypnotherapist is flexible enough to modify his style of suggestion according to the needs of a given patient, not according to his own interests and biases.

How, then, does the hypnotherapist choose between directive, permissive, and Ericksonian styles of suggestion? The degree of hypnotic susceptibility and the treatment goal are useful criteria. Where the purpose is symptom removal, one can use a directive style of hypnosis with very highly hypnotizable patients. A permissive style is most useful for most people, namely, moderately and low hypnotizable patients and all those who need more than just symptom removal, that is, a reorganization of the personality and the development of strategies to help them cope with their life problems and inner conflicts. The Ericksonian style is especially useful for poorly hypnotizable patients, patients with otherwise intractable symptoms, and those resistant to more straightforward approaches.

Choosing a Treatment Modality

Another important decision in treatment planning pertains to the treatment modality. The therapist must choose among *individual, group,* or *family* hypnotherapy and may often combine any of these with teaching the patient self-hypnosis. Each of these modalities reflects differences in the relative emphasis given to the private and the public domains of the therapy process. Symptoms can be viewed from the perspective of either the inner life of the patient or the outer, communal context of his life. The total structure of a symptom comprises both the inner (private) and the outer (public) domains (Rutterman, 1983).

Individual hypnotherapy and self-hypnosis place emphasis on the private domain. The events of the patient's inner life are explored, with the goal of symptom change or emotionally corrective relationship; but their influence on the patient's wider, real-life community context is seldom emphasized in a systematic way. It is, however, given emphasis in group and family hypnotherapy: Interaction within the context of a community, an artificially constructed community (group therapy), or the real-life community in which the patient lives (family) is given prominence over access to the patient's private world.

There are no clear guidelines for choosing among individual, group, or family hypnotherapy, or for determining when to use self-hypnosis as an adjunct to any of these. The choice between the individual or the family modality hinges on whether therapeutic change is viewed as contingent on intrapsychic reorganization, as in individual hypnotherapy and self-hypnosis, or on situational rearrangements, as in family therapy (Ritterman, 1983). Depending on the nature of the group, group hypnotherapy can serve the goal of either intrapsychic or situational change. Change on an intrapsychic level does not guarantee change on an interpersonal or contextual level, nor vice versa. Usually, the choice of a modality reflects the therapist's decision about the primary locus of difficulty (intrapsychic or interpersonal) in a given patient.

Because of the lack of established criteria, some recommendations are in order. Individual hypnotherapy is indicated for most clinical problems. There are a few exceptions. Hypnotherapy, combined with nonhypnotic family therapy and sometimes hypnotic family therapy, may be indicated when the patient's symptomatology is tied up in a family system and it can be clearly established that the symptom has meaning within this family system. Group hypnotherapy may be indicated for habit change when prevailing cultural systems support the maintenance of destructive habits. Here the group becomes a supportive subculture that fosters habit change and attempts to prevent relapse, as, for example, in smoking or weight gain. Supportive groups are also especially valuable when the goal of therapy is to make sense out of unusual life events, such as in the treatment of posttraumatic stress disorders. The group is also indicated when the therapeutic goal is attitude change, alteration of beliefs, and patient education. Guidance and persuasion are stronger in a group than in an individual setting because cognitive dissonance operates in the service of attitude change. In addition, groups are useful when the goal is to enhance interaction with others and to foster improved social skills. In a group, patients can learn about how they interact with others, and they can gain feedback from one another that will help improve their social skills and help correct maladaptive ways of relating to others. Group members also learn from, and form valuable identifications with, one another. The group has the advantage of peer pressure, a strong catalyst for change and maintenance of change.

Self-Hypnosis.   The therapist also must decide whether to incorporate self-hypnosis into the overall treatment plan. In the permissive approach, self-hypnosis is often used as an adjunct to the hypnotherapy sessions, because the therapist wishes to enhance the patient's sense of responsibility for and mastery of the treatment outcome (Fromm & Eisen, 1982). In hypnotherapy, much of the clinical work is done in self-hypnosis in the later stages of treatment.

Self-hypnosis is usually introduced into the treatment after the patient has been hypnotized several times by the therapist and has become familiar with a range of hypnotic phenomena. The majority of patients find self-hypnosis difficult at first. Many complain that they cannot hypnotize themselves effectively or are unable to attain a satisfactory depth of trance on their own (Fromm et al., 1981). In these initial stages, it is helpful to the patients to let them hypnotize themselves in the presence of the hypnotherapist before they practice at home. The hypnotherapist can give a few encouraging and structuring suggestions as needed. Another method is to have the patient imagine hypnotizing someone else deeply and then imagine himself becoming as hypnotized as the imagined person. In self-hypnosis some patients imagine the hypnotherapist sitting next to them and giving them suggestions; others subvocalize their own suggestions; still others produce the experience by imagining it, for example, seeing or feeling their arm levitate, or by simply "letting go" (of conscious control), without explicitly speaking suggestions to themselves.

At first, patients are likely to ask questions about what to do in self-hypnosis. They can be told to induce a comfortable level of trance and then to enjoy the experience in whatever way they wish. When patients practice at home, they must free a special time for themselves and find a quiet place without distractions. It is a good idea to plan a phone call so that the patient can report his first self-hypnotic experience at home to the therapist before the next office visit. If the patient had difficulty with self-hypnosis, the therapist can then offer suggestions so that subsequent home practice proceeds well and so that the patient does not become discouraged and stop practicing self-hypnosis at home. If the patient continues to have difficulties with home practice, the therapist tape records some hypnotherapy hours and the patient can listen to the tapes at home.

At first, the patient should not use self-hypnosis to work on the problem that brought him into therapy. Self-hypnosis is a skill; it must be learned before it can be applied. Patients who immediately use self-hypnosis to continue the work of the heterohypnotic therapy are likely to be disappointed when they fail to get the same insights as they do when they are with the hypnotherapist. In that case, they become discouraged and may discontinue practicing self-hypnosis. To enhance their sense of self-efficacy, patients should at first use self-hypnosis only for relaxation and enjoyment. After they have become quite familiar with it and as confidence grows, the transition will be made naturally to a more therapeutic use of self-hypnosis.

Group Hypnotherapy.   Two approaches combine hypnosis with group treatment: (a) individual hypnotherapy with nonhypnotic group therapy and (b) hypnotic group therapy, also called group hypnotherapy. Group hypnotherapy can be classified into three types, depending on the goals of treatment. First is *symptom-specific group hypnotherapy,* the goal of which is to educate the patient to the nature of the symptom (Ivanov, 1977; Ludwig, Lyler, & Miller, 1964) and to provide a systematic and often highly structured protocol for the steps of treatment. The theoretical background for this kind of group is often learning theory. This model of group hypnotherapy has been applied to the treatment of anxiety and phobias (DeVoge, 1975), psychophysiological disorders (Ivanov, 1977), and habit disorders (Kline, 1970). Treatment usually includes patient education in the waking state, formal periods of relaxation training and hypnotic inductions, and a systematic protocol of hypnotic and posthypnotic suggestions that guide the patient toward symptom change (Wolberg, 1948). Second is *dynamic group hypnotherapy* whose goals are to uncover unconscious processes and foster emotionally corrective experiences with group members and the group therapist. Such groups are usually less structured than symptom-specific groups. The theoretical background for these groups is dynamic psychology.

A distinction can be made between hypnotic group therapy and hypnosis in a group setting. In the former, the group is viewed as an entity in its own right. Individual patient concerns and personal problems are subordinated to the themes emerging from the entire group (Levendula, 1963;

Reardon, 1971). Hypnotic suggestions are often worded in very general terms so as to be relevant to all group members. In hypnosis in a group setting, on the other hand, the individual is given primacy. The therapist sets individualized goals for each patient. After a general induction, specific suggestions are given to each patient. This group, though not technically a group in the sense of fostering group dynamics, nevertheless takes advantage of the presence of the patients to enhance suggestibility through a contagion effect (Fox, 1960; Ludwig et al., 1964). Privacy is respected so that group members need not share their experiences with other group members. It is possible to design a dynamic hypnotherapy group which strikes a balance between group themes and individualized dynamics. Such a group utilizes individualized uncovering and ego-strengthening suggestions, but also focuses on working through the transferences that develop among group members and toward the group leader. Specific suggestions can be given to recover affects and memories in individual group members and to increase communication and interaction among group members (Serlin, 1970). Finally, there is *demonstrative group hypnotherapy,* which involves a therapeutic interaction between the therapist and one or more patients while the others in the group watch as an audience. Hypnodrama, an offshoot of psychodrama, is an example (Enneis, 1950; Greenberg, 1977). The demonstration is usually followed by a discussion with the audience.

The hypnotherapist who wishes to utilize group hypnotherapy as the modality must decide which type of hypnotic group is best for his therapeutic goals with a particular group of patients. The optimal size for any group is six to eight patients. Care must be taken in the composition of the group, and particular technical parameters may be introduced to deal with disruptive group members, such as those who excessively abreact. Most group sessions last 1 to 1 ½ hours and include opening remarks and discussion, group hypnotherapy, nonhypnotic discussion of group themes, and discussion of homework assignments (if any). Hypnosis ordinarily is not used during *every* group meeting. Serlin (1970), in an excellent example of dynamic group hypnotherapy, recommends using hypnosis in an ongoing group primarily when there is evidence of increased resistance or at a propitious moment for change in the group.

A serious problem in any type of group hypnotherapy is to strike just the right balance between privacy and group cohesion. Many patients resist group hypnosis because they fear rejection, or criticism, or invasion of privacy. Just how much one should respect the patient's private experience during group hypnosis, or in subsequent discussions, is a matter of judgment. Those who err on the side of protecting privacy may sacrifice group cohesiveness (Ludwig, 1964); those who foster increased group cohesiveness by encouraging the sharing of private experiences may intrude on the patient's boundaries and increase resistance to group hypnosis.

Some hypnotherapists combine individual hypnotherapy with nonhypnotic group therapy. This is particularly useful in the treatment of post-traumatic stress disorders (e.g., incest and war trauma), where hypnosis within the group would be too overwhelming but where group support is nevertheless desired.

Family Hypnotherapy.   Family hypnotherapy is the modality of choice when the symptom-bearing patient is actively involved in a couple or family system and it can be ascertained that the symptom is not primarily an expression of intrapsychic, but rather of interfamily, conflict. Through the symptoms, the patient attempts to reconcile contradictions in the communication patterns for the entire family and thereby—though suffering—is maintaining the family's equilibrium.

When the patient presents with symptoms caused by intrapsychic as well as by family conflicts, the hypnotherapist must choose between individual hypnotherapy combined with adjunctive, nonhypnotic family therapy or hypnotic family therapy. In the former, dynamic hypnotherapy is used to explore the meaning of the symptom to the individual patient. In nonhypnotic family therapy, the therapist explores the ways the symptom functions in the family context. Hypnosis is used directly during family therapy sessions in order to effect both intrapsychic changes and changes within the family dynamics.

Hypnotic family therapy begins with a family assessment. The therapist observes the interaction of family members in order to discover contradictions in the communications within the family. He also looks out for assignments of rigid roles of family members. The therapist tries to learn how the patterns of communication and role assignment contribute to symptom formation in the identified patient. According to Ritterman (1983), certain patterns of communication within families "induce" symptoms in the identified patient through indirect forms of suggestion. The goal of hypnotic family therapy is to develop "counterinductions." In this mode of treatment, the therapist uses indirect, covert forms of suggestion during family sessions. These hypnotic suggestions are directed either at specific symptom-bearing family members or to the entire family. Formal trance induction of the entire family or some of its members is sometimes used, but is not typically necessary when indirect suggestions are employed as the ongoing medium for change. In hypnotic family therapy, the therapist uses trance to increase the receptivity of individual family members to new and less rigid beliefs and expanded repertoires of behavior and attempts to move the entire family system to less contradictory and maladaptive communications and patterns of relationship.

A word of caution: Hypnotic family therapy is a very recent development, an offshoot of Ericksonian hypnosis (Ritterman, 1983), and because not much is known about it, it should be used judiciously. While hypnotic family therapy can be a powerful vehicle of change on both the intrapsychic and interpersonal levels, it is a virtually uncharted area of hypnotherapy. The possibly harmful effects of hypnotizing several family members simultaneously in front of one another (breakdown of boundaries, intrusion of privacy) have not been adequately investigated yet. Hypnotherapists must be sensitive to these potential hazards. With this sensitivity they can, for example, increase boundaries between family members in hypnosis and develop private domains for individual members of the family.

Hypnotherapy with Children.   A long-neglected field of hypnotherapy that is finally coming into its own is hypnotherapy with children. Starting with Liébeault (1866, 1889), there was a flurry of interest in child hypnotherapy between 1880 and 1900, particularly in France. A decline of work in this field that lasted from 1900 to about 1960 was followed by a revival of interest in child hypnosis and child hypnotherapy, particularly in the United States. This renaissance was due largely to the work of four Americans: G. Gail Gardner, Josephine R. Hilgard, and Karen Olness, talented and thorough clinician-researchers at the forefront of developing hypnotherapy techniques specifically for working with children; and Perry London, who developed the first children's susceptibility scales in 1962. In 1981, Gardner and Olness published their pioneering book, *Hypnosis and Hypnotherapy with Children,* a book that in the few years since its publication already has become a classic. It is to be recommended enthusiastically to all those who want to use hypnosis with children, whether as hypnotherapists or as researchers.

In child hypnosis, imagery plays an even greater role than in adult hypnosis. Children live naturally much of the time in a world of imagery. Of course, in each case the imaginative techniques used must be fitted to the child's age, personal style, and needs. Various other aspects of ego strength are also used to advantage; the child's desire for stimulation, for mastery, for being well, and for social interaction. The sensitive hypnotherapist can employ hypnosis to help children cope with a great variety of emotional problems. Among them are learning difficulties; behavior disorders; temper tantrums, hair pulling, nail biting, prolonged thumb sucking; phobic reactions, including school phobias, needle phobias, and animal phobias; shyness; nightmares and sleepwalking; anorexia nervosa and posttraumatic amnesias; and habit disorders, stuttering, enuresis, tics, and drug abuse.

In addition, hypnotic imagery can be employed to help the child distance and dissociate himself from his physical pain—for instance, in cancer or burn cases, or when the child has to undergo minor surgery or a dental procedure. Hypnosis can help the child to relax, to focus his attention on pleasant or exciting imagery and thereby become unaware, or less aware, of the pain. Children suffering recurrent or constant pain can be taught self-hypnosis so that they have at their disposal a tool for self-help to use whenever they need it. Hypnosis can also be employed with a variety of pediatric medical problems, such as asthma, diabetes, urine retention, and hemophilia. Above all, it can help the terminally ill child to face death with dignity (Gardner, 1976) and to improve the quality of his life during the time he still has to live. As Gardner has shown touchingly and beautifully, growth is possible even in the face of death.

In child hypnotherapy, the child's inner world of imagination is used for stimulating ego strength, coping, and mastery. The wise child hypno-therapist conceives of his role not as the omnipotent healer, but as a guide who helps children develop their own imagery and other cognitive skills they possess but may not have been aware of, or used enough, so they can learn to cope with and master their problems. Hope, joy, and a deep trust in the child's ability to help himself climb up the developmental ladder, as well as great warmth, love, and understanding of children are essential for the successful child hypnotherapist.

Although since 1960 respectable progress has been made in the area of child hypnotherapy, which had lain fallow for so long, the field still is a frontier. It offers many opportunities to undertake pioneering, as well as confirming or disconfirming, research and to develop new clinical applications.

Combining Hypnotherapy and Psychotherapy in the Same Hour

Most hypnotherapists, and particularly hypnoanalysts, do some waking-state psychotherapy during the same hour they do hypnotherapy or hyp-noanalysis. Usually one begins with the waking state, after a little while induces trance, and then does some waking-state therapy again to inte-grate and make conscious the gains achieved in the altered state. Another way of combining hypnotherapy and psychotherapy in the same hour is by helping the patient to alternate between hypnotic and nonhypnotic states several times within the hour. In hypnoanalysis, the patient is routinely told before each awakening that he now can bring up with himself into the waking state as much of the material he has uncovered or experienced in hypnosis as he deep down within himself (i.e., unconsciously) knows he will be able to face when awake. This leaves him the choice of keeping out of waking awareness (i.e., repressed) affects or traumatic events that he is not yet able to deal with in his normal waking life.

Another way of combining hypnotherapy and psychotherapy can also be combined by alternating hypnotherapy or hypnoanalysis hours with waking psychotherapy hours, usually one hypnotherapy hour to two or three waking psychotherapy hours. At some stages of the therapy, one may use a higher ratio of hypnotic hours; at other phases, a lower one. When there is blocking, hypnosis is a useful device to get through the impasse, but only if the patient agrees to the use of hypnosis.

THE HYPNOTHERAPY CONTRACT

Hypnosis involves certain contractual aspects between the patient and the hypnotherapist (Hodge, 1976). Before induction, during the induction, and during the deepening procedures, as well as during the phase in each hour that is devoted to the treatment itself, a series of agreements are made, implicitly or explicitly, between the patient and the therapist. These comprise a set of expectations to which both parties agree—the patient expects the therapist to follow certain procedures (induction, deepening, etc.), to which he then will respond by going into trance (provided the therapist-patient relationship is a trusting and secure one).

Foremost among these agreements is that the trance state is time limited and that no matter how much the patient may enjoy this altered state, he will return to reality and the waking state after a set period of time. The contract also stipulates that hypnotherapy is used to afford the patient a special opportunity to get better and to solve his problems faster. If, for whatever reasons, it makes him get worse or extremely anxious, the mutual contract implies that the therapist will stop hypnotherapy—at least temporarily—and revert to using another method of psychotherapy with the patient.

Frequency and Duration of Hypnotherapy

Hypnotherapists and hypnoanalysts usually see their patients once or twice a week for approximately one hour. Some of this time, usually the beginning and the end of the hour, is taken up with waking-state therapy; and some time, of course, with induction and deepening of the trance.

Most hypnotherapists and hypnoanalysts adhere to the traditional 50-minute hour. Some directive hypnotherapists use less time, roughly 20 minutes, because they view hypnotherapy primarily as giving directions and posthypnotic suggestions. Some permissive hypnotherapists expand the traditional 50-minute hour to 60 or 75 minutes, seldom longer. The session is lengthened because it is difficult to fit all aspects of combined hypnotic and nonhypnotic therapy into a 50-minute format. The therapeutic work to be accomplished in the session includes: the opening phase, that is, the patient's opening (nonhypnotic) comments and the therapist's assessment of and response to these; the trance induction, its utilization and its termination (including instructions for posthypnotic suggestions); and a nonhypnotic discussion to facilitate integration of the trance experience.

Hypnotherapy usually takes less time than other types of psycho-therapy, much less than psychoanalysis. But rarely can a patient be cured in one hour. In general, what can be accomplished in psychoanalysis in 3 years usually will take only 3 to 6 months in hypnoanalysis. And often a patient can be helped with physical pain or with symptom amelioration in 6 to 10 hypnotherapy hours.

Posthypnotic Suggestions: An Implicit Contractual Agreement

The posthypnotic suggestion constitutes another, implicit, contractual agreement between patient and therapist. Often it is what the patient is asking for more than anything else when he comes for hypnotherapy and begs the hypnotherapist to give him a suggestion that will make his migraine pass, stop his overeating, or relieve his emotional pain. The desired contract here reads: If you give me the right suggestion, I will follow it.

Posthypnotic suggestions are given while the patient is in hypnosis and take effect *after* the patient has returned to wakefulness. If they are hypnotherapeutic suggestions, their effect is intended to be longlasting. Posthypnotic suggestions are usually given with the added remark, ". . . but you may forget that I told you so." The effectiveness of posthypnotic therapeutic suggestions is greater when the patient can feel that they stem from his own decisions, not from what he has been told to do. To be told to do something evokes resistance in some people, particularly adolescents, and it is for this reason that therapists often help the patients repress the knowledge that the suggestion was given to them by someone else.

Posthypnotic suggestions are designed to influence the patient's be-havior beyond the hypnotherapy hours and often have considerable influ-ence on the patient's everyday life. It is especially important, then, that the therapist word posthypnotic suggestions carefully and remember exactly what posthypnotic suggestions he has given. Because the patient is likely to take the posthypnotic suggestions literally, there is a danger that mis-takes in wording might have unintended effects. Therefore, it is good practice for the therapist to record all posthypnotic suggestions verbatim and ask the patient to describe his experiences in consecutive weeks in order to see how the experiences may have been influenced by the posthypnotic suggestions.

PROFESSIONAL PRACTICE AND ETHICS[1]

The ethical standards governing psychotherapists and researchers, such as the American Psychological Association's Ethical Principles of Psychologists (1981), of course apply also to hypnotherapists, hypnoanalysts, and all who work in the field of experimental hypnosis for research purposes. The fact that a person in trance is more suggestible, less vigilant—and thus perhaps also more vulnerable and less able to stand up for himself—places additional ethical requirements on the hypnotist to protect the hypnotized person from harm caused either by the hypnotist's suggestions or by the patient's own strong affects that might overwhelm him.

Uncovering Without Piercing Defenses Too Quickly

Because hypnosis is a regression in the service of the ego, and because in hypnosis the patient makes contact with the unconscious more rapidly and more deeply than in waking therapies, the hypnotherapist is in the both advantageous and perilous position of being able to uncover deeply unconscious wishes and defenses, even when the patient is not yet ready to face the unconscious wish or to give up the defense against it. In waking therapy, premature confrontation is more easily handled by the patient than it is in hypnosis. That the patient has disclosed the unconscious conflict to the therapist in the hypnotic trance does not mean he is able or ready to deal with the material yet or to face his naked self in the mirror of waking self-awareness. Therefore, the conscientious and permissive hypnoanalyst who respects his patient will not demand—as even Freud did—that the patient bring up into the waking state all the unconscious material that came into awareness in the hypnotic state. Rather, before helping the patient back into the waking state, the permissive hypnotherapist will say, "When you return to the waking state, you will be able to bring up with you as much as you will be able to face," thus encouraging the patient to remember previously unconscious material, but at the same time respecting the autonomy and the wisdom of the patient's own protective unconscious, which may decide that the time is not yet ripe to allow material that would be too upsetting to enter ordinary awareness.

To Give and Not to Take Away

An important part of the beliefs held by most—though not all—contemporary hypnotherapists can be expressed in the maxim: Give to the patient—do not take away! For instance, although it is possible to help a certain percentage of obese patients to lose weight by suggesting to them in trance that sweets and fatty foods will make them feel nauseated, the great majority of contemporary hypnotherapists prefer to tell obsese patients in trance that they do not derive enough enjoyment from eating because they stuff great amounts of food into their mouths without giving all their taste buds a chance to savor it. They then go on to suggest that in the days and weeks to come, the patients will find that instead of stuffing their mouths full of food, they will move every bite, slowly, from one place on the tongue to another, until each of the taste buds has gotten the full enjoyment of the food. The patients will find, the hypnotherapist says, that after a few bites, they have gained so much enjoyment from what they have eaten that they will be satisfied and will not need to eat until the next regular meal, when the same thing will happen. They will feel proud of themselves for overcoming their weight problem. Thus, the therapist does not take away pleasure; he gives the patient new and more appropriate means for instinctual gratification. In addition, he attempts to strengthen the healthy pride the patient feels in mastering the overeating.

The philosophy and value system of the contemporary hypnotherapist can be expressed as follows: It is the task of the therapist to enrich the patient, to help expand the ego span, and to foster pride in the ability to cope and master; it is not for the therapist to forbid, to restrict, or to make a person into an obedient slave who just follows the advice or restrictive suggestions of the hypnotherapist. The hypnotherapist should not attempt to shape the patient in his own image.

It is characteristic of persons in hypnosis to have a strong desire to please their hypnotist and to want to acquiesce in the hypnotist's request. This is due partly to the heightened ego receptivity in trance; but it also can be caused by the fact that very strong transferences, particularly father and mother transferences, develop quickly in the hypnotized person. This puts an added moral responsibility on the hypnotist: he must not exploit the tendency of the patient towards "obedience" and indeed must guard the welfare of the patient even more strenuously than he would with the ordinary psychotherapy patient. The personal welfare of the patient must always come first, even if it interferes with a great research idea or project of the hypnotist. Sometimes this can present a real dilemma for the hypnotherapist/researcher.

Abuses and Their Prevention

There are certain abuses against which hypnotists must guard themselves. In the main, these abuses are:

1. Coercing the patient to behave in discordance with his or her moral convictions and principles.
2. Seducing or coercing a hypnotized patient into a behavior or act that could be dangerous.
3. Sexually seducing a hypnotized patient.
4. Age regressing a patient to a so-called previous life.
5. Inappropriate and indiscriminate use of age *pro*gression.
6. The training of laypeople who do not have a broad background in the healing arts.

We all have moral principles, which we think of as absolutes. However, our moral imperatives depend to some extent on the situation in which we find ourselves. There have been long and heated disputes in the field of hypnosis (cf. Erickson, 1939, & Watkins, 1947) about whether the hypnotist can coerce or induce a person who has good moral standards to commit a criminal act in trance or posthypnotically. Experiments (Watkins, 1947) have shown that it is possible, but only when the hypnotist creates for the patient by vivid description *a situation in which such amoral behavior would be moral.* The hypnotist must describe this situation so vividly that the patient feels himself to be literally living it and it becomes "real" to him. In Watkins' experiment, an American World War II private with a very good Army record was hypnotized in 1945 in a psychology laboratory in the U.S. in the presence of an American lieutenant colonel. The soldier was told, "Look there, behind that tree! There is a dirty Jap! He has a bayonet in his hand! He's coming at you!" The experimenter had placed the lieutenant colonel about ten feet in front of the private. The private dove at the lieutenant colonel in a flying tackle and with both hands nearly strangled him. He was not antagonistic towards his superiors, as soldiers were during the war in Vietnam, nor did he violate his own conscience. He was attacking what *was* to him a Japanese soldier, the enemy, not an officer in the U.S. Army.

If a hypnotist induced or coerced a patient to commit an immoral act, it clearly would be an abuse of hypnosis. But what if the purpose of such coercion were a good one? What about the hypnotist who has a group of paitents with strong racial prejudices? Does he have the right to influence his patients in this receptive, open-minded hypnotic state to give up their prejudices and give them up for good? Laboratory research (Rosenberg, 1959) has shown that it is possible to change racial prejudice by means of hypnosis. Whether or not this would be an abuse if done in the hypnotherapy of, let us say, a member of the Ku Klux Klan is not easy to answer.

It is certainly an abuse of hypnosis if a hypnotist coerces a hypnotized person into destroying himself. For example, some years ago, a physician/ hypnotherapist who was having an extramarital affair with a woman whom he wanted to marry hypnotized his wife and suggested to her that she was developing a headache. When the headache would become very severe, he told her, she would swallow all the pills in the bottle he had put in her lap. They would make her fall asleep, so she would not feel the pain any longer. After a little while she reached for the pills and took them all. It was a lethal dose.

Sexual seduction of a hypnotized patient is, of course, an abuse. It seldom happens nowadays, certainly much less frequently than the general public assumes. However, there are occasional cases where the hypnotherapist misuses his function, not consciously and perhaps with good therapeutic intentions, but unconsciously in order to gratify his own sexual needs. To give an example: A very beautiful young woman shied away from sexual contacts. She went to a male hypnotherapist, who found her to be an extremely good hypnotic subject, able to go into deep stages of trance. He began a regular hypnoanalysis. In the sixth hour, as she lay on the couch with closed eyes, in deep trance, he became aware of the fairness of the skin of her face framed by her long, shiny black curls. Fleetingly, his own associations were of Snow White and of Sleeping Beauty. He suddenly bent over and kissed her fully on the mouth, before he even became aware of thinking of himself as Prince Charming. The patient roused herself, slapped his face, and cried out, "How dare you . . . !" The therapist sheepishly said, "I really did it only to help you get over your fear of men." In later supervision, however, he could recognize that he had overstepped the boundaries of good hypnotherapy.

Indiscriminate and careless use of age regression is unprofessional. The attempt to age regress a patient for therapeutic purposes to a previous life is a gross misuse of hypnosis—there is no scientific way in which the existence of reincarnation ever can be proven. All the evidence so far shows that hypnotic subjects who allow themselves to be pushed by the hypnotist into so-called former lives choose the century they somehow gather the hypnotist is particularly interested n and then make up a story about their life in that century. Employing hypnosis for age regression to earlier existences is simply too sensational and lacks the possibility of scientific verification. It, therefore, falls into the category of abuses of the technique.

In general, the profession of hypnotherapy frowns upon any sensational use of hypnosis. The early history of hypnotherapy, it is true, was one of sensationalism. Dramatic discoveries were made, and often higher hopes and promises for cures were raised than could be kept. Since the end of World War II, however, the profession has tried to keep a low profile, to avoid sensationalism, and to establish a large body of solid research on the phenomena, the characteristics, the realistic possibilities, and the limitations of hypnosis and hypnotherapy.

Age *pro*gression should be employed only rarely, with even greater care than age regression, never indiscriminately or with self-destructive patients. When asked in hypnosis to progress to an age 3 or 5 years hence, the patient who has turned hostility inward is likely to picture himself severely ill, in an accident, or dying. When that time of life eventually does come around, the patient may unconsciously feel compelled to fulfill the self-made prophecy and destroy his own life by, indeed, becoming involved in a fatal accident or illness. Patients may also make other, milder pathological prophecies for themselves, which later they unconsciously feel they have to live up to. Therefore, if one uses age progression in hypnotherapy at all, it is wise to use it only in connection with ego integrative suggestions of healthy growth and coping. Otherwise, we cannot see any therapeutic value in age *pro*gression.

It is relatively easy to learn how to induce hypnosis. It is much harder to learn how to use it wisely and therapeutically. That requires a broad professional background in the healing arts and in psychodynamics. Stage hypnotists and other laypeople, however, have trifled with hypnosis for a long time, mainly for sensational display. Many of them fancy themselves to be hypnotherapists and advertise themselves as such. Physicians and psychologists across the country have warned that the irresponsible practices of these laypeople endanger the public interest, and attempts have been made to outlaw them. But in most states these attempts fail because the lobbies of the lay groups are more powerful, more afffluent (and probably politically more astute) than those of the professionals. In some cities even police officers are being trained in hypnotic induction, deepening, and uncovering techniques, presumably to obtain information to solve crimes. Police officers have neither the necessary broad understanding of psychology and psychopathology, nor the knowledge that would enable them to differentiate between real memories and pseudomemories. In addition, police officers frequently have such strong views as to who is likely to be the guilty party in a crime that they easily and inadvertently can bias the hypnotized subject's memories, even if they do not intend to do so. The profession, therefore, views with great alarm the training of police officers and has urged its members not to teach hypnosis to police officers and laypeople (Society for Clinical and Experimental Hypnosis,

Code of Ethics, 1981). The exception with regard to laypeople is, of course, the teaching of self-hypnosis to patients. But patients are always warned to use it only on themselves, not on others.

In summary, hypnosis is an altered state of consciousness characterized by a regression in the service of the ego along with increased access to the unconscious. This makes it possible to achieve lasting therapeutic results faster in hypnosis than in the waking state. Hypnosis is also a state of decreased vigilance and a decreased ability to defend oneself against demands made by the therapist. This vulnerability involves dangers if a patient is in the hands of a poorly trained, incompetent, or unscrupulous therapist, who may abuse hypnosis. In general, the same human and moral values that guide the responsible therapist with the patient in the ordinary waking state must guide him with the patient in hypnosis—only more so. The contemporary permissive hypnotherapist does not superimpose his own will or personality onto the patient but supports him, helps him face the frightening parts of his unconscious, shows him where his own inner, and often unknown, resources lie, and thus helps him to cope with conflicts, master them, and gain full autonomy and freedom from fear.

6 Techniques of Hypnotherapy

THE FUNDAMENTALS OF HYPNOTHERAPY

Respecting the Ground Rules of Psychotherapy

The behavior and experiences of patients in trance are certainly unlike those in the waking state. Skilled clinicians previously unfamiliar with hypnosis typically react with a mixture of anxiety and fascination the first time they discover the special parameters that hypnosis introduces into the clinical situation. Because of the unusual nature of trance, even skilled clinicians feel like novices when first learning clinical hypnosis and unfortunately often temporarily suspend their years of clinical experience when they begin to learn about hypnosis.

Any clinician who inquires into hypnosis should be reminded that hypnosis itself is not a clinical procedure; it is an adjunct to psychotherapy, a parameter that may be introduced into the therapy. By introducing hypnosis into psychotherapy, one brings in new expectations, a new, special relationship (which we have called the hypnotic relationship), and the special nature of the altered state of consciousness that is called trance. It is imperative that the hypnotherapist understand how hypnosis changes the ongoing process of psychotherapy; it is equally imperative that he retain a sound knowledge of the nonhypnotic psychotherapeutic process within which the hypnotic practices are embedded. Unfortunately, some practitioners—mostly those who have had little training in psychotherapy—become narrowly specialized as 'hypnotists.' Lacking a comprehensive understanding of the field of psychotherapy, and sometimes lacking much experience as therapists, such practitioners indiscriminately use hypnosis for every presenting problem. To them, hypnotherapy is limited to direct and indirect suggestions for symptom removal.

The proper use of hypnosis, however, is set well within the context of psychotherapy. The clinician should have a sound theoretical orientation and sufficient experience in the practice of psychotherapy to know how to integrate hypnosis into his ongoing work. It is important that the hypnotherapist behave professionally, respecting the basic principles of psychotherapy when using hypnosis. Like the psychoanalytically oriented therapist, he must adopt an anonymously neutral stance. He must never use hypnosis in a manipulative way that could be detrimental to the patient's welfare. In the therapeutic alliance, the hypnotherapist uses hypnosis in the context of an emotionally corrective relationship. He attempts to understand the patient's verbal and nonverbal communications and develops a formulation for helping him with his problems. Realistic goals are set within four broad treatment areas: changing maladaptive patterns of relationship and behaviors, fostering awareness of and tolerance for repressed and disavowed affects, developing insight into the cause and perpetuation of problems, and helping the patient to develop his strengths and coping strategies. The clinician wishing to utilize hypnosis must be familiar with the operation of transference in psychotherapy, especially since hypnosis intensifies the transference.

Hypnotherapy and Hypnoanalysis

Brief hypnotherapy can be done from either a hypnobehavioral or a hypnodynamic perspective. In the literature both are often called "hypnotherapy," and we do so in this book too. The course of the treatment is usually from five to 20 sessions. Dynamic hypnotherapy, also called brief hypnoanalytically oriented psychotherapy, employs uncovering techniques and requires sensitivity to the transference. It differs from hypnoanalysis in length of treatment as well as in the way in which the clinician works with the transference. In hypnoanalysis (see chapter 9) the transference is systematically explored. Hypnodynamically oriented psychotherapy, or hypnotherapy from a dynamic perspective, also requires that the therapist be aware of and interpret the transference, usually in a limited and circumscribed way. In hypnoanalysis, the goal is total personality reorganization; in hypnodynamically oriented psychotherapy, the goal is more circumscribed, namely, relief of suffering by means of symptom amelioration or alteration of maladaptive behaviors and patterns of relationship. Both dynamic hypnotherapy and hypnoanalysis use the same uncovering methods.

Special Parameters of Conducting Psychotherapy in Trance

The introduction of hypnosis into some segment of the therapy hour significantly alters the nature of the therapeutic process in many ways. The interchange between the patient and therapist is considerably altered when the patient closes his eyes to go into trance. Like nonhypnotic patients who begin psychoanalysis on the couch—only more so—hypnotic patients report a greater awareness of their own internal world and concomitantly less awareness of the subtle nuances in the interchange between patient and therapist, which are part of the face-to-face interaction. The patient can no longer see the therapist and judge from the therapist's facial expression how the emotional interaction between them is proceeding. This is one of the reasons that transference reactions develop so quickly and become so strong in hypnosis.

Because in trance patients tend to be less inclined to talk than while awake, the therapist may need to use specific instructions to encourage the patient's spontaneous verbalization. For example, he may say to the patient, "Perhaps you did not think you could talk in trance, but you will be able to talk freely about whatever you are experiencing. You will be able to describe your experiences, if asked to do so. Now you can see this for yourself. . . . Describe to me what this experience is like." If the therapist wants the patient to visualize a scene, he says, "Describe the scene as it unfolds."

Sometimes it is advisable to teach the patient an open-eyed trance. For this, a deep state of trance is required. To assess the depth, the hypnotist uses a state report (Tart, 1970b), say, form one to ten, ten representing the deepest state imaginable. After the patient reports a sufficiently deep state, say, eight, the hypnotist says, "In a moment I will ask you to open your eyes. Although you will do this, it will not lighten your level of trance, In fact, the longer you keep your eyes open, the deeper you will go. Now, I will count to five and your eyes will open." After the patient opens his eyes, the hypnotherapist gives the signal for the state report. If the patient does not report a deep state, the instructions are repeated with a slight modification: "Each successive time you open your eyes you will go deeper." The hypnotist repeats the opening and closing until the desired depth is achieved. Although most hypnotherapy work is conducted with closed eyes, an open-eyed trance is useful in certain instances, notably during free play in an age regression and with schizophrenics, many of whom are fearful of being abandoned when they cannot see the therapist.

The therapist must structure the sequence of suggestions so that the meaning of the patient's symbolic communications becomes clear to the patient as well as to the therapist. The ground rules for interpretation in trance are not unlike those used in interpreting in nonhypnotic psychotherapy: the therapist does not guess wildly, but patiently waits and offers an interpretation only when reasonably assured, through the unfolding material, that the interpretation is accurate. The difference between trance and nontrance interpretation is that the trance allows the therapist to speed up the interpretive process. When unsure what the unfolding material means, the therapist can ask for additional symbolic material. Or he may give direct suggestions to clarify the meaning: "The meaning will become clearer and clearer to you, and you will soon be able to tell me. . . ."

One of the most difficult skills for beginning hypnotherapists concerns the clinical decision making during hypnotic work. Decision making is based on a "utilization approach" to the clinical material (Erickson, 1959). If the hypnotherapist structures the sequence of suggestions appropriately, nearly all the information needed can be drawn from the clinical material as it unfolds in trance. If, for example, the therapist is unsure what direction to take, he can suggest a scene that will convey "something more about the problem" or a hypnotic dream "about the direction that will best help you."

Beginning hypnotherapists also have difficulty with the spontaneity of the material unfolding in the trance. They are often uncomfortable, too, with the intensity of the affect and the regressive dimension of the therapeutic exchange. Rather than working with the emerging material so that it can be integrated into consciousness, the beginner may try to suggest away the feelings. The skilled hypnotherapist welcomes the intensity that typically accompanies psychotherapy in trance because it can become a motivating force for genuine therapeutic change.

Special Consideration when Conducting Therapy in Trance

As outlined in the previous chapter, the typical hypnotherapy hour can be divided into three distinct phases: the opening phase in the waking state, the trance work, and the closing integration in the waking state. During the opening phase, the therapist tries to assess the influence of the previous therapy hour on both the patient's everyday behavior in the interim and the way the patient presents in the current hour. The therapist should be attentive to the possible effects of previous posthypnotic suggestions and to the way the patient has assimilated the previous therapy work. During the trance work, the therapist structures suggestions in accordance with the therapeutic goals, while being mindful of the special parameters that the trance introduces into the therapy. Just before ending the trance work, the therapist may, when it is indicated, give a posthypnotic suggestion and a suggestion for partial posthypnotic amnesia. The therapist should terminate the trance well before the end of the hour and leave enough time for waking integration of the trance work.

If the trance work has involved uncovering, the therapist should assess how much of the affect-laden material the patient does or does not recall in the waking state. The purpose of the nontrance discussion is to help the patient integrate the new material into consciousness, which sometimes necessitates conducting the therapy in and out of trance a number of times. If the trance work involved insight, the nontrance discussion facilitates the patient's waking understanding of the material. If the trance work was intended to modify the patient's behavior, the nontrance discussion helps prepare the patient for behavioral change in everyday life. Whatever the short-term goal of the trance work, the therapist always must realize that the strong affects and transference feelings evoked by the hypnosis are in some way also carried over into the nontrance part of the therapy hour.

Technical Errors in Brief Hypnotherapy

A number of technical errors are commonly made in hypnotherapy. We will not include here the errors made when inducing hypnosis (see chapter 3) nor the problems of countertransference that may occur in long-term hypnoanalysis (see chapter 7). Here we discuss only the errors of brief hypnotherapy.

Experienced therapists just beginning to use hypnosis in their clinical practice are likely to use the wrong style of suggestion. All too often they adopt a familiar style from other, nonhypnotic systems of therapy for use during trance. We do advocate that the therapist not forget his clinical wisdom, but we also advocate some modification in the style of wording suggestions and interpretations. Some therapists reflect back the patient's hypnotic communication in a client-centered manner. They fail to appreciate that a reflecting statement made when the patient is in trance becomes a suggestion. If the therapist reflects, "So you feel bad today," he should not wonder why the patient takes a turn for the worse. The patient has literally responded to the suggestion to feel bad. Some therapists use a nonhypnotic inquiry style in trance instead of reframing the questions as suggestive statements. When learning hypnotherapy, it is understandable that the clinician should draw upon his fund of clinical knowledge. Yet, some of this knowledge is not applicable to conducting hypnotherapy.

The therapist may also be too directive and not permissive enough. When the therapist is too active, he fails to utilize the patient's own inner symbolic processes and coping resources. In working with fantasy productions, the therapist may suggest specific images to the patient when it would be preferable to give more open-ended suggestions. In the worst instances, the fantasy productions are completely those of the therapist, not the patient, and the uncovering process can become obstructed. The therapist may too eagerly suggest specific ways for the patient to cope instead of drawing the coping strategies from the patient's own ego-syntonic resources. Even though such therapist-produced imagery may be temporarily effective, it can impede the development of self-efficacy so integral to a fully successful outcome.

A related problem pertains to following through with the plan of suggestions. The directive therapist worries too much about where to go next and what to say. At a loss for what to do next, the therapist conjures up some new suggestion and introduces into the therapeutic process elements alien to the patient. The therapist must learn to trust the patient's inner resources. Frequently, he can draw each step in the unfolding clinical material from them.

Empathic failures in hypnotherapy occur when the therapist fails to show sensitivity to the patient's feelings or to understand accurately and to interpret correctly the unfolding material. Inasmuch as affect is seldom subtle in hypnotherapy, empathic failures are less a matter of misreading the affect than of distancing oneself from the intensity of the patient's feelings. Some hypnotherapists are too quick to become overprotective or to suggest away negative affect. The therapist must learn to distinguish between intense affect and overwhelming affect.

Deleterious effects can result from a patient's misunderstanding of a posthypnotic suggestion. For example, a therapist gave the following posthypnotic suggestion: "You will have a dream this week about whatever is upsetting to you at this time." The patient called two days later, complaining that she had been unable to go to sleep since the last session. She took the posthypnotic suggestion literally, as a command to have an upsetting dream and was afraid to go to sleep. The hypnotherapist must take care to word posthypnotic suggestions in a clear and unambiguous manner, and must anticipate as much as possible the various ways his posthypnotic suggestions could be interpreted or misunderstood by the patient.

TECHNIQUES OF DYNAMIC HYPNOTHERAPY

Projective techniques in hypnotherapy enable the patient to produce imagery or fantasies that reveal unconscious meanings. Hypnoprojective methods are used in the service of an uncovering approach to therapy, where the goal is to gain insight into dynamics associated with a particular symptom, behavior, or relationship problem. Some hypnoprojective methods rely heavily on imagery and visualization to uncover unconscious meaning; others, on motor expression (such as automatic writing).

Hypnoprojective Techniques

Cloud Technique.   The therapist introduces the Cloud Fantasy (see chapter 4) and modifies it to make it a projective method:

> Look closely at the clouds now. . . . The clouds look like something or remind you of something. . . . As you look at the clouds more carefully, you can see something in them . . . something that has to

do with the problem we are working on. . . . Now, what do the clouds look like? [Patient describes.]

Crystal or Mirror Gazing.   The patient is taught to open his eyes during trance in such a way that it does not disturb the trance. Upon opening his eyes, he looks upon a crystal glass or mirror placed so that it reflects the blank ceiling and is told:

Look into the crystal [or mirror], and you will begin to see things vividly in it. . . . You will see things before you that somehow relate to your problem, and you will be able to describe to me what you see (Wolberg, 1945).

The Anagram Technique.   The hypnotherapist says to the patient:

In front of you is a box containing all kinds of letters, perhaps like those in a Scrabble game. Imagine reaching in and taking a handful of the letters. In a moment I'll ask you to imagine throwing the letters up into the air. Some of them will land face up so you can see the letters. Some will land face down so no letter will be visible. The letters that land face up will form a word. The word will somehow be connected to your problem. You will be interested to see what the letters will say. O.K., now throw the letters, and tell me what you see.

The Theatre Technique.   The Theatre Technique is adapted from Wolberg (1948). The patient can symbolically express or project the unconscious meaning of the symptom or problem into the play's unfolding action. First, induce sufficient relaxation. Next, have the patient visualize the theatre, which serves as the basis of the projection:

Now, imagine yourself seated in a very comfortable chair. As you sit in that chair, you will notice how much more relaxed you are becoming. More and more relaxed and comfortable . . . relaxed and comfortable. . . . When you feel deeply relaxed, the index finger on your right hand will lift [wait for signal].

Now, perhaps you would not mind looking around you. You will see that you are in a theatre seated in a chair from which you have a clear view of the stage, perhaps seated in the second or third row. While you can see the stage clearly, you will notice that the curtain is closed. Notice what the theatre is like. Perhaps you could describe now what the theatre looks like. [Patient describes, therapist accents sensory description.] Now, what kind of curtain does the theatre have? [Patient answers.] Yes, that's right; it has a [name color, etc.]

curtain. Now, observe the stage. You are curious about what is going to happen behind the curtain. Soon the curtain will open, but not quite yet. When it does, you will notice that a play is taking place on the stage.

The play will somehow be about [name problem or symptom]. Although you may or may not see at first exactly how the play relates to your [problem or symptom], nevertheless, the play will somehow be about your [problem or symtom]. You will be able to watch the play with interest, and you will be able to describe what happens as the play unfolds. Yet, no matter what happens on the stage as you sit in the audience, you will remain as relaxed as you now are. You will be reassured to know that you will remain as relaxed as you are even after the play begins, because it is only a play. [The patient as experiencer of the possibly upsetting play and the patient as the relaxed observer of the play are here dissociated from each other.] I'll count from one to ten, and, as I do, the curtain will open. Are you ready to see the play? O.K. Let's see. One . . . two . . . the curtain is beginning to rise . . . three . . . . . . ten. Now, describe what is happening in this play as it unfolds.

The patient describes the action. The therapist listens for the ways it relates to the patient's problem. Then the therapist suggests that the curtain close.

Sometimes defensive operations interfere with the response. A patient may report that the rope broke and the curtain went down again. This is a signal to the therapist to go slowly. The patient is saying that he is not yet ready to uncover the unconscious meaning of the problem. Sometimes the patient reports that the curtain has opened but nothing is happening on stage. The failure to see the play also is defensive. It cannot be a deficiency in the ability to visualize, because the patient has just finished describing the details of the theatre. In this case the therapist continues:

Look carefully to the sides of the stage, and you will sense some activity. . . . Do you sense this yet? [If patient says yes, proceed; if patient says no, say:] O.K., you will notice that the scenery from the play is about to be set up . . . it is coming out onto the stage. . . . What kind of scenery is it? [Patient responds.] Soon some people will come out onto the stage, and the play will begin . . . your index finger will rise when the play has begun.

Often patients will respond to such structuring. If the patient persists in seeing nothing, the therapist respects the need for the defense and discontinues the visualization.

An advantage of the Theatre Technique is that a play usually has several acts. This enables the therapist to structure the experience so as to gradually uncover the meaning of the problem. The therapist continues to suggest the second act to the patient. If the patient has not been upset by the first act, the second act can proceed without the need to dissociate the observing and experiencing parts of his ego:

> I'll count from one to ten again, and, as I do, the curtain will open. This time you will watch the second act of the play. You will learn something more about your (problem) as the play continues, and you will be able to describe to me what happens as it unfolds. This time you will find yourself getting more absorbed in the play. As you sit in your chair in the audience, you will begin to notice that the play is evoking certain feelings in you that you identify with the characters in a certain way. Now, the curtain is about to lift . . . one . . . two . . . it's beginning to lift up . . . three . . . . . . ten. Now, describe what is happening in the act as it unfolds (patient describes act). O.K. Now, the curtain is closing, and you are aware once again of sitting in the chair deeply relaxed.

The therapist may continue with several additional acts, each time exploring something more about the problem. The final act usually poses more or less of a solution to the problem. This final act is intended to uncover the patient's unconscious coping strategies:

> I'll count from one to ten again, and, as I do, the curtain will open. You will watch the closing act of the play. The play will reach its conclusion. This act will somehow suggest a solution to your problem [or an effective way to cope with your symptoms]. Although at first you may or may not know exactly how the play suggests a solution to your problem, nevertheless, it will do that. Now, the curtain is about to open . . . one . . . two . . . three. . . . It is beginning to lift . . . four . . . . . . ten. Now, describe what is happening in the play as it continues. [Patient describes.] O.K., now the curtain is closing, and the play has come to an end. Notice how you feel about the play you have just seen. You will be able to describe the feeling. [Patient describes feeling.]

The next task is to help the patient understand the meaning of the play. The play is a symbolic representation of the dynamic meaning of the patient's problem as well as of the patient's unconscious resources for coping with the problem. Sometimes the meaning of the play is readily apparent; sometimes it is disguised. The therapist gives the patient a graded hypnotic or posthypnotic suggestion for insight:

> As you reflect on and discuss the play with me now [or after you awaken from hypnosis], you will come to understand the meaning of

the play more and more: how it relates to your problem and how to suggest a way to handle the symptom [or presents a solution to the problem]. You will come to understand its meaning when you are ready to understand it.

It is very important to respect the patient's defenses and to suggest that the patient understand the meaning only when he is ready to understand it. By the therapist's wording the suggestion in this permissive, non-authoritarian way, the patient comes to understand the meaning when he is able to integrate it into consciousness.

The Television Technique.   An alternative hypnoprojective technique is the Television Technique. The visualization is constructed similarly to that of the Theatre Technique:

> Now, imagine yourself seated in a very comfortable chair. It is a very comfortable chair. In fact, as you sit in it, you will notice how much more relaxed you are becoming . . . more and more relaxed . . . and comfortable. . . . When you feel very relaxed, the index finger of one of your hands will lift up. [Therapist waits for signal.] Fine, now you are very relaxed. Imagine that the chair is in front of a television set. You can see the TV set clearly in front of you, although the TV is not yet turned on. Describe to me what the TV looks like. [Patient describes.] . . . . Now, imagine that you have a remote control device in your hand which can turn the TV on or off, change the channels, or adjust the volume. Soon I will ask you to turn on the TV set, but not quite yet. You are curious to know what is on the TV.

After it is clearly established that the patient is able to visualize the TV, the therapist suggests a pleasant, relaxing program:

> Now, in a moment I'll ask you to turn on the TV set so that you can watch the program. The program will be very interesting and enjoyable to you. As you watch this program, you will find yourself feeling more and more comfortable and relaxed. O.K., you can turn on the TV set. Describe the program as it unfolds. [Patient describes the program.] Fine. Now, in a moment I'll ask you to switch the channel of the television. On another channel you will be able to watch another program. The next program will somehow be about your problem [or symptom], although you may or may not know at first exactly how the program relates to your problem. O.K., now, turn the channel and describe the program as it unfolds. [Patient describes.]

Here again, defensive operations may interfere with the response. The patient may fail to report another program. This would indicate that he is not yet ready to uncover the unconscious meaning of the problem. If the patient reports a program but says it has nothing to do with his problem, the patient is most likely defensive and unconsciously stating a need for disguise. In that case, a number of programs are used. Each represents "some aspect of the problem."

When the produced show seems to be very bland, the patient can be told that certain programs may evoke feelings in him or that he may identify with the people in the show and feel what they really feel. The volume control can symbolically represent a feeling dial: the patient makes the feelings more or less intense by turning the feeling dial up or down, as needed.

The advantage of the Television Technique is that the patient can switch programs. Therefore, it can be used in a number of different ways. In an uncovering therapy, each program can symbolically represent a different aspect of the patient's problem. A patient with a traumatic neurosis or a phobia can readily switch back to the relaxing program or adjust the volume of feelings as necessary, so as not to become overwhelmed. In a hypnobehavioral treatment, the patient can first generate a relaxed state by watching the pleasant program and then can turn to another channel, to a program somehow connected with one of a number of feared situations but one low along a continuum of least-to-most-feared situations. It is progressively suggested that he switch to more anxiety-arousing programs, or back to the relaxing program, when needed and then again to progressively more fear-arousing situations along the stimulus continuum. (Hypnotic desensitization is discussed at greater length in chapter 8.)

Old Picture Technique

Imagine you have discovered a very old painting. You can tell it is very old by the antique frame, although it is hard to see the picture. The picture has been painted over many times and is now covered with layers of dust and cobwebs. Describe to me as much of the picture as you can see. [Patient describes.]

Now, begin dusting off the layers of dust from the painting, very slowly, one layer at a time. You will notice that it becomes a little clearer . . . a picture emerges that has something to do with your problem. As it becomes clearer and clearer, you will be able to describe it to me. [Patient describes.] Now wipe off the next layer, and another picture will emerge that has something more to do with your problem. . . . As it becomes clear, you will be able to describe it to me. [Patient describes.]

The patient continues to remove layer after layer. All layers projectively and symbolically represent life experiences or feelings unconsciously associated with the patient's problem.

Sidewalk Superintendent

As you walk along the street, you come to a construction site. There is a wall around the construction site so you can't see how the building is being constructed. . . . You discover a crack in the wall through which you can take a peek. The construction somehow relates to your problem, although it may or may not be clear to you exactly how. Now, take a peek . . . look through the crack and see how the building is being constructed. Describe what you see. [Patient describes.]

The building is a symbolic representation of the patient's problem. Moreover, it symbolically represents ego structure and coping mechanisms. In reporting how the building is being constructed, the patient gives clues to or gains insight into current and potential coping mechanisms.

Techniques Involving the Motor System

Unconscious motivation can be expressed through the motor system, just as it can be expressed in imagery and fantasy. Patients communicate their responses to the ongoing therapeutic process through facial displays and posture. In turn, the therapist can give suggestions that utilize ideomotor phenomena as a means of uncovering. Since most hypnotizable patients are responsive to ideomotor phenomena to some extent, ideomotor phenomena offer a useful tool for exploring the dynamics associated with a particular problem. Ideomotor techniques include the Chevreul Pendulum and the Finger Signaling Techniques (Cheek & LeCron, 1968), Automatic Writing, and Automatic Drawing (Wolberg, 1945).

The Pendulum.   The therapist introduces the Chevreul Pendulum to the patient, as described in chapter 4. While the patient watches the pendulum swing, the therapist takes care to suggest each of the four possible movements of the pendulum: a clockwise circle, a counterclockwise circle, a straight line from right to left, or toward and away from the patient. Enough care is taken so that these four movement patterns are readily distinguishable from one other. Both the patient and the therapist must be able to recognize each pattern. The patient practices with the pendulum one or more times until each pattern emerges immediately upon suggestion and can be recognized readily. Next, the therapist suggests that each of the four movement patterns can have a different meaning. One means yes; another, no; still another, I don't know; and the last, I don't want to answer. To check whether the patient understands the instructions and is responsive to the suggestions, the therapist asks the patient a question, the answer to which is an obvious yes. The therapist says, "Is the pendulum now swinging?" Having established the patient's responsiveness, the therapist introduces the idea of the unconscious by saying:

> On some level your inner mind knows things of which you are not consciously aware. In fact, your inner mind knows all about your problem [or symptom] and everything that has contributed to your developing this problem [or symptom]. Your inner mind also knows exactly what would help you most with this problem [or symptom]. The pendulum is an extension of your inner mind. The movements of the pendulum can express what your inner mind knows, even though you are not consciously aware of what it is expressing.

Sometimes the therapist, wanting to get a fuller dissociation, suggests that the pendulum knows all about the patient's problem. It is the pendulum, not the patient, that knows about the problem. The patient's defenses are respected.

Next, the therapist addresses questions to the patient. The wording of the questions requires some skill. Questions must be worded so they can be answered with yes, no, I don't know, or I don't want to answer. The therapist frames questions about the patient's problems, about coping strategies, about the nature of the transference, and anything else he needs to know about the patient.

The pendulum is a very useful technique. Cheek and LeCron (1968) claim that it works for 95% of patients.

Finger Signaling.   Finger signaling can be used in ways similar to the pendulum response. It has the added advantage of not needing paraphernalia like a pendulum. The patient's fingers are used instead. The simplest form is levitation of a finger to signal successful response to a hypnotic suggestion. If the therapist is suggesting waves of relaxation, for example, a finger signal can be used to indicate when the patient is sufficiently relaxed. The hypnotist says:

> . . . and when you are relaxed enough to your satisfaction, the index finger on your hand will lift up all by itself.

If the therapist has suggested a dream, the finger signal indicates when the dream is finished:

> You will be able to let me know when the dream has finished, even though you are asleep, because the index finger on your hand will lift by itself.

It is a good idea to suggest a particular finger, so the therapist knows which finger is likely to move. This is especially necessary if the movement is subtle. If the movement is too slight for the therapist to be sure it really has occurred, an additional suggestion is given:

> The finger will lift up completely, by itself, so that its movement can be clearly seen. If you understand this instruction, the finger will lift up now. [Patient lifts finger.]

A failure to respond sometimes indicates that the question was worded ambiguously. Once the patient demonstrates a successful response, subsequent finger signals are likely to be clear. A successful response is an involuntary one usually a slow, jerky movement of the finger. If the patient simply lifts the finger voluntarily, the ideomotor signal is not tapping into unconscious motivation. The phrase, "all by itself," is added to increase involuntarism. Finger signaling is one of the main tools of the hypnotist and is not necessarily a hypnoprojective method by itself.

Another simple form of hypnoprojective signaling involves a yes–no response. The patient is told that the index finger on one hand will lift all by itself to indicate yes; the index finger on the other, to indicate no. The therapist can use such signals to take the guesswork out of how to proceed with the therapy. If the patient feels uncomfortable during a guided fantasy, for example, the therapist says:

> On some level you know exactly what is best for you . . . if you are really ready to proceed, the index finger on your right hand will lift all by itself; if it seems better to stop for now so that we can learn about what is making you anxious in other ways, the index finger on your left hand will lift all by itself. Now, one of the index fingers will lift up.

A more elaborate form of hypnoprojective finger signaling involves the yes, no, I don't know, I don't want to answer format used in the pendulum (Cheek & LeCron, 1968). Four fingers are used for each possible response. The patient is told that the fingers represent the inner mind.

Automatic Writing.   Because writing is an overlearned motor habit, it can be used readily as a hypnoprojective method. Automatic writing (Muhl, 1952; Wolberg, 1945) is the ability to write and express ideas without conscious awareness of either the act of writing or the ideas being expressed. A more complex behavior than simple finger signaling, automatic writing requires careful coordination of the finger and hand movements as well as an integration with ideational processes. Yet, it is not especially difficult to learn and can be easily taught to patients. Many people exhibit automatic writing when they doodle or scribble while talking on the telephone or listening to a lecture. The ideas and feelings being expressed in the doodle usually are not conscious, nor are those expressed in automatic writing.

The first step is to dissociate the dominant hand from the rest of the body:

> The hand you write with experiences a peculiar sensation. As I touch it [therapist encircles wrist], the hand from the wrist down no longer feels like part of your body. The hand is comfortable but detached from your body.
>
> The fingers are just beginning to move all by themselves . . . at first the movement is subtle . . . the movement in the fingers grows. . . . Now, the entire hand and fingers move all by themselves as if pushed by some inner force of their own.

The therapist waits until the finger movements are visible and clear. The therapist may also ask the patient to move the fingers of the other hand and describe the comparison. If a difference is noted, the therapist places a board or writing tablet on the patient's lap, lifts the dominant hand onto the board, and gives more suggestions for writing:

> As the hand continues to move all by itself, it begins to move more and more the way it does when it writes. Whenever a pen or pencil is placed in the hand, it will begin to write all by itself. Whenever the pen is removed, it will stop writing.

It is wise to dissociate the experience of writing from the conscious observation of it. For this, a distraction task is used. The patient is engaged in a fantasy, watches an hallucinated movie, or reads an hallucinated book while the writing is going on:

> You need not concern yourself with what the hand is doing. A pleasant scene [movie, book] will come to mind, and you will be able to describe it to me. The more you absorb yourself in the scene [movie, book], the less you will be aware of what the hand is doing. In fact, soon you will have no awareness of what the hand is doing.

The therapist gives a graded suggestion to increase the clarity of the writing by alternately removing the pen from the patient's hand and returning it several times and saying:

> Each time the hand senses the pen in it, it will write more and more clearly. Soon the hand will write legibly . . . the hand will write words . . . more and more clearly each time.

Once the automatic writing is developed, the therapist introduces the idea that the hand can be the spokesman of the unconscious:

> The hand knows everything about you . . . the hand can remember all your experiences. . . . If you cannot consciously remember something, don't worry because the hand knows everything about you anyhow. . . . The hand knows about your problem and what has contributed to this problem. . . . If there are things that are too painful for you to know, the hand knows these things already and can express them in its movements, even though you are unable to remember these things.

Then the writing and simultaneous distraction task are repeated.

Some patients have difficulty with automatic writing. If the hand fails to move when the pen is placed in it, more practice is needed to develop spontaneous hand movements before the signal is introduced. If the hand moves but fails to write, the therapist suggests to the hand that it will write something specific. If the hand writes illegibly, the therapist suggests it will write words more and more clearly. If the patient is conscious of the writing, the therapist keeps the patient busy by having him describe every detail of the distracting fantasy so that the patient is talking continuously as the hand writes. With some practice most patients can produce automatic writing.

The writing, however, is hardly the same as writing in the waking state. The hand usually moves rapidly across the page, but sometimes it goes very slowly. The therapist must remember to move the writing tablet. Otherwise, the writing is illegible simply because most patients fail to move the hand along the page and all the words are written on top of one another. But it would be a mistake for the therapist to assume that the writing is meaningless. Automatic writing is a form of cryptic communication, the language of the unconscious, and its expression is by primary process operations. For defensive purposes, words are often disguised by misspelling, condensation, or fragmentation. The words often run together or are embedded in scribbles.

One way to appreciate the cryptic nature of automatic writing is to have the patient, while still in trance, read what he has written. The patient is asked to open his eyes in trance and to look at the writing. Then the therapist says, "The longer you look at it, the clearer it will become. As you look at it, words will suggest themselves to you." The patient is also asked to point to each word as it comes to mind. An alternative is to give a posthypnotic suggestion that the meaning will become clear after the patient has awakened and is ready to understand it. One patient who scribbled heavy black lines over a page said there was no writing. He was rehypnotized and asked to interpret the meaning of the lines while in trance. The patient readily pointed out the word "war" embedded among the black scribbles. Subsequently, upon awakening, the patient began to recall traumatic war experiences and connect these to his symptoms.

Automatic Drawing. Suggestions for automatic drawing (Wolberg, 1945) follow the same format as those for automatic writing, except that the hand is encouraged to *draw* freely. In drawing, the patient expresses, nonverbally and symbolically, unconscious wishes, fears, and motivations. Sometimes unconscious processes are revealed more clearly in drawing than in writing. The drawings are more like the productions of children than of adults. Patients can be given suggestions to interpret the meaning of these productions in trance, or posthypnotic suggestions can be given that the meaning will become clear over time as the patient is ready to understand it.

Guided Imagery

Guided imagery is one of the main tools of hypotherapy and is a powerful tool for uncovering the unconscious conflicts and transference perceptions (Horowitz, 1970; Kubie, 1943; Reyher, 1963; Shorr, 1972). Imagery reveals these undercurrents more clearly than secondary process, logical, reality-oriented thinking because images mobilize less resistance (Volt, 1970) and involve less censorship (Horowitz, 1970) than secondary process thought. Moreover, since imagery and affective experience are interrelated (Singer, 1966), imagery is a direct means to gain access to the world of emotions.

The hypnotherapist can either work with spontaneous imagery, or he can suggest it. He may suggest a standard scene that symbolically could represent some underlying conflict as the starting point of the imagery work (Caslant, 1921; Desoille, 1966; Frétigny & Virel, 1968; Leuner, 1969). For instance, the therapist can suggest that the patient imagine himself walking in a pleasant meadow, traveling along a path, in a forest or up a mountain, or exploring an unfamiliar house. Sometimes a scene from a recent dream is used (Epstein, 1981; Johnsgard, 1969). An alternative approach is to facilitate spontaneous imagery (Bonny & Savary, 1973; Jellinek, 1949; Watkins, 1976). The patient is given an open-ended suggestion, for example, "Imagine a scene" or "Float along in a cloud until it carries you to a special place." The scene emerges spontaneously in the stream of consciousness, and the patient describes it as it unfolds.

In working with either suggested or spontaneous imagery, the therapist attempts to deepen the patient's absorption in the experience in a number of ways. The therapist repeatedly asks for the details of the scene: "Notice what is around you," "See what is there," or "You'll notice something else." As mentioned before for inductions, it is important to structure the suggestion for imagery so that all the sense modalities are involved. If, for example, the patient is walking in a meadow, the therapist says:

> Notice what you see around you. . . . Listen, do you hear the sound of the birds yet? . . . Take a deep breath. . . . What is that smell? . . . You can feel the touch of the earth [or grass] beneath your feet. . . . Notice what it feels like.

The patient should be encouraged to participate fully in the scene, not just look at it. If the patient is commenting on the scene from some remote stance, the therapist says, "Do you see yourself in the scene yet? . . . Soon you will find a way to imagine yourself in that scene. . . . When that occurs, describe to me what you are doing." Enhancing the emotional participation in the scene is especially important: "Notice more carefully what it feels like to be in [name scene], and the feeling will become increasingly more real to you." With such suggestions the patient learns to become fully immersed in the imaginal world.

The therapist attempts to create a climate in which the patient can enter the internal world of imagery. The wise therapist encourages the patient to share his fantasy and builds it into the heterohypnotic patter (Eisen & Fromm, 1983), for the imagery produced by the *patient* reveals the patient's personality structure, his problems, and possible solutions that are *right for him*. It gives the therapist the building blocks for therapy. The patient learns to scan the stream of consciousness and to identify imagery as it occurs.

The patient must also learn to identify the various modes of imaginal experience: frequently the imagery is very visual; sometimes it is more thoughtlike; and sometimes it is more auditory, tactile, olfactory, gustatory, or kinesthetic. The therapist should avoid the implication that only visual imagery is valid. He should make it possible for the patient to feel free to report the full range of imaginal experience in the stream of consciousness. The therapist should establish the expectation that the patient is to discover and report his imaginal experience as it unfolds, regardless of the mode in which the imagery is experienced.

As the patient becomes familiar with the emerging images and fantasy productions, the therapist directs his attention to several other features of the experience. He encourages the patient to be receptive to the emerging imagery. He urges the patient not to try consciously and intentionally to make up a narrative. The experience of imagery should be immediate, spontaneous, and involuntary. The patient then becomes increasingly able to absorb himself in the imaginal experience without interfering with its arising from the unconscious by reflecting on it or analyzing it. Once he has learned to produce imagery easily, the patient can be told to pay more careful attention to *how* the imagery unfolds over time: The therapist may say: "Notice how the imagery unfolds. . . . You will find that more and more, as time passes, a story begins to unfold," or: "A scene will unfold, and yet new things continue to emerge, and you will describe what happens." In this way the therapist tries to strike a balance between the extremes of disconnected spontaneous imagery and purposeful secondary process narration. Between these extremes is an imaginal experience that allows for both continuously emerging spontaneous images *and* their appearing in a thematic manner. When images unfold in this way, it is easier for both the patient and the therapist to understand their underlying meaning. With the therapist's taking care in establishing the right set and giving the patient a little practice, most patients can develop some skill in allowing imagery to unfold.

In addition, the patient must, as the imagery arises, learn to verbalize it in such a way that it does not interfere with either the spontaneity of the images or with their unfolding. The hypnotherapist encourages the patient to report the experience continuously, as it happens, and interjects comments as necessary. Good imagery work is a kind of dialogue. The therapist does not bombard the passive patient with suggestions on what to imagine, nor does the patient simply free associate to a silently listening therapist. The therapist is a kind of companion and guide to the patient as he explores the world of imagery. Although at first the patient's world of imagery may seem alien to patient and therapist alike, the therapist serves not as a translator but as a guide, who introduces the patient to the landmarks of this world of imagery. Most of the interpretive and integrative work is done in the waking state.

To facilitate the spontaneous unfolding of imagery, the therapist must adopt a particular perspective toward the imaginal experience. The role of the therapist is primarily to amplify the experience, not to suggest it. Therefore, in most instances the therapist tries to avoid suggesting specific images or scenes to the patient. If, for example, the patient reports walking along a path in a forest, the therapist should not say, "Soon you will see your father on this path." Open-ended suggestions are used whenever possible: "As you walk further along the path, something or someone will appear to you. When that happens, you will be able to tell me what or who it is." If the patient reports being in a dark cave, the therapist might suggest that the patient "explore the cave to see what is there." If the patient reports a light off in the distance, the therapist might suggest, "Go toward the light and see what happens." In each case, the therapist either stimulates exploration of what is immediately presented or encourages the patient to generate additional images, scenes, or fantasy productions. The objective is for the patient to continuously generate imaginal experiences. Comments such as "Look further into that . . . ," "See what happens next . . . ," "Explore that and see what happens" are frequently used to facilitate the unfolding of imagery. Sometimes the therapist may simply suggest that the imagery change: "Soon the scene will change, and you will be able to describe what changes." These suggestions are simple enough, but their effect is significant: the patient remains oriented to a continuously unfolding and changing process.

As the imagery unfolds, strong affects typically emerge. The therapist helps the patient become aware of these affects and to tolerate their intensity. He says, "Notice how you feel as you walk along the road." The therapist also helps the patient gain insight into the imagery as a symbolic representation for underlying conflicts and transference feelings: "And as you continue to reflect on this [name scene], its meaning will become more and more clear to you." The progressive integration of affects into consciousness, as well as the gradual understanding of what the imagery symbolizes, is essential to the process of working through.

Sometimes resistance to imagery work is encountered. A patient may refuse to report the imagery experience or may talk excessively about irrelevant thoughts so as to avoid imaging. Other patients report the unfolding imagery experience, but only up to a point—then the imagery either disappears entirely, becomes disconnected and fragmented, or occurs very rapidly so that it becomes impossible to report. When resistances like these occur, the therapist focuses on the underlying affect. A suggestion is given to amplify the affect. Symbolic resistances also occur as the imagery unfolds. The patient may report an obstruction. For example, he may report that while walking down a path in a forest, he sees that a tree has fallen across the path. The therapist tries to work with these symbolic resistances in a symbolic manner and suggests, "Soon you will find a way to continue" or "Soon the scene will change." The patient is likely to discover a way around the fallen tree or to report taking another path.

Guided imagery is a powerful uncovering technique, a symbolic process through which underlying conflicts are both revealed and concealed. The underlying wishes, as well as the transference perceptions, are often thinly disguised and can be readily interpreted (M. Horowitz, 1970; Kubie, 1943b; Reyher, 1963; Silberer, 1951). In many instances of trance, however, interpretation is not really necessary. How the imagery unfolds has its own wisdom. It represents a kind of problem-solving activity in which various defensive operations against, as well as solutions for, unconscious conflicts are successively rehearsed, as they are in nocturnal dreams (French & Fromm, 1964/1986), and various possibilities for future courses of action are practiced (Singer, 1979). Hypnotic imagery unfolds in much the same way as a musical score, with variations on a theme. Each variation in the imagery sequence is a new approach to the problem. In the overall sequence there are natural resolution points. Some clinicians believe that just as the musical score with its variations leads to a conclusion, the imagery will find its way to an effective solution of a problem if allowed to unfold without interference (Leuner, 1969; Watkins, 1976). Some believe that the unfolding process is intrinsically curative and interpretation is not necessary (Bonny & Savery, 1973; Watkins, 1976). While there is certainly some truth to this point of view, it is also true that imagery themes frequently need interpretation out of trance and sometimes in trance.

Hypnoprojective Techniques Incorporated into Guided Fantasy

Sometimes it is advisable to incorporate hypnoprojective methods directly into ongoing guided fantasy. For example, if the patient describes walking along a path in the woods or along a road, the therapist can simply suggest, "And as you walk along, you will encounter things along the way that will somehow relate to the problem we are working on." If the patient describes entering a house, the therapist suggests, "You will discover things in each of the rooms [or in a special room] that somehow relate to the problem you have. The patient may also imagine walking down a street, where he notices a number of houses. One house in particular captures his attention. As the patient enters the house, he notices a corridor with a number of closed doors. He opens one of the doors and in the room discovers something about his unresolved problems. The possibilities are infinite. All that the therapist need do is listen carefully to the patient's unfolding fantasy, look for material that has projective potential, and use it creatively.

Hypnotic Dreams and Word Associations

Hypnotizable patients are responsive to suggestions to dream in trance and give a range of responses from spontaneous thoughts to images, to daydreams, to dreams that are like geniune nocturnal dreams. The patient usually believes he has genuinely dreamt and that the dream informs him of his inner life. Hypnotic dreaming enables the patient to gain access in a symbolic manner to unconscious conflicts and to self- and object representations. Hypnotic dreams are a convenient type of "forced fantasy" (Ferenczi, 1926), by which the clinician can directly inquire into unconscious processes.

To help the patient produce a hypnotic dream, the hypnotist begins by telling the patient that he is becoming increasingly drowsy and sleepy. (It is a good idea to avoid suggesting to the patient that he will actually fall asleep, since that is unlikely to happen):

> In a moment I'll stop talking. When I do, you will notice that you are becoming increasingly drowsy and sleepy . . . drowsy and sleepy . . . very drowsy. . . . As you become increasingly drowsy, your mind will wander off . . . you won't need to try to think about anything . . . your mind will simply wander off because you are so drowsy. . . .

Next, the hypnotist gives the suggestion for the hypnotic dream per se:

> At some point soon . . . as your mind wanders . . . a dream will spontaneously come into your mind. . . . You won't have to try to have a dream . . . the dream will come all by itself because you are so drowsy and sleepy. . . . It will be a dream like the kind you have at night. . . . As soon as the dream comes to an end, the index finger on your hand will lift up by itself . . . that will be a way to signal to me that the dream has ended. As soon as the dream ends, you will be able to recall it in detail and to describe it to me. . . . Now, I'll stop talking. . . . Notice how drowsy and sleepy you are becoming. . . . Soon the dream will come. . . .

There is silence for a few minutes. When the patient's finger levitates, the hypnotherapist says, "Now you can tell me the dream." If the patient fails to lift the index finger after a reasonable amount of time, the hypnotist suggests: ". . . soon the dream will have come and gone and the index finger will lift." If the patient has not yet started to dream, the suggestion stimulates dreaming. If the patient has begun to dream, the same suggestion is an impetus for him to finish the dream. In the initial work with hypnotic dreams, it is a good idea to suggest that "a vivid daydream or dream will come into your mind." Wording the suggestion this way leaves the option open; more patients respond successfully.

The patient may give any of several responses to suggestions for hypnotic dreams: all are clinically relevant. Sometimes the patient gives embellished reminiscences, sometimes static images, and sometimes sequences of unconnected images. More hypnotizable patients in medium-deep states of trance produce daydreams in which the images revolve around a central theme that is available to consciousness. In deep states of trance, patients produce dreams very much like nocturnal dreams in structure and content. These dreams both reveal and conceal unconscious conflicts, yet the disguises are thinner than in ordinary dreams (Brenman, 1949).

If the patient fails to produce a real dream, the suggestion is repeated over a number of sessions. Each time the suggestion is modified slightly so as to evoke mental products progressively more like nocturnal dreams, along a continuum from secondary to primary process manifestations. For example, the hypnotist can simply suggest that a "spontaneous thought" will come to mind when the patient gets drowsy. Then it can be suggested that a "daydream" will come to mind, and finally "a dream like the dreams you have at night."

Hypnotic dreaming can be used for many purposes. It is a kind of "psychic weather report" about the ongoing therapeutic process. Once it is clearly established that the patient has the ability to produce hypnotic dreams, he can be told to dream about a particular problem (Schroetter, 1951). The hypnotist modifies the suggestion as follows:

> . . . a dream will spontaneously come to mind. . . . In fact, a particular dream will come into your mind. . . . While it may or may not be clear to you at the time you are dreaming, the dream will somehow deal with your problem or symptom (name problem).

The patient can also be told to dream about the therapeutic relationship: ". . . the dream will somehow be about the therapy" or "about hypnosis" or "about our working together." These dreams are useful indicators of the status of the transference at any given moment in the therapy.

After the patient has reported the dream, the hypnotherapist asks for associations to it and helps the patient understand its unconscious meaning. (For further elaboration, see chapters 7, 8, and 9.)

Word associations produced in trance are another way to gain access to unconscious processes. The patient is told:

> In a moment I'll count from one to five. The next time you hear the number "five," thoughts, images, or feelings will come spontaneously into your mind about [name the symptom or problem]. One . . . two . . . three . . . four . . . five. . . . Now, what comes to mind? [Patient reports.]

Patients seldom fail to report associations. The suggestion to produce "thoughts, images, or feelings" gives the patient considerable freedom in the nature of the associations produced and is more likely to produce a positive response.

Working With Affect

Emotions and their communication are an integral part of the psychotherapeutic process. Affect amplifies certain aspects of experience so they can be attended to with greater care (Tomkins, 1962/1963). It is a means to communicate to others, primarily through facial display patterns,[1] so that they will respond. The continual verbal reporting of emotional experiences makes both the patient and the therapist aware of changes in the patient's internal world. For example, affects signal changes in the patterns of discharge of conflicting impulses, as revealed in the fantasy productions. Emotions also signal significant shifts in the representational world (Sandler & Rosenblatt, 1962). They signal which images of the self and others are activated at any given moment. Through affects, the patient and therapist learn where to place emphasis in the process of understanding.

For certain patients, the task of hypotherapy is to widen the range of affective experience and to foster appropriate and effective channels for their expression. For other patients, the aim of hypnotherapy is to help them modulate the intensity of emotions within an optimal range—in other words, to learn to amplify or diminish the strength of emotional experience as necessary. In the clinical situation, especially in hypnotherapy, the task often is to help the patient develop tolerance for and integration of emotional experience. Affects are not isolated but, on the one hand, are embedded within the matrix of memories and fantasies about accumulated life experience and, on the other hand, are integrated with the internal images of self and others derived from the internalization of significant relationships. Still another task of therapy is to help the patient modify the relationship between affects and associated memory impressions, fantasies, and self- and object representations. Hypnotherapy holds a certain advantage over psychotherapy in working with affect, first, because the trance state makes possible greater access to affective experience and, second, because hypnotic suggestions allow for careful structuring of the intensity of affects, their expression, and their relationship to cognitions.

Enhancing Affective Experience and Its Expression.   Hypnosis has been used to induce specific emotions in normal subjects (Hodge & Wagner, 1964). In the clinical situation the hypnotherapist's task is not to suggest specific emotions to the patient but rather *to bring the patient's current emotional experience into full awareness.* Patients are often only dimly aware of the emotional undercurrent in interactions with others; the psychotherapy process is no exception. They become aware of emotions only at discrete moments in the ongoing exchange. Apart from these moments, they have little conscious awareness of the continuous affective experience. The therapist can help patients bring these underlying emotions to the point of consciousness (Rosen, 1953) and also help them to recognize the specific emotions accurately. To ease the entry of underlying

---

[1] Of course, when the patient is in hypnosis and his eyes are closed, only the therapist benefits from these means of communication.

emotions into awareness, the hypnotized patient is told, "Notice now what you feel as you experience this scene" or "When I count from one to five . . . by the time you hear me say, 'five' . . . you will begin to feel whatever emotion is associated with the [name symptom or problem]."

Bringing the undercurrent of feeling to the point of consciousness is only the first step. Many patients have difficulty in accurately recognizing certain affects and in verbalizing them. To enhance recognition and verbalization, the hypnotist says:

> A specific feeling will become clear to you . . . It will become clearer . . . and clearer . . . You will be able to recognize exactly what this particular feeling is . . . and you will be able to describe it to me . . . Now, what is it that you are now feeling?

It is especially important to give an open-ended suggestion—not to suggest a particular emotion to the patient but to amplify the patient's awareness of the emotion of the moment. Usually the patient will report experiencing a particular emotion. Should the patient continue to have difficulty finding words for the feeling, the hypnotist says:

> I will count slowly from one to five . . . by the time I reach five, a word or two will come into your mind spontaneously . . . a word or two which exactly express what you are now aware of feeling. . . . [Therapist counts]. . . . Now, tell me what it is you are feeling.

The hypnotherapist also helps the patient to experience the affect fully so that its visceral, cognitive, and motor (expressive) components are well integrated:

> As the feeling becomes clearer and clearer to you, notice more carefully exactly how you experience this feeling in your body . . . notice what sensations you experience in your body as you feel [x] . . . notice where in your body you hold this feeling . . . notice the muscles in your face, and you will see just what muscles hold this feeling . . . now, notice what goes through your mind as you feel [x]. . . . You will discover certain thoughts, images, or memories spontaneously passing through your mind about this feeling.

Those instructions are standard procedure and can be employed whenever the patient describes a symptom or a behavioral problem, is involved in a fantasy production, or experiences some sort of shift in the psychotherapeutic process. By using this procedure strategically during the course of the therapy session, the therapist helps amplify a variety of affective experiences associated with the psychotherapeutic process.

Another technique used by the hypnotherapist is *affect intensification* (Rosen, 1953). The hypnotist says:

> When I count slowly from one to five . . . with each number you will begin to feel "x" more and more intensely . . . with each number you hear, the feeling will grow stronger and stronger. . . . By the time I reach five, you will feel it in your body as strongly as it is possible to bear. . . . Now . . . one . . . two . . . three . . . four . . . five. Notice what you feel, and you will be able to describe it to me.

This technique is especially useful when a patient spontaneously reports a feeling emerging in the course of the therapy session. The therapist uses hypnotic suggestions to help the patient recognize the feeling and to intensify the experience of the feeling within certain limits. To safeguard the patient from being overwhelmed, the therapist can use an ideomotor signal:

> If at any point in the counting the intensity of the feeling seems too much to bear, the index finger of your hand will lift all by itself, and that will be your way of signaling to me not to count beyond that point.

Hypnosis can also *enhance affects* the patient has discovered. Affects are expressed through certain defined groups of facial muscles, supplemented by the limbs, through visceral responses largely mediated through the autonomic nervous system, and through complex behavioral patterns. The experience of an affect is not the same as its expression. It is not always necessary to encourage expression of the affect in behavior, though encouraging its communication in words is usually therapeutic. For example, the hypnotherapist should not say, ". . . and as the feeling gets stronger and stronger, you will find yourself compelled to do something." This kind of suggestion encourages discharge in the form of abreaction or acting out. When the suggestion is worded this way, the expression of rage, sexual acting out, or panic states is commonly observed (Rosen, 1953). The patient is likely to cry or laugh or have violent emotional outbursts, which are not themselves therapeutic. A better way to word the suggestion is to say, ". . . and as the feeling gets stronger and stronger, you will find an appropriate way to communicate it." This kind of suggestion encourages appropriate channels for expression, communication, and understanding. Emphasis is on the therapeutic relationship, not on discharge itself. When suggestions are worded as we advise, the patient finds effective ways to communicate to the therapist the affective experience of the moment and to elicit an empathic response.

Affect Tolerance. Even without specific suggestions to intensify the affect, the experience of emotions during trance is often very intense. It is as if the trance state itself represents a generalized amplification of affect. Against this background of intensified affect, feelings sometimes emerge which are difficult for the patient to tolerate. Patients not only become more able to experience affects, they have strong reactions to these affects.

Hypnotic relaxation can also attenuate intense affects. The therapist should first distinguish whether it is in fact the patient, not the therapist, who is uncomfortable with the intensity of the affect—beginning hypnotherapists all too often "suggest away" meaningful affective experiences by urging the patient to relax. If, however, it is appropriate to tune down the affect, direct suggestions for relaxation are useful:

> . . . with each breath you will find yourself becoming more and more relaxed . . . with each exhalation you are able to let out the tension in your body more and more . . . you notice yourself becoming more relaxed now . . . soon you will be very relaxed. . . .

Another method of attenuating affect is the Clenched Fist Technique, described in chapter 4.

Hypnotic use of fantasy and imagery is yet another way to help the patient tolerate the affect:

> When I count from one to five, a very pleasant scene will come to mind . . . you will find yourself in a very comfortable and safe place. . . . One . . . two . . . three . . . four . . . five . . . now, where are you?

Once the patient describes the safe place, the hypnotist reminds the patient that he can return to it whenever the fear of being overwhelmed begins to come up:

> No matter what you are experiencing now or fear you might experience, you need not worry because you can always return to that safe and comfortable place.

Patients typically report seeing the ocean, mountains, or the woods as soothing locations.

An alternative method which symbolically conveys that affect modulation is under the patient's voluntary control is the use of an affect dial:

> Now, picture a dial or knob . . . the kind of dial you might use to control the volume of your stereo system or television set. . . . It has numbers on it from one to ten. . . . This dial controls the intensity of your emotions. Whenever you feel something, you will notice that the dial shows numbers from one to ten, one being very mild, ten being so intense it is unbearable. The rest of the numbers are somewhere in between, feelings of moderate intensity. Now, at which number is the dial set as you feel [x]? [Patient answers.]. . . . Imag-

ine now that your right hand is lifting up all by itself and moving toward that dial . . . the fingers touch the dial . . . you can see how the fingers wrap around the dial. The body and the hand know exactly the intensity of the feelings you are capable of tolerating at this time. . . . Notice how the hand begins to turn the dial one way or the other . . . as it does, you will notice a change in the intensity of your feelings. . . . Now, where is the dial set now? [Patient answers.] Notice how you feel. [Patient answers.]

The hypnotist can also suggest that the dial turn clockwise to increase the intensity of the feelings and counterclockwise to decrease it. The hypnotist gives a posthypnotic suggestion that whenever the patient anticipates being overwhelmed, he can visualize the dial and notice how the hand automatically turns the dial to a point where he can tolerate the affect.

Another alternative is to use soothing imagery. Open-ended suggestions are given: "Something will come to mind that gives you comfort . . . you will find yourself doing something that is quite soothing and comforting." Patients typically report listening to music, reading, eating, or being comforted by friends, relatives, or the therapist.

Dissociation and Ego States

According to E. R. Hilgard's (1974) neodissociation theory, cognitive operations are hierarchically organized. These operations include an executive function, which plans and directs behavior, and a monitoring function, which observes these operations and allows some of them to become conscious, but not others. In the normal waking state, these operations are well integrated; in trance, the organization is altered. The executive and monitoring functions change. Some aspect of the self that is normally out of awareness may plan and direct behavior; some aspect of experience normally out of awareness may come into consciousness.

Dissociation is a property of the hypnotic trance useful to the clinician as an uncovering method and as a means to modulate the intensity of affects or sensory experiences, notably pain. Through dissociation, a painful aspect of experience can be at least partially kept out of conscious awareness while it is recognized on another level.

Spontaneous dissociative symptoms function in the service of defense to keep traumatic memories out of consciousness. Such experiences become split off from the mainstream of consciousness, although they may still exert an influence on thought processes and behavior in some way (Janet, 1924). With hypnosis, dissociative process can be controlled. Dissociation can be suggested, and the dissociative experience structured in certain ways to support the patient's defenses during the uncovering and integrative work of therapy. The therapist can utilize dissociation in three ways: (a) dissociating the experiencing and observing parts of the ego (Fromm, 1965a, 1965b), (b) eliciting a hidden observer (Hilgard, 1977), and (c) evoking a particular ego state (Edelstien, 1981; Watkins & Watkins, 1979).

Dissociating the experiencing ego from the observing ego is one way of diminishing affect or temporarily rescuing the patient who feels overwhelmed by affect:

> You can let that part of you which feels so strongly [is afraid of being overwhelmed by frightfully strong feelings] step out of you now and go into the yard while *you* sit here in the chair by the window and watch what that person out there is doing.

It is extremely important that the "I" remain with the observing ego and the frightening, ego-dystonic part that is overwhelmed by affect run amok be designated as "that" (alien) dissociated part, not the other way round (Fromm, 1965b).

Eliciting a hidden observer is another way to use dissociation. Ernest Hilgard (1977) has used the hidden observer in his research on hypnotic analgesia. Deeply hypnotizable subjects in trance were given instructions for analgesia and then were exposed to an objectively very painful stimulus, such as immersing a hand in ice water for several minutes. The hypnotized patient responsive to analgesic suggestions reports little or no pain. However, in order to find out whether a patient experiences pain that is beyond conscious awareness, the hidden observer instruction is given as follows:

> In a little while I will touch your shoulder. When you feel the touch on your shoulder, you will come into contact with some hidden part of yourself, a part unknown to the part of you that is now hypnotized. That concealed part of yourself may have some awareness of the pain you would have experienced if you were not hypnotized as you are now. That part will be able to describe the experience that went on while you were hypnotized and did not feel the pain. When I remove my hand from the shoulder, that part will recede again, and you will experience yourself as you now are: hypnotized and unable to feel pain. All right. [Therapist puts his hand on patient's shoulder. Patient's hidden observer describes experiencing distressing pain. Therapist removes hand. Patient feels no pain and says so.]

Although the patient consciously does not feel or report pain, the "hidden observer" is quite aware of both the pain sensations and the pain distress. The sensation of pain is concealed from consciousness in trance except when the hidden observer is used.

The hypnotherapist may also wish to evoke particular ego states believed to be defensively dissociated from consciousness. An ego state is part of the overall self system, which includes certain experiences (Klemperer, 1965) and certain configurations of perceiving, thinking, and feeling that are integrated around a common principle (Watkins & Watkins, 1979) within its domain. It has its own boundary within the overall self system. The self system is composed of a number of ego states, in much the same way as the United States is composed of separate states. In some patients, certain ego states have become repressed (Klemperer, 1965). They are split off from consciousness, and carry on a quasi-autonomous existence, but they exert an influence over the feelings and behavior of the main personality. Some ego states are directly implicated in the formation of symptoms. Hypnosis is a vehicle for activating an ego state and restructuring the overall relationship between ego states. During trance, the executive and monitoring parts of the self system can become translocated into the previously dormant ego state. To activate an ego state associated with a particular symptom or problem, the therapist says:

> I wish to speak to that part of you which causes you to [name the symptom or problematic behavior]. I will touch you on the right [or left] shoulder [or count to five], and when I do, the part of you that causes you to [therapist names patient's problem] will begin to speak. That part of you will know when the symptom first appeared and what purpose it serves. When I remove my hand, you will once again experience yourself as you now are. [Therapist puts his hand on patient's shoulder or counts. Patient describes symptom from perspective of the deviant ego state. Therapist removes hand from the shoulder.]

The therapist tries to reframe the function of the pathological ego state in more adaptive, healthier ways (Edelstien, 1981).

Watkins and Watkins (1979) and Edelstien (1981) recommend giving proper names to these ego states; they maintain that such ego states have specific ages and genders. We, however, caution against personifying an ego state. We agree with Neisser (cited in Sheehan & McConkey, 1982 p. 255) that naming ego states divides consciousness as if each ego state were a separate person. It can foster splitting of consciousness, rather than its integration. Such iatrogenic effects are observed in hypnotherapy with multiple personalities, where identifying and naming the so-called personalities may not so much activate as actually create the parts (Gruenewald, 1984). The goal of the hypnotherapeutic work is integration of ego states, not their separation.

Revivification and Age Regression

Some of the most valuable uncovering techniques at the disposal of the hypnotherapist are *revivification* and *age regression*. Hypnotic suggestions for revivification and age regression enable the hypnotizable patient to gain access to past experiences. The hypnotherapist can structure the suggestions so as to explore experiences at different developmental ages and to learn how these experiences have contributed to the patient's current problem. The patient reexperiences the event with affect like that accompanying the original event (Sheehan & McConkey, 1982) and from the perspective of the self-experience characteristic of the given developmental age (Nash et al., 1979). Suggestions for age regression are a direct means to gain access to affect-laden experiences of the past that pertain to the patient's problems.

Revivification and age regression are related phenomena. They represent degrees of the patient's response along a continuum from lesser to greater regression. Revivification is the reliving, in the current trance state, of a past experience in a compelling and literal way (Sheehan & McConkey, 1982). Even though the quality of revivification is emotionally more compelling than that of a mere memory, or even hypermnesia, the patient views and describes the event from an adult perspective and remains oriented to the therapeutic context. The patient is aware of who the therapist is, of being hypnotized, and of sitting in a chair (Cheek & LeCron, 1968).

Age regression is even more compelling. It is a literal, though often only partial, reinstatement of earlier modes of functioning and behavior in addition to the reliving of earlier affective experiences. The patient experiences himself as really *being* the child, to whom what happened in childhood again happens now. And as he did not know the therapist then, he is unaware of the therapist *as* a therapist. An age-regressed patient may also be unaware that he is sitting in a chair, hypnotized. He may hallucinate the environment of the suggested age and events in question. The patient is likely to activate the self- and object representations characteristic of the suggested age (Nash et al., 1979). Usually the patient manifests the cognitive and perceptual functions roughly characteristic of the suggested age (Reiff & Sheerer, 1959). The multilingual patient may recover a forgotten language he spoke in childhood (Fromm, 1970; Sheehan & McConkey, 1982). To a great extent, age regression represents a partial and temporary reinstatement of childhood modes of functioning and behavior.

Before attempting an age regression or revivification, the therapist must interview the patient to get an overview of the main events of the patient's history. The therapist must be vigilant for signs of traumatic experience. The patient is asked if there is any age or time of life he wishes not to reexperience and the reasons why not. He is assured that these episodes will be avoided during the age regression. The therapist also asks the patient what he consciously recalls of the intended period of the regression and tries to ascertain the patient's interests and activities at that time to incorporate them into the suggestions. Having obtained the information, the therapist selects an approach to the suggested regression. Revivification and age regression can be produced in any of the following ways: (a) direct suggestions for regression, (b) the affect bridge, (c) fantasy methods, and (d) confusion methods.

Direct Suggestions for Age Regression.   Direct suggestions for age regression can be used with highly hypnotizable patients who have a demonstrated ability for regression. Sometimes simple counting can be used:

> Now think about the time when you were [specify the age; or specify the place or event]. Soon you will begin to feel just as you did when you were [x] years old, doing [y]. With each number I count from one to five, you will find yourself going back, back in time, back to when you were [x] years old, doing [y]. One . . . you are going back into the past. It is no longer (state present month and year) but earlier. . . . Two . . . much earlier . . . going back in time. . . . Three . . . getting younger and younger. . . . Four . . . soon you will be [x] years old doing [y]. . . . Five . . . you are now [x] years old. . . . Where are you? What are you doing? Describe what it is like. [Patient responds.]

The same sort of direct suggestion can be used without counting. A finger signal is used instead. The patient is simply told to go back to [x] years old, doing [y]. When the patient feels that he is once again [x] years old, the finger will lift by itself.

It is a good idea to anchor the regression to a particular time period or event, at least for the initial regressive experiences. The more affectively important the event, the better the regression. In experimental hypnosis, holidays and birthdays are good events the hypnotist might choose. Experiences in school in a particular grade, or at a specified age, are also commonly selected by the hypnotist as anchoring events. Anchoring helps the patient make the experience real and concrete and produces a more complete regression. Once the patient becomes skilled in responding to suggestions for regression, the hypnotherapist leaves the suggestions more open ended. The patient usually regresses to what is more affectively salient in the context of the ongoing therapeutic process.

The Affect Bridge.   The affect bridge (Watkins, 1971) is one of the best ways to produce age regression. It is a way of uncovering memories and fantasies associated with a particular affect. Before starting the age regression, the hypnotist suggests a particular emotion [z], for example, happiness, sadness, anger, or fear. Next, suggestions are given to amplify the intensity of the affect of [z]. The affect bridge will not be effective unless a particular feeling is both salient and experienced with some intensity. Then, the evoked strong affect is used as a bridge to the past. The patient is told to imagine that he is traveling along that bridge of [z] to a time earlier in his life when he felt exactly the same: "This feeling will become a bridge to your past. You will find yourself traveling along that bridge of [z]" [name feeling] "now . . . traveling along that bridge of [happiness]. The therapist waits for a while and then asks: "Where are you now?" The patient says he is [x] years old and blissfully relates the happy experience he—that [x]-year-old child—now is having. The therapist then says: "And now, along that same bridge you can go back even further, to an even earlier time when you feel just that happy." With the same affect bridge, manifestations of a particular affect state (e.g., depression, or rage, or happiness) can be traced through various developmental periods within the same hypnotic hour.

Sometimes the therapist suggests a specific affect as the medium for the regression. At other times the therapist may work with a feeling of unknown origin that emerges spontaneously in the course of the therapy. In that case, also, the hypnotist first intensifies the feeling and then uses the affect bridge to trace the feeling back. He may leave the suggestion open ended: ". . . to (a) time(s) early in your life when you felt just as you now do. . . ." or the therapist can word the suggestion specifically to uncover the origin of the feeling: ". . . to the very first time you ever experienced that feeling." There is a certain advantage in leaving the suggestion open ended. It helps to explore the full matrix of memories and fantasies in which the feeling of the original experience was embedded.

Age Regression Through Fantasy.   Various kinds of visualizations can be used to produce age regression (Cheek & LeCron, 1968). The patient may imagine himself floating in a magic boat down a river of time. Each milestone he passes represents the previous year. The boat moves faster and faster along the river until it stops at a designated year. Or the patient may visualize a grandfather clock. The clock's face is a panel showing the years. The patient imagines the hands of the clock turning in reverse very quickly, each year changing to the previous one until a designated year is reached. Still another method is to have the patient imagine a book of time, with the book opened at the current date. Each page represents a month of the patient's life. The patient imagines quickly flipping the pages back until the designated time is reached. Another visualization especially useful for children is a time machine. The therapist builds a "time machine" in the playroom, and the child sits in it. The therapist adjusts the dials and tells the child that he will go back to a particular time or event.

Age Regression Through Confusion.   Confusion techniques can produce or enhance regression (Erickson, 1964b). Confusion techniques entail plays on words and irrelevancies introduced into the flow of hypnotic communication to produce disorientation to time and place. The confusion method is especially useful for patients who find it difficult to let go of their orientation to time. The hypnotist systematically structures the suggestions so that the past, present, and future blend together in a confusing way. Presumably the patient is shaken from his ordinary temporal frame of reference and is able to adopt the temporal frame of reference designated by the therapist. Table 6.1 illustrates Erickson's brief summary of the confusion method used to produce age regression:

TABLE 6.1
The Use of the Confusion Technique to Induce Age Regression

I am so very glad you volunteered to be a subject	Joint participation in a joint task
You probably enjoyed eating today	Irrelevant–most likely factual
Most people do though sometimes they skip a meal	A valid commonplace utterance
You probably ate breakfast this morning	The temporal present
Maybe you will want tomorrow something you had today	The future (an indirect implication of a certain identity of the past and of today with the future)
You have eaten it before, perhaps on Friday like today	The past and the present and a common identity
Maybe you will next week	The present and the future
Whether last week, this week or next week, makes no difference	The present, future and past all equated
Thursday always comes before Friday	Irrelevant, non sequitur, and valid
This was true last week, will be true next week, and is so this week	Irrelevant, meaningful and true but what does it mean? (Subject struggles mentally to put a *connected* meaning on all this future, present and past all included in a meaningful statement which lacks pertinence
Before Friday is Thursday and before June is May	How true: But note use of *present tense* in relation to today's yesterday and to May

But first there is "whan that Aprille with its shoures soote"	Here comes April of the past (remote past) and it also *pinpoints a particular area* in the subject's life—*his college days*. (An item of fact predetermined—it might have been in high school—but to introduce Chaucer creates a problem of relating it meaningfully to what has been said, but this is a confusing task
And March followed the snows of February but who really remembers the 6th of February	Back now to March, then to February and one does (present tense) remember February 12th, 14th and 22nd. February 6th only offers confusion (It has been predetermined that February 6th is not a birthday or some such event, but if it is meaningful this serves only to impel the subject to validate that day also)
And January 1st is the beginning of the New Year of 1963 and *all that it will bring*	Thus is given a memory task. *It will bring June* (already here) but slipping unaccountably into the remote future because January is given a present tense
But December brought Christmas	True, valid vivid memories of the past December and the implied coming of the year of 1963
But Thanksgiving preceded Christmas and all that shopping to get done and what a good dinner	November, 1962 with an *impending urgency to do something in the coming December* an emotionally valid dinner memory, all of 1962. (And there have been many New Years, Christmasses and Thanksgiving Days, all strongly emotionally tinged)

From: Erickson, 1964b, Reprinted by permission

Improving the Quality of the Age Regression. Suggestions can be designed in various ways to improve the quality of the regression and to achieve genuine age regression rather than revivification. To increase the likelihood of reinstating previous modes of functioning over current adult functioning, the therapist can directly suggest:

> You will find yourself thinking, acting, feeling, and behaving like a child of [specify suggested age]. No matter what you find yourself doing, you will experience yourself exactly as you did when you were [x] years old. You will temporarily forget your current ways of thinking, acting, feeling, and behaving until the next time you hear me say these words, "Soon you will find yourself growing up again."

He may also suggest a change in the body image, especially for regression to childhood:

> You are younger and younger, and your body is getting smaller and smaller . . . your arms and legs seem smaller and smaller . . . your

whole body seems smaller and smaller . . . the room which you are in seems so large as you look around. . . .

The reinstatement of previous modes of functioning is for the most part quite unstable. The regressive experience characteristically fluctuates between revivification and elements of genuine age regression (Greenleaf, 1969). In order to bias the fluctuation in favor of genuine age regression, the therapist must help the regressed patient temporarily suspend his orientation to the therapeutic context and adopt the context of the regressed situation. The hypnotist does this in a number of ways. Once the therapist has suggested the regression, he should give the patient enough time to orient himself to the new level of functioning. The hypnotist should pause before giving any further suggestion. A graded suggestion is also useful: ". . . and the longer you find yourself to be [x] years old, the more you will actually experience yourself once again as an [x]-year-old." A finger signal may be added: ". . . and whenever you feel exactly the way you did when you were [x] years old, the index finger will lift up." As most patients did not know the hypnotist when they were children, he must explicitly suggest an alteration in the way he is perceived. An open-ended suggestion will allow the patient the freedom to imagine the hypnotist in a way that best fits the internal experience of the age regression: "I will be a person you know and like. Who am I?" The age-regressed patient may say that the hypnotist is a teacher, a relative, a sibling, a parent, a friend. The hypnotist then uses information from the patient's history to play the part chosen for him as well as possible.

Thus, the hypnotist structures the situation to favor a context congruent with the regressed situation, giving task-appropriate suggestions that will elicit childlike responses. Giving suggestions that demand adult-appropriate response will interfere with genuine age regression. For instance, if the patient is regressed to the age of 5 years, the therapist must relate and talk to the patient as if he were talking to a 5-year-old. And he must word the inquiry with the regressed patient in the present, not in the past tense—not "What happened?" but "What is happening?" Talking to the patient in the present tense, as if the childhood experience were happening right now, favors the occurrence of a genuine age regression over revivification. The therapist must also treat the patient as if the patient were a child. To develop a context appropriate for the age regression, the therapist may need to engage the "child" in fantasy, sit down on the floor and play a game with him, or behave in other ways roughly equivalent to the developmental age of the regressed patient.

Some highly hypnotizable patients with a talent for age regression may manifest two additional features of age regression. If they are capable of an open-eyed trance, they may open their eyes and hallucinate a childhood setting to which they are regressed. That is, they perceive the office in which they currently are as if it were, say, their school room. Yet, they also see the therapist's office when they open their eyes. Because of trance logic (Orne, 1959), perceiving two realities with open eyes simultaneously is not necessarily a problem for the age-regressed patient (Sheehan & McConkey, 1982). Other patients are capable of experiencing themselves simultaneously as the regressed child and the observing adult (Fromm, 1965a; Laurence & Perry, 1981). Still others, by dividing the ego into an experiencing part and an observing part (Fromm, 1965b), alternate between the experience of the regressed child (genuine age regression) and the observing adult (revivification). Such patients can be given "hidden observer" (Hilgard, 1977) suggestions to help them achieve a fuller age regression:

> Now, often it is possible for people who are hypnotized to comment in some way on their experiences, what they are feeling at the time, the various sensations and experiences they feel while they are hypnotized. You're back in the classroom and 5 now, and you are deeply hypnotized. In a little while I am going to tap you on the shoulder. When I do that, I want that other part of you that can comment on these experiences to tell me what you are feeling at the time, just simply tell me what's happening. When I tap you on the shoulder again, the other part of you will go, and you will be right back to where you are now, 5 years of age. So, when I tap you the first time, the other part of you can tell me what you are feeling and thinking and when I tap you again you will be back, to 5 years of age. I'll tap you the first time now. Describe to me the feelings and thoughts you have at this moment. (Sheehan & McConkey, 1982, p. 126).

When regressing a patient to a very young age, it is a good idea to have the patient imagine being in a warm and safe setting, perhaps being surrounded by warm blankets or feeling the comforting presence of the mother or Teddy Bear. Because a very young child does not understand language, the hypnotherapist must also prearrange a nonverbal signal to bring the patient back to the verbal level, where he understands language: "The next time you feel the touch on your arm like this [therapist touches patient], you will no longer be 6 months old but will be [therapist names an older age]."

A number of signs distinguish genuine age regression from revivification:

1. Developmental somatic functioning. In genuine age regression to very young ages, the childhood Babinsky reflex, the grasping reflex, and

random movements typical for infants often reappear as nonvolitional reflexes and outside the patient's awareness.

2. Cognitive and perceptual functioning: (a) The patient writes and draws like a child; (b) the voice becomes childlike; (c) the patient responds to suggestions with increased literalness and concreteness; (d) cognitive tasks evoke childlike responses, for example, telling time by saying, "The big hand is on one. . . ."; (e) the patient spontaneously plays with paints, dough, dolls, and other toys during a free play period.

3. Functioning of self and object relations: there is reinstatement of the self-experience and perception of others characteristic of the suggested age.

Time Distortion

Some hypnotizable patients respond to the suggestion that time seems to be passing slower or faster than usual. The hypnotist may suggest, for example, that the patient imagine watching an entire TV program as the therapist counts from one to ten. On completion of the count, the patient reports the entire program, often in considerable detail. Through time distortion the patient is able to engage in a great deal of imaginal activity in a very brief span of clock-time. Yet, the patient believes that the activity progressed at a normal rate. Although it is unlikely that the patient's thought processes have speeded up (Johnson, 1976), his subjective estimate of time passage is considerably altered (Barber & Calverley, 1964). According to the hypnotic S's and patient's report, the TV program does not instantaneously flash into his mind, but rather seems to unfold continuously at a natural rate. The patient believes the program to be real (Cooper & Erickson, 1959).

In preparation of time distortion, the patient is told to clear his mind of any activity:

> Now, any scenes that you've been seeing are disappearing from view. They have now disappeared, and your mind is now blank (Cooper & Erickson, 1959, p. 25).

Because time distortion works best when patients are deeply absorbed in their imaginal activity, it is also a good idea to introduce a suggestion for the fading of the generalized reality orientation:

> During these experiences you will be completely unaware of your surroundings in the waking world (Cooper & Erickson, 1959, p. 33).

To facilitate the concentration necessary for time distortion, the patient should be told to remain motionless and by no means should be asked to report while the imaginal activity is going on.

The sequence for the suggested time distortion is: (a) a suggestion for time distortion itself, (b) a suggested imaginal activity, (c) a signal to start and stop the time-distorted interval, and (d) a request to report the activity after it is completed. The simplest form of suggestion is some variation on the theme "a short interval will seem like a long interval": "Every minute will seem like 5 [or 10 or 15] minutes" (Kraus, Katzell, & Krauss, 1974; Wolberg, 1945). An alternative method introduces the notion of a "special time" to the patient:

> Now I'm going to give you much more time than you need to do this. I will give you 20 seconds of world time. But in your special time, these 20 seconds will be just as long as you need to complete your work. (Cooper & Erickson, 1959, p. 171)

A third approach is to give an open-ended suggestion, which the patient terminates with a finger signal:

> It will seem to you that you are spending as much time as you wish without having to hurry doing something that you enjoy. And when it is finished in a few seconds of clock time, the index finger will lift up.

It is especially important that the hypnotist suggest that the patient need not hurry.

The patient may engage in any kind of imaginal activity during the time-distorted interval. Cooper and Erickson (1959) classify these activities into continuous (e.g. drawing) and completed (e.g. finishing a report) activities.

Time distortion is useful for uncovering in therapy. The therapist, for example, might suggest that the patient watch a TV program about his problem under time-distortion conditions. Given the suggestion of time acceleration, the patient reports considerable detail after a brief interval of clock time. Time distortion can also be an adjunct in the development of coping strategies. The patient is told to imagine a scene or a series of scenes in which he discovers ways to cope with his problem effectively. The patient may report newly discovered, considerably detailed coping strategies after a very brief period of clock time.

A specialized use of time distortion is the technique of pseudo-orientation in time (Cooper & Erickson, 1959). After disorienting the patient to current time, the therapist tells the patient that the seconds, minutes, and hours are quickly passing. The patient is oriented to "sometime in the future," as if it were the current time. Pseudotime orientation enables the patient to experience as reality whatever he imagines or wishes to accomplish or have happen in the future. Through pseudotime orientation, for example, the patient can be projected into a future time when he will be symptom free. The patient is told that seconds and minutes will pass very quickly and that he soon will find himself sometime in the future, able to describe what is happening in his life since the therapy has ended, and pleased about his accomplishment. Of course, time progression suggestions should be used only when one can attach a hopeful, healthy note to them.

For patients who do not respond readily to simple suggestions for time distortion, additional suggestions are necessary. Sometimes the patient should be prepared for time distortion with suggestions designed to disorient him with respect to ordinary time, for instance, with a direct suggestion that "time is dragging" or "speeding up" (Wolberg, 1945). More effective is Erickson's (1964) elaborate confusion technique, discussed earlier in this chapter. Sometimes training is necessary, for which a metronome is a useful aid. The metronome is set at a rate of one stroke per second, and the patient is told so. A bit later, the patient is told that the metronome will slow down until its rate is one stroke every 5, 10 . . . 60 seconds: "It's going slower and slower . . . slower and slower." Then the patient is asked to estimate how fast the metronome is going. With practice, some patients are able to experience the metronome subjectively at a rate of one stroke per minute, even though the metronome continues at the fixed rate of one stroke per second. Cooper and Erickson (1959) report that it took from 3 to 20 hours to train their subjects.

Amnesia and Hypermnesia

Posthypnotic amnesia is the temporary inability to recall, upon awakening, some or all of the experiences one has had while in trance. Where extremely painful emotional material is involved, the clinician may explicitly suggest a posthypnotic amnesia, or posthypnotic amnesia may even occur spontaneously (Kline, 1966). Typically, posthypnotic amnesia, whether suggested or spontaneous, is selective, that is, it is specific to certain memories. With traumatic events, however, posthypnotic amnesia may be general; the patient may not remember anything that transpired in trance after he closed his eyes.

Experimental subjects experiencing posthypnotic amnesia are unable to recall certain events of the trance, yet they are aware of the presence of the unavailable material (Evans & Kihlstrom, 1973). Experimental (laboratory) posthypnotic amnesia is more accurately a form of suppression in which the patient actively inhibits the search and retrieval mechanisms of memory, either by being too relaxed to recall the events or by actively distracting himself from the memory (Spanos & Bodorik, 1977). Whichever strategy is used, it is involuntary, at least for hypnotizable subjects (Williamsen, Johnson, & Ericksen, 1965), and disrupts the normal organization of recall (Evans & Kihlstrom, 1973). Patients are simply unable to bring the suppressed material into conscious awareness. They report, "I can't remember much of that. . . ." Or they may rationalize their inability to remember it: "It's not worth the effort of recalling it." Posthypnotic amnesia persists despite demands to remember the events (Sheehan & McConkey, 1982). If the hypnotist has used a release signal, the posthypnotic amnesia is mostly, but not entirely, reversible upon signal (Kihlstrom, 1977).

The inability to recall is compounded in the clinical situation. Patients may recall repressed material in trance. When given a posthypnotic suggestion to remember only what they are ready to remember in the waking state, many patients fail to recall some or all of the material upon awakening. However, it is difficult to know how much of the failure to recall is due to *re*pression, that is, letting the material sink below the repression barrier again, and how much may be due to *sup*pression, according to the mechanisms by which posthypnotic amnesia functions with laboratory subjects. The patient who represses material typically is unaware of the existence of the repressed material, whereas a patient who suppresses it is somehow aware that the material exists but cannot get at it. In some cases, the inability to remember is a mixture of repression and suppression.

Suggested posthypnotic amnesia is especially effective as a protective device while uncovering traumatic memories and intolerable affects. Hypnotherapy patients often feel that they are expected to remember the events of trance. Even where these events are painful, they may try to comply with the assumed demand to remember at the risk of becoming overwhelmed (Wolberg, 1945). The clinician is well advised to respect their defenses and even, when appropriate, to suggest suppression through posthypnotic amnesia. We recommend the clinician routinely use suggestions for *partial* posthypnotic amnesia: The best way to do this is to say, "And when you awaken from hypnosis, you will remember only what you are ready to remember" or ". . . are able to handle." On awakening, some patients remember everything; others have amnesia for unconscious material so conflictful or painful they are not yet able to face it in the waking state. Partial posthypnotic amnesia also alerts the clinician to the painful areas the patient is not yet able to bring into consciousness and that, for a while, he should not touch.

Graded suggestions can also be given for posthypnotic amnesia: "After you awaken from hypnosis, you will find youself reflecting on this material and will be able to remember it and understand its meaning more and more over time as you become ready to remember and understand it." The amnesia dissipates as time passes and as the patient is able to integrate the material. Sometimes the therapist may use a release signal: "And you won't be able to remember it until you return to this office and sit in the chair." Whatever material the patient develops amnesia for usually can be brought into awareness again the next time the hypnotist asks the patient for it in trance. The hypnotist may use a series of trance inductions as a means to integrate the material into consciousness over time by suggesting in consecutive hypnotherapy hours:

> Each time upon awakening, you will forget a little less of this than before.

Hypermnesia is the increased ability to remember in trance past experiences one is unable to recall in the waking state. The hypermnestic patient remembers the experience during trance, but does not relive it (as he does with revivification). During trance, one utilizes search and retrieval mechanisms different from those used in the waking state. Normally unavailable, often affect-laden memories spontaneously come into awareness. Although hypnosis generally does not improve memory, except for certain kinds of meaningful material (Dhanens & Lundy, 1975), recall is considerably enhanced for events that are both personally meaningful and emotional (Udolf, 1981). Patients have ready access to those memories most relevant to the clinical situation. They recall, sometimes in considerable detail, significant experiences they have completely forgotten. The recalled experiences are sometimes inaccurate, but even when inaccurate, the material recalled is clinically significant in the way the patient recalls it. The inner meaning to the patient, even in a fantasy reconstruction, is what is important and must be understood.

Hypermnesia can be spontaneous, or it may be suggested. Spontaneous hypermnesia is quite common. The hypnotist may also give a hypnotic suggestion for hypermnesia:

> In a moment I will begin counting slowly from one to five. With each number you will notice a change in your memory. You will no longer recall things in your usual way of remembering. Your memory will change with each number I count. When I reach five, you will be able to recall [specify event or experience in question]. One . . . your memory is changing now. . . . Notice what this is like. . . . Two . . . something is happening in your mind. . . . Three . . . it is coming back now . . . you can feel it as if it were on the tip of your tongue. . . . Four . . . very soon you will be able to remember. . . . Five . . . now, tell me what you remember.

The patient then reports the hypermnestic experience, usually describing it as coming into awareness suddenly at the count of five. Hypermnestic recall circumvents the search and retrieval mechanisms used in the waking state, such as anchoring the event to its context or its temporal relation to other events. Hypermnestic experiences have a sense of immediacy about them.

To terminate the hypnotic suggestion for hypermnesia, the therapist says that the patient's way of remembering things is returning to normal.

Posthypnotic Suggestions

Posthypnotic suggestions are made during trance but are intended to have their effect after the trance has been terminated. A posthypnotic suggestion is a type of persistent effect (Sheehan & McConkey, 1982). A patient responsive to posthypnotic suggestions manifests a specific effect sometime after awakening from hypnosis, usually but not always after some time has elapsed. The patient typically feels a compulsion to follow the posthypnotic suggestion and may or may not be aware that he has made a response. Responsiveness to posthypnotic suggestions is a specific area of hypnotic talent, which some patients may lack. Others may fail to respond, even when capable of doing so, because they partially inhibit the response. Resisting the compulsion to respond, they become uncomfortable. Then they should be told to make the response anyway. After enacting the response, patients usually report feeling relieved.

Some posthypnotic suggestions elicit a response only when a prearranged signal is given: "Whenever I tap twice like this [taps twice]. . . ." or "The next time you sit in this chair. . . ." or "When I say the word, 'state,' you will do. . . ." The behavioral response to a cue-released posthypnotic suggestion is self-limited. The patient involuntarily makes a brief response when the signal is given, and the posthypnotic command is followed only when the signal is given or repeated. Some (e.g., Erickson, 1941) believe that the patient lapses into a spontaneous trance at the signal, for the brief duration of the response to the posthypnotic suggestion. Other posthypnotic suggestions elicit a response within a set time frame: "When we discuss this upon awakening but before the therapy hour ends today. . . ." or "Before our next appointment, you will do. . . ." Still other posthypnotic suggestions elicit a gradual or cumulative response over time. These are graded posthypnotic suggestions: "As time passes. . . ." or "In the future [x] will happen more and more" (e.g., ". . . you will feel more and more confident about your own abilities").

Some posthypnotic suggestions are designed to change the patient's mental state. For example, the patient may be told to think or feel in a particular way about his problem, a way that will lead to greater understanding. Other posthypnotic suggestions are intended to elicit a particular behavior. Other posthypnotic suggestions demand very specific responses, such as clearing one's throat upon a tapping signal. Still others are open ended. They allow for a wide range of responses, and the patient gives the response that best suits him at that time. For example, the hypnotist may say, "As time passes, you will notice some change in your symptoms."

The hypnotist must take special care in wording the posthypnotic suggestion in order to ensure the proper response. The strength of the response, or its lack, is contingent on a number of factors, which vary with the hypnotic subject. First, the patient must possess talent for posthypnotic responses. The patient's ability for posthypnotic suggestion can be tested by first giving a very simple posthypnotic suggestion, such as clearing the throat or coughing upon a signal, and then by a series of increasingly complex posthypnotic suggestions. In this way, the patient also is given the opportunity gradually to develop skill for posthypnotic responses (Kroger & Fezler, 1976). Second, the patient must have the motivation to respond. The hypnotist must word posthypnotic suggestions to be congruent with the patient's values, so that the patient will find it desirable to try to respond. Third, the patient must feel capable of the posthypnotic response. By fulfilling progressively more difficult posthypnotic suggestions, the patient develops confidence in posthypnotic ability. Conversely, particularly in a group situation, subjects are unlikely to respond to posthypnotic suggestions that make them self-conscious. For instance, during a class demonstration of hypnosis, a subject given a posthypnotic suggestion to take his shoe off upon a signal may fail (or refuse) to respond, owing not to inability, but to embarrassment. Special care must be taken, too, to word posthypnotic suggestions to avoid self-consciousness. The hypnotist may say, "And you will do this without thinking about it . . . without any self-consciousness . . . without hesitating . . . in a way that seems perfectly natural to you."

The strength of a posthypnotic response also depends on the hypnotic communication itself. It must be communicated clearly so that the patient knows exactly what response is intended. The posthypnotic suggestion must also be worded to increase the involuntarism of the response. Many people believe that posthypnotic suggestions fail if the patient remembers the posthypnotic suggestion upon awakening. It is not uncommon for a patient to say, "I didn't do it because I remember what you told me." However, many patients respond to posthypnotic suggestions even when they remember them. Suggested or spontaneous amnesia for posthypnotic suggestions may indeed increase the likelihood of a response as well as the involuntarism of the response because conscious reasoning is bypassed (Cheek & LeCron, 1968, p. 47), but amnesia is not a necessary condition of a posthypnotic response. It is better to word the posthypnotic suggestion by saying, ". . . it is not necessary to remember" than by saying,

". . . you won't be able to remember." Wording it in the former way is more permissive and leaves the choice of whether or not to remember to the patient.

The therapist may choose from a variety of types of posthypnotic suggestions according to the patient's clinical need. In nonhypnotic therapy, the insights and behavioral changes occurring in the sessions do not necessarily generalize to the patient's everyday life. The therapist is confronted with the very real limitation that therapeutic changes may not affect the "other 23 hours." Therapeutic posthypnotic suggestions are applicable to events in the patient's everyday life beyond the hypnotherapy hour. In this sense, posthypnotic suggestions offer the clinician the advantage of being directly able to help the patient improve how he feels and behaves in real life outside the therapy hour.

Posthypnotic suggestions serve the clinician in a variety of ways. They can be used to gain or enhance insight: "After you awaken, you will find youself reflecting on what you have just experienced, and the meaning of this will get increasingly clear to you as you are ready to understand it." They can be used to extend the uncovering and working through process beyond the therapy hour: "And you will have a dream about your problem this week and will remember it upon arrival at the next therapy hour." Posthypnotic suggestions can also directly affect symptoms: "As time passes, you will experience less and less pain. And although you may still feel something, it will not be experienced as pain." This wording can be used both for physical and emotional pain. Posthypnotic suggestions can enable the patient to adopt a new behavior in everyday life subsequent to work in the hypnotherapy hours. The patient may respond successfully to desensitization of, say, a speaking phobia, with a hierarchy of visualizations in trance. Posthypnotic suggestions can reinforce the actual behavioral change between the hours. The patient with difficulty in public speaking can be told in trance, "The next time you find yourself at the speaker's podium, you will remain relaxed as you now are and will be able to speak effectively as you just have imagined doing." Posthypnotic suggestions can facilitate ease of reinduction of hypnosis: "And each time you are hypnotized, it will be easier and easier for you to enter as deep a state of trance as you are in now. This will happen more and more quickly each time." Posthypnotic suggestions can also foster self-efficacy: "As time passes, you will become increasingly confident in your ability to. . . ." or ". . . you will feel stronger about. . . ."

Hypnotized people take suggestions very literally. Wording that is too sloppy or specific can be dangerous, as the following vignette illustrates:

A medical student who was an experimental subject was given the following posthypnotic suggestion: "Next Wednesday at 3:00 p.m. you will feel a compelling urge to go to the library here and read the current issue of the *Journal of Neurology*. But you will forget that I told you so."

The posthypnotic suggestion seemed innocuous enough. The experimenter, a novice in hypnosis, assumed that on a Wednesday afternoon at 3:00 p.m. a medical student would be in the medical school complex, and it would not hurt him to do a bit of extra reading in the library. The medical school was located near a very busy highway.

On Thursday, the student called her, very upset, to tell her that he had nearly killed himself the previous afternoon at 2:45 p.m. by suddenly making a U-turn against the traffic on a six-lane highway. He had been on his way home, needing to go home earlier than usual that day, and all of a sudden he felt *compelled* to go to "our medical school library to read some stupid neurological journal." He said he could not understand why he had made that U-turn in busy traffic; two oncoming cars in full flight just barely avoided hitting his car and smashing it. He had the feeling his "acting so recklessly" must have had some connection with the hypnosis experiment in which he had been a subject the day before, but he really did not know. Could the experimenter throw some light on the matter?

Ego-Strengthening Procedures

Ego-strengthening suggestions are designed to increase the patient's ability to cope with his difficulties or to encourage him to stand on his own feet (Hartland, 1965). There are three kinds of ego-strengthening suggestions: (a) general ego-strengthening suggestions, (b) specific ego-strengthening suggestions to facilitate the discovery and enhancement of the patient's inner coping strategies, and (c) specific suggestions to foster the patient's sense of self-efficacy.

General ego-strengthening suggestions are intended to foster the ego state characterized by an increased sense of well-being. The hypnotist uses a graded posthypnotic suggestion:

> As each day passes, you will find yourself getting less and less depressed, discouraged, or nervous . . . as each day passes, you will find yourself getting more and more cheerful and happy . . . more and more calm and relaxed. You will be more and more content with yourself and accepting of yourself than you have previously been able to do.

The therapist may also use hypnoprojective methods (dream, theatre) to help the patient discover coping strategies:

And soon a scene [or dream] will come to you. As the scene [or dream] unfolds, it will suggest ways in which you can effectively cope with your problem. The scene [or dream] will somehow be about a way [or ways] in which you will be able to deal with your difficulty and [name problem]. Although you may or may not know exactly how this scene [or dream] is about ways to deal with your problem, nevertheless, the scene [or dream] will open up for you ways to deal with the problem.

The therapist collects one or more coping productions from the patient until new and potentially effective coping strategies clearly have emerged. These are reflected to the patient as suggestions. The therapist also gives suggestions to enhance the coping strategies: He says, "You will find these to be more and more effective" or "It will automatically occur to you to do or think of [specify coping strategy] whenever you notice [name problem] beginning to occur."

Self-efficacy is a critical component of therapeutic change. The hypnotist can increase self-efficacy with direct suggestions: "You are becoming more and more confident and competent" or "Notice how you are becoming increasingly confident in your ability to resolve your problem . . . your confidence is increasing each time you practice self-hypnosis."

Ego-strengthening suggestions, while seemingly simplistic, are quite valuable. Hartland (1965) and many others believe that in certain instances ego-strengthening suggestions alone can bring about a successful treatment outcome without the need of symptomatic or dynamic hypnotherapy. Some patients experience spontaneous alleviation of symptoms when they feel strong enough to cope without the symptoms. Direct suggestions for coping, therefore, are sometimes more effective than direct suggestions for symptom change.

7
The Theory and Practice of Hypnoanalysis

As stated before in chapter 5, the hypnotherapist begins the treatment of most patients by employing symptomatic, hypnodynamic, (hypno-analytically oriented) approaches, or both. If these short-term approaches work, they will save the patient time and money. If they do not work, the therapist may decide to use hypnoanalysis, a relatively long-term treatment. It is modified psychoanalysis conducted while the patient, at least for part of the time, is in the hypnotic state (25% to 70% of the total treatment time). Because hypnosis enables the patient to make contact more easily with unconscious material and also intensifies the transference, hypnoanalysis works faster than psychoanalysis alone. What can be accomplished in psychoanalysis in 3 years usually can be done in hypnoanalysis in 1 year.

Hypnosis is not employed during every hour, or necessarily for the full duration of any therapy hour because the hypnoanalyst must help the patient work through the material in the waking state, too. Insight, we feel, is more effective and leads more readily to permanent change when it becomes fully conscious and does not occur only in unconscious or preconscious awareness. In addition, the transference in the hypnotic state may not be the same as that in the waking interaction between the patient and therapist, and both need to be interpreted. In some hypnoanalyses, trance is used only sporadically, at intervals of several months.

THE PSYCHOANALTIC THEORIES AND THEIR APPLICABILITY TO SPECIFIC NOSOLOGIC CATEGORIES

Psychoanalysis has existed for a century now. It originally revoled around the libido theory and was modified as other psychoanalytic theo-

---

[1] Earlier versions of some parts of this chapter appeared in *The International Journal of Clinical and Experimental Hypnosis*, 1968, *16*, 77–84; *Psychoanalytic Psychology*, 1984, *1*, 68–71; and Wester, William C. Wester II and Alexander Smith (Eds.) (1984). *Clinical Hypnosis: A Multidisciplinary Approach* (pp. 142–154). New York: Lippincott. Adapted by permission.

ries were added. By now a broad braid of four strands constitutes the fabric of psychoanalysis: the libido theory; ego psychology, which Freud (1923) also originated; object relations theory, which began in England in the late 1940s and in the United States in the 1950s; and the theory of the self, or the theory of narcissism, starting in the 1960s. According to the libido theory, the motivation behind all behavior is pleasure-seeking; ego psychology stresses the seeking of the joy that comes with the mastery of difficulties; object relations theory views pleasure-seeking behavior as the seeking of an "object," that is, making relationships, finding someone to love and be loved by; whereas self theory supplants libido theory by holding that the motivation of behavior is the development of self-experience and self-actualization, and the seeking of admiration. Depending on the nature of the patient's illness, one or another of these theories—more often a combination of all or some of them—will form the base of the hypnoanalytic treatment of a particular patient.

Classical Psychoanalysis—The Libido Theory

In the late 1890s, Breuer treated Miss Anna O, a classical case of hysteria, which was of great interest to Freud, with whom Breuer frequently discussed it. From Anna O's case, Freud discovered the existence of the unconscious, and psychoanalysis was born (Breuer & Freud, 1895/1955).

Classical psychoanalysis is to be understood as a reaction to the time in which it arose. It was a revolt against the Victorian era, with its stifling, too proper, too restrictive rules of behavior and its denial of the existence of female and infantile sexuality. Freud fought for the recognition of sexuality and its acceptance as an instinct, an all-human need, a vital drive. He believed it to be the source of all human energy. The libido theory states that all energy comes from the id and that the aim of the drives is to seek pleasure and avoid pain.

Freud postulated that the unconscious is the reservoir of the drives and that there were two basic inborn drives: libido, the erotic-sexual drive and aggression. Accordingly, the basic human emotions, which express these drives, are love and hate.

Classical psychoanalysts believe that the two sources of all conflict are environmental taboos and the person's own superego, which is the internalization of external moral demands. Freud (1908/1959) believed that conventional "civilized" morality led to repression of instinctual needs and wishes, preventing them from coming into consciousness and achieving normal gratification.

In his Topographical Model, the first model of the personality he developed, Freud (1900/1953) conceived of the personality as consisting of the unconscious (the deepest layer), the preconscious, and the conscious.

His method of therapy was based mainly on helping the patient make the unconscious become conscious; that is, helping the patient to bring repressed or otherwise defended-against wishes, feelings, thoughts, and memories into conscious awareness and squarely face them.

Ego Psychology

Between 1917 and 1923, Freud became aware that the Topographical Model of personality was inadequate. He (1923) therefore developed the Structural Model of the personality, comprising the id, the ego, and the superego. The id is totally unconscious; the ego and the superego has unconscious, preconscious, and conscious parts.

The ego organizes and structures information in relation to the outside world, such as perception, thinking, memory, and erects and maintains defenses. (For further elaboration, see A. Freud, 1936, and Hartmann, 1968.) The superego—the conscience—represents the internalization of parental prohibitions and values, what one feels one *ought* to do or *ought* to be. The ego ideal had earlier been introduced as that part of the personality representing the person that one aspires to be.

A new strand was being woven into psychoanalytic theory, namely, ego psychology. Psychoanalysts became interested not only in uncovering unconscious material, but also in the *structure* of the personality, particularly in the ego's role as intrapsychic mediator between the id and the superego and between the id and the outside reality. Psychoanalysts also became more interested in the inner strengths of the patient and the strategies their patients used to adapt to reality, to cope with it, to master it, or to change it into a better reality for themselves and others.

Object Relations Theory

By the late 1940s, a third strand was being added to the psychoanalytic braid—the theory of object relations. Object relations theorists (Fairbairn, 1952; Fraiberg, 1969; Guntrip, 1969; Kernberg, 1968, 1976; Modell, 1968; Mahler, Pine, & Bergman, 1975; Winnicott, 1953; Jacobson, 1973) believe that libido is not primarily pleasure-seeking, but rather object-seeking: We forever seek someone to love and be loved by. It is relationships with people that constitute true libidinal goals, not simply relief of tension or pleasure. The impressions and internal images we form from our interactions with people are "object representations." Object representations constitute an integral part of psychic structure. The internal matrix of images of others is the "representational world." In an object relationship a person invests his feelings of love or hate in another. To be able to make permanent object relations requires stability of the internal representation

of "the other" (Erikson, 1984), that is, object constancy. Object relationships develop from impressions of early infant–caregiver interactions
as the infant begins to move away from the early symbiotic mother–child
relationship. Mahler and her associates (1975) regard the entire life cycle
as a more or less successful process of distancing oneself—and internalization of—the lost "good" symbiotic mother people are eternally
longing for.

In object relations theory, the process of separation and individuation
(Mahler *et al.,* 1975) is much more important than conflicts about gratification of instinctual needs. But it does not totally eclipse them.

The Theory of the Self

Beginning in the 1960s, a fourth strand was added to the psychoanalytic
braid of theories: the theory of the self (Kernberg, 1975; Kohut, 1966,
1971, 1972, 1977; Lichtenberg, 1975; Ornstein, 1974). Ego psychology had
concerned itself for 40 years with the four parts of the personality (id, ego,
superego, and ego ideal), as if they were four separate people living
together and fighting among one another within one house, the total
personality or the "self." The self has a certain identity throughout its life
cycle (Erikson, 1968). Psychoanalysts became aware that even though
they knew a good deal about the components of the personality, they knew
very little about the whole, the self.

Moreover, they no longer were seeing many patients suffering from
neuroses; most patients had personality disorders. The narcissistic personality emerged as a new diagnostic phenomenon in the 1960s and 1970s.
These patients complained of feelings of emptiness and lack of self-worth.
But beneath their conscious feelings of worthlessness, they had unconscious feelings of grandiosity.

Particular times produce particular emotional illnesses. Just as the
Victorian Age, which did not allow women and children to become aware
of their sexuality, produced the hysterias, so the post-World War II era
produced the narcissistic personality as a general phenomenon among the
young. Children born after 1945 have never known a world without the
atom bomb and the abysmal fear that the nuclear holocaust will come
before they have a chance to grow up and take their place in the world.
Many of these people come from affluent homes, where they were mate-
rially indulged but emotionally deprived. The nuclear family and family
closeness were in a state of disintegration during their early childhood.
Their parents had lived through the Depression and war. They were
upwardly mobile and had developed strong expectations of the kind of life
they wanted for their children. But they failed to attune themselves to their
children's early separation-individuation needs (Mahler *et al.,* 1975) and to

show admiration for the accomplishments of their developing children—especially when these needs and accomplishments were at odds with the parents' expectations. The effect on the children was impairment of self-esteem. In the late 1960s, psychoanalysts began to analyze narcissistic and borderline patients and learned a great deal about the development of the self as an integral part of psychic structure. The most important authors in the development of this new area of psychoanalysis are Kohut (1971, 1977), Kernberg (1975, 1976), Masterson (1976, 1981), Bach (1977), and Adler (1981, 1985).

Applicability of the Four Psychoanalytic Theories to Specific Nosologic Categories

Contemporary hypnoanalysis uses any or all four strands of psychoanalytic theory, depending on the case. In working with neurotic patients who present with relatively circumscribed symptoms, the hypnoanalyst helps the patient into trance and then conducts an uncovering therapy based on classical libido theory and ego psychology. With narcissistic and borderline personality disorders, that is, patients who suffer from developmental arrests (Stolorow & Lachman, 1980), the hypnoanalyst puts the main emphases on correcting deficits in psychic structure, on working through conflicts around separation-individuation, and on developing the twin capacities to form stable object relations and maintain a cohesive self. Object relations theory and self theory address directly these issues. In working with psychotic patients, the hypnoanalyst does not attempt to uncover conflicts but does try to facilitate ego building or "progressive structuralization" (Gedo & Goldberg, 1973), by combining therapeutic methods based on ego psychology, object relations theory, and self psychology. All four psychoanalytic theories can be used in hypnoanalysis, the emphasis on one or the other depending on the case. Frequently more than one of the four psychoanalytic theories will underlie the hypnoanalytic treatment of the same case at different points (see chapter 9).

DIFFERENCES IN MENTAL FUNCTIONING BETWEEN THE WAKING STATE (PSYCHOANALYSIS) AND THE HYPNOTIC STATE (HYPNOANALYSIS)

Primary Process and Secondary Process

Freud (1900/1953) differentiated two modes of mental functioning, which he called primary process and secondary process. Primary process is the mental functioning typical of early childhood, before reality orientation and language have developed. The small child lives in a world not yet structured according to the reality principle. He thinks and acts as if anything were possible, even the impossible. Logical contradictions do not exist for him yet.

The main form of thinking in primary process is preverbal imagery (Ehrenzweig, 1953). In primary process functioning, energy is highly mobile and can be readily shifted. Functioning is still fluid and undifferentiated, and "interpenetrating condensations . . . can therefore . . . reconcile incompatible things" (Ehrenzweig, 1964, p. 381). Several ideas are often represented by a single image or, if language is used, by the possibility for a double meaning of a word or phrase. These phenomena are common occurrences in nocturnal dreams and in hypnosis, states in which the GRO has faded, and in jokes. (See the example of the pea "pot" and "pod" in this chapter.)

Slowly, as the child learns more about the reality around him, a new mode of functioning develops, the secondary process. Secondary process thinking is logical and sequential. Most often it is thinking in words and sentences, in language rather than in imagery. It results from the impact of reality and is reality oriented.

Primary process thinking is not given up when secondary process thinking develops. Both continue to interact: even in the adult waking state, our thoughts are hardly, if ever, devoid of some minor form of imagery; and even during nocturnal dreaming or in deep states of hypnosis, some traces of realism and logic can be found.

In the hypnotized adult, the typically strong increase in imagery over that in the waking state represents a reestablishment of the dominance of primary process functioning, with a regression in the service of the ego to the mode of cognitive activity characteristic of the early period of life. It is a shift downwards on the continuum from secondary process towards primary process (Fromm, 1978–79).

The Modes of Ego Functioning: Ego Activity, Ego Receptivity, Ego Inactivity, and Ego Passivity

The psychoanalytic theory of activity and passivity of the ego was initiated by Rapaport in 1953 (in Gill, 1967, pp. 530–568) and Hart (1961), and extended by Fromm (1972) and Stolar and Fromm (1974). The concept of ego receptivity, an important and exciting concept, was later added to Rapaport's scheme by Deikman (1971) and discussed with regard to the role it plays in hypnosis by Fromm (1976, 1977, 1979). Rapaport differentiated ego activity and passivity from active and passive behavior. He thus advanced psychoanalytic theory and provided an exciting, important distinction. Hart showed that the feeling of choicelessness is the center element of ego passivity. The ego is active or autonomous when the person can make an ego-syntonic choice; it is passive or lacks autonomy when the person is overwhelmed by instinctual drives (Rapaport, in Gill, 1967, pp. 530–568), by demands coming from the environment (Fromm, 1972), or by the superego (Stolar & Fromm, 1974).

Essentially, the issue of activity and passivity of the ego is tied to the concept of coping or failing to cope. There are two forms of coping: sovereign, masterful coping and protective, or defensive, coping. In both, the ego is active and maintains autonomy. In masterful coping, the ego actively meets the demands coming from the instincts, from reality, and from the superego and handles them creatively, or at least sovereignly, at its own pace and convenience. In protective coping, the person defends against these demands, but the action lacks free, smooth, and sovereign mastery. It presents only mastery of a lower order, namely, the best that can be done under the circumstances—a compromise. We define ego activity with regard to hypnotic trance as a volitional mental activity during trance. It is not the same as behavioral activity. Each can occur without the other. In heterohypnosis it can be a decision *not* to go along with what the hypnotist is suggesting or to go along with it because one *wants* to do it. In self-hypnosis, it can be a self-suggestion.

When the patient submits to ego-dystonic demands coming from the instincts, from the external world, or from the superego, the ego is passive. The patient goes along with the demands, even though he does not want to or because he feels overwhelmed and experiences that he *has* to submit. Both are forms of ego passivity. Ego passivity of the latter type occurs characteristically in psychoses, panic, catastrophic reactions, and brain washing; and in heterohypnosis when an authoritarian hypnotist forces a patient into doing, feeling, or experiencing something he definitely does not want to experience (Fromm, 1972). We define ego passivity as a state in which the patient feels overwhelmed or helpless and is unable to master the situation or exert active ego control. It is usually accompanied by unpleasant affect.

However, not all states in which active control and voluntarism are relinquished are states of ego passivity. Many are characterized by ego receptivity. In ego receptivity, critical judgment, strict adherence to reality orientation, and active, goal-directed thinking are held to a minimum, and the person allows himself to let unconscious and preconscious material float freely into his mind. There is an openess to experiencing, which William James (1892/1961) would have characterized as watching the stream of consciousness flow by. Ego receptivity is the prevailing state in heterohypnosis; it also occurs frequently in self-hypnosis (Fromm, Skinner, Lombard, & Kahn, in preparation). In heterohypnosis, the patient opens himself to the hypnotist and is more receptive to the therapist's suggestions than he would be in the waking state. Hypnotic suggestibility really is nothing more than heightened ego receptivity (Fromm, 1979). For self-hypnosis, we are defining ego receptivity as the patient's heightened ability to let unconscious or preconscious thoughts, feelings, or imagery come into awareness. Ego receptivity implies that the "gates" to primary process thoughts and images have opened more widely than they do in the waking state. Ego receptivity generally is an ego-syntonic state.

In the active ego mode, the organism is able to manipulate the environment. On the other hand, the receptive mode is organized around intake from the environment rather than its manipulation. In the receptive mode, one allows things to happen; one does not make them happen. Cognitively prelogical thought and imagery predominate over formal conceptual thought. The barriers between conscious awareness and the unconscious and preconscious are lowered, leading to a greater availability of unconscious material.

A fourth mode of the ego, which to our knowledge has not been reported before in the scientific literature, is ego inactivity. We do not know whether it exists in heterohypnosis, but we have come across it in our research on self-hypnosis (Fromm, Skinner, Lombard & Kahn, in preparation). It is the subject's feeling that while he has been in trance, nothing has been going on in his mind, and he has been doing nothing. A subject reporting about a self-hypnotic session, for instance, may say, "For 20 minutes nothing happened" or "I remained in trance without suggesting anything for quite a while, and I experienced nothing."

PRACTICE

Hypnoanalysis with neurotic patients has three parts: (a) uncovering unconscious conflicts, memories, affects, thoughts, and so on, against which the patient is defending himself—without piercing defenses too quickly; and (b) the "working through," which leads to (c) integration, mature coping, and mastery. In psychoanalysis, transference, a regressive phenomenon, is considered to be one of the most important tools for helping the patient. It is important also in hypnoanalysis, in all three parts of the hypnoanalytic process, the uncovering, the working through, and the healthy reintegration.

Uncovering the Unconscious Sources of Conflict

Classical psychoanalysis employs mainly four techniques for uncovering, all of which can be used in hypnoanalysis. They are: (a) free association; (b) dream interpretation; (c) interpretation of defenses and resistances; and (d) transference analysis.

Free Association

The hypnoanalyst uses free association very similarly to the psycho-analyst, except that in the hypnotic state associations more frequently appear in the form of imagery. Imagery is primary process mentation. It comes more directly from the unconscious than do most verbal associations given in the waking state. Conflicts, wishes, and defenses are more thinly disguised in hypnotic imagery, and thus the therapeutic process is accelerated (Reyher, 1963). Like the imagery of the nocturnal dream, hypnotic imagery—unless it is quite reality oriented—is the form in which free association takes place in altered states of consciousness (Fromm, 1984, p. 67). Patients who do not spontaneously report images should be encouraged to become more aware of all the different images that go through their mind in the hypnotic state and to report them, regardless of whether or not there seems to be a logical connection between them. Free association—mainly through images, but also through free verbal association—occurs in the uncovering process as well as in the working through and integration processes in hypnoanalysis. The following vignette is an example of how *imagery* in hypnosis can sometimes help a patient more than *verbal* free association in the waking state.

A graduate student at one of the Big Ten universities had become disenchanted with studying and wanted to leave the university. He felt vaguely depressed and listless and could not concentrate. The night before his hypnoanalytic hour, he dreamt that he saw a pot full of peas. In the waking state he was asked to free associate to it and said, "All peas look alike" and "I don't like pea soup." No other associations ensued, and he said he could not figure out the dream. When helped into trance, he produced a dream in which he dived into a lake. At first the water seemed to be muddy, but as he dived deeper, it became clearer and clearer. (The increasing clarity pictured his coming closer to understanding the dream.) At the bottom of the lake was a beautiful palace with a throne room. The throne was empty, but there were many people in the room: vassals, knights, beautiful ladies, and also many contenders for the throne. In the hypnotic dream, the patient tried very hard to get onto that throne, to win it for himself. He felt a strong need to be the king and struggled hard to get up to that throne ahead of all other contenders. Suddenly he said, "Oh, I know what this image and my dream of last night mean: I want to be better than everyone else. I want to be admired; I want to be the 'king.' But here at this university I am just one among many. We are all like peas in a pod. We are all more or less equally gifted. I want to be better than everybody else. I am depressed because I do not get the adulation of my peers, as I did in high school and in the small college I went to. I am not 'the best.'" Then, as an aside, he gave a verbal association, saying, "Isn't it interesting that in the dream there appeared a pot full of peas, in hypnosis a pod. Apparently I played with words without knowing it."

Dream Interpretation

The second classical psychoanalytic technique is dream interpretation. Freud (1900/1953) called the nocturnal dream "the royal road to the unconscious."

In dream interpretation one differentiates between the manifest and the latent content of the dream. The manifest content is what the dreamer actually sees or hears or does in the dream; the latent content is the unconscious or preconscious thought processes underlying the manifest content. Freud compared the total dream work to a mountain range partially submerged in the ocean, with the manifest content representing the tops of the highest mountains visible as islands above the surface of the sea. The latent content is comparable to the part of the mountain range that is submerged below the ocean's surface. In dream work, symbolism, condensation, displacement, and substitution are used rather than logical and formally organized thought. Therefore, the meaning of a dream often seems quite unintelligible at first.

The dreams of patients in therapy deal with conflicts—mainly, in Freud's view, with unresolved childhood conflicts. According to Freud (1900/1953), dreams represent a "primary wish-fulfilling process," which is interfered with by the "dream censor," that is, the conscience. In Freud's view, the motivating force for the dream is the instincts, which strive for expression and gratification; but the instincts are in conflict with the conscience.

Thomas French and Erika Fromm (1986) place more emphasis on ego processes in the dream and on its cognitive structure. They conceive of the dream as an ego function, a problem-solving attempt of the unconscious and the preconscious ego. The thoughts closer to consciousness show up in the manifest content; the more deeply unconscious thoughts are hidden beneath the surface, in the latent content. French and Fromm have also demonstrated that dreams are reactions to, and expressions of, a current conflict, a "focal conflict," that is, one in which the dreamer is involved in his *present* life situation. The dream may have roots in the past, but people do not dream about the past as such. The past has to be reactivated in the present, in the interrelationship of the patient with real-life figures, *here and now*. It is the here-and-now situation that gives rise to a disturbing wish within the patient. This disturbing wish in turn leads to and is in conflict with a reactive motive—guilt, fear, pride, shame, or a counterwish. Every dream contains one or more successful or unsuccessful attempts to solve the conflict (Fromm & French, 1962).

In initial attempts to interpret the dream, the psychoanalyst or hypnoanalyst often finds himself in a situation like that of Monsieur Broussard when he discovered the Rosetta Stone. The message of the dream—or parts of it—are written in hieroglyphs (the language of the patient's unconscious). It must be translated faithfully into the language of the waking state (the language of the conscious). How does the interpreter go about this task?

The interpreter should not just decode "symbols," for example, think that every oblong object is a penis symbol. Like the *good* translator of poetry from a foreign language and culture, who faithfully and artistically tries to recreate in the language of the translation the specific poetic atmosphere and quality of the original poem, so the dream interpreter must also recreate the dream's specific elusive atmosphere in order to make the dream meaningful to the patient's conscious mind.

Dream interpretation, like the understanding of the hypnotic patient's verbal and nonverbal communications, calls upon intuition. It requires also scientific self-discipline and the willingness to evaluate critically and conscientiously the ideas and hypotheses one has arrived at intuitively. The therapist must constantly check and recheck whether his intuitive hypnotheses about the meaning of the dream are really supported by the manifest content of the dream and the associations, need modification or refinement, or should be discarded because they are wrong.

In dream interpretation, the hypnoanalyst enjoys a distinct advantage over the psychoanalyst, who must wait, often for weeks, for the dream reports the patient brings in. Often there are none for quite a while. And psychoanalysts are always faced with the fact that much of the content of dreams—even those remembered—has been repressed, forgotten, or distorted. In hypnosis, however, there are a number of tools available to facilitate and improve working with dreams:

1. The hypnoanalyst can hypnotically induce dreams during the hypnotic session, dreams that the patient reports immediately after they are dreamt.

2. The hypnoanalyst can suggest that the patient dream about a particular conflict or problem the therapist is trying to help him solve.

3. If the patient has not come to a solution by means of the dream, the hypnoanalyst can ask him to dream it again—perhaps with a different manifest content—and to try again to cope with the same problem, either in a different manner or on a different level. The therapist can encouragingly tell the patient that he will find better and better solutions in his continuing attempts at re-dreaming (Sacerdote, 1978).

4. The hypnoanalyst can suggest that the patient will be better able to understand the symbolism and meaning of his dreams as time goes on.

In addition to these four useful ways of employing hypnotic dreams, the hypnoanalyst has two other valuable techniques at his disposal. First, in hypnoanalysis (in contrast to psychoanalysis), the analyst recourse to the posthypnotic suggestion. The hypnoanalyst can give the patient a posthypnotic suggestion that during the week to come he will dream some important dreams at night, which, even if he should forget them, will rise into consciousness and be remembered by him as soon as he steps into the therapist's office the next week. Then the therapist can explore with the patient the full dream product and interpret it, rather than being forced not to work with dreams because the patient forgets them.

Finally, it happens not infrequently in hypnoanalysis that when the patient—particularly one who is only in light trance—is asked to dream during the current hour, he will hypermnestically remember an old nocturnal dream he had never reported before. Usually this is a very important dream he had earlier repressed. Or he may produce a hypnotic daydream, which also can be gainfully interpreted.

As Freud (1900/1953) said, the dream is the royal road to the unconscious, but the dream is only one of many roads. Hypnosis is another. The psychoanalyst, whose patient is not in hypnosis, talks to the conscious ego, and only through the dream and slips of the tongue does the patient's unconscious communicate directly with the psychoanalyst. When the patient is in hypnosis, particularly in deep hypnosis, the hypnotist can also get directly to the patient's unconscious by means of imagery, age regression, and hypermnesia; and the patient's unconscious can answer directly. Therefore, hypnosis can bring about improvements or cures more quickly.

Dealing with Defenses and Resistances

The interpretation of defenses and resistances, an essential part of psychoanalysis as well as of hypnoanalysis, should be handled carefully, gently, and respectfully. While often it is clear quite early what the patient is defending against, defenses should not be pierced too quickly. Like underlying wishes, defenses often are expressed through imagery. The following case, as reported by one of the authors (E. F.), illustrates:

A highly sensitive, artistic graduate student, who wanted to become a writer or a musician, came for hypnoanalysis because he wanted to know whether he was a homosexual. He had both homosexual and heterosexual fantasies but never dared to approach either men or women and led a totally celibate life. He told me about his father, a Midwestern farmer, who wanted his son to step into his footsteps and who objected to the son's choice of profession.

Consciously it was clear to the patient that his father conceived of his artistic interests as being 'feminine.' But I had the feeling that much more was involved in this patient's doubts about his sexual identity and his need to keep away from any sexual contact. Using the Theater Technique, I suggested, when the patient was in a rather deep trance, that we would go to a theater, sit down in our seats, and see a play that in some ways was connected with his problem. I described the beautiful red velvet curtain that was now being pulled up. As it was going up, the patient suddenly said, "Uh-uh, the rope broke. The curtain has fallen down." I tacitly recognized this as a defense. The patient was not yet ready to look more deeply at his problem. I explained that he could relax some more while the curtain was being repaired, a process I described in elaborate imagistic detail. A little later I said that the rope was now repaired, the play could begin, and the curtain again was being pulled up. When the curtain was halfway up, the patient informed me that the rope had broken again. Not only that, he said, but now a gold-colored metal curtain had come down, too, totally shutting the stage off from vision. Thus, through imagery, the patient told me in unmistakable terms that he still needed to protect himself from finding out more about the roots of his problem, that he was not yet ready for such uncovering. It would have been wrong to pierce this defense at that time. So I dropped the subject for a while.

A month later we again went through the imagery of going to a theater. This time no curtain fell. The patient saw on the stage an older man who was sexually attacking a young boy. This brought up a hitherto totally repressed memory from when he was between 9 and 12 years old. He had had to sleep in the same bed with his grandfather who a number of times attempted to abuse him sexually. The patient could now see the deeper dynamics of his homosexual fears: his grandfather's incestuously abusing him in preadolescence.

In psychoanalysis the most common forms of resistance are blocking and coming late to an appointment. In hypnoanalysis they are: refusing to go into trance or avoiding it, not allowing oneself to "let go," lightening the trance, blocking, and the production of imagery that symbolizes resistance (e.g., an iron curtain falling down).

In hypnoanalysis, interpretation of resistances is not necessarily pursued as assiduously as it is in psychoanalysis. At times the hypnoanalyst interprets resistances, but more often, he accepts their existence silently and does not draw them into the focus of interpretive activity. The hypnoanalyst notes the patient's resistances, and he notes when the patient resists. Then the hypnoanalyst tries to think of ways to word his therapeutic suggestions so that the patient does not need to resist. Only if this does not work does the hypnoanalyst draw the patient's attention to his resistance so that they can analyze it together. On the whole, in hypnoanalysis one makes somewhat less of resistance as a cornerstone of therapy than one does in psychoanalysis. Morcover, because in the hypnotic state the subject or patient characteristically has a strong wish to cooperate with the hypnotist and to please him, resistances are not quite as frequent as they are in waking-state psychoanalysis.

Transference

Transference is a psychoanalytic term indicating that the patient distortedly perceives, unrealistically feels about, and behaves toward his therapist according to the impressions formed about significant figures in childhood. He sees his therapist—who is part of his current world—through the tinted glasses of the past. Whether the glasses are rose colored or dark, the patient unconsciously tries to re-enact with his therapist important relationships he has had with others earlier in life (Fromm, 1968). In psychoanalysis one speaks of positive and negative transferences: A patient who is in a period of positive transference loves and idealizes his therapist; in a negative transference he hates him. Both kinds of transferences have to be worked through.

Transference feelings, very strong in psychoanalysis, are even stronger in hypnotherapy and hypnoanalysis. Hypnosis brings into focus, even more rapidly and more deeply than psychoanalysis does, conflicts and repressed affects associated with internal object representations.

There are three major general categories of transference: (a) neurotic transferences; (b) selfobject transferences, and (c) psychotic and borderline transferences. For the best advantage to the patient, each category requires a separate method and procedure.

The Neurotic Transference.   Neurotic transferences are based on stable internal representations of self and others, in which patterns of repetitive maladaptive behaviors are associated with affective distortions in the perception of others as well as with disavowal of certain of one's own impulses and affects. Neurotics do form stable object relationships—an ability lacking in borderline patients and in psychotics. But neurotics have difficulties in these relationships. The reason is that they often unrealistically transfer to people in their current environment feelings they had toward their parents or siblings in the past.

In neurotic transferences, three subtypes can be found: (a) infantile dependency transferences, (b) oedipal transferences, and (c) sibling transferences.

The hypnotic situation tends to foster infantile dependency transferences, especially in the beginning. Frequently the patient who comes for hypnotherapy expects the hypnotist to take care of him, to solve all his problems, while he, the patient, is "asleep." Such a patient wants to be dependent. Unrealistically, he sees the hypnotist as the omniscient, omnipotent parent. He may fantasize that he is being held in the therapist's arms, nursed, and rocked. Transference feelings are unrealistic; in the transference the patient may overlook such "minor" details as the real sex of the therapist. He can make a man into a mother figure, a woman into a father figure. In either case, he may want the hypnotist to make decisions for him, as his father or his mother used to do when he was a child. The patient expects to be taken care of, either as he was taken care of in his early childhood by his parents or as he wishes he had been.

The oedipal complex has two sides: the desire to have a love relationship with the parent of the opposite sex and the desire to win the object of one's love away from the parent of the same sex, whose wrath one fears. Similarly, the oedipal transference in hypnosis can take two forms: seduction (ingratiation) or fierce competition coupled with death wishes. In hypnoanalysis, all of these archaic feelings are transferred to the hypnotherapist. A female patient may fantasize that the male hypnotist lures her to him, holds her in his strong arms, seduces her. Another may bring a lawsuit against her male hypnotherapist for supposedly having attacked her sexually while she was in a trance. In the latter instance, wish and fear have merged into one fantasy, which to the patient has in turn become a psychic reality. When such a woman patient was between the ages of 3 and 5, she experienced the normal oedipal wish of every little girl: that her father take the initiative and have a sexual relationship with her. But she has not resolved this oedipal wish; in her unconscious it keeps throbbing, and later she transfers this wish to the hypnotist. She wishes to be seduced by the male hypnotist. In bringing suit, she is unconsciously revenging herself on the therapist/father for *not* having seduced her. She blames the seductive wish on the hypnotist, transferring to him the unfulfilled hope she had for her father. Being in trance, "asleep," and not actively doing the seducing, makes it more possible in her own mind to rid herself of the responsibility.

Frequently in hypnoanalysis the patient acts out old sibling rivalries through a transference. The patient becomes very competitive. For example, one of the authors (E. F.) had a hypnoanalysis patient, a woman in an allied profession, who had one sister. The patient never went into more than a very light trance with me. In her first hour she asked me to teach her autohypnosis. I did. Subsequently she told me several times that at home, when practicing autohypnosis, she could get herself into a much deeper state than I could help her enter. Clearly, sibling rivalry here reared its head: "I can do better than you can."

Would it have been helpful to interpret the sibling rivalry to the patient in hypnosis? I do not think so. She would have felt uncomfortable, ill at ease, guilty. Competitiveness can become a useful tool, provided the therapist does not feel the need to be the patient's savior. If the patient also can use autohypnosis effectively, why not let her? In traditional psychoanalysis, one analyzes all transference phenomena. In hypnoanalysis it is sometimes wiser not to make the patient aware of every transference feeling that comes up. At times one can do more constructive work by utilizing transference feelings in hypnoanalysis than by analyzing them. In the case of this patient with the need to outshine me, I praised her while she was in heterohypnosis for her competence in autohypnosis. I told her how pleased I was that she was learning to help herself go into trance, and I even suggested that at home, in the evening, she put herself into a much deeper trance than I could put her in—and that memories and images would come to her that would shed new light on her major problems, alcoholism and compulsive overeating. Moreover, what she would bring in during each hour following self-hypnosis would furnish ample material for the hypnoanalysis. Later I could suggest to her that she would soon find herself as competent in dealing with her problems as she was in putting herself into trance.

In addition to the three above-named general categories of neurotic transference, there are, of course, more specific transference feelings and reactions worthy of examination. For example, a patient whose mother had suddenly died one night when he was 4 years old and asleep had great difficulty going into anything but the lightest stages of trance. Every once in a while he exhibited in his light trances a curious, minute, pulling-up movement of his head and shoulders—as if he wanted to alert himself or prevent himself from going down into a deeper trance. At the end of most of his hypnotic sessions, he would become very solicitous about me, asking me how I felt, wondering whether I was tired, remarking that he must be a strain on me. As he was my last patient of the day, we often left the building together, and he would always insist on carrying my brief case or my books to my car. At first I thought this was gallantry, but then I realized that the behavior, both in and out of trance, was an expression of the same transference reaction: The patient pictured me as weak, was afraid I might die and leave him . . . as his mother had done. Further hypnoanalytic work revealed his unconscious fantasy that his mother had died because she had had to work too hard to support him. The father had deserted the mother a few months after the patient was born.

When he next made this curious head and shoulder movement in trance, I quietly said to him, "You don't need to be afraid of making demands on me. I am strong. I am not going to die." The patient heaved a great sigh, relaxed, and immediately went into much deeper trance. I then interpreted to him that he imagined he was responsible for his mother's death.

In the hypnoanalysis of patients on the narcissistic-borderline-psychotic continuum, the therapist takes on a much more active role in *making* himself into a transference object that fulfills the particular needs of these patients—and even their changing needs at different times—than he does when treating the neurotic patient. Only in that way can he help them correct their developmental deficit and move on to growth and maturation.

The Selfobject Transference of the Narcissistic Patient.   Patients with narcissistic pathology superficially function well in relationships. But they suffer from a deficit in self-esteem and associated feelings of worthlessness. They compensate with an unconscious grandiose self-image and feelings of elation. If in the rapprochement period (ages 16–25 months) of the separation-individuation phase of development (Mahler *et al.*, 1975) the caregiver frequently was unable to gauge and gratify the toddler's alternating needs for autonomy and dependency—which can change from moment to moment—and to admire the child's attempts at coping, mastery, and self-expression, lasting deficits in self-esteem result.

Narcissistic personalities form transferences characterized by this developmental failure. The narcissistic patient's self-esteem is highly vulnerable to the therapist's limitations and occasional failures in empathy. The mildly narcissistic patient reacts to these failures with disappointment and anger; highly narcissistic patients, with disillusionment and rage (Kohut, 1972). Nevertheless, the narcissist is capable of forming a stable selfobject transference (Adler, 1981, 1985; Kohut, 1971, 1977; Gedo & Goldberg, 1973). A selfobject is a person the young child selects and uses to provide functions that are essential for the development of self-esteem, functions he as yet is unable to provide for himself. Narcissists suffer from a developmental deficit in self-esteem, for which they attempt to compensate by obtaining from the therapist, through the selfobject transference, what they have not yet internalized, namely, feelings of self-worth and healthy pride in their own accomplishments. To the extent that the therapist provides "mirroring" (Kohut, 1971) and admiration, the narcissistic patient experiences well-being; whenever the therapist fails to do that, self-esteem plummets, and the patient becomes depressed. The self-esteem of narcissistic people is dependent on what others think of them.

The hypnoanalyst must actively put himself in the role the mother did not fulfill satisfactorily in the patient's preoedipal childhood. At least for a while, he must empathically be the always available mother, who thinks so highly of her child and admires the child so much that the patient can begin to develop solid self-confidence.

The Borderline Transference.   The patient with borderline personality organization manifests a deficit in the integration of object representations. Failures in the two earliest subphases of the separation-individuation period (Mahler, 1972)—via the repeated extremes of emotional abandonment or overprotectiveness (Masterson, 1976) on the part of the caregiver and considerable inconsistency in the caregiving (Mahler et al., 1975)—contribute to deficits in the structuralization of the internal world. Object representations remain poorly integrated or are split. "For the borderline personality, the choice in close relationships is between attachment that symbolizes engulfment and loss of identity, and separation that evokes feelings of loss and abandonment" (Copeland, 1986, p. 158). In borderline patients, object representations are highly unstable and vulnerable to fragmentation. Borderline patients form transferences characterized by these developmental failures. Unlike narcissistic patients, borderline patients are unable to form stable selfobject transferences (Adler, 1981, 1985). The transference is, instead, characterized by boundary diffusion, splitting (Kernberg, 1975), panic states (Buie & Adler, 1982), and transient loss of or fragmentation of self- and object representations (Giovacchini, 1979). The hypnoanalyst must provide a safe and facilitating environment in which the patient can recapitulate the development of the early subphases of the separation-individuation period (Mahler et al., 1975) with a better parent figure and in which he can explore his own self, in the relationship with the hypnoanalyst, in a safe climate, or what Winnicott (1965) has called a "holding environment." The hypnoanalyst must provide soothing when the patient is anxious; he must help to develop object constancy and overcome "splitting"; he must freely and unstintingly give a great deal for a long time. The hypnoanalyst should provide for the borderline (and the psychotic) patient an emotional environment that is nurturing, stable, protective, and constant. He must "hold" the boundaries of reality as the good mother does when she holds the infant, so that the patient can fully internalize a sense of demarcation between the "me" and the "not-me," the self and the other.

Baker (1981), Fromm (1984), and Copeland (1986) have found that the hypnoanalyst must be much more active and directive in building up the therapeutic scenario for the borderline and the psychotic than for the neurotic or even for the narcissistic patient. By asking the borderline patient to visualize the distorted bad self- and object representations that have been internalized, the hypnoanalyst can help the patient bring these representations into awareness and find ways to deactivate them or integrate them with the good ones in healthy ways. As a transference object, starting at a somewhat earlier developmental level than he needs to do with narcissistic patients, the hypnoanalyst must help the patient to overcome splitting and develop solid object and self-constancy. Once progress in treatment has made possible the internalization of the hypnoanalyst as the good object, the therapist also at times must put himself in the position of the sometimes frustrating mother figure who cannot fulfill *all* of the patient's demands. He can do that only when the patient's ego structure has become stable enough so that the hypnoanalyst is integrated in the patient's inner life and is perceived as a constant object, in place of the alternating good and bad object of earlier phases of treatment. In chapter 8 we discuss the newly developed methods for the hypnoanalysis of narcissistic, borderline, and psychotic patients. To repair the developmental deficit, the therapeutic process with such patients should parallel the phases of normal preoedipal development.

The Psychotic Transference.   The psychotic patient forms a transference based on poorly developed object representations (Modell, 1968) and a lack of a cohesive sense of self. The boundaries between the internal representations for self and others are barely differentiated (Blatt & Wild, 1976; Jacobson, 1973). At times the psychotic is unable to distinguish clearly between the self and the other, or between the self and the world. His representational world is poorly differentiated and poorly integrated. Unassimilated internal representations, or introjects, often carry on a quasi-autonomous existence. A variety of these unintegrated introjects become activated at different times and influence the psychotic's perception of others in a fluid and unstable manner (Volkan, 1976). The internal images on the basis of which the psychotic perceives the therapist during the hours are often distorted, frightening, grotesque, and fragmented; at other times, the therapist may be perceived in equally unrealistic, idyllic terms (Blatt, Schimek, & Brenneis, 1980; Smith, 1977). These highly unrealistic perceptions are rudimentary adaptive attempts by the patient to construct a positive, albeit distorted, representational world by forming a psychotic transference. The psychotic patient creates for himself an illusory environment oriented around his own needs and wishes (Modell, 1968).

Until recently it was generally assumed by psychoanalysts that psychotics can form neither object nor transference relationships. Therefore, it was assumed, they could not be analyzed. Burnham, Gladstone and Gibson (1969) opened up new vistas for the psychoanalytic treatment of psychotics. Although the object relations of the psychotic are at times very distorted and unstable, he nevertheless still has some capacity for object relationships. The psychotic patient does form a different type of transference. Burnham and his associates have conceptualized the basic problem of the psychotic transference by calling it the need-fear dilemma. The psychotic needs others in order to define himself as a person, apart from them. However, the psychotic fears that by making contact with "the other" (Erikson, 1984), he will be swallowed up, lose his own weakly established boundaries, and merge with the object. Because he fears this, he attempts to withdraw from all object relationships. But, then again, by withdrawing, he loses "the other," whom he so desperately needs to preserve the self. The dilemma of the psychotic is that he continually alternates between seeking self-definition through an external object and fearful withdrawal from it. He behaves in the same way in his relationship with the therapist. Like transference manifestations with other types of patients, this pattern of relationship can be interpreted and worked through in the transference in hypnoanalysis.

Countertransferences

Therapists, too, sometimes look at patients through the distorting lenses of the past. They may feel for and about certain patients, and react to them, as if these patients were important figures from their own past. If, when this occurs, the hypnoanalyst does not become aware of his own unconscious countertransference feelings toward the patient, the therapy suffers. The therapist must either analyze his countertransference immediately and resolve it quickly, or he must transfer the patient to another therapist (Fromm, 1968).

A few years ago, a college student came to me (E. F.) with a request for hypnotherapy. He could not concentrate, he said. He could not do his homework. In a few weeks he would have to pass his comprehensive examinations. I liked the boy on sight, and I took him on for therapy.

The patient had little hypnotic talent and experienced only extremely light stages of trance. In general, I had the impression that he felt it was all up to the hypnotist; she could do the work for him, both his homework and the hypnotic work. I saw him three times and tried with all means at my disposal to help him go into trance. During the second hour it occurred to me that the boy's head looked from the back like that of one of my brothers. I also became aware of a feeling of slight resentment toward the boy. The resentment was mixed with a feeling of fondness.

When in the third hour the feeling of resentment grew, I decided that I had to do some self-analysis after the hour. The physical resemblance to my brother struck me more and more: the boy had black hair and large, light, luminous eyes—like my brother. He looked as my brother had looked as an adolescent. And suddenly it dawned on me why I felt resentment. For years my brother had induced me to do his homework for him. He had been a very difficult adolescent, and in his quarrels with the authority figures—our parents—I always had to be the go-between who would pull the "chestnuts out of the fire" for him.

I had analyzed the countertransference, and under normal circumstances I would have been able to continue to do therapy with this young man. But at that time circumstances beyond my control made me particularly careful about perhaps unresolvable reminders of such a countertransference. Just a few weeks before, my brother, who lived on another continent, had suddenly become seriously ill. I knew his illness was terminal and progressing rapidly. Chances were that his death would throw me into another countertransference reaction to the patient, namely, that I would transfer all my love for and resentment towards the lost brother onto the patient (at least during the mourning period). For these reasons, it was in the best interest of the patient to transfer him to another hypnotherapist.

The story has an epilogue. The countertransference danger I had thought might possibly occur, indeed did occur, as an unconscious process. Three years later, while driving my car, I noticed a young man on a bicycle. I thought I recognized him as a hypnotic subject whom one of my students had used once in class half a year before. I also thought I remembered that the young man had indicated he would like to be a subject in other experiments. I honked my horn, beckoned him to come over, stopped the car in the middle of the street (holding up traffic), and asked the young man whether he would be willing to come and be an experimental subject for me. I did not recognize him as a former patient until he said something about therapy. Then I suddenly remembered the "resemblance" to my brother, which had been clear to me then, but which was not really much of a resemblance.

It is not usually my habit to beckon young men on the street, nor to collect experimental subjects in this way. I unconsciously had attempted to revive a relationship with the object of my brother-countertransference, in order to replace the relationship with my brother, who had died 3 years earlier.

Pregenital Parent Countertransferences.   Several main kinds of countertransference feelings and attitudes occur in therapists. There is the hypnotist who has never quite given up his early childhood belief in the omnipotence and omniscience of parents. He transfers this devout attitude of God-likeness from his parents onto his patients and feels they know all he thinks about while he is hypnotizing. If he is an experimental researcher, he may be unrealistically convinced that his subjects can sense his hypotheses and what results he hopes to obtain in his hypnotic experiments. He may insist on double-blind procedures in his hypnotic experiments. Although unconscious communication between the hypnotist and the patient or subject can exist, it remains to be examined in each case whether unconscious communication or the hypnotist's countertransference fantasy was at work.

Another form is the Oedipal-Sexual Countertransference. The male hypnotherapist who talks to most patients in a seductive manner, regardless of what the patient's needs are, belongs in this category. As a hypnotherapist, he is a Don Juan. He has never overcome the disappointment of his mother's oedipal rejection and now seeks to seduce many instead of the one who did not accept him in his father's stead when he was 3 or 4 years old.

A variation on this theme is the objectively competent hypnotherapist who is subjectively plagued by self-doubt. He fears that he cannot help a patient or that the patient will see through him and recognize him as a "fraud." The little boy who played doctor when he was 5 years old or the little girl who dressed up in her mother's dress and high heels indeed was a "fraud." They pretended to be grownups and feared being "cut down to size" after a while by the real adults in their environment.

The hypnotist constantly plagued by self-doubt can also be a narcissistic personality suffering from feelings of lack of self-worth. The other side of the coin is the narcissistic hypnotherapist, who grandiosely thinks he cures all of his patients within a few hours (and does not follow them up).

A third form, Sibling Countertransference, can be found in the hypnotherapist who—again, regardless of the *patient's* needs—turns every hypnotherapy hour into a contest he must win. He must win by getting the patient into deep trance, even though the patient prefers or needs only lighter trances; and win by wresting away all of the patient's secrets, symptoms, and conflicts without respecting the patient's more healthy defenses or the patient's need for different timing. Frequently this countertransference attitude goes back to competition with the father or to sibling rivalry and the childhood wish to be the winner in the peer group. There are, of course, other types of sibling and parent countertransferences. As Gruenewald (1971b) has shown, the hypnotherapist's unresolved dependency needs, unconscious conflicts about aggression, and need for power and control can impede effective hypnotherapy.

Transferences are useful material in hypnoanalysis. The hypnotherapist uses them to point out to the patient that he stands with one foot in the past—which makes it difficult for him to walk in the present, cope with his current situation, and enjoy life to the fullest. Countertransferences are obstacles to helping the patient, because, when unrecognized and unconscious, they cause the therapist to see the patient unrealistically, as if the patient were partially a re-edition of a beloved or hated figure out of the hypnotist's past. The hypnotherapist must recognize, analyze, and resolve his countertransferences without delay, or he cannot help his patient.

Countertransferences When Treating Narcissistic, Borderline, and Psychotic Patients.   Working with narcissistic patients is always difficult and easily can lead to a number of specific countertransferences (see Doroff, 1976; Giovacchini, 1972; Kernberg, 1975; Kohut, 1971). Kernberg conceives of a continuum of countertransference reactions ranging from those related to the neuroses to those in response to psychotic reactions, "a continuum in which the different reality and transference components of both patient and therapist vary in a significant way" (Kernberg, 1975, p. 54). However, there is a qualitative difference between therapists' countertransferences to neurotic patients and their countertransferences to the severely narcissistic, borderline, and psychotic patients. With patients in the latter three categories, the therapist's reaction is not so much due to specific problems in his own past as it is to the patient's intense or chaotic transference violating the therapist's boundaries and privacy. The tremendous demands the narcissist makes upon the therapist's time and patience, the patient's unwillingness to "let go," and his exploitativeness (of which the patient often is quite unaware; see the case history in chapter 9, this volume), his unconsciously attempting existentially to annihilate the therapist (Doroff, 1976) cause anger and resentment in the therapist. Frequently they bring him to the point where he loses his patience or becomes so fed up that he gets rid of the patient prematurely. Some therapists are unable to impose any limits and consequently accumulate more and more resentment against the patient, which certainly does not help the therapy. Such patients in their transference activate primitive object relations and in turn evoke in the therapist a strong emotional response. The therapist feels that the patient is imposing on him for very long times the preoedipal role of the mother who is supposed to have no other interests than caring for him and mirroring his achievements. Like many mothers of very young children, the therapist feels robbed of individuality and freedom, tied down by the patient, resentful of the patient's wanting to chain the transference object to himself, and fears he will lose his identity as a person in his own right. Such emotions may temporarily interfere with the therapist's neutrality.

Thus, what usually in the literature is called the countertransference to psychotic, borderline, or narcissistic patients is really the therapist's here-and-now reaction to patients who attempt to take away his freedom and autonomy. In the current psychoanalytic literature such feelings toward patients who suffer from developmental deficits also are called countertransference. We think this is a misnomer and would prefer to restrict the term "countertransference" to its original meaning, namely, the therapist's seeing the patient in an unrealistic way by transferring onto him characteristics of people who were important to the therapist in his own childhood.

The hypnoanalytic methods described so far in this chapter derive from psychoanalytic uncovering techniques for neurotics or psychoanalytic techniques for helping patients suffering from developmental deficits. That is, we have described so far how the hypnoanalyst uses psychoanalytic tools while the patient is in trance. These tools are strengthened by the increased production of imagery and primary process (Gruenewald, Fromm & Oberlander, 1979) that are essential features of the hypnotic state, as well as by the possibility of giving the patient permissive, open-ended suggestions to encourage him to employ more of his inner potential for problem solving and growth than he ordinarily makes use of in the waking state.

FURTHER HYPNOANALYTIC TECHNIQUES

In addition to employing the four classical methods derived from psycho-analysis (free association, dream interpretation, dealing with defenses and resistances, and transference analysis) as well as principles based on object relations theory and self psychology, hypnoanalysts make use of phenomena specific to the hypnotic state or to altered states of con-sciousness in general, which enable them to help their patients faster than would be possible when the patient is awake and reality oriented. We are referring here to such hypnotic phenomena as age regression, hyperm-nesia, automatic writing, dissociation, and heightened imagery. They have been invested by hypnoanalysts with psychoanalytic substructures that serve as guidelines for their use in hypnoanalysis and in dynamically oriented hypnotherapy. The most important of these techniques are:

(a) Age Regression
   i)   for the recovery of repressed memories and affects
   ii) for tracing earlier developmental stages of personality organi-zation
(b) Hypermnesia for the recovery of repressed memories
(c) Guided imagery and spontaneously arising heightened imagery
(d) Dissociation of the observing ego from the experiencing ego
(e) Automatic writing, drawing, and painting

They are genuine phenomena of the hypnotic state, phenomena that hypnoanalysts use psychodynamically to help the patient uncover, face, and integrate disturbing material previously held under the repression barrier or otherwise defended against.

In chapter 4 we gave the wordings, in chapters 5 and 6 we discussed how and when these techniques are employed in psychoanalytically oriented hypnotherapy. Because these techniques are used in the same way in hypnoanalysis as they are in psychoanalytically oriented, more short-term hypnotherapy, we shall not describe them again in this chapter.

THE PROCESSES OF INTEGRATION, GROWTH, AND MASTERY

Once the therapist has helped the patient gain insight into his conflict, he must help him resolve it. He must help him gain the strength to master and overcome his difficulties so that he can build for himself a new, productive, joyful life. The real purpose of hypnoanalysis is to facilitate maturity and continued growth.

Classical psychoanalysis originally conceived of maturity as a final plateau of growth reached by the healthy person at the end of adolescence. Through Erik Erikson's work (1950; 1984), however, psychoanalysts have learned that growth continues throughout the normal life span. In full adulthood, even in old age, it still can be either facilitated or hampered.

Certain ego psychological concepts can be applied in hypnoanalysis to facilitate personal growth. They are: (a) the use of imagery and fantasy, (b) the Ego Ideal Technique, and (c) coping, mastery, and the joy of functioning at one's full level of competence.

The Use of Imagery and Fantasy, and the Rehearsal Technique

Human beings have two types of fantasy: (a) symbolic fantasy (imagery), which is the cognitive mode of the unconscious ego, and (b) reality-testing fantasy, the fantasy one uses to plan ahead for realistic situations, thinking out what one might say or do in a difficult situation one has to face. The hypnotherapist employs both types of fantasy. He makes use of symbolic imagery in hypnotherapy by, for instance, symbolizing to the patient the process of his movement from illness towards health as a wide and turbulent river the patient has to cross or as a mountain he has to climb. Reality testing in fantasy may be used to deal, for example, with a flying phobia. The hypnotherapist may describe for the patient, step by step, the details of his driving to the airport, checking his bags, going through the security check, entering the plane, settling himself down comfortably with a book, and finding that book so engrossing that throughout the whole trip his attention is riveted to it and he is not aware of any discomfort about flying. Or, in hypnosis, the hypnotherapist may put a patient who is afraid of being interviewed for a new job through a rehearsal of that dreaded interview, step by realistic step. By putting him through such a rehearsal several times, that is to say, *by testing reality in fantasy* in the hypnotic state, the therapist can help him to gain mastery in reality. Reality testing in fantasy in the presence of the supportive hypnotherapist leads to the development of coping mechanisms previously not available to the patient (Frankel, 1976). In his imagery in hypnosis, the patient gains mastery over the feared situation. This mastery enables him then to approach the realistic situation with greater courage and with much more confidence about being able to handle it. Thus, the patient transfers the sense of success from the imagined to the real situation on the basis of the simple principle, "Nothing succeeds like success."

Why and how can fantasy in hypnoanalysis help the patient find better solutions to his problems? In the normal course of healthy growing up, a central regulating factor arises, which Hartmann (1958) has called the "inner world"—the world of imagery, fantasy, memory, and thinking. The inner world makes possible a two-step adaptation process: temporary withdrawal from the external world followed by return to the external world with improved mastery. The inner world allows one to step back, look, and think things over—and then to act with improved mastery. Hartmann called this process an "adaptive regression;" Kris (1952) called it "regression in the service of the ego," a psychoanalytic concept on which Gill and Brenman (1959) based their theory of hypnosis. For the limited duration of the hypnotic hour, the patient lets reality fade into the backgound of his awareness, engages in his inner world of imagery, gains insight or relaxation, and then returns to the world of reality, frequently with improved mastery.

In the ordinary waking state one must be reality-oriented and must think mostly in reality-oriented, logical ways. Hypnosis, because it is an altered state rather than the reality-oriented waking state, gives the therapist a better chance to use fantasy (i.e., imaginative thinking in visual, auditory, or other sensory forms) instead of or in addition to logical, sequential thought. This is so because in hypnosis the patient functions much more frequently with his unconscious ego than he does in the waking state. Learning to go into hypnosis can be compared to learning to snorkel. To the beginning snorkeler, a whole new world opens up: the brilliant, colorful world of life below the surface of the tropical oceans—an enchanting new world. Similarly, to the person in hypnosis or in self-hypnosis a totally new world, his own inner world, opens up. If he is healthy, he will get enormous enjoyment from looking at his inner world. If he is emotionally sick, the experience may not be so enjoyable, but hypnoanalysis can help him to deal with and tame his inner-world monsters. It may also help him to become aware of resources and assets within himself which before may have lain untapped and unrecognized below the surface.

The Ego Ideal Technique

Another psychoanalytic concept we have found most useful to work with in hypnoanalysis is the Ego Ideal. Psychoanalytic ego psychology differentiates between the superego (the conscience) and the ego ideal. "The superego's main function is to set boundaries; the ego ideal sets goals" (Stolar & Fromm, 1974, p. 301). The ego ideal represents what one hopes to be or strives to be. If one does not reach one's level of aspiration, one feels shame—shame about not being as grown up, or as competent, or as perfect as one would like to be.

The hypnoanalyst can help a patient learn to cope with something he dreads by literally bringing the ego ideal into the therapy, as if the ego ideal were a real person. For instance, the hypnoanalyst may suggest to the patient that someone who looks very much like him and who is the person the patient would *like* to be, steps into the room, sits down at the other end of the couch, and tells how he has joyfully and competently mastered the goals the patient would like to reach. Here is an example: Kate, a female medical student, had a fear of blood. She fainted whenever she saw it, but she wanted to become a physician. The hypnoanalyst brought into the office her ego ideal (whom they named Melissa), a competent young woman physician, able to bandage a child's bleeding wound or to do surgery when needed. "Melissa" told Kate that she had scheduled surgery for a patient and that she must now go over to talk to the patient for a while and see that he was wheeled into the operating room. Then it was suggested to Kate that she felt an irrepressible urge to move into the body of "Melissa" and that safely encased in "Melissa" she was going to watch the surgery "Melissa" would perform on the patient. After repeating this scenario, with variations, in the next therapy hour, the hypnoanalyst let Kate feel so relaxed about the operation while watching from within "Melissa's" body that she now could step out of "Melissa" in the (imaginary) "operating room" and assist "Melissa" with the surgery. Still later, the patient was encouraged to perform the surgery in imagination by herself and then told that she would be able to do it in reality "when the right time would come." She did 2 weeks later, and has been able to do so ever since. The ego ideal can be an excellent tool to help hypnoanalytic patients achieve competence and mastery of fear or conflict.

Coping, Competence, Mastery, and the Joy of Functioning

People feel pleasure when efficient action enables them to cope with challenges and to master them. Coping refers not only to a person's attempt to deal with conflicts, but also to the manner of dealing with novel situations and with challenges in the environment (Murphy, 1962). Coping is the successful meeting of challenges. And challenges are the spice of life. It is this pleasure in competence and mastery that the hypnoanalyst attempts to stimulate in the patient during the integration phase of the therapy.

In supportive therapies, including many types of hypnotherapy, part of the therapist's task is to help the patient to alleviate anxiety, tension, and conflict. However, not all tension in life is undesirable. Quite the contrary. Tension can be joyful, as is the tension in foreplay and in the sexual act. And joyful tension is at least part of what one experiences in the creative process, the ecstasy part of the "agony and the ecstasy." Any theory of personality that leaves out the pleasure of functioning, the joy of being able to do something well, ignores a multitude of processes that are characteristically experienced by children and by dedicated adults. One may teach, do research, climb mountains, ski, play a strenuous and hard game of tennis, or row in a race—not because it is one's job and one is paid to do it or because one thinks one ought to do it for one's health, but because it is fun, because it is exciting, because one passionately *wants* to do it. There is joy in ego functioning at increasingly higher levels of competence.

CONCLUSION

The hypnoanalyst has several advantages not available to the psycho-analyst. In psychoanalysis, improvement or cure is brought about by a three-fold procedure: uncovering, working through, and new integration. The same three procedures are essential in hypnoanalysis, but the arsenal of dynamic techniques that can be employed to help the patient change is larger, because methods not available in the waking state (or, in the case of imagery, less available), such as age regression, hypermnesia, imagery, dissociation, and automatic writing can be used. In hypnoanalysis the therapist helps the patient to go back and uncover the historical roots of conflicts. In the transference situation he allows the neurotic patient to re-experience repressed memories and disavowed affects, bring them into conscious awareness, and cope with them productively. In addition, he makes it possible for the patient with developmental arrest to develop more mature internal self- and object representations (see chapters 8 and 9, this volume). He helps patients work through their difficulties by means of the transference relationship, guided or spontaneously arising imagery, suggestions that the patient dream consecutive dreams leading to increasingly better solutions of his problem, dissociation of the observing from the experiencing ego, the Ego Ideal Technique, and the testing of reality in fantasy—until the patient eventually arrives at a solid new personality integration. On the other hand, when the hypnoanalyst has decided that relatively short-term, hypnoanalytically oriented hypno-therapy will suffice, he does not go back to uncovering all or most of the historical roots of conflict, but can take a here-and-now or teleological approach, and work with hypnoanalytically oriented methods only.

The trance state adds a new dimension to psychoanalytic treatment. Hypnoanalysis is based on psychoanalytic libido theory and ego psychology and is now adding the major newer developments in psychoanalytic theory (object relations theory and Self Psychology) to its armamentarium. On the other hand, hypnoanalysis is contributing to the elaboration of psychoanalytic theory in several respects, namely, increasing the understanding of primary and secondary process operations and the nature of ego receptivity, ego activity, and ego passivity (Fromm, 1972, 1977b, 1978–79, 1979; Gill & Brenman, 1959; Gruenewald et al., 1979; Levin & Harrison, 1976).

In hypnoanalysis many more tools can be employed to bring about cure than in psychoanalysis. The hypnoanalyst attempts to help the neurotic patient achieve new harmony within himself; that is, among his drives, conscience, ego ideal, and ego. He tries to help the patient with a developmental deficit to gain object constancy and benevolent internalized object representations and to establish a cohesive self so that he can grow and develop further. He can help patients in both categories develop new methods of coping so they can master their environment—perhaps even improve it—or adapt to it joyfully.

Hypnoanalysts have borrowed some of their treatment procedures (such as dream interpretation and the analysis of the transference and countertransference) from psychoanalysis. But they have also taken phenomena that can be produced only in a altered state of consciousness (e.g., age regression, hypermnesia, heightened imagery) and creatively employed them in the service of uncovering unconscious sources of conflict and suffering, working through the problems, and integrating and mastering them.

8

Clinical Applications of Hypnotherapy and Hypnoanalysis

HYPNOTIC TREATMENT OF NEUROTIC SYMPTOMS

Anxiety States and Anxiety Neurosis

Anxiety states are characterized by cognitive, visceral, and motoric changes (Zilboorg, 1933). The anxious patient presents with a distinctive feeling of apprehension or dread. He also typically reports a variety of autonomic symptoms: shortness of breath, increased heart rate, dizziness, flushes or pallor, hot flashes or chills, a dry mouth, sinking feelings in the stomach, and stomach cramps. Alternations in motor functioning are also common: shaking, tremors, weakness of limbs, and restlessness. When patients are anxious, attention and concentration are impaired. Thinking becomes less clear. According to Schur (1953), anxiety reactions involve a regression in cognitive functioning. On the one hand, anxiety represents a regression in evaluation; situations that are potentially only mildly dangerous are interpreted as being traumatic. On the other hand, "resomatization" occurs (Schur, 1955); like the infant, the patient reacts to real or fathomed danger primarily with somatic discharge and temporarily loses the capacity for secondary process thinking about the potential danger. Anxious persons seldom articulate their reasons for feeling so anxious, but they experience strong visceral reactions.

Anxiety states must be distinguished from normal, purposive fear (Rosenberg, 1949). Most learning necessitates an optimal level of arousal. The normally anxious person experiences optimal tension and prepares for the challenge of learning. The pathologically anxious patient is overcome by a debilitating anxiety state he is unable to master. These anxiety states are often attack-like in nature. The normally anxious person experiences an increased arousal appropriate to the situation, such as an examination or before an operation. The pathologically anxious person usually does not know the source of his anxiety, or if he believes he knows the cause consciously, his perception is often incorrect. Because the source is unclear, anxiety is accompanied by excessive worry.

The numerous theories regarding generalized anxiety disorders and panic states fall into three categories: psychodynamic, behavioral, and biological. According to Freud's (1926/1959) classical psychodynamic theory of anxiety, anxiety is a "response to internal danger." However, for defensive purposes (Rosenberg, 1949), patients frequently attribute the anxiety to external sources. Fenichel (1945) used the analogy of a dam to explain the mechanism of defensive operations against forbidden impulses that strive towards discharge. Anxiety is felt when impulses threaten to break through the dam of defenses and flood into consciousness. Psychodynamic treatment of anxiety neurosis, therefore, aims at uncovering of unconscious conflicts that cause the anxiety symptoms.

According to the behavioral learning theories (Levis & Hare, 1977; Watson & Raynor, 1920; Wolpe, 1958), anxiety states are a result of conditioning. Patients "learn" to be anxious through repetitive pairing of initially neutral stimuli with an autonomically arousing event until the neutral stimuli themselves elicit the anxiety response. Some patients "learn" anxiety vicariously by watching others being excessively anxious (Bandura, 1969). Clarke and Jackson (1983) suggest that learning to be anxious is most likely to occur when the threat to survival is great. Behavioral treatment is based on reduction in autonomic arousal or on counterconditioning.

Systematic desensitization (Wolpe, 1958) combines both features into a single treatment. Biological treatment is focused on the disregulation of the autonomic nervous system in patients vulnerable to panic attacks. For these patients who may manifest deficits in the metabolism of limbic neurotransmittors, certain antidepressant medications, notably Imipramine, have been effective (Carr & Sheehan, 1984).

Unfortunately, there are as yet no adequate means to predict which approach is best suited to the treatment of anxiety disorders. Perhaps there are distinct subgroups for which specific dynamic, behavioral, or pharmacological interventions work best. A combination of treatment approaches is indicated for some patients. Psychodynamic conflicts or biological vulnerability may originally have caused the anxiety, and conditioning factors may later have contributed to maintaining it. Only a combination of treatments brings relief for such patients.

Hypnotic treatment begins with the exploration of the efficacy of direct suggestions. Some patients respond readily to simple, graded posthypnotic suggestions. The patient is told, "After you awaken from hypnosis you will find yourself becoming less and less anxious as time passes" (Stein, 1963). The Clenched Fist Technique is another direct approach. For example, a 32-year-old married man came to the clinic in an acute state of panic. He worked in a factory that made machine parts. He had recently agreed to change the nature of his daily work activity by switching to piecework, for which he was paid by the quantity of parts made successfully during a given span of time, rather than by the hour. Although he experienced piecework as added pressure, he felt that he had to take the job because his wife was expecting their first child. The patient's father had worked in the same factory until retirement and also had done piecework. Because the patient was unsophisticated about therapy and desired immediate relief, the Clenched Fist method was used. The patient entered hypnosis by means of eye fixation. Trance was deepened with the staircase technique, following which the patient imagined floating on a couch. He was instructed to dream about his anxiety. Then he was told to make a fist and to imagine all the tension in his body flowing into his hand until the hand made a tighter and tighter fist. When the patient reported that all the tension had been stored in the fist, he was instructed to let the tension go quickly and imagine it being released outside of him. The patient was also given a posthypnotic suggestion that whenever he noticed the onset of anxiety at work, he should leave his machine, imagine the tension flowing into his nondominant fist, and then release it. A 6-month follow-up showed that the single session had helped him find relief. The anxiety still occurred, but he was able to use the method to control it. The patient's history and the hypnotic dream had suggested that the impending birth of his first child, along with his taking the same job as his father, activated unconscious oedipal conflicts. However, the quick success of the Clenched Fist method made it unnecessary to explore these conflicts in extended hypnotherapy. More often than not, anxiety symptoms can be treated by brief interventions aimed at symptom alleviation.

Typically, anxiety symptoms are treated by some form of anxiety management training (Suinn & Richardson, 1971). Behavioral therapists have demonstrated the efficacy of training patients in methods that attempt to help patients to cope with anxiety. The patient first is taught to relax and then to produce relaxation in a variety of imagined anxiety-provoking situations. Emphasis is on learning a way to cope with the anxiety as it is experienced. For example, a 24-year-old married female reported panic attacks. She was also anxious about being hypnotized and was unable to concentrate with an eye fixation induction. After being reassured that she could leave her eyes open, she responded readily to various ideomotor suggestions (magnets, arm drop, and arm levitation), after which she spontaneously closed her eyes. She was able to achieve a deep state of relaxation when waves of relaxation flowing over her were suggested. In her next session, she was able to enter trance readily with nothing but the waves of relaxation method. She was also taught to control anxiety by regulating her breathing. In the third session, she was asked to imagine herself in situations in which she felt anxious and then to use the tools she had learned to control her anxiety. She was given a posthypnotic suggested to use the waves of relaxation and deep breathing whenever she noticed the onset, or increasing levels of, anxiety symptoms in everyday life. She was also encouraged to strengthen her anxiety management skills through daily self-hypnotic practice. In the fourth session, suggestions were given to increase anxiety during trance, following which she was told to use the techniques she had learned to alleviate anxiety. She did this confidently and terminated the treatment.

Sometimes it is necessary to explore unconscious conflicts associated with anxiety symptoms. For instance, a 35-year-old married female reported debilitating panic attacks that occurred when her husband was away from home on a business trip. Hypnotically induced waves of relaxation and deep breathing brought little relief after six sessions. The Theater Technique was introduced as an uncovering procedure. In trance the patient was told that she would see a play, which "would somehow be about her panic attacks". In the first act she saw a frightened woman alone in a big house. A burglar was breaking into her bedroom. In the next act she was told she would learn "something more about her panic attacks." She saw a woman meeting a strange man in a park. Later in the act a woman was flying a kite. Asked to focus of her feelings while watching the play, the patient said she felt "excited." After three additional hypnotherapy sessions, the patient came to realize her wish for an affair. She had always suspected her husband, who was often away on business trips, had numerous affairs. She, however, could not allow herself the same "excitement." The anxiety symptoms diminished as she gained insight into her sexual wishes and subsequently negotiated a different relationship with her husband through couples' therapy.

Phobias

Phobias are characterized by a disproportionate amount of anxiety generated by the phobic object or situation. Unlike generalized anxiety reactions and panic states, where the precipitating events are unclear and unpredictable, phobic reactions are associated with well-defined stimuli and situations. When confronted with the phobic object or situation, the person predictably becomes anxious or panics. There are various ways to classify phobic stimuli. Marks (1969) distinguishes between external phobias (animal phobias, social phobias, e.g. speaking phobias), miscellaneous situational phobias, (such as flight phobias and fear of heights), and agoraphobial and internal phobias (fear of illness, such as cancer phobia, and obsessional fears, e.g. fear of being contaminated or fear of making obscene gestures). Although phobic stimuli vary, all phobias share certain common features: fear and avoidance (Rachman & Hodgson, 1974) and worry (Liebert & Morris, 1967). Intense fear is experienced with contact or anticipated contact with the phobic stimuli. Avoidance refers to the behavior associated with the phobias. Phobic patients restrict their behavior to avoid contact with the phobic stimuli. The extent of avoidance may be limited to specific stimuli, or there may be more generalized patterns of inhibition. While attempting to avoid the phobic stimuli, phobic patients are nevertheless preoccupied with the object of their phobias and sometimes unconsciously seek contact with these stimuli (Laughlin, 1967). Worry characterizes the patients' cognitive state. Patients may worry excessively about coming into contact with the feared animal or about encountering the feared situation; so much so that it may interfere with their ability to think clearly. Worry about successful performance is especially problematic in test anxiety and in public speaking phobias.

As with the anxiety disorders, psychodynamic, behavioral, and biological theories have been advanced to account for phobic symptoms. All contain some degree of validity. According to the psychodynamic theories, phobias are symptoms formed to compensate for inadequate repression. They represent an attempt to bind anxiety by displacement and projection. For example, in Freud's (1909/1955) famous case Little Hans, Hans developed a phobia of horses. The underlying oedipal conflict was between Hans' wish to kill his father and his fear of retaliation. The death wish was displaced onto the phobic object, in this case a horse, and then projected: The horse had the death wish and would kill him by falling on him. As long as the phobic objects or situations can be avoided, the anxiety is bound. The phobic person who comes in contact with or anticipates contact with the feared stimulus suffers an anxiety attack.

According to learning theory, phobic behavior is a learned, conditioned emotional response. In John Watson's famous case, Little Albert is an 11-month-old boy conditioned to fear rats. Watson repetitively paired an anxiety-producing noise with the presence of a tame laboratory rat until the rat also caused anxiety (Watson & Raynor, 1920). According to the biological theories, the phobic state represents a deficit in neurotransmitter metabolism associated with the function of the autonomic nervous system. Each theory represents a partial truth, and both are more or less applicable to certain populations. There are many patients in whom unconscious conflicts have caused phobias and in whom the phobias are maintained by conditioning. This subgroup of patients, the largest subgroup, presents the greatest challenge, because it is difficult to decide whether to begin with a symptomatic intervention based on learning theory, for example, desensitization, or to use a direct, dynamic, uncovering mode of hypnotherapy. We recommend a three-step treatment process: (a) direct hypnotic suggestion; (b) symptomatic hypnotherapy; and (c) dynamic hypnotherapy or hypnoanalysis.

Direct hypnotic suggestions can be useful with phobic patients. Marks, Gelder, and Edwards (1968) gave their phobic patients "a forceful suggestion" that their phobias would gradually disappear. Naruse (1965) suggested to champion athletes who suffered from stage fright that they would among other things, become indifferent to the opinions of others. S. Horowitz (1970) hypnotized snake phobics and gave them suggestions that they were "no longer frightened by harmless snakes" (p. 106). In each case, simple, directive hypnotic and posthypnotic suggestions proved effective for certain patients.

Where direct suggestions are ineffective in the first treatment sessions, the therapist switches to hypnotic desensitization. Frequently it is unnecessary to explore the underlying dynamics, as many phobias can be effectively treated with brief symptomatic interventions. The therapist begins by constructing a hierarchy of phobic situations. The patient is hypnotized and taught deep relaxation by means of waves of relaxation or deep breathing. After the patient has attained some proficiency in relaxation, he imagines a phobic situation low on the hierarchy. Hypnosis offers an advantage over nonhypnotic desensitization because the capacity for visualization is enhanced (Deiker & Pollock, 1975; Glick, 1970). It is advisable to teach the patient a scale for the degree of anxiety experienced during the procedure. The patient may use a fear thermometer (Walk, 1956) reporting a number from 0 to 10, from complete calm to absolute terror. Both patient and therapist can thus assess the degree of anxiety elicited during any stage of the imaginary exposure. It is important for the patient to visualize the phobic situation in detail (Clarke & Jackson, 1983) and for the therapist to extend the duration of the imagery for as long as the patient can tolerate it. If the patient becomes distressed, suggestions for relaxation are given. In subsequent sessions the patient imagines encountering progressively more fearful situations higher on the heirarchy until he achieves the goal of deep relaxation during visualization of even the more feared situations. Many patients show improvement before they imagine the most anxiety-provoking items on the hierarchy (Lang, Lazorik, & Reynolds, 1965; Marks et. al., 1968). Direct feedback about the progress attained while maintaining relaxation in the face of the imagined anxiety situation is a crucial element in the treatment (Lang et al., 1965). It is also very important to give graded suggestions for actual contact with the phobic situations on the hierarchy. When the patient shows some response to imaginary contact with the phobic situation (hypnotic desensitization) the therapist gives posthypnotic suggestions to utilize the relaxed state when encountering real-life phobic situations lower on the hierarchy than those currently mastered in imagination. Hypnotic desensitization offers an advantage over nonhypnotic behavioral desensitization because posthynotic suggestions can influence the patient to make contact with the phobic stimulus in real life (Deyoub & Epstein, 1977; Gibbons, Kilbourne, Saunders, & Castles, 1970).

Clarke and Jackson (1983) distill the clinical wisdom gained from the hundreds of clinical experiments on phobias to three points: "(1) get the patient to reenter the phobic situation; (2) let him do it under the right conditions; and (3) let him remain there until there is a noticeable decline in anxiety" (p. 195–196). Hypnotic systematic desensitization has proven successful with flight phobias (Kroger & Fezler, 1976; Rosenthal, 1967); animal phobias such as snake phobias (Daniels, 1976; Lang el at., 1965; O'Brien, Cooley, Ciotti, & Henninger, 1981) and dog phobias (Spiegel & Spiegel, 1978); injection phobias (Daniels, 1976); a bleach phobia (Deiker & Pollock, 1975); and test anxiety (Spies, 1979). Successful outcome is indicated by reduced anxiety and related changes in dream content and, above all, by reduced avoidance behavior.

It is not always necessary to carry out step-by-step desensitization with hypnotizable patients. Whereas Kroger and Fezler (1976) emphasize that the therapist must desensitize the patient one step at a time, others have demonstrated that the hypnotizable patient can be introduced to a number of progressively more anxiety eliciting stimuli within the same session, sometimes all at once (Deyoub & Epstein, 1977). Because information processing in hypnosis is nonsequential, the patient may be able to master progressively more difficult items on the hierarchy simultaneously. Some (Gustavson & Weight, 1981; Spies, 1979) have argued that for this reason hypnotic treatment usually proceeds much more quickly than nonhypnotic behavorial desensitization. Spiegel and his colleagues (Spiegel, Frischholz, Maruffi, & Spiegel, 1981; Spiegel & Spiegel, 1978) described a successful approach to flight phobias. The patient imagines the plane to be an extension of his body and then imagines himself pleasantly floating. He is given instructions to practice "floating with the plane" and viewing the plane as an extension of his body in self-hypnosis until he gains a sense of mastery and control. In hypnotic sessions, Deyoub and Epstein (1977) and Shaw (1977) had their flight phobia patients imagine the entire flight in its chronological sequence (not in hierarchical progression of least to most anxiety-eliciting events). Deyoub and Epstein claim that hypnotizable patients are able to develop a "new Gestalt" for successful mastery of the entire sequence of behaviors involved in flying. All-at-once rehearsal places emphasis on successful mastery. Surman (1979) had his hypnotized patients rehearse phobic situations as if beginning from the point of having mastered the situation without becoming anxious. In addition, he used suggestions to give the patient confidence. He calls this approach "post-noxious desensitization."

The Television Technique is especially useful in rehearsal. For example, a 15-year-old boy who was failing mathematics and Spanish came to hypnotherapy for test anxiety. He responded readily to hypnosis. The patient imagined sitting in front of the TV set, watching a program that absorbed his attention and made him feel very relaxed. He was told to switch channels and look at another program in which he would see himself sitting at his desk at school, somewhat anxiously, about to take an examination. Suggestions were given to amplify the affect until he felt as anxious as he usually felt at the onset of an examination. He was then told to switch the channel to a relaxing program and stay with it until he became relaxed. On another channel, he was told, he would see himself studying with careful attention and a clear mind. Posthypnotic suggestions were given that whenever he noticed the anxiety, he would automatically imagine his relaxing television program and then imagine the show about studying with a clear mind, until he was able to recall what he had studied as appropriate to the examination questions. The patient practiced self-hypnosis daily between examinations and utilized weekly quizzes for practice. He mastered his examination fear in four hypnotic sessions and received a C in mathematics and a B in Spanish.

An analogous approach entails Hypnotic Time Distortion. Tilton (1983) described treating a case of flight phobia by using pseudotime orientation, and Deiker and Pollack (1975) describe the treatment of a patient with a bleach phobia in which the patient was asked to imagine herself sometime in the future as if leaving her last therapy session after having overcome her former fears. Logsdon (1960) age regressed a patient to a time prior to the onset of the phobia so that the patient could recover the memory of successful coping. In such cases the patient uses the new orientation in time to gain a sense of mastery over the phobia.

Another approach to mastery is through Hypnotic Flooding Techniques. The hypnotized patient is exposed to the most intensely anxiety-eliciting stimuli imaginable until the anxiety is diminished. The therapist suggests vivid images of the most feared situations. Cancer phobia (O'Donnell, 1978) and homophobia (Scrignar, 1981) have been successfully treated with Hypnotic Flooding. However, flooding methods should be used only infrequently and then with caution. They are generally not liked by patients and carry the danger of overwhelming the patient.

Still another approach to mastery is the Ideal Self Technique. A singer with stage fright imagines herself as a successful opera singer performing perfectly on stage. Posthypnotic suggestions are given for the patient gradually to become more and more like the ideal image (Mordey, 1965). Especially for patients lacking in feelings of efficacy the "My Friend John" approach (Erickson, 1964c) is an alternative to the Ideal Self Technique. The patient thinks of someone else who unlike the patient is able to effectively cope with the phobic situation. Bakal (1981) used this approach successfully with flight phobias. The hypnotized phobics were taken step-by-step through the entire flight.

Hypnosis can be combined with cognitive therapy for phobics who are worried about test performance and for whom this is a critical issue. Defeatist thinking and excessive worry greatly exacerbate test anxiety (Meichenbaum, 1972). Boutin (1978) used a method called rational stage directed hypnotherapy to treat test anxiety patients. The therapist helps the patient in the waking state to identify defeating and irrational thoughts associated with taking tests. Then the patient is hypnotized and rehearses taking the test in fantasy. During the rehearsal, the patient engages in "cognitive restructuring," in which he develops self-enhancing thoughts to counteract his usual negative thoughts about taking the test. The patient then practices cognitive restructuring in real life while taking examinations.

Bakal (1981) has illustrated how the news media subliminally reinforces negative thinking with regard to flight phobias. Airline travel is fraught with death imagery from the "final boarding call" to the airline "terminal." Hypnotized patients rehearse in fantasy the stages of a flight, during which the hypnotist points out such negative words. He teaches the patient to be aware of these words and not to let them become detrimental suggestions; then he helps the patient develop a more rational perspective.

Another cognitive hypnotherapy approach is to help the patient adopt a new perspective on his fears. Spiegel and Spiegel (1978) treat agoraphobic patients by giving them the following message in hypnosis: "(1) Gravity can be my security; (2) my feet lock me into this magnetic gravity; (3) this downward pull stablizies my movement" (p. 269).

Similarly, they help patients with dog phobias to restructure their fear of dogs and distinguish between tame dogs and wild animals. Sometimes humor is helpful (Clarke & Jackson, 1983). Cohen (1981) successfully treated a male patient who had a fear of bovine sounds by suggesting that the patient see humor in the situation. The therapist handled the patient's avoidance behavior by having the patient in trance imagine he was making a documentary movie on cows. Eventually the patient was able to come into close contact with cows without becoming anxious.

We recommend using hypnotherapeutic imagery to facilitate coping. The phobic patient should imagine a relaxing scene, followed by one in which he encounters the phobic object or situation and becomes anxious. After returning to the relaxing scene, the patient is told that another scene or series of scenes will come to mind which "will suggest effective ways of coping with the phobic situation." The patient symbolically communicates coping strategies in these scenes. The material from these hypnoprojective images and narrations is used to refine coping strategies, which can be suggested to the patient in trance and incorporated into successful rehearsals in fantasy as well as into posthypnotic suggestions encouraging real-life encounters with phobic situations.

The majority of phobias can be successfully treated in ten sessions with hypnotic systematic desensitization, all-at-once rehearsal, or any of the methods previously mentioned. It is not always necessary to uncover unconscious conflicts associated with the phobia. The goal of most hypnotherapeutic treatment of phobias is mastery, not insight (Spiegel & Spiegel, 1978). Cohen (1981), for example, successfully treated his patient with the bovine-sound phobia in two sessions by using a symptomatic approach, even after the patient had alluded to the relationship between the bovine-sound phobia and his conflicts with women.

Sometimes, however, resistances arise, and symptomatic treatment reaches a plateau. Then dynamic hypnotherapy is indicated (Edelstien, 1981). The hypnotherapeutic techniques discussed in chapter 6 are useful.

Wolberg (1948) treated a woman with an anxiety neurosis by giving her hypnotic instructions to dream and then to produce associations to the dream. Through such explorations the patient gained insight into the relationship between discovering her husband's affair and the onset of her anxiety symptoms. O'Brien et. al., (1981) recommend posthypnotic dreaming to overcome plateaus in the treatment of phobic patients. Often the nature of the conflicts, as well as potential resolutions, are contained within the dream content. Schneck (1966b) used the Theatre Technique and hypnotic dreams to uncover an incest experience associated with the development of a germ phobia. Crasilneck and Hall (1975) recommend regressing patients to the age when the sympton first appeared. Van der Hart (1981) used ego state therapy to treat a patient with a fear of dead birds. Clarke and Jackson (1983) recommend a "scene-within-a-scene technique" (p. 225) for extremely anxious patients. The patient is instructed to have a daydream about the phobic situation within a relaxing scene. For example, he may imagine lying in the sun on a beach until he feels very relaxed. A daydream about the phobic situation is then suggested. If the patient becomes upset, he is reminded that he is at the beach, pleasantly relaxing. Gustavson and Weight (1981) used the Theater Technique and age regression to uncover fears associated with a slug phobia. Scott (1970) treated a patient with a bird phobia by age regressing the patient to the childhood event associated with the phobic anxiety. Subsequently the patient was desensitized following a procedure similar to that previously described. We utilize the combination of dynamic hypnotherapy and hypnotic desensitization for many patients.

There is very little controlled-outcome research on the hypnotic treatment of phobia. In his review, McGuinness (1984) concluded that hypnosis is an effective adjunct to the treatment of phobias, but that methodological pitfalls prevent accurate assessment of the results. Most studies use a very small sample of patients (e.g. Glick, 1970). Exceptions are the Spiegel et al. (1981) study of flight phobias which reported some improvement in 52% of the patients, and the studies on agoraphobia by Van Dyck, Spinhoven, and Commandeur (1984a, 1984b). Lang et al. (1965) compared hypnotic desensitization and a pseudotherapy control in the treatment of snake phobias. Only the hypnotically desensitized patients (not placebo controls) showed reduction of fear; but the positive treatment outcome was not related to hypnotizability. This experimental study counters Kazdin & Wilcoxon's (1976) claim that desensitization contains no specific therapeutic ingredient beyond expectation of change. Other studies have shown treatment outcome to be related to hypnotizability (S. Horowitz, 1970; Spiegel et al., 1981). Still other studies have compared nonhypnotic behavioral desensitization to hypnotic treatment of phobias. In these studies, nonhypnotic desensitization worked out better than direct hypnotic suggestion (Marks et al., 1968) or guided imagery (Melnick & Russell, 1976). However, results showed improvement over nonhypnotic systematic desensitization when hypnosis was used as an adjunct to desensitization (Woody, 1973) or when all-at-once rehearsal was employed as the hypnotic intervention (Gibbons et al., 1970). In another study by Spies (1979), nonhypnotic systematic desensitization and hypnosis were equally effective, but hypnotic treatment was faster.

Several investigators have identified patient characteristics and particulars in the treatment procedure which predict a successful outcome: patients who are monosymptomatic and not debilitated by pervasive anxiety (Daniels, 1976); patients who show a successful response to the majority of items on a desensitization hierarchy (Lang et al., 1965); and patients who show positive changes in their dreams during the treatment (O'Brien et al., 1981).

Agoraphobia

Agoraphobia, literally fear of the marketplace, has more accurately been defined as fear of being away from a place or object representing safety (Snaith, 1968). Snaith proposes that the term agoraphobia be replaced with the term "nonspecific security fears". He argues that intense anxiety is the central factor in agoraphobia and that the phobic content is secondary to the anxiety. Agoraphobics manifest panic in a wide variety of settings ranging from wide open spaces to confined places. Although the situations in which the anxiety is experienced vary markedly, agoraphobia, nevertheless, constitutes a specific syndrome distinct from other types of phobias (Snaith, 1968). The cluster of symptoms common to agoraphobics include: intense and unpredictable panic states (Clark & Jackson, 1983); generalized free-floating anxiety (Burglass, Clarke, Henderson, Kreitman, & Presley, 1977); depression (Burglass et al., 1977); depersonalization (Roth, 1959); obsessions and compulsions (Snaith, 1968); and hypochondriasis (Snaith, 1968). Like other adult phobias agoraphobia is often associated with a history of an unstable family background and school phobias (Snaith, 1968). More than other phobics, agoraphobics have a greater incidence of childhood behavioral problems, such as nightmares, fear of the dark, difficulty in making friends, and sensitivity to emotional hurt (Thorpe & Burns, 1983). A high proportion of agoraphobics (83%) associate the onset of the syndrome with a traumatic event that threatened their health, life, or security; another 13% report onset associated with pregnancy and childbirth (Roth, 1959).

Agoraphobia may constitute a kind of "separation phobia" (Clarke & Jackson, 1983). Emmelkamp (1979) reports that agoraphobics typically come from stable but overprotective families, a history that may contribute to a conflict over dependency. Agoraphobia may be a manifestation of underlying conflicts over abandonment (Chambless, 1978). Goldstein and Chambless (1978) have provided the most comprehensive explanation of agoraphobia. In their combined psychodynamic and behavioral reformulation of the agoraphobic concept, they cite four general features:

1. Fear of fear: A slight fear acts as a stimulus to additional fears, and the patient becomes afraid he will lose control (faint, get a heart attack, etc.). 2. A low level of self-sufficiency: Agoraphobics are highly dependent and sometimes cannot venture into the world without a familiar person (called a phobic partner), a walking stick, a bicycle, or other transitional object (Marks, 1969). 3. Misapprehension of the causal antecedents of uncomfortable feelings: Agoraphobics have little understanding of their internal lives (unconscious and preconscious motivations). 4. Onset of symptoms in the climate of notable conflict: Agoraphobics often are unaware of interpersonal conflict but usually experience an attack following interpersonal strife.

According to Goldstein and Chambless's (1978) approach combining psychodynamic and behavioral principles and Clarke and Jackson's (1983) hypnobehavioral approach, treatment must address both the panic attacks and the extreme avoidance behavior. Systematic behavioral desensitization to anxiety-eliciting situations (Goldstein & Chambless, 1978; Wolpe, 1958) and cognitive behavioral therapy (Clarke & Jackson, 1983; Emmelkamp *et.al.*, 1978) have been consistently ineffective with agoraphobics. In rare cases where systematic desensitization has been successful, the treatment was very lengthy (Thorpe & Burns, 1983). Some clinicians have, therefore, tried to adapt desensitization techniques to the needs of the agoraphobic. The agoraphobic needs to find ways to alleviate the intense panic and fear of losing control. Zaccheo and Palmer (1980) have constructed a desensitization hierarchy not to phobic situations but to the fear of loss of control itself. Goldstein and Chambless (1978) recommend constructing hierarchies for the sensations of fear and panic themselves. Cognitive therapeutic approaches may be useful when the patient is taught to make statements about increased self-control in hypnosis (Clarke & Jackson, 1983). Clarke and Jackson also recommend helping the patient to discover the role of hyperventilation in maintaining the panic state. They recommend teaching the patient breathing techniques to counter this tendency. In any event, the patient must learn some means of directly alleviating his panic and the thoughts associated with it.

The main emphasis of treatment, however, relates to the agoraphobic's avoidance behavior. According to Wilson (1984), all successful treatment methods for agoraphobics have an "instigating function" by facilitating "corrective activity" (p. 93). In other words, the treatment of agoraphobia, in contrast to other phobias, must stress real-life exposure. The treatment begins with the construction of a hierarchy of easier-to-more-difficult environments (Clarke & Jackson, 1983). Construction of the hierarchy should take into consideration the distance from safe and familiar areas, access to safe places and support from phobic partners; and contingencies that might prevent return to safety during exposure (p. 315). An excellent example of a hierarchy for the hypnotic treatment of the agoraphobic is found in Clarke and Jackson (1983, Appendix B). The patient is hypnotized and taught coping skills for managing anxiety states, for example, waves of relaxation, deep breathing, imagery of safe and familiar surroundings. The patient may also choose to use a transitional object, such as a walking stick, for the initial life exposure. Next, the patient actually ventures out into the feared environment. In graded life exposure, the patient first ventures into easy environments (for example, looking out the door of his home), and then he really goes out. If the patient is unable to tolerate any real-life exposure, treatment begins with preparatory hypnotic rehearsal in fantasy. In a self-management approach to life exposure, the patient is instructed to stay in the designated environment for an extended period, say, 90 minutes, which is more effective than brief exposure (Stern & Marks, 1973). The patient learns to tolerate the situation until his fear diminishes. He is not allowed to terminate the exposure except under extreme duress. An alternative approach is to have the patient walk away from the clinic or the office until he becomes anxious. Or, in the therapist-centered approach, the patient ventures into the feared environment accompanied by the therapist. Whatever the approach, feedback, and encouragement by the therapist are essential in the initial stages of real-life exposure (Leitenberg, Agras, Thompson, & Wright, 1968). If the patient becomes anxious, he is instructed to utilize coping strategies to manage the anxiety (Clarke & Jackson, 1983). Posthypnotic suggestions, previously given, increase the likelihood of the patient's remembering to draw upon coping strategies during anxious moments. If the patient becomes overwhelmed and retreats before anxiety diminishes, the treatment will not necessarily be set back, provided the therapist helps the patient view the event as a learning experience and adopt a positive set in the subsequent treatment sessions (Thorpe & Burns, 1983). Treatment always proceeds along the hierarchy from easier-to-more-difficult environments until the patient is able to tolerate being in difficult environments for extended times without experiencing anxiety.

If the treatment reaches a plateau, it may be necessary to use dynamic hypnotherapy to uncover unconscious conflicts associated with the agoraphobia. According to classical psychoanalytic theory, the conflict in patients suffering from agoraphobia usually is an exhibitionistic-seductive one: Unconsciously they wish they would (and fear they will) expose themselves on the street to strangers and seduce them sexually. More contemporary psychoanalytic studies suggest conflicts associated with separation-individuation. Gruenewald (1971a) describes the hypnoanalytic treatment of a 58-year-old female with a 40-year history of agoraphobia. The patient was unresponsive to hypnotic suggestions for sympton relief, which involved rehearsal in fantasy of exposure situations. She did, however, respond favorably to suggestions to strengthen her coping mechanisms and to suggestions designed to uncover feelings and memories associated with the agoraphobic symptoms. Typically, hypnoanalysis of agoraphobia reveals conflicts around both separation and fears of inability to control impulses.

The outcome studies on nonhypnotic behavioral treatment of agoraphobia with graded real-life exposure are impressive. Wilson (1984) states that improvement rates range from 66%–84% in the many studies he reviewed. Barlow, O'Brien, Last, and Holden (1983) report a 68% success rate. Chambless and Goldstein (1978) report a 22% success rate, which increased to 71% at a one-year follow-up period. Other studies have likewise reported increased improvement in the months and years following successful treatment (Emmelkamp & Kuipers, 1979). However, few patients are ever *completely* cured (Wilson, 1984). Instead, with behavioral and hypnobehavioral treatment, patients learn skills to tolerate separation fears and venture into the world. Further venturing into the world provides positive feedback to maintain the treatment gain and assists in the resolution of the separation fears. Real-life exposure works better than placebo treatment (Wilson, 1984) or systematic desensitization (Emmelkamp, 1979). Although claims have been made for antidepressant medication in the treatment of agoraphobics, 20% of the patients refuse medication (Telch, Teaman, & Taylor, 1983) and 27%–50% suffered relapse after termination of medication. Medications clearly diminish depressed mood, but they are less effective in reducing the panic attacks and avoidance behavior associated with agoraphobia (Mavissakalian & Barlow, 1981). Unfortunately, there are as yet not enough reliable outcome data comparing the hypnotic and nonhypnotic treatments of agoraphobia. Although Clarke and Jackson (1983) give a detailed protocol for the hypnotic treatment of agoraphobia, they do not report outcome statistics, and it remains unclear whether hypnosis offers any advantage over the established behavioral treatments other than the obvious advantage of providing relief at a faster rate.

Hysteria: Conversion Reactions

Conversion reactions are symptoms involving voluntary musculature and special senses (e.g. vision and hearing) (Charcot, 1886). They differ from psychophysiological disorders in that they pertain to defenses against conflictual impulses (Breuer & Freud, 1893/1955) or painful affects (Ziegler & Imboden, 1962). The body becomes the arena for the symbolic expression of these impulses and the defenses against them. The somatic symptom itself both reveals and conceals the underlying impulse. There are many types of conversion reactions. The most common conversion symptoms involving the musculature include: psychogenic seizures, contractures, tics, partial or complete paralyses, and aphonia. The most common conversion symptoms involving the senses include focal blindness, hysterical deafness, anesthesia, conversion pain, and conversion skin disorders.

Because of the involvement of voluntary musculature and the senses in conversion symptoms (Charcot, 1886; Janet, 1889:), dynamic hypnotherapy has been the treatment of choice since Charcot (1892) and Breuer and Freud (1883/1955). Because a variety of ideomotor and sensory alterations can be produced in hypnosis, the clinician is able to affect directly and exactly those organ systems implicated in the conversion reaction. Moreover, inasmuch as hypnosis is a means gaining access to memories, fantasies and affects not readily available to consciousness, hypnosis becomes the main tool for uncovering the nature of these conflicts. An uncovering, not a behavioral, approach to hypnotherapy is generally indicated when one is dealing with conversion symptoms. In certain cases, hypnosis also can help in validating the diagnosis of conversion because conversion symptoms generally respond to hypnotic suggestions, whereas organic symptoms do not. For example, Schwarz, Bickford, and Rasmussen (1955) used hypnotic suggestions to elicit seizures from hypnotized patients who had psychogenic but not genuine (EEG-validated) seizures. During seizure activity, the hysterical patients had normal EEGs. Patients with hysterical blindness "see" in trance under certain conditions.

Patients with psychogenic seizures usually manifest movements and convulsions that superficially resemble an epileptic seizure but are different from it in several important respects. The patient with psychogenic seizures does not lose consciousness and resists attempts to open his eyes. Reflexes are normal during the seizure. Moreover, the patient usually avoids bumping into objects during the seizure and more often than not has the seizures in the presence of others. During the seizure, the patient exhibits muscular rigidity, twitches, convulsions, and peculiar postures, bodily movements and facial expressions. He is also disoriented. The movement during the seizure is often a characterization of sexual intercourse or resembles aggressive posturing. This is so because the seizures are associated with conflictual sexual and aggressive impulses.

The goal of hypnotherapy is to uncover and work through the conflicts associated with the seizures. After the patient becomes familiar with hypnosis, various hypnotherapeutic methods are utilized, such as hypnoprojective methods, hypnotic dreaming, free associating, and age regression. Rosen (1953) described the treatment of a 30-year-old woman with psychogenic seizures. Hypnoprojective methods, notably the Theater Technique and hypnotic intensification of affect, were used to explore the seizures, which were found to be a form of sexual acting out. Similarly, Bernstein (1969) described the treatment of adolescent girls whose seizures were associated with conflicts about sexual relationships with boyfriends. Glenn and Simonds (1977) described the treatment of a 13-year-old girl whose seizures began during the heightened sexual awareness of early adolescence. They were able to induce seizures with hypnotic suggestions. The patient was encouraged to produce imagery and to learn to express conflicts in fantasy rather than somatically. She also was given posthypnotic suggestions to prevent subsequent seizures by pressing her thumb and forefinger together at the onset of an attack. Whereas the conversion seizures in each of these cases were associated with the activation of infantile neurotic conflicts about sexual impulses, seizures can also begin subsequent to traumatization (Schneck, 1959). LaBarbera and Dozier (1980) describe a number of cases in which the seizures in adolescent girls initially appeared after an incest experience and subsequently were precipitated by sexually charged situations. Caldwell and Stewart (1981) present a case in which latent homosexual conflicts were activated in a young man following traumatization by rape. The patient's seizures cleared up after brief hypnotherapy. However the patient did not disclose his homosexual conflicts directly nor work through the traumatic experience during the hypnotherapy. Caldwell and Stewart remind us that seizures can sometimes be treated without dealing with the dynamics. Of course, not all psychogenic seizures are associated with sexual impulses. Lindner (1973) describes two cases in which age regression was used to revivify the feelings experienced during the first convulsive experience. Lindner was also able to evoke and terminate the seizures with direct hypnotic suggestions. In each case, the uncovering made it clear that the seizures occurred because the patient had disavowed aggressive impulses.

Less dramatic disturbances in the musculature can occur, for example, conversion tics and contractures. Wolbery (1948) traced a nasal tic in a 13-year-old boy to an unconscious desire for anal attack and the rejection of this impulse. Gardner (1973) described the symptomatic treatment of an 8-year-old girl with frequent eye fluttering episodes. The patient was given direct hypnotic suggestions and posthypnotic suggestions to "keep her eyes open more and more." To aid this process the girl was given several tasks in which she had to watch things very attentively. Trenerry and Jackson (1983) used direct posthypnotic suggestions effectively to treat a patient with involuntary spasms of the neck and back. In each hypnotic session, the patient was told she would experience the spasms for progressively shorter periods of time. Treatment continued until the spasms had disappeared.

Direct hypnotic suggestions are sometimes useful in treating hysterical paralysis. Bryan (1961) treated a patient who had "lost" the use of his legs by giving him posthypnotic suggestions that he would be able to walk satisfactorily after 10 days had elapsed. Fogel (1976) treated several patients who suffered from asomatognosia (inability to recognize the existence of parts of the body) by giving them direct hypnotic suggestions to become aware of that part of the body as part of the self and that it would continue to belong to them. Moskowitz (1964) used hypnotic suggestions to increase arm strength in treating a patient who had lost the strength of his arm. Erickson (1954) describes several cases of hysterical paralysis treated by symptom substitution. In each case the suggestions were given to reduce the paralysis of the arm to a weakness in a hand or finger. Abraham (1968) used guided imagery to treat a patient with hysterical paraplegia. The patient imagined himself at a beach, with very cold sea water touching his feet. He imagined contracting his feet to avoid the cold and became so absorbed in the fantasy that he actually lifted his legs. Once the patient was able to lift his legs in the waking state, he was rehypnotized, and cognitive restructuring was used so that the patient could consciously accept the use of his legs. Spiegel and Spiegel (1978) describe several cases of paralysis having been precipitated by traumatic events later uncovered in hypnotherapy.

In hysterical blindness the subject believes himself to be partially or totally blind yet is usually able to negotiate the world adequately. The hysterically blind patient defends against 'seeing' something in his unconscious and learns to maintain the blindness through operant conditioning (Brady & Lind, 1961). As with other conversion reactions, a dynamic uncovering approach to hypnotherapy is indicated in most cases. Greenleaf (1971) describes a case, rich in detail, in which the blindness was associated with conflicts about getting angry ("seeing red"). Wilkens and Field (1968) present two cases where age regression, scene visualizations, and hypnotic dreams revealed the blindness to be associated with conflicts around dependency and helplessness. In a number of cases of blindness, the hypnotic uncovering disclosed a relationship between the symptoms and a previous traumatic incident. Patterson (1980) treated a young man whose loss of vision occurred after a traumatic incident in which his sister was blinded. Wolberg (1948) used hypnotic dreaming and associative techniques to trace the blindness of a 27-year-old woman to several layers of trauma: first to a dormitory fire and then to the original traumatic event, witnessing a train crash and seeing someone die. Incest can provoke hysterical blindness. A 10-year-old girl was referred to the clinic for psychological testing with a diagnosis of focal blindness of unknown origin. Her inability to generate images other than butterflies on the Rorschach or to tell stories other than naming the characters on the TAT suggested massive repression. While she was drawing, it was suggested that she was drawing with a magic pencil. The "wiggly pencil" was able to draw all by itself. She was told that the pencil knew all about her, knew even things that might otherwise upset her, but that she need not concern herself with these things because the wiggly pencil could take care of itself by drawing. Over the next few sessions, the girl produced a series of drawings about incestuous involvements with her father. As she gradually became conscious of the meaning of the material uncovered through the automatic drawing, the blindness cleared.

There have been fewer reported treatments of hysterical deafness. Hurst (1943) and Kodman and Pattie (1958) used direct suggestions. Patients were instructed to listen more attentively, and the hearing loss was explained as a problem of not listening. Malmö, Davis, and Barza (1954) were able to cure a 19-year-old girl with hearing loss through nonhypnotic conditioning and waking suggestion. Pelletier (1977) describes an interesting treatment of aphonia, or the inability to speak, with a combination of dynamic hypnotherapy and conjoint couple's treatment. The patient was able to recover her ability to speak only in hypnotic age regression. The regression failed to reveal any childhood conflicts associated with the aphonia but did reveal marital conflicts. The patient literally felt unable to speak to her very busy husband. Therefore, Pelletier initiated conjoint couple's therapy in which the husband learned ways to help her speak to him.

Other sensory alterations may occur: anethesias, conversion pains, skin diseases. For example, a 30-year-old woman with chronic pain of 15 years' duration was hypnotized to learn pain coping strategies. When treatment reached a plateau after several sessions, the therapist switched to an uncovering approach to hypnotherapy. The Theater Technique disclosed a history of child abuse and several episodes of abandonment by the mother. The patient also reported an intensification in pain during separations from her family. The pain literally was her way of abusing herself. The physical pain also necessitated her living with her mother on account of her disability and thus prevented the emotional pain of separation. In this sense the pain, being a direct expression of conflict, constituted a conversion symptom.

Another patient, also 30 years old, was seen in hypnotherapy for recurrent lip sores. The therapist first approached the treatment symptomatically. The hypnotized patient was asked to imagine applying a special hallucinated salve to the sores. Though the application of the imaginary salve resulted in immediate relief, the sores usually returned. After three sessions the therapist switched to an uncovering approach. Hypnoprojective procedures revealed that the patient had been in an unhappy marriage for more than 10 years. She and her husband had sexual relations only infrequently. Because of her strict Catholic background, she sought the counsel of a priest. She did not feel it proper to divorce her husband. The priest, who had had some counseling training, saw her regularly over a number of months. The patient developed an intensely eroticized transference toward the priest but could not reveal her fantasies to him. She abruptly left treatment with him and developed the lip sores shortly afterwards. The conflicts associated with the symptom formation became clear to the hypnotherapist from the uncovering work, although the patient could not consciously accept this knowledge. The lip sores represented a wish to kiss the priest (displaced upwards from a wish for genital intercourse with him). As the hypnotic uncovering proceeded, the patient also abruptly terminated treatment with the male hypnotherapist after a total of six sessions. She told the hypnotherapist in a follow-up telephone conversation that she had achieved some symptomatic relief through acupuncture. She did not seek additional psychotherapy nor had she contacted the priest.

Dissociative Symptoms

Dissociative symptoms involve alterations in consciousness and memory. The alterations in consciousness include fugue states and hypnoidal states. The memory alterations (amnesias) may apply specifically to certain events or periods of time or may be generalized and encompass one's sense of identity. Dissociative symptoms are manifestations of defensive operations in which the contents of experience are actively removed from memory recall or consciousness. Dynamic hypnotherapy or hypnoanalysis are the treatments of choice. The hypnotherapy techniques described in chapter 6 allow the conflictual material to emerge gradually into consciousness in a symbolic form until it can be integrated and no longer needs to be disavowed.

Amnestic episodes are frequently associated with neurotic conflicts. For instance, a psychologist was seen for constantly misplacing his beeper. He was given direct suggestions for hypermnesia along with suggestions for hypnotic dreams about the location of the lost object. He was able to locate the beeper after a single hypnotic session but also learned about the conflicts associated with its loss. The psychologist was treating a severely disturbed patient who called his office many times a day. The psychologist "lost" the beeper in an effort to stop the calls and was unaware of his anger at the patient. The uncovering work enabled him to gain insight into the countertransference feeling he harbored toward the patient. Of course, amnestic episodes can also be associated with trauma. For example, Crasilneck and Hall (1975) describe the treatment of a 17-year-old girl who became amnestic after being raped.

Hypnosis is also useful in treating various alterations of consciousness. Symptomatic treatment can sometimes be effective. A student asked for hypnotherapeutic treatment of a symptom that bothered her: in many of her classes she would "fall asleep." Some probing by the hypnotherapist made it clear that the patient in these instances was neither bored by the lecturer nor overtired and sleepy—she was dissociating, going into a hypnoidal state. But why? We were puzzled to find that the patient had these dissociative episodes only in the classroom and in the library, never anywhere else. Further questioning revealed that she came from a lower class family of little education and that she felt she would alienate herself from her beloved parents by getting a higher education. This was discussed with her in and out of hypnosis. In addition, the posthypnotic suggestion was given to the patient that she would hear an alarm clock ring any time she felt the prodromal signs of the dissociative state come up. She improved rapidly. The entire treatment took two sessions.

When symptomatic treatment of disturbances in consciousness fail, it is sometimes necessary to explore the underlying dynamics. Kaplan and Deabler (1975) used age regression in the treatment of a 25-year-old man with "blackouts" associated with violent rage attacks. The patient was regressed to the time that each episode had occurred in order to explore the events preceding the spell. In each instance, the blackout was associated with the patient's fear of his aggressive impulses. In another case, a patient was treated for "spaciness." The Theater Technique revealed the spaciness was related to his fear of oedipal strivings. The patient subsequently realized that he became spacy just prior to sexual intercourse or when speaking with his boss at work.

Obsessive-Compulsive Symptoms

Hypnosis has a poor success rate with obsessive/compulsive symptoms. When symptoms are embedded in the rigid obsessive/compulsive personality structure, the prognosis is poor; symptoms are relatively circumscribed, the prognosis is better. For example, a 28-year-old woman, somewhat overweight but not really obese, wanted to lose weight and get rid of a compulsive symptom: every afternoon at 3 p.m. she felt *compelled* to leave her job and get herself a large milk shake, even though she really did not like milk shakes. In an age regression via the Affect Bridge (Watkins, 1971) utilizing the affect of craving, she found herself at various points between the ages of 2 and 5 lying in a darkened room on a hard sort of table under a big machine after having had to drink a very large glass of something that looked like a milk shake, but "tasted awful." She now relived—and in the waking state remembered—that as a child she had had a congenital malformation of the stomach for which she had to have periodic X-ray examinations. The hypnotherapist age progressed the patient to her real chronological age and interpreted to her in trance that the milk shakes represented the barium solution she had been required to drink before the X-rays were taken and that she still wanted to be the obedient little girl who drank the barium solution even though it "tasted awful." This interpretation was also made to the patient in the waking state. After 3 hours of further hypnotherapy, the compulsive craving for milk shakes totally ceased. It never returned. And within a couple of months the patient, without any further therapy, lost the weight she wanted to lose.

DEVELOPMENTAL HYPNOTHERAPY WITH SEVERELY DISTURBED PATIENTS

The Treatment of Psychotic, Borderline, and Narcissistic Conditions

Several theoretical advances in psychoanalysis in the past decades have contributed to the recent interest in the hypnotherapy of severely disturbed patients. These advances are loosely tied together within the perspective of "developmental lines," a theoretical focus that began with Anna Freud's classic paper of 1965, "The Concept of Developmental Lines." The viewpoint that grew out of this seminal paper has been equated with structural psychoanalytic theory (Gedo & Goldberg, 1973) and, clinically, with the treatment of developmental arrests (Stolorow & Lachman, 1980). It attempts to synthesize important aspects of object relations theory, self psychology, ego psychology and affect development theory into a comprehensive framework for the clinical assessment and treatment of psychotic and borderline patients.

Each of the many versions of a developmental lines approach has its own terminology, despite attempts at an integrative view (Blanck & Blanck, 1974; Gedo & Goldberg, 1973). Nevertheless, it is possible to draw certain basic assumptions. Each line of development charts the emergence of a specific developmental potential through a sequence of epigenetic stages. Thus, we may posit separate lines of development for the consolidation of a sense of self (Kohut, 1971; Lichtenberg, 1975; Ornstein, 1974), for internalized object representations (Horner, 1979; Jacobson, 1972; Kernberg, 1968; Mahler et. al., 1975; Modell, 1968), for affect (Brown, 1985; Emde, Kligman, Reich, & Wade, 1978; Isaacs, 1984; Sroufe, 1979), and for the defenses (Vaillant, 1977). Each developmental line is thought to contribute to the formation of psychic structure, and human development in toto is seen as "progressive structuralization" along multiple lines (Gedo & Goldberg, 1973). Freud (1933, p. 84) used the metaphor of crystal formation to illustrate how psychic structure proceeds from a fluid, undifferentiated state to a solid, structured state to build what has since been called the "representational world" (Sandler & Rosenblatt, 1962).

Psychopathology, especially that of those illnesses now called "severe disturbance" (schizophrenia, affective psychosis, and personality disorders), is reconceptualized as a failure in normal human development along one or more developmental lines. Developmental deficits are sometimes associated with genetic-maturational difficulties but more often are connected with repetitive maladaptive interactions with the holding environment (Winnicott, 1965), so that psychic structure fails to form properly. Psychological conflicts and defenses against these conflicts may also contribute to failures in the normal progression of developmental lines. A severely disturbed patient's seemingly bizarre symptoms or behaviors can, then, be interpreted as adaptive, as compensatory structures (Kohut, 1971). For example, a patient's self-destructiveness may be an attempt to feel alive (Perry, 1980); command hallucinations may be ways to develop an executive function (Larkin, 1979). Such a view of psychopathology is radically different from the consensual symptom descriptions of the DSM III (American Psychiatric Association, 1982). Assessment of deficits in self- and object representations or in affect is not as clear cut as the observation of symptoms, and can be made only through an evaluation of an unfolding therapeutic relationship (Kohut, 1971; Ornstein, 1980–81).

The concept of developmental arrests has profound implications for therapy. Outcome studies of nonhypnotic therapy with severely disturbed patients (schizophrenics) have convincingly shown that dynamic uncovering therapies, which focus on interpretation of symbolic content, are not very effective (May, 1968). In contrast, a therapy that focuses on failures in structure formation instead of content interpretation holds considerable promise. The therapist who has formed a stable therapeutic relationship with a severely disturbed patient can use this relationship to establish a common language through which both patient and therapist can come to understand the nature and experience of the patient's structural deficits—the lack of a sense of self, unintegrated representations of others, and incapacity for awareness and tolerance of affect—and work toward the goal of helping the patient develop mature psychic structures. From this perspective, it is more accurate to speak of the therapist's primary task as structural interpretation (or ego building) rather than dynamic interpretation, and the patient's internal process as adaptation and assimilation, not defense against impulses. Symptoms and behaviors, for example, hallucinations, may not be something to rid the patient of, but to understand, even utilize, for what they disclose about the developmental task(s) the patient must still accomplish.

Furthermore, in the therapy of severely disturbed patients, structuralization can take place only in the context of a stable therapeutic relationship in which there is a solid alliance, a realistic perception of the interaction, an opportunity for working through the specific transference—whether a psychotic transference (Burnham et al., 1969), a borderline transference (Adler, 1981; Kernberg, 1968; Masterson, 1976), or a narcissistic transference (Bach, 1977; Kohut, 1971)—and an opportunity for internalization of certain qualities of the therapeutic interaction, which contributes to structure formation (Leowald, 1973; Meissner, 1981).

The Use of Hypnosis in the Treatment of the Severely Disturbed Patient

Although originally it was believed that severely disturbed patients were not hypnotizable (Abrams, 1964), we know now that they do not differ essentially from normal people in their susceptibility to hypnosis. In fact, some severely disturbed patients are sufficiently hypnotizable to merit the consideration of hypnotherapy as an intervention.

The position set forth here is that hypnotherapy can indeed be useful in the treatment of the severely disturbed patient—with some qualifications: Only highly hypnotizable patients should be selected; hypnotherapy should be well embedded in the context of a stable ongoing therapeutic relationship; and hypnotherapy is set within a developmental framework.

When these qualifications are taken into account, hypnosis can indeed be useful primarily because of the patient's great access to sensations, imagery, and memories (Fromm et al., 1981)—precisely those processes that play the largest role in the formation of psychic structure (Sandler & Rosenblatt, 1962). Imagery, sensory awareness, and memory are important tools in the hypnotic work with severely disturbed patients in conjunction with the ongoing (often nonhypnotic) working through of the transference. They facilitate internalization.

Boundary Formation.   Implicated in severe disturbance, especially schizophrenia, is a developmental deficit in boundary formation, "the capacity to maintain a separation between independent objects and between representations of independent objects" (Blatt & Wild, 1976, p. 6). According to Blatt and Wild, the normally developing child passes through a sequence of discrete stages in boundary formation (articulation of the perceptual field, or segregation of space; differentiation of inside and outside; segregation of categories for developing concepts about the perceived world). The child who has mastered these stages has achieved stable boundary formation, which is a prerequisite for the development of both the intellectual operations outlined by Piaget (1969) which take as their foundation grouping and categorizing operations associated with boundary formation, and the internal self- and object representations described by Jacobson (1973), Kernberg (1976), and Modell (1968), which presupposes boundary differentiation between self and others.

Since the development of both thinking and internal self- and object representations presupposes boundary formation, it is not surprising that the manifest symptoms of schizophrenia include disturbances in both of these areas. A significant developmental failure in boundary formation contributes to the lack of differentiation characteristic of chronic undifferentiated schizophrenia. The fragmentation of boundaries or ego dissolution characteristic of acute psychosis (Bowers, 1974; Federn, 1952) could be interpreted as the achievement of a degree of boundary formation that is unstable and breaks down under stress.

Schizophrenics with boundary deficits develop various compensatory strategies. Just as normal children segregate spaces for themselves to form psychological boundaries, some schizophrenics use the walls of rooms as coextensive with their bodies in the attempt to shore up boundaries. Walking out of an interview could be understood as using locomotion to establish greater distance to preserve unstable boundaries. The negativism characteristic of some schizophrenics could also be seen as an attempt to establish boundaries.

Using hypnotic visualizations, one can help highly hypnotizable schizophrenics to capitalize on such compensatory strategies to further the development of boundaries. Such a patient was a 32-year-old chronic paranoid schizophrenic who constantly felt that he was under the influence of others or that others deliberately wanted to harass him in public situations. He first learned in nonhypnotic therapy to use locomotion literally to establish distance from others, for example, by walking to the other side of the street when he feared others would walk into him or by leaving a restaurant when he was afraid others would harass him. In subsequent hypnotic therapy he learned to visualize himself floating inside a protective bubble with solid, durable boundaries at a sufficient distance from the therapist to preserve his own boundaries so that he would not need to fear he would merge with the hypnotherapist. He visualized the bubble at various distances and locations in imagined and real interactions, first with the therapist and then with others. Although in the beginning the bubble tended to break up readily, later it collapsed only in intense emotional interactions. Eventually, he learned to judge spatial distance so as to keep the bubble intact, without fragmentation, in most daily interactions. At that point he responded to the hypnotist's suggestion to "fit the bubble around the skin" as a step toward the formation of a stable body image. Such visualizations practiced repeatedly in hypnosis and self-hypnosis contributed to the patient's feeling "more real than I ever have." Another hypnotized patient, a borderline, visualized herself capable of expanding and contracting the walls of the therapy office until she found a safe and comfortable distance between herself and her therapist.

Hypnotic visualizations that aid boundary formation include:

1. **Safe Space Imagery.** The patient repeatedly visualizes a series of safe and protected imaginary environments until he is consistently able to generate, upon a signal, the experience of being contained within a safe and protected space.

2. **Regulation of Closeness and Distance.** The patient in trance visualizes himself in relation to the therapist (and others). Each time, he is instructed to regulate the imagined distance between himself and the therapist (and others) until he finds the distance that is most comfortable to him. For example, the patient imagines floating in his bubble at various distances from the therapist until he locates just the right distance. Or he may imagine expanding and contracting the imaginal space in which he and the therapist are contained until he discovers the right distance. The patient is symbolically given control over the distance between himself and the therapist.

3. **Barrier Imagery.** The patient uses imagery to clearly demarcate boundaries around the body, for example, solid boundaries around the imagined bubble or protective barriers around the safe space. These visu-

alizations must be practiced repeatedly until signs of boundary formation can be observed.

Body Image Formation.   Also implicated in Schizophrenia is a deficit in the formation of the body image, that visceral/kinesthetic representation derived from enteroceptive, tactile, and kinesthetic impressions. Like the development of boundaries, the formation of the body image requires a passage through several stages from the formation of representations for bodily experience, to the coalescence of these into partial body images, and ultimately to the development of an integrated whole-body image with clearly demarcated boundaries (Brown, Sands, & Jones, 1985; Lichtenberg, 1978; Mahler & McDevitt, 1982).

A developmental deficit in body image is reflected in the inability of those most severely disturbed to develop representations for bodily experience, of those moderately disturbed to develop only a partial and fragmented body image, and of those least severely disturbed to develop a body image that, although cohesive and integrated, is nevertheless unstable. Regardless of the level of body image development, the body image is vulnerable to further disintegration during psychotic episodes (Bychowski, 1943). Schizophrenics who fail to develop even partial body images may compensate with stereotypic posturing and grimacing, which can be understood as repetitive proprioceptive and sensoriperceptive stimulation so as to form fleeting memory impressions of bodily experience. Somatic delusions, however inaccurate, may be attempts to form more elaborate memory impressions of bodily experience, something akin to the formation of partial body images in the normally developing child. For schizophrenics who form unstable whole-body images, collecting body products (clipped nails or hair and feces), skin picking, and mirror gazing, may be attempts to counteract their fear of bodily disintegration.

Hypnosis can be used to stimulate the processes that lead to the formation of the normal body image in patients. Preparatory nonhypnotic therapies—yoga (Clance, Mitchell, & Engelman, 1980), physical exercise (Darby, 1970), and especially movement and sensory awareness training (Mosey, 1969)—are indicated for patients who are deficient in forming memory impressions from bodily experience. For highly hypnotizable schizophrenics, the hypnotist can combine sensory awareness and imaginal methods to enhance the development of a normal body image. He can suggest a series of fantasies involving body surface stimulation, such as being cuddled, bathed, or played with, or he can give suggestions to increase awareness of internal body sensations, such as being hungry or in pain. The patient is asked to identify and describe the resulting surface and internal bodily sensations evoked by the imagery.

The development of partial body images can be facilitated in hypnosis by having the patient repeatedly focus attention on certain body parts and on different internal body areas (left and right, top and bottom). The patient should try to discriminate the sensations associated with the inside and outside of the body. The patient is also instructed to scan the body surface systematically to identify the changing sensations. It is important for the patient to practice the body scan until he can readily "outline" the body's surface through immediate sensory experience.

The development of the whole-body image can also be stimulated in hypnosis by having the patient describe sensations associated with a series of movement exercises he imagines himself doing, movements that become progressively more complicated and purposeful. He also can fantasize dancing in front of a mirror and describe sensations evoked by making the imagined coordinated muscle movements. These hypnotic visualizations may be supplemented by real movement and sensory feedback exercises. For patients with unstable body images, barrier imagery can also be suggested. (A more detailed discussion of the stages of hypnotic reconstruction of the body image can be found in Brown, Sands & Jones, 1985.)

Development of Object Representations.   A developmental deficit or regression in object representations has been implicated in the various types of severe disturbance—schizophrenia (Bychowski, 1952; Modell, 1968; Volkan, 1976), affective psychosis (Jacobson, 1973), and borderline personality disorder (Kernberg, 1968). Having successfully negotiated the several stages in the structuring of object representations, or internal representations of others, the child develops the ability to integrate and retain the positive and the negative schemata of the self as well as those of the other. The child no longer needs to see people as either "all good" or "all bad." He now is capable of ambivalence and can love people, notwithstanding their faults, and can accept himself for what he is.

The schizophrenic, on the other hand, fails to develop a stable, integrated representational world, as can be seen in a variety of clinical phenomena: fluidity of representations and doubles (Volkan, 1976), free-floating introjects (Bychowski, 1952; Kernberg, 1976), the re-fusing of self- and object representations (Jacobson, 1973), auditory hallucinations (Modell, 1948), and splitting off the "bad" parts of the self and externalizing them in order to prevent "contamination" of the good part of the self by the bad. High functioning schizophrenics and borderlines do develop an integrated representational world which, nevertheless, is unstable and may disintegrate under stress like a crystalline structure breaking into pieces (Modell, 1968). Patients with personality disorders presumably form a stable representational world, but the internal representations are split (Kernberg, 1968, 1976).

Severely disturbed patients formulate a number of compensatory strategies in their attempts to construct a representational world. Just as during the symbiotic stage the normally developing child constructs the representational world through fantasies of merger (Jacobson, 1973) and omnipotent investment of the physical world with the contents of wishes (Modell, 1968), so does the schizophrenic patient attempt to compensate through psychotic fantasies (Jacobson, 1973). In these fantasies the therapist's sole purpose (in the view of the patient) is to meet all the patient's needs. He becomes the patient's entire world, and the patient hardly differentiates between himself and the therapist. Such fantasies signify regression to the very early mother–child relationship. Schizophrenic patients often harbor these psychotic fantasies outside the patient–therapist interaction (Blatt et al., 1980) and resist disclosing them to the therapist (Smith, 1977). Although the psychotic transference is commonly viewed as a potentially negative therapeutic reaction, some writers (Blatt et al., 1980; Little, 1960) have interpreted them as adaptive attempts to recapitulate the normal developmental task of the symbiotic stage, wherein merger in fantasy and omnipotent wishes are the means to establish a base of positive images from which the representational world can be (re)constructed. In a similar vein, others (Larkin, 1979; Modell, 1948) have interpreted auditory hallucinations as a revival of aspects of wished-for interactions in an attempt to create a gratifying internal world. Patients with lower level personality disorders, who presumably have developed an integrated but unstable representational world, utilize transitional objects and transitional modes of relationship (Arkema, 1981; Horton, Lovy, & Coppolillo, 1974) in order to stabilize that world. While patients with personality disorders at a higher level have a stable representational world, they fail to internalize certain functions (e.g., the regulation of self-esteem) and form dependent relationships to provide the missing functions by means of narcissistic object choice (Kohut, 1971; Reich, 1973).

The Hypnoanalysis of Patients with Developmental Deficits

Elgan Baker (1981), a psychologist-hypnoanalyst, has devised a protocol of seven consecutive steps for the hypnoanalytic treatment of psychotic patients. Fromm (1984) has extended it by one step and has shown that the more advanced steps can be used in the hypnoanalysis of borderline and narcissistic patients. Copeland (1986) has refined it. The eight steps of the protocol are:

Step 1. Hypnosis is induced. When the patient shows posturally or verbally that he feels relaxed, he is helped to imagine that he is alone and involved in some pleasant activity of his choosing. Throughout the hypnoanalytic hours in this phase, the hypnoanalyst suggests from time to time feelings of comfort and well being.

Step 2. Because the psychotic patient wishes to merge with "the other" (Erikson, 1984) but also fears the other person would destroy him or abandon him, it is important to let the patient recognize that the therapist is (peacefully) present even when he is not seen. The hypnotized patient again is instructed to visualize himself after he has closed his eyes and is in trance feeling comfortable, then after a while to open his eyes and look at the hypnoanalyst for a moment and close them again. Both Steps 1 and 2 may have to be repeated over quite a few hours.

Step 3. While continuing to give suggestions for feelings of relaxation and well being, the hypnoanalyst now asks the patient in trance to develop visual images of the therapist. Frequently that is difficult, especially, for psychotics and borderlines. In such cases, the hypnoanalyst should ask the patient to produce images that can serve as symbols for the therapist or as imaginary "transitional phenomena" (Winnicott, 1965). For instance, the hypnoanalyst may suggest that the patient imagine an object from the therapist's desk or the hypnoanalyst's name written on a blackboard; only after this visualization has been achieved regularly and easily, is the patient asked to imagine seeing the hypnoanalyst himself. The purpose is to help the patient eventually to develop visual images of the therapist as a separate person, alive and whole. It is the initial step toward object constancy.

Step 4. Here the measure of proximity between patient and hypno-analyst in the patient's imagery is left to the patient. Initially, psychotics and borderlines often imagine therapist and patient on opposite sides of a lake or on separate mountaintops with a chasm between them. It may take several weeks before they can visualize themselves in the same room with the hypnoanalyst. But gradually the hypnoanalyst can help the patient decrease the distance in the image while maintaining relaxation and comfort.

Step 5. This is perhaps *the* most important step in the whole series. It requires the hypnoanalyst to prove himself to the patient for many months, and sometimes years, to be a nurturing, protecting, supportive, empathic, and gratifying "good" parent figure, who sees the patient's good and admirable sides. Interactional fantasies can be suggested in which the hypnoanalyst takes the role of the "good" object. This role must be taken on by the therapist actively and with real empathy and sincerity. It is a step that will help the patient begin to introject the good object and to see himself as a "good me." In the imagery, interactional fantasies should be emphasized in which the hypnoanalyst provides the nurturing, "holding environment" (Winnicott, 1965) for the patient. For quite a long time the hypnoanalyst has to provide soothing and comfort. Toward the end of this period, the patient's adult ego can be enlisted to help provide the soothing and consolation for the suffering-child part of the patient. This is often done in connection with spontaneous or induced age regression.

Step 6. In this step, the hypnoanalyst helps the patient to externalize, in a controlled way, and rework distorted object representations. The patient is asked in the hypnotic state to visualize the "bad" object representations he has internalized, and to externalize them and let them go.

For instance, the patient may be told that now he can look deep inside of himself, as with an X-ray, where he can see the old image of the "bad" parent. When he sees it clearly, he is told that he can take the image of the "bad" parent out from within himself and find a new place for it, sometimes to integrate it in a new way, sometimes to let it go. For example, he may attach it to a balloon that he can allow to float away, or he can put it into a box and "shelve it" for good. The hypnoanalyst should also suggest to the patient that he keep within himself those parts of the parent that he can now recognize as good. And it can be suggested that the patient now visualize himself in the mask of the "bad" child, who sometimes may have provoked the parents' anger and thus became deprived, but who now can tear off the constraining mask of the "bad" small child and really grow and unfold all the good potential he has within himself (Eisen & Fromm, 1983).

In general it is preferable, as much as possible, to let the patient's own imagery and visualizations come up and then to guide them in the therapeutic direction.

Step 7. As stability of ego functioning grows, other significant love and hate objects appear in the patient's hypnotic imagery. Continued emphasis is placed on the integration of positive and negative interpersonal experiences, and on achieving solid, separate self- and object constancy.

Step 8. This step helps the patient to gain control over splitting as a defense, to integrate love and hate objects solidly, and to consolidate the gains made. The therapist explains to the patient in the waking state that a mother cannot always gratify a child's needs, that some frustration of dependent wishes leads to the child's moving towards autonomy and growth, that all people have both good characteristics and bad ones, and that people can be giving even when they withhold. He can help the patient to see that the world is not black and white. He can now point out how the patient has transferred to the hypnoanalyst and other people in his current adult environment his early defense of splitting the beloved parent (who sometimes had to frustrate him) into an "all-good" and an "all-bad" object; and how unrealistic it is to see people at times as all-good and at other times as all-bad. Unrealistic feelings and fantasies that have a destructive effect on the patient and his environment can now be talked about and made ego dystonic, so the patient will not revert to this defense in the future.

In the hypnotic state the patient may be asked to look carefully at these unrealistic feelings in imagery, to bundle them up, put them in a can marked "trash," throw them from a bridge into a fast-flowing river, and let them float away. Or various fantasies and guided images can be used in hypnosis that emphasize bonding the "bad" image of the mother with the now safely internalized good image of the therapist. In this phase, the patient must constantly be shown that the good relationship with the therapist is not destroyed by this merger and that the therapist continues to stand by him.

The purpose of Step 1 is to allay the patient's fear of being engulfed and annihilated by the therapist; that of Step 2 is to lay the groundwork for the concept of separateness of object and self. Step 3 serves to help the patient develop visual images of the hypnoanalyst as a live, whole, and separate person; Step 4, to aid the patient to imagine himself and the therapist comfortably together. In Step 5, the hypnoanalyst takes on a very nurturing, protective stance, so that the patient can conceive of him as a gratifying "good" object that he internalizes and that helps him to gain a positive self-image. In Step 6, the hypnoanalyst helps the patient to externalize distorted self- and object representations; in Step 7, to integrate love and hate objects; and in Step 8, to achieve solid, separate self- and object constancy and to gain control over splitting as a defense.

This eight-step protocol for the hypnoanalytic treatment of patients who have suffered a deficit along the developmental line of the self is a real innovation in the practice of psychotherapy. Although the underlying ideas about the different types of transferences and the different grades of developmental deficits in the psychotic, the borderline, and the narcissistic patient clearly stem from psychoanalytic object relations theory and self theory, the technique itself is a contribution made to the field by hypnoanalysis.

Psychotics are afraid of entering interpersonal relationships because they wish to merge with the other person but at the same time fear that they either will be engulfed and destroyed by the other or destroy him. With psychotic patients, hypnoanalysis therefore should start with Steps 1 and 2.

The borderline patient is farther along the road to object constancy than the schizophrenic. Therefore, hypnoanalytic work with borderlines can be started with Step 3 or 4. But in all hypnotic work with psychotics as well as with borderlines, it is imperative to start each hypnotic session with the induction of relaxation and comfort.

With the narcissistic patient, the sequence can begin with Step 5.

The Development of Self-Representations

According to Lichtenberg's (1975) integrative theory of self-development, the three discrete groupings of self-representations—the body self, the differentiated self- and object representations, and the grandiose self—converge at a critical point of development into the cohesive sense of self. The development of the cohesive sense of self in childhood (Lichtenberg, 1975) and its later reformulation as a sense of identity in adolescence (Erikson, 1959) mark a milestone in normal human development. The experiential consequences of the cohesive sense of self are profound: it lends coherence to personal experience (Kohut, 1971), it provides a stable frame of reference ("I") around which to orient experience in the world (Spiegel, 1959), and it gives continuity to experience over time and across changes in state and context (Lichtenberg, 1975).

Developmental arrest or regression, which results in failure to synthesize or keep synthesized a cohesive sense of self, is present in psychosis (Kohut, 1977; Wexler, 1971). Some psychotics, especially chronic schizophrenics, fail to develop a cohesive sense of self; others, some acute schizophrenics, have an unstable sense of self or a false self (Winnicott, 1960), which easily fragments under stress and under the developmental task of identity formation characteristic of adolescence (which presupposes an intact self-structure) (Bowers, et al., 1961). Lacking this sense of self, the psychotic's experience does not cohere. The patient has no personal frame of reference. He experiences the world from the outside in rather than from the inside out. Experience is discontinuous, each moment entirely new and strange. A clear sense of personal history is absent.

Hypnosis is a useful adjunct to ongoing therapy when the goal is the construction of a cohesive sense of self and the psychotic is hypnotizable. First, it aids the establishment of an internal frame of reference. Bowers et al. (1961) nearly 30 years ago described an hypnotic treatment designed to help the psychotic patient to make contact with the "sense of 'I am,'" believed to be hidden and protected. She called this poorly developed frame of reference the "little me." Hypnosis provided a permissive context along with explicit suggestions to foster the growth of this self-experience. Spontaneous experience of genuine needs and feelings and encouragement of the ability to play in trance were vehicles to develop the sense of self as a frame of reference.

The self psychologist Khan (1972) has described a very similar process in nonhypnotic psychoanalytic treatment to facilitate growth of self-experience for patients suffering what he called "the privacy of the self." Self-denying attempts to comply with the analyst and use the analyst as a frame of reference were interpreted until the patient was able to "disregard" the analyst in favor of playful exploration of the self.

Hypnosis can be used, too, in developing a sense of continuity in life experience and identity. Bowers et al. (1961) described the use of age regression in the full service of structural repair. Age regression to various points in one's personal history is a means of bringing a variety of emotion-laden life experiences to conscious awareness. The structural work can be enhanced on termination of the trance. The therapist and patient must work to organize these life experiences into a continuous life story.

Through repetition of hypnotic age regression and nonhypnotic ordering of the recovered experiences, the patient gradually comes to realize the continuity of a personal history. Patients can be encouraged to make the developing sense of continuity concrete by writing these events into an autobiography.

Affective Development. Still another deficit to be found in schizophrenic and borderline patients is in the area of affect, whose development first occurs as a dimension of perceptual maturation—the child is intensely interested in novel, complex, and changing stimuli. Proceeding through the various stages of this domain, the child learns to sustain interest in processing discrepant stimuli (Izard, 1977) and to regulate internal tensions (Greenspan & Lourie, 1981) by manifested states of pleasureable or unpleasurable activation. In the symbiotic phase, during which the child forms a bond with the caregiver, the child develops self-awareness (Lewis, Brooks, & Haviland, 1978). As the autonomic nervous system matures, the child applies this self-awareness to distinguish between internal and externally caused sensations, as well as to discriminate a variety of visceral changes as the capacity for primary emotional experience develops—moods (Tronick, Ricks & Cohn, 1982) and the 8-month anxieties (Campos et al., 1978).

At some point an important integration takes place and primary affective experience becomes associated with developing self- and object representations, on the one hand (Emde et al., 1978; Kernberg, 1968; Novey, 1959), and becomes organized within a matrix of affective memories and concepts, on the other (Klein, 1967). As cognition develops, the nascent visceral experiences are given greater specificity. A variety of specific emotional states gain definition. The infant now possesses the capacity for a wide range of affective experiences and later develops the capability for affective tolerance through internalization of the repeated soothing responses given by the caregiver (Mahler et al., 1975; Tolpin, 1971).

If a developmental failure occurs at the earliest stage, the schizophrenic may lack the fundamental sense of aliveness from which a sense of existence and motivation are derived (Perry, 1980). If the failure occurs during the stage of discrimination of visceral experiences, the schizophrenic may manifest a failure in the capacity for emotional experience.

Self-destructive behavior such as cutting or burning, compulsive masturbation, and violent or bizarre sexual activity are attempts to compensate for affective failure. Such behavior creates, even for only brief moments, a sense of aliveness. Schizophrenics also try to infer internal affective states through symbolic reading of external cues, such as changes in others' facial expression or gestures and through their own observable tension level (Perry, 1980).

Hypnosis can facilitate the development of affect. Highly hypnotizable schizophrenics can learn to acquire a state of intense interest in which they carefully scan the body surface and the internal milieu to identify the stream of novel and changing sensations for longer and longer periods. They also learn through practice to feel these sensations with greater and greater intensity.

For one such patient, the result of months of such hypnotic practice was a sense of aliveness and awareness of intense energy shifts within the body. Continuous practice resulted in spontaneous panic attacks, a yet unmodulated form of anxiety. The patient then learned under hypnosis to identify internal sensory perceptions in a more refined way, that is, to specify various patterns of bodily sensations and their different bodily locations (Mason, 1961). Hypnotic suggestions evoked spontaneous vivid visual imagery, memories, and thoughts in association with the patterns of bodily sensations. Thus the patient learned to link differentiated somatic experiences with cognitive processes eventually to integrate affective experiences. At that time she reported that her usually racing thoughts had slowed down. A number of specific affects became available in association with specific life events, for instance, sadness and anger, and later pleasurable affects related to a sense of well being. With the aid of posthypnotic suggestions to reinforce the work, she was taught to gain quick access to a variety of specific emotions and associated fantasies and memory material. It was then possible to treat her further in ongoing nonhypnotic therapy. (For a more complete discussion of the specific hypnotic techniques to develop affective experience, see Brown, 1985.)

Treating the Seriously Suicidal Patient with Developmental Hypnotherapy

People make serious suicide attempts for essentially two reasons: They lack a sustained sense of connection to others, and they lack internal mechanisms to soothe and comfort themselves. The socially isolated and interpersonally impaired patient is at the greatest risk of suicide (Fawcett, Leff & Bunney, 1969). These patients complain of being incapable of loving and being loved. They are unable to find gratification in relationships, even truly caring relationships. Relationships are a source of discomfort, not of pleasure. This deficit in human connection probably represents some form of impairment in the development of object relations (Maltsberger & Buie, 1980).

Patients at high risk for suicide also complain of experiencing an unusual degree of pain in daily life. They live in constant fear or misery, from which they find little relief. This inability to find comfort and peace probably signifies an underlying deficit in affect tolerance and in self-soothing mechanisms. The normal child develops soothing mechanisms during the separation-individuation phase of development by internalizing the comforting provided repeatedly by the caregivers during affective storms (Tolpin, 1971). Adults vulnerable to intense panic and distress states presumably have failed to develop adequate self-soothing mechanisms. Even when they are not in an affective storm, the world is seldom experienced as a safe and secure place.

According to Maltsberger and Buie (1980), there are three motives for suicide: revenge, riddance, and rebirth. Revenge suicide is object related— the patient is trying to manage aggressive impulses by getting back at someone. When revenge suicide is attempted, it may be lethal but is not consistently fatal. Because the patient maintains his sense of connection to others, he may survive the attempt even if the connection is through intense hatred. Riddance suicide, the most common of serious suicide types, is motivated by the desire to rid oneself of the pain of existence. Rebirth suicide patients seek soothing in fantasy and believe that other realms, or death itself, will provide the soothing that is lacking in human existence. They actively seek death as a compensatory strategy to resolve the deficit in self-soothing and to disengage from relationships.

From a developmental perspective, treatment of the seriously suicidal patient entails correction of the deficits in relatedness and self-soothing. Hypnosis can serve as an adjunct to the therapeutic work by presenting the patient with a series of structured visualizations designed to facilitate the repair. It goes without saying that management of acute suicidal behavior is through hospitalization and medication, where indicated. Beyond this, the ongoing treatment of the seriously suicidal patient begins with an assessment of the patient's soothing capacities, by asking how he finds peace and comfort. Some people utilize transitional objects and related behaviors to gain the soothing they seek; personal journals, reading, music, shopping, and substance use are among common soothing objects and activities. Others rely on transitional space. They feel secure only in a dark, safe place, or in wide, open spaces, or in a natural environment (like a forest or the oceanside). Still others utilize transitional modes of relatedness: identification with characters in novels, relating to an imaginary companion, developing a crush on someone, relating to a pet, or finding a relationship with God through prayer.

These transitional modes of relatedness are adaptive in that they allow the individual to sustain a sense of connectedness to others at a safe distance from the conflicts experienced in real, everyday relationships. The therapist first lets the patient name for him all the transitional objects and phenomena he has utilized at various points in his life and then lists them in hierarchical order. The patient is hypnotized and asked to imagine a comforting scene until some degree of comfort is attained. Often the patient will need to repeat the visualization many times to generate any sense of comfort. The therapist may also need to experiment with various types of soothing imagery until he hits upon the most effective. Seriously suicidal patients at first have difficulty experiencing any soothing, and, of course, the difficulty itself exemplifies the developmental deficit. Because of the hopelessness and helplessness accompanying serious suicidal wishes, the therapist must actively structure the exercises and convey the expectation that they will in time be effective.

Eventually even the highly suicidal patient should find some form of soothing imagery. If not, the therapist can directly introduce transitional objects to the patient. These are durable objects or activities that provide a sense of soothing—a paperweight, writing in a personal journal or listening to music when upset. The earliest visualizations typically involve transitional space rather than people. The goal at this stage is to establish some experience of soothing at an imaginal level. The patient learns to retreat to his safe and protected place whenever he experiences discomfort. The patient is encouraged to practice self-hypnosis and to generate the safe internal place as needed, even many times a day. Once the patient acquires some skill in imagining a comforting, safe space, the therapist introduces new imagery, telling the patient to imagine other ways of feeling safe, comfortable, and at peace. The therapist also encourages fantasy involvement, for example, finding comfort by the ocean or in the forest. The aim is to expand the range of soothing imagery available to the patient.

At some point, a shift from transitional space to transitional modes of relatedness is indicated. The patient begins to imagine soothing derived from some form of relatedness—God, a pet, an imaginary companion, a once trusted friend. The patient practices generating a soothing experience through imaginal relatedness. The patient becomes able to imagine soothing in association with the therapist and the process of therapy. He reports thinking about the therapist, the process of therapy, or the hypnotic trance when upset and then feeling some comfort. Later the patient is able to develop an internal capacity for self-soothing and a sense of connectedness to the therapist. Then, the patient and the therapist examine more closely the vicissitudes of self-soothing. They scrutinize the situations in which the patient was or was not able to sustain a sense of comfort. The goal is to help the patient maintain self-soothing in a more continual manner and in a variety of life situations without relapse.

As the sense of connectedness to the therapist and then to others strengthens and self-soothing mechanisms have been internalized, the patient's suicidal risk greatly diminishes. This structural repair happens in the context of an ongoing therapeutic relationship, through which internalization occurs. It is difficult to apportion the relative contribution of the therapeutic relationship on the one hand, and the series of hypnotic visualizations on the other, to the overall outcome of the treatment.

Conclusion

All that has been discussed in this section suggests that it is time to reconsider hypnosis in the treatment of the severely disturbed patient. In the past 10 years the hypnotizability of some schizophrenics has been well documented (Lavoie, Sabourin, & Langlois, 1973; Pettinati, 1983). Yet, it has not been clear how to utilize hypnotizability for clinical gain with such patients. The recent convergence of psychoanalytic ego psychology, object relations theory, self psychology, and affect development theory into a more comprehensive developmental lines perspective for the treatment of severe disturbances offers the needed theoretical rationale for such treatment.

The usefulness of developmental lines theory in hypnotherapy with severely disturbed patients depends primarily on the accuracy of the developmental assessment. To the extent that it is possible, the therapist must understand which lines of development are deficient and at which stage(s) the deficits occured. Subtle developmental assessment of this sort is not as easy to make as are the descriptive symptomatic assessments that are used in the DSM III (American Psychiatric Association, 1980). Development is best assessed by evaluating how the clinical material unfolds over time in the therapy relationship (Kohut, 1971). Since hypnotherapy with severely disturbed patients is advocated only after preparatory nonhypnotic therapy, the therapist is likely to have a wealth of clinical material available to make such an assessment. Furthermore, the therapist can be guided by the spontaneous compensatory strategies evident in the patient's behavior. The goal in each phase of therapy is to match the hypnotic interventions with the specific developmental tasks the patient is trying to accomplish.

We have advocated here using hypnotherapy after preparatory nonhypnotic therapy, that is, where conflicts around control in the psychotic transference (Burnham, et al., 1969) are offset by a strong alliance or have been otherwise worked through. Others introduce hypnosis early in the treatment of the severely disturbed patient, using special parameters to reduce complications (Baker, 1981; Scagnelli, 1975, 1976, 1977). The goal of hypnotherapy with severely disturbed patients is genuine structural change, for example, the formation of boundaries or a stable body image, the development of differentiated and stable self- and object representations, resulting in a cohesive sense of self, and the capacity to experience and tolerate genuine affect. Structural change means the alleviation of psychotic symptoms (first-rank symptoms and thought disorder) and behaviors associated with borderlines (the incapacity to tolerate aloneness and panic states). The schizophrenic patient develops a subjective sense of aliveness and connectedness to others. Behaviorally, these patients develop the ability for meaningful work and for sustaining caring relationships beyond the therapy. The borderline patient develops a more realistic capability for relationships and the capability to bear intense affects. Such changes, felt subjectively by the patient, can be identified by the therapist and recognized by significant others as well.

HYPNOSIS AND POST-TRAUMATIC STRESS DISORDERS

Traumatic neurosis, and post-traumatic stress disorder (PTSD), are syndromes arising from exposure to extraordinarily stressful situations. According to DSM III (American Psychiatric Association, 1980), PTSD is induced by events generally outside the range of normal human experience, events so stressful that they can produce symptoms in almost anyone exposed to them. Events that typically cause PTSDs fall into two classes: natural disasters (tornadoes, earthquakes, volcanic eruptions, storms, floods, fires, and animal attacks); and human aggression (assault, rape, burglary, kidnapping, hijacking, political incarceration and torture, war, and holocaust). These situations are so removed from ordinary, everyday experience that therefore even the healthiest of people are ill equipped to cope with them.

Exposure to extraordinary circumstances produces a predictable cluster of symptoms, though not always pathological. With respect to many traumatic events, the course of these symptoms is typically short lived. These symptoms represent the patient's attempt to adapt to the unusual circumstances and to integrate the experience. Horowitz (1976) has described the typical course of recovery from stress. According to his information-processing model of traumatic response, many of the symptoms of PTSD are biphasic. The initial reaction of outcry is typically followed by either denial or the intrusive state. Over the course of time, the patient alternates between denial and the intrusive state until the experience is worked through. The frequency and intensity of the symptoms gradually diminish, and, on completion of this process, the symptoms disappear.

Sometimes the duration of symptoms is prolonged, their manifestation is excessively intense, or their working through is blocked (Horowitz, 1974, 1976). The normal post-traumatic response can become pathological, when (a) the patient's degree of control over the symptoms is called into question, (b) he becomes excessively preoccupied with the symptoms, or (c) the symptoms have a severe impact on the various areas of his life functioning (Green, Wilson, & Lindy, 1985). The diagnosis of pathological PTSD is made when the normal process of recovery is blocked and the symptoms remain for prolonged periods of time, sometimes decades.

The typical symptoms of PTSD include cognitive, affective, and behavioral manifestations. During the denial phase, cognition is restricted. The patient is virtually incapable of fantasy productions and is amnestic for significant events in his life history. General affective numbing is the hallmark of PTSD during the denial phase. Severe trauma affects the ability to utilize affects as signals (Krystal, 1984). PTSD is also characterized by a generalized behavioral inhibition in many life spheres. The patient tends to restrict activities, narrows his range of interests, and withdraws from social interactions. He may become quite detached from life. In cases of extreme trauma, such as the Nazi holocaust, the patient may seem to be a "walking corpse" (Niederland, 1968) and responds as if "dead to the world" (Murray, 1967). During the intrusive phase, the patient suffers from intrusive, unbidden recurring thoughts and ruminations and from hypermnestic flooding. Affect storms, for example, panic and rage attacks, frequently overwhelm the person. Traumatization can impair the capacity for affect tolerance. Behaviorally, there is a strong tendency to re-enact the traumatic situation in current life. The risk of repetition extends beyond the individual. The intergenerational risk subsequent to traumatization is well documented for children of incest survivors (Gelinas, 1983) and of holocaust survivors (Danielli, 1985). Table 8.1 summarizes the typical phasic alternation between denial and intrusive symptoms.

PTSDs are characterized by a variety of other symptoms. Chronic anxiety or depression is extremely prevalent (Krystal, 1984; Niederland, 1968), so prevalent in fact that PTSDs are often misdiagnosed as depression in those patients who present during the denial phase. Poor self-care is an outcome of severe traumatization (Krystal, 1984). Substance and alcohol abuse are extremely prevalent among traumatized persons, who use the substances in an attempt to cope with intolerable affects (Brende, 1984; Lacoursière, Godfrey, & Ruby, 1980; Nace, Meyers, O'Brien, Ream, & Mintz, 1977). Somatization is also very common. There is a high incidence of conversion reactions and psychophysiological disorders

TABLE 8.1
Typical Manifestations of PTSD

I. Information-Processing Model: Cognitive, Affective and Behavioral Symptoms
  A. Symptoms of the Denial and Intrusive Phases of PTSD

	Phase	
Psychological Mode	*Denial*	*Intrusion*
Cognition	amnesia	hypermnestic flooding
Affect	numbing	affect storms
Behavior	inhibition	compulsion to repeat

  B. Other typical symptoms
    1. Atypical dream life
    2. Dissociative episodes
  C. Symptoms Prevalent in Disguised PTSD
    1. Chronic anxiety and depression
    2. Substance and alcohol abuse
    3. Somatization and conversion reactions
    4. Cognitive impairment
    5. Acting out and antisocial behavior

II Psychobiological Model: Autonomic Hyperactivity
  A. Conditioned hypersensitivity to stimuli
  B. Sensation-seeking
  C. Addiction to trauma

III. Structural-Developmental Model: Fluid Character Pathology
  A. Impaired relationships; estrangement from others
  B. Arrested self development (restriction of interests and activities)
  C. Complicated mourning reactions and rage reactions (associated with loss of real and transitional modes of relatedness)
  D. Internalization of Negative Introjects (killer-self, victim-self introjects, identification with death)
  E. Self-as-object experience
  F. Primitivization of group relationships

IV. Structural-Developmental Model: Disregulation of Impulse
  A. Hypo- and hypersexuality
  B. Extreme inhibition of aggression (chronic passivity); chronic irritability; episodic assaultiveness

among PTSD patients (Krystal, 1968). Traumatization may also contribute to a variety of more or less serious cognitive deficits, such as impaired concentration, forgetting, cognitive disorganization, and confusion, and, in children, learning disabilities. Dissociative states are another hallmark of PTSD. Whether in the denial or in the intrusive phase, traumatized patients have an atypical sleep and dream life. A history of repetitive nightmares or, less frequently, frightening day images whose content is associated with the trauma are the most reliable signs of PTSD (Kramer,

Schoen, & Kinney, 1984). People with PTSD are also prone to lapse into dissociative states, such as flashbacks, in which they re-experience the trauma when exposed to events that resemble or symbolize some elements of the actual traumatic situation. Acting out (Pynoos & Eth, 1985) and antisocial behavior (Scurfield, 1985) are often signs of PTSD, especially in adolescents.

There are a number of psychological sequelae of exposure to extraordinarily stressful events. Traumatization often shatters some of the basic assumptions one holds about the world and about human relationships. Most normal persons perceive life as meaningful. Most have relatively intact self-esteem. Most people also think of themselves as invulnerable to harm and persist in the belief that tragedy always happens to the other person. Exposure to a traumatic event shatters these ordinary beliefs (Janoff-Bulman, 1985).

Most natural disasters are unpredictable; most traumata caused by human destructiveness are senseless. Whether or not a particular person is directly affected by a trauma is often purely a matter of chance. Survival or death in combat, natural disaster, or holocaust occurs more or less on a random basis. The randomness and senselessness of these events disrupt the everyday belief that life is meaningful and that events are causally related (Krystal, 1968). Survivor guilt is the typical consequence of the person's difficulty in accounting for his chance survival and other's harm or death (Krystal, 1968). The experience of survivor guilt becomes all the more complicated when the person was forced to make unnatural moral decisions about who would live or die (Krystal, 1968).

People often experience unusual degrees of helplessness during the trauma, an experience that erodes the normal tendency to view oneself as an effective and esteemed person. Traumatized people live in fear of recurrence of disaster (Burgess & Holmstrom, 1974; Janoff-Bulman, 1985; Krystal, 1984) or expect abuse from others (Summit & Kryso, 1978). Their basic trust in the world is shattered (Lifton, 1968). The most common experience is of vulnerability and unsafety (Davis & Friedman, 1985). They may overreact to or even catastrophize everyday hassles. This catastrophizing of everyday life occurs because their fundamental perception of control over the environment has been destroyed (Kelman, 1945), and dissonance has been created between the perception of ordinary reality and that of the traumatic reality (Shatan, 1985). It becomes very difficult, for example, for a survivor of incest experiences or of a political holocaust to reconcile the previously held perception of a just world with the extraordinary tragedy to which he has been exposed.

Not all psychological sequelae, however, are negative. Because of the extraordinary nature of their encounters, survivors of severe trauma can teach fundamental truths about evil, injustice, human dignity and higher values (Scurfield, 1985). Some gain a rare wisdom and compassion while suffering and find the strength to endure it in order to tell their story to the world. However, this outcome, contingent upon healthy recovery, is rare. The more common psychological outcome is the "conspiracy of silence" characteristic of most post-traumatic adjustment (Krystal, 1968; Lister, 1982).

The aforementioned symptoms, typical of most prolonged PTSD, represent only part of the overall domain of post-traumatic sequelae. The list of diagnostic criteria for PTSD in DSM III (American Psychiatric Association, 1980) is strongly biased toward patients who present intrusive symptoms (Laufer, Brett, & Gallops, 1984). Many people exposed to trauma manifest a disguised presentation (Gelinas, 1983). Their only obvious symptoms are chronic low-grade depression, substance abuse, somatic complaints, and sometimes, when detected, a disturbed dream life. Horowitz's (1974, 1976) biphasic stress response model conveys more of the scope of the typical stress symptoms. However, both models fail to account for the more serious consequences of traumatization, namely, enduring biological and characterological alterations. The DSM III and Horowitz's accounts of PTSD limit the description of effects largely to the cognitive, affective, and behavioral spheres. Recent research has shown that the overall domain of traumatic effects should include at least several additional areas: biological consequences and characterological effects.

Exposure to extraordinarily stressful stimuli can produce persistent changes in biological response mechanisms. The organism responds to threatening stimuli with sympathetic arousal. Chronic repetitive exposure to especially overwhelming stressors can cause a sustained hypersensitivity to stimuli (Bychowski, 1968). The person is readily prone to startle sensitivity. He becomes vulnerable to sympathetically mediated increases in heart rate, systolic blood pressure, and muscle tension and the release of a cascade of humoral agents (norepinephrine, dopamine, endogenous opioids (Anisman, 1978; Van der Kolk, Boyd, Krystal, & Greenberg, 1984). This enduring "physioneurosis" represents a "presistent defect in the emergency control system" (Kardiner, 1941, p. 987) in which the organism has become conditioned (Dobbs & Wilson, 1960; Kolb & Mutalipassi, 1982) to produce sympathetic arousal at slight or no provocation. Some people remain in a chronic state of sympathetic andrenergic hyperactivity. Others may also actively seek additional traumatization in order to recreate the heightened sense of arousal. Voluntary sensation seeking, addiction to trauma, and mistreatment are common in populations of certain severely traumatized people, such as Vietnam veterans (Van der Kolk et al., 1984).

For the normally developing child, the formation of the representational world depends on an average expectable environment (Hartmann, 1958), a "good enough" maternal holding environment (Winnicott, 1965), and consistent mirroring interactions with the primary caregiver (Kohut, 1971). Within this context internalization can take place (Meissner, 1981), through which the child assimilates qualities of the interaction with others and develops a cohesive self and a matrix of internal representations of others. "Progressive structuralization" occurs (Gedo & Goldberg, 1973). The maintenance of psychic structure also depends on an average expectable environment and "holding" (Winnicott, 1965) interactions with others. Certain man-made traumatic situations, notably wars and holocausts, are circumstances in which neither the environment is predictable nor people act as human beings ordinarily do. These traumata represent total destruction of the structures of the world (Lifton, 1968). War and holocaust set the conditions for psychic destructuralization—a reversal of growth along the normal developmental lines of self- and object representations and of affect. Regardless of whether the premorbid personality adjustment was normal or pathological, an unpredictable, severely terrifying, and dehumanizing environment can precipitate the development of "fluid character pathology" (Parson, 1984) in previously normal people. In other words, even when the boys who are sent off to war come home alive and physically healthy, they may come home as very disturbed boys. Evidence suggests that certain environments may cause character disorders or even psychoses. Psychotic decompensation and permanent character change were reported, for example, in a subgroup of Nazi holocaust survivors (Bychowski, 1968; Niederland, 1968; Venzlaff, 1968). Characterological changes are especially likely to occur when the traumatized person has had the experience of being made into an object, that is, has been treated in inhuman ways (Krystal, 1968), or finds himself acting in ways that challenge his idealized self-image (Kelman, 1945).

Wars, holocaust, and sometimes other forms of victimization result in a loss of relationships and transitional modes of relatedness (Fox, 1974; Haley, 1985a). During war and other chronically life-threatening situations, people tend to form intense narcissistic relationships with peers and authorities to cope with the fear of annihilation. Because war buddies or fellow victims of a political holocaust are likely to die, rage reactions and complicated mourning reactions are quite common (Fox, 1974; Meerloo, 1968). For Vietnam combatants, disillusionment with commanding officers and with the government and resultant lethal rage reactions (Fox, 1974), and for holocaust victims severe inhibitions toward aggression and assertiveness, are all too common experiences.

Persons who have experienced war and holocaust repeatedly bear witness to humans behaving in nonhuman ways. Watching or participating in murder or repeatedly being the victim of torture or starvation has a profound impact on the ongoing development of the representational world. A person may internalize a killer-self after being given permission to kill during a war (Brende, 1984; Parson, 1984) or a victim-self after exposure to traumatization (Krystal, 1968; Parson, 1984). During the traumatic episode he may experience primitivization of group relationships, in which he is reduced to a mindless member of a primal horde in a regressed combat unit or may become a blind and ruthless perpetrator of atrocities on his own people in a holocaust camp (Meerloo, 1968). Where the person is exposed to daily life threats, as in guerrilla warfare or a holocaust camp, death itself is introjected. Identification with death is a common reaction in such instances, a presence that colors everyday experience (Niederland, 1968; Shatan, 1973). Pathological introjects such as these tend to become split off from the conscious matrix of representations and maintain a quasi-autonomous existence. Such splitting interferes with the overall integration of the psyche. Furthermore, certain life events can reactivate these introjects years later. The person may find himself repeatedly acting out the victim role in relationships or lapsing into a dissociative state, in which he assaults another.

A chronically unpredictable and dehumanizing environment disrupts the process of self-development. Arrested self-development (Parson, 1984) can take many forms: identity diffusion (Parson, 1984), lesions in the self-concept (Buchenholz & Frank, 1949), depersonalization (Jacobson, 1971), fragmentation of the self (Parson, 1984); impaired autonomy (Brende, 1984), and alteration in the structure and content of the self-representations (Parson, 1984).

One of the most common results of dehumanizing traumatizations—whether rape or holocaust—is the experience of the self-as-object (Parson, 1984). As repeated experience of the self-as-object becomes assimilated into the self-representation, the individual undergoes a number of personality changes: increased emotional detachment (Lifton, 1968), chronic passivity (Krystal, 1968; Morrier, 1984), severe impairment of healthy competitive strivings (Krystal, 1968), inhibition of intellectual pursuits, restriction in the range of life activities (Krystal, 1968; Kilpatrick, 1985), impaired attachment behavior (Krystal, 1968; Parson, 1984), and impaired self-care (Krystal, 1968, 1984).

Chronic exposure to life-threatening events may precipitate the formation of pathological self-representations, such as the "slave self" in holocaust survivors (Krystal, 1968) or identification with death in the life of Hiroshima survivors (Lifton, 1968). Another is the illusion of invulnerability (Parson, 1984). Combatants are sometimes observed to develop defensive grandiosity. They unrealistically believe that they cannot be harmed by the enemy and unwittingly put themselves in extreme danger.

Traumatization that occurs during childhood may result in a premature acceleration of development. A common pattern associated with childhood incest is parentification, in which the incest victim is selected to bear the roles and functions of the parents in numerous ways. Parentification interferes with the spontaneous use of childhood play, which is important in the development of self. Another common consequence of childhood trauma is role confusion within the family. Traumatization during adolescence may cause arrested adolescent development (Haley, 1985b; Krystal, 1968). When it occurs during adulthood, the individual may, in an effort to restore continuity to self-experience, resort to overidealization of his life history prior to traumatization (Futterman & Pumpian-Midlin, 1951). The overall result of severe traumatization is an arrest in the development of the self, a reversal in the development of the self, or pathological self-development.

Repeated exposure to unpredictable and dehumanizing traumatic situations may impair affective development and drive regulation. For example, the systematic challenge to social inhibitions against the expression of aggression encountered, in basic training, followed by the permission to release rampant aggression during active combat, may significantly alter the otherwise normal regulation of aggressive impulses in soldiers. A typical consequence of war experience is chronic irritability (Kardiner, 1941; Kolb & Mutalipassi, 1982), and where homecoming ceremonies designed to resocialize the returning veteran fail, as they have with Vietnam veterans, an enduring outcome may be vulnerability to episodic violent outbursts and sadistic behaviors (Fox, 1974; Krystal, 1968, 1984). In the extreme situation where the normal expression of aggression is repeatedly suppressed, as in a Nazi holocaust camp, the long-term outcome for the survivor may also be "chronic reactive aggression" (Hoppe, 1962). Whenever the traumatizing environment repeatedly forces extreme inhibition or release of aggression, the impairment to the normal regulation of aggression may long outlast the traumatic situation.

Similarly, repeated traumatization may interfere with the normal regulation of sexual impulses. The overstimulation of a child by incest or molestation may result in a condition of sexual hyperarousal and a sexualization of behavior. If the child is not treated, this disregulation of sexual functioning may persist into adulthood and take the form of either hypersexuality or extreme inhibition of sexual desire (Burgess & Holstrom, 1974; Donaldson & Gardner, 1985; Gelinas, 1983). Sexual dysfunction as a consequence of exposure to a terror-ridden environment has also been reported for a subgroup of adult Vietnam veterans (Figley, 1978) and for holocaust survivors (Krystal, 1968).

The overall domain of post-traumatic sequelae includes cognitive, affective, and behavioral symptoms and also enduring biological and characterological effects. It is useful to distinguish between simple PTSD and complicated PTSD. Simple PTSD is based on the principle of cognitive processing of the traumatic experience. The typical cognitive, affective, and behavioral symptoms of simple PTSD are time limited. When normal cognitive processing of the traumatic experience is blocked, simple PTSD symptoms sometimes are either prolonged or delayed. Nevertheless, simple PTSD rests on the assumption that resolution *can* occur if the conditions are established that facilitate processing of the event. Complicated PTSD, or post-traumatic decline (Titchener & Knapp, 1978), rests on a different assumption, namely, that resolution is impaired so that even where cognitive processing of the trauma is not blocked, recovery does not necessarily occur. In complicated PTSD, enduring and perhaps irreversible changes have occurred in the regulation of the autonomic nervous system and of impulse control, and in the structuralization of the ego. Recovery from complicated PTSD is possible only in the context of a long-term therapeutic relationship where internalization takes place.

We are gaining increasing understanding of the conditions that contribute to the development of both prolonged or delayed PTSD, on the one hand, and complicated PTSD, on the other hand. These factors are summarized in Table 8.2. According to Horowitz (1974), the extent of the symptoms is a function of the intensity and duration of the traumatic situation. We define the intensity of a traumatic situation by the degree of disorganization it causes the individual in any area(s) of his life. Traumatization may occur when there is displacement from a familiar place to an entirely new and unpredictable or terror-ridden environment (Gleser, Green, & Winget, 1981; Parson, 1984), such as the environment of guerrilla warfare of Vietnam, the Nazis' disrupting ordinary life and displacing the Jews to death camps, or the total destruction of the known "world" in Hiroshima (Lifton, 1968). Traumatization may also involve the complete breakup of a known community, a fact well-documented in the 1972 Buffalo Creek dam disaster (Erikson, 1976; Gleser et al., 1981; Newman, 1976), or the loss of cultural belief systems, as in POW and brainwashing experience (Lifton, 1961).

Certain types of traumatic situations also disrupt normal social relationships. A common contributor to acute PTSD symptoms is the loss of wartime buddies (Haley, 1985a). In some wars, like Vietnam, the intentional discouragement of a wartime buddy system and the consequent extreme isolation of combatants were significant factors in the prevalence of delayed PTSD (Laufer et al., 1984). In fact, the severity of symptoms is directly related to the extent to which loss is experienced (Lindy, Grace, & Green, 1984; Wilson, Smith, & Johnson, 1985). Clinical research on PTSD strongly suggests that social support and the response of the people in the recovery environment are key factors in recovery (Burgess & Holmstrom, 1976; Figley, 1978; Green et al., 1985; Haley, 1985b; Janoff-Bulman, 1985; Lindy et al., 1984; Scurfield, 1985). More pervasive is the loss of normal

TABLE 8.2
Factors Contributing to Complicated PTSD

I. Intensity of Trauma
   A. Degree of disorganization of:
      environment
      community
      cultural belief systems
      social supports
   B. Meaning
      natural vs. human disaster
      degree of moral conflict

II. Duration

III. Speed of onset of trauma; coping during traumatization

IV. Frequency (cumulative trauma)

V. Developmental time

VI. Coping style
   A. Availability of coping strategies
   B. Degree of perceived control
   C. Agency/role during traumatization

VII. Exposure to death, destructiveness, and atrocity
   A. Threat to life; fear of bodily injury
   B. Exposure to atrocity and abusive violence
   C. Extent of dehumanization

social supports, which occurred in the Nazi and Cambodian holocausts, with the systematic decimation of entire families. The Nazi and Cambodian holocausts, Hiroshima, and Vietnam stand out as the greatest incidences of delayed and complicated PTSD, it seems to us, because each situation caused extreme disorganization in every sphere—environmental, communal, and social.

Others have attempted to define the intensity of a traumatic situation in terms of the idiosyncratic meaning or appraisal given to the situation by the individual (Green et al., 1985).

Speed of onset, duration, and frequency also affect the seriousness of the symptoms. The person who is suddenly exposed to a traumatic situation without time to prepare is more likely to manifest symptoms than someone who is able to predict and therefore mentally prepare for possible tragedy (Wilson et al., 1985). The duration of traumatization is also significant. For example, length of combat exposure alone correlates significantly with severity of PTSD symptoms (DeFazio, Rustin, & Diamond, 1975; Laufer et al., 1984). Whereas most disastrous events are time limited, some people (e.g., soldiers) exposed to repeated trauma develop a virtual trauma career (DeFazio et al., 1975; Wilson et al., 1985). Frequent trauma is cumulative and is more damaging than a single traumatic experience (Khan, 1963; Laufer, Frey-Wouters, & Gallops, 1985; Niederland, 1968; Scurfield, 1985; Wilson et al., 1985). Living with the constant threat of a "potential for recurrence" (Wilson et al., 1985) may be as harmful as an actual occurrence. The effects of real or potential cumulative incest or child abuse illustrate this point.

A strong predictor of the severity of PTSD is the developmental stage at which traumatization occurs. More pervasive cognitive, affective, behavioral, and characterological changes are likely to occur when a person is traumatized during the formative years and when the individual is in the midst of a normal developmental transition. For example, incest is more damaging to characterological and cognitive development in younger than in older children (Pynoos & Eth, 1985). Sending troops off to war during the normal phase of adolescent identity formation contributes to complicated PTSD reactions, for example, arrested development of the self and identity consolidation (Haley, 1985b; Wilson et al., 1985).

One's style of coping with trauma bears a significant relationship to the manifestation of PTSD. The availability of coping resources and the degree of perceived control determine the extent to which the traumatic situation is or is not processed. One's role at the time of the traumatic event also plays a part. For example, some of the most severe sufferers of PTSD are those required to play a passive role in the face of extreme exposure to grotesque bodily damage as in the case of body counters during natural disasters and war, and POWs who endure torture passively. The degree of moral conflict inherent in the situation, for example, deciding the life and death of others, also predicts complicated PTSD (Haley, 1985b; Wilson et al., 1985).

Numerous studies have shown that the severity of symptoms is a function of the degree of threat to life and fear of bodily injury (Adler, 1943; Lindy, et al., 1984; Wilson, et al., 1985). Exposure to grotesque bodily damage, as in the case of jobs requiring repeated contact with death (e.g., grave registration, medical combat evacuation, body counting, and bagging), greatly increases the likelihood of complicated PTSD (Laufer et al., 1984; Taylor & Frazer, 1982). The single, most important predictor of complicated PTSD, however, is exposure to abusive violence or atrocity (Haley, 1985b; Foy, Sipprelle, Rueger, & Carroll, 1984; Laufer et al., 1985; Strayer & Ellenhorn, 1975). The extent of dehumanization entailed in the passive witnessing of or active participation in atrocity completely reverses the normal conditions of holding and mirroring relationships required for the maintenance of structuralization of the ego. Atrocity stands out as the primary risk factor for complicated PTSD.

Traditional hypnotherapeutic treatment of PTSD is based on abreaction. Hypnotic abreaction has a long history. It was pioneered in the 1870s by Janet (1925) and in the 1880s by Breuer and Freud (1983) for the treatment of hysteria. It was used to some degree in the treatment of "shell shock" victims in World War I (Brown, 1920) and to a much greater extent in the treatment of "war neurosis" in World War II (Buchenholz & Frank, 1949; Fisher, 1943; Grinker & Spiegel, 1945; Kubie, 1943a; Leahy & Martin, 1967; Silver & Kelly, 1985; Simmel, 1944; Watkins, 1949; Wolberg, 1948) as well as the PTSD of Vietnam veterans (Balson & Dempster, 1980). Abreaction assumes an hydraulic model of the personality. According to this model, the symptoms of PTSD are believed to be a consequence of repressed emotions. The goal of treatment is therefore to facilitate free expression of pent-up emotions. Watkins (1949), for example, likened hypnotic abreacation to lancing a boil. A related goal is the recovery of amnestic material or memory reconstruction. Hypnosis is used to gain access to the repressed emotions and to allow the patient to re-enact the traumatic situation(s). Often the traumatic events must be "relived" a number of times in trance before resolution is achieved.

Although hypnotic abreaction may be of limited use in certain cases of acute stress symptoms, we do not recommend this treatment; in particular, we do not recommend that the therapist intentionally encourage dramatic emotional expression. Since PTSD is characterized by an alternation between denial and intrusion, the hypnotherapist who encourages emotional expression is increasing the patient's risk for intrusive experiences. The patient may become overwhelmed or fear being overwhelmed and may terminate treatment prematurely. Since most PTSD patients fear loss of control, the therapist's encouragement of emotional displays merely intensifies that fear and does not facilitate working through of the trauma. In the transference, the therapist is seen as trying to retraumatize or otherwise inflict pain on the patient. The prevalence of negative therapeutic reactions is extremely high in abreactive hypnotherapy of PTSD (Spiegel, 1981). There are more failures in the treatment of PTSD than in many other therapy areas (Kelman, 1945), mainly when the abreactive model is employed in the treatment of complicated PTSD.

We strongly agree with Horowitz (1973) that the primary emphasis of the treatment should be *integration,* not emotional expression. Facilitation of conscious emotional experience (something different from emotional expression) is useful at a certain phase of the treatment, but emotional experience must be regulated so that the patient can handle the disavowed affects (Buchenholz & Frank, 1949; Horowitz, 1973; Lindy et al., 1984). More recent hypnotherapeutic treatment of PTSD has tended to emphasize progressive uncovering, working through, and integration, which enable the patient to gain a sense of control over the intrusive experiences while he completes cognitive processing of the trauma (Brende & Benedict, 1980; Silver & Kelly, 1985; Spiegel, 1981).

Treatment begins with a careful assessment of the nature of the PTSD. Because PTSD patients present with either denial or intrusive symptoms, they are easiest to diagnose during the intrusive phase of the illness. In fact, if strict DSM III (American Psychiatric Association, 1980) criteria are used, a definitive diagnosis of PTSD is possible only during the intrusive phase. However, it is easy to miss a diagnosis of PTSD when the patient is in the denial phase. Many patients manifest disguised PTSD. Because PTSD patients may be amnestic for significant portions of their personal history, the clinician may fail to detect evidence of trauma when taking the history.

Hypnosis can be a useful diagnostic tool for cases of disguised PTSD. Patients with disguised PTSD often have unusual reactions to the initial hypnotic experience. Sometimes when the patient is first hypnotized, the traumatic memories dramatically intrude into consciousness, as if the patient were re-enacting the trauma with its full emotional intensity. Patient and therapist alike may be surprised by the appearance in consciousness of the previously forgotten trauma. Sometimes the patient does not remember the trauma but experiences a generalized anxiety upon being hypnotized—the ideational content of the trauma has been defensively dissociated from the affect connected with the trauma. In either case, the patient experiences very intense affect in the first hypnotic sessions before developing any sense of control over the hypnotic experience. He is likely to become frightened of hypnosis and may avoid future hypnotic experiences.

Sometimes the patient is able to ward off intrusion of the traumatic experience into consciousness by suppressing hypnotic ability. While some therapists have observed no difference between the hypnotizability of normals and that of PTSD patients (Spiegel, 1981), others claim PTSD patients are more hypnotizable than normals (Brown, 1920) because of the shared elements of dissociation in both PTSD and hypnosis. We have observed that, at least for a subgroup of disguised PTSD patients, hypnotizability is suppressed. These patients initially appear to be poorly hypnotizable and become increasingly restless during the hypnotic induction. However, once the trauma has been identified and partially integrated into waking consciousness, they show dramatic improvements in hypnotizability. The extremes of very poor hypnotic responsiveness and agitation, on the one hand, and very quick response with the sudden emergence of intense affect or traumatic re-enactment, on the other hand, during initial hypnotic experiences are often diagnostic of disguised PTSD. To prevent the patient from developing a negative attitude toward hypnosis, or having a harmful experience with hypnosis, it is important in such cases to delay the use of hypnosis in favor of waking imagery. The therapist helps the patient to understand the untoward reaction to hypnosis as an example of PTSD symptomatology.

The primary goal of treating simple PTSD is to facilitate normal cognitive/affective processing of the trauma so the patient can recover (Horowitz, 1973). The treatment is phase oriented. The therapist helps to establish the conditions under which to reconstruct the traumatic events and make sense out of the experience. The working through process is gradual. In the first phase the therapeutic work is conducted in the waking state. It begins with a discussion of the patient's current symptoms. An occasional patient may during the interview recall all or part of the traumatic situation so that hypnosis is unnecessary (Futterman & Pumpian-Mindlin, 1951). In such a case the patient continues to rework the traumatic experience in the waking state until the symptoms subside.

In most other cases, hypnosis is introduced first as a means of relaxation. The therapist intentionally builds in a delay to intrusive recall by telling the patient explicitly that hypnosis will not be used at this point to recover the events of the trauma. Waves of relaxation and relaxing imagery are then introduced. The patient is encouraged to use self-hypnosis to generate a relaxed state whenever he is tense or uncomfortable. Uncovering the memories and affects associated with the trauma is approached indirectly with hypnosis. Guided imagery is introduced. The therapist avoids suggesting scenes in any way associated with the trauma. The patient is encouraged to allow the seemingly neutral imagery to emerge spontaneously. The sequence of images that unfolds over one or more sessions usually occurs as a series of representations of the trauma in progressively less and less disguised symbolic forms. Guided imagery eases the patient into cognitive/affective processing of the trauma at the symbolic level. Gradually the patient achieves partial recovery of the traumatic memories and some conscious memory or re-experiencing of the affects associated with the trauma. Emphasis is given to waking integration of the partially recalled experience. Other indirect hypnoprojective techniques are used, such as cloud gazing and anagrams.

As the patient begins to make sense of the experience and the symptompicture stabilizes, the therapist approaches uncovering more directly. Now each hypnotic session can begin with guided imagery. The therapist looks for those aspects of the imagery experience associated with anxiety or other salient affects. Then the therapist amplifies the affects and uses the Affect Bridge Method to explore earlier times when the patient felt much the same way. Further aspects of the traumatic situation reveal themselves. Emphasis is again on waking integration of having experienced the trauma. The experience is reworked a number of times until the cognitive/

affective processing approaches completion and the PTSD symptoms fully disappear. In some cases, such as those involving mugging, this can be done in five sessions.

The goals of treating complicated PTSD are multiple. Treatment is designed to correct the dual pathology, that is, both the cognitive/affective symptoms and the enduring characterological (and sometimes biological) changes. Treatment occurs in stages (Brende, 1984; Parson, 1984; Scurfield, 1985). The goals are: (a) stabilization of the symptom-picture; in order to (b) facilitate cognitive/affective processing of the trauma; and (c) facilitate structuralization, correcting the damage to self-development and of object representations, and the integration of drives; a further goal is (d) to reduce the biological vulnerability to stress response. When treating complicated PTSD, it is necessary to adopt a stage-model of treatment. Table 8.3 summarizes the five stages we have identified in the treatment of complicated PTSD.

The first goal of treatment is to assist the patient in stabilization (Brende, 1984; Parson, 1984). Patients who do not have a disguised form of PTSD are vulnerable to disruptive intrusive experiences—overwhelming affective storms, eruption of intrusive memories, flashbacks and disturbed dreaming, somatization, and the compulsion to repeat the trauma in everyday behavior. Surprising as it may seem, these patients, although aware of the trauma, seldom associate the symptoms with the experience of a past trauma. The therapist must educate the patient about the nature of the recovery process from stress (Scurfield, 1985). According to Leventhal and Everhart (1979), anxiety is a function of inefficient information-processing. In some patients, anxiety greatly diminishes when they are provided with accurate information regarding the nature of their symptoms.

Hence, disaster victims are given a description of the typical PTSD symptoms and are told that such a traumatic event would produce similar symptoms in anyone. The therapist openly discusses the typical psychological consequences of PTSD—shattered illusion of invulnerability, loss of control over everyday events. The patient is encouraged to read about the traumatic events and about others' typical reactions to these events. For example, patients read the popular and professional literature about the Vietnam war, adult rape, and so forth. The aim is to provide the patient with a conceptual framework for his symptoms, with the hope of alleviating anxiety.

Beyond patient education, the first therapeutic interventions are directed toward the manifest symptoms themselves. Patients are taught to keep a daily record of typical symptoms—anxiety attacks, somatic reactions, nightmares, and the like. Patients discover the impact of these symptoms on their everyday lives. They also develop a repertoire of coping

TABLE 8.3
Stages of Treatment of Complicated PTSD

Disguised Presentation	Nonhypnotic Methods	Hypnotic Methods
I. Stabilization of symptoms	Patient education Self-monitoring of symptoms Learning coping strategies Stress management Pharmacotherapy Supportive therapy Group therapy Establishing a therapeutic alliance	Hypnodynamic therapy is contraindicated during this phase Exploration of coping strategies Hypnotic and Selfhypnotic relaxation Ego-strengthening
II. Integration A. Controlled uncovering	Supportive therapy Waking guided imagery	Protective and soothing imagery Transitional imagery Symbolic working through with: Guided imagery Hypnoprojective methods Dissociation of observing and experiencing ego Suggested partial amnesia Affect amplifications and attenuation Age regression Suggested hypermnesia
B. Integrating introjects	Transference work	Hypnotic imagery Age regression Ego state therapy
III. Development of self	Playful exploration Autonomous pursuit of new interests/activities Selfobject transference Reassigning responsibility for the traumatic event(s) Differentiation of values	Rehearsal in fantasy of new interests/activities Working through body image distortions Ideal self transference Ego-strengthening
IV. Drive integration	Neurotic Transference Adjunctive Assertiveness training or sex therapy	Hypnodynamic uncovering
V. Enduring biological sensitivity	Pharmacotherapy Learned psychophysiological control (biofeedback)	

strategies. The therapist assesses the patient's typical means of coping with these symptoms, reinforcing the patient's most effective coping strategies and helping the patient devise new coping strategies. A concrete problem-solving approach is used, or what has been called "limited-objective therapy" (Tanay, 1968). The patient is also taught some means of relaxation, which may entail progressive muscle relaxation (Brende, 1984; Brooks & Scarano, 1982; Keane, Fairbank, Caddell, Zimmering, & Bender, 1985) or self-hypnosis. A regular program of exercise may also be introduced. Where the patient fails to stabilize, pharmacological interventions may be indicated (Kolb, Burris, Cullen, & Griffiths, 1984; Van der Kolk, et al., 1984). Every attempt is made to give the patient a sense of control over his symptoms and restore his sense of confidence. The treatment model used at this stage is a combination of behavioral stress management and supportive therapy, sometimes together with pharmacotherapy.

Providing the patient with concrete tools to stabilize his symptoms is the first major step in establishing a working therapeutic relationship based on trust (Haley, 1974). Because trust in the world has been shattered for the PTSD patient, it is especially important for the therapist to provide a tangible basis for this trust. Over the weeks, months, or sometimes years it take the patient to stabilize, the patient is beginning to internalize a good object relationship. Because PTSD patients experience isolation from others, it is advisable, whenever possible, to encourage them to attend a survivors' group, such as a Vietnam rap group (Brende, 1984; Shatan, 1973) or an incest survivors' group (Herman & Schatzow, 1984). Group therapy provides a sense of community; it enables patients to overcome feelings of stigma by encountering others with equally extraordinary experiences. In the accepting environment of the group, members work together to understand the impact of traumatization (Scurfield, 1985).

Hypnosis is used with great caution during the stabilization phase, if it is used at all. An uncovering approach in hypnotherapy and certain other nonhypnotic methods, such as implosion therapy, are contraindicated because any method that facilitates uncovering at an early phase can lead to further disorganization (Van der Kolk et al., 1984). If the patient persistently re-experiences intrusions, hypnosis is to be avoided altogether at this stage in favor of waking therapy.

Otherwise, hypnosis can be used in a limited way as an adjunct to supportive therapy. One use of hypnosis is to facilitate the exploration of coping strategies for symptoms. Another involves teaching the patient a skill in self-hypnotic relaxation (Brende & Benedict, 1980). Still another involves the repeated use of ego-strengthening suggestions to enable the patient to increase his sense of control and restore lost confidence (Silver & Kelly, 1985). If hypnosis is used, the therapist must be alert to the potential for recurrence of disruptive intrusive experiences. Hypnosis is *not* always indicated at the early stage of treatment of complicated PTSD. Patients sometimes communicate this to the therapist by declining to use or continue with hypnosis at some point early in the work.

The second phase of the treatment, *after* stabilization, is the uncovering phase. The decision to initiate uncovering is based on (a) some alleviation of certain PTSD symptoms, for example, anxiety; (b) restoration of a modicum of control and confidence; (c) return of interest in hypnosis; and (d) spontaneous return of memories and affects associated with the traumatic event. Sometimes several years of nonhypnotic therapy are required to achieve stabilization.

Furthermore, uncovering does not happen all at once. It occurs as a progression in which the patient is exposed to varying "doses" of disavowed affects and memories as he is able to process and integrate them into conscious experience (Horowitz, 1973; Lindy et al., 1984). Fluctuations are characteristic of the unfolding treatment. The patient uncovers a bit and steps back to process it. This stepping back should not be construed as resistance but as an adaptive attempt to further the processing. The patient uncovers some material in hypnosis and then takes a number of sessions of waking therapy to assimilate it before returning to hypnotic uncovering. Weeks, months, and sometimes years pass before the patient returns to hypnotic uncovering. The therapist must accept this as the natural course of therapy with complicated PTSD patients. Each episode of uncovering is a partial recall. The overall uncovering phase entails a continuous working and reworking of the partially recalled material until the entirety of the disavowed experience can be integrated into ongoing everyday life. Some clinicians have described the uncovering process as a type of "controlled regression" (Brende, 1984; Spiegel, 1981). Hypnosis offers an advantage over narcotherapy by permitting finer control over the uncovering process than is possible with drugs (Silver & Kelly, 1985). The therapist is advised to use hypnosis only for a part of each therapy session and to allow ample time for waking integration. He may also alternate between short periods of trance and waking therapy a number of times in the same session and over a number of sessions. Further, some patients, especially Vietnam veterans who were "conditioned" to be hypervigilant, prefer open-eyed trance experiences.

Uncovering therapy begins with a preparatory period during which the therapist teaches the patient how to use hypnosis safely. First, hypnosis is used to explore protective and soothing imagery. The patient is told to imagine a place where he feels especially safe and protected. A series of such scenes is explored. The patient is encouraged to generate and enjoy safe and protected scenes in daily self-hypnotic practice until he develops skill at quickly generating a variety of soothing experiences. The Vietnam veteran might imagine a special "hootch," safe from mines and sniper fire; the incest victim might imagine a safe room or a small island that no one has access to. The safe place is subsequently used for the induction of hypnosis. This Safe Place Induction symbolically conveys to the patient that hypnosis can be a safe, not a frightening, experience.

Transitional imagery is also used. The hypnotized patient imagines scenes with people who can be trusted. Images of war buddies, fellow survivors, friends, and therapists typically are reported. Sometimes pets and god-imagery are reported. The use of transitional objects is encouraged. For example, patients may use personal journals as a kind of transitional object. They are instructed to write their experience in a journal when they experience anxiety. The journal is a concrete representation of the continuity of personal experience throughout the symptomatic period.

With patients who are vulnerable to disruptive intrusions, the therapist proceeds slowly and cautiously. The therapist should not proceed with controlled uncovering until a repertoire of safe imagery is clearly established. The best approach is indirect, with the therapist using guided imagery not directly associated with the traumatic event. The imagery is allowed to unfold spontaneously over a number of sessions as the aspects of the trauma are slowly revealed and accepted into consciousness. By helping the patient first to work through the traumatic experience(s) on a *symbolic* level, the hypnotherapist (respectfully) works *with* the defenses but does not challenge or pierce them too early. If the patient becomes symptomatic, the therapist returns to waking, nonhypnotic imagery, which allows less precipitous access to repressed material than hypnotic imagery. With patients with complicated PTSD it is not uncommon to conduct months of therapy without hypnosis but with guided waking imagery. Hypnosis is reintroduced as the symptoms diminish or when the patient once again requests it.

Hypnoprojective methods such as the Theatre and Television Techniques are also quite useful. The therapist suggests that the patient see a safe and protected scene on television or a stage. Then the therapist suggests that the patient see "something that he is ready to understand about the trauma" on another channel. Spiegel (1981) recommends envisioning a split screen in which the traumatic scene is viewed on one side and a scene involving something the patient can do to protect himself on the other side. Silver and Kelly (1985) suggest an imaginary videotape with which the therapist can suggest stopping the action or instantly replaying a part of the scene. In any event, the use of an hallucinated television, theatre, or videotape allows the patient to experience aspects of the trauma at a distance.

We also suggest that the patient use an hallucinated remote control device to regulate the volume of the television and turn the channels. The patient is told that he can turn to the safety and protection channel whenever he wishes. He also is told that by turning the volume dial of the control device up or down he can regulate the intensity of emotions associated with the trauma as needed. Thus he learns to control the intensity of emotional experience. Sometimes patients develop images and other signals to assess the intensity of the affects and warn of the possibility of becoming overwhelmed: a meter with an arrow that can move from a safety zone to a warning zone, an ideomotor signal (a designated finger that lifts automatically just before the experience cannot be tolerated), a protected vehicle that transports the patient to the traumatic scene and returns to a safe sanctuary as needed.

Dissociating the observing from the experiencing ego is standard procedure with PTSD patients. The observing part of the ego is asked to remain calm and attentive while the experiencing part relives certain aspects of the traumatic situation. The hypnotherapist can carefully regulate the degree of dissociation in the service of uncovering and of integration. He may suggest greater dissociation when the material has the potential of becoming overwhelming. As the patient demonstrates ability to cope with the material, the therapist may suggest remerging of these two facets of the ego to facilitate integration.

Another means of regulating the uncovering process is the use of suggestions for posthypnotic amnesia. With PTSD patients it is absolutely necessary to close each hypnotic session with the suggestion, "You'll remember only what you are ready to remember" or "You will come to understand this over time as you are ready to understand it." Suggestions for partial posthypnotic amnesia can be balanced against suggestions for insight, such as, "You will come to understand the implications of these events for the meaning and course of your life."

PTSD patients go through periods during the uncovering and the integration phases in which defenses are strong. They may report a paucity of associations, lack of fantasy productions, or inability to remember anything. There may be a distinct lack of affect. Depression and somatization may predominate during these periods. When these episodes occur, the therapist places greater emphasis on uncovering techniques, while not losing sight of the protective procedures employed throughout the therapeutic work. When working with guided imagery, for example, the therapist employs suggestions to amplify the emerging affects and then uses the Affect Bridge Technique to trace these affects back to the traumatic situation(s). Age regression can be introduced for direct recovery of aspects of the traumatic experience. Systematic age regressions to different developmental periods preceding, during, and following the traumatization(s) reinforce the sense of continuity disrupted by traumatization and also situate the trauma within the context of the overall life development of the patient.

When resistances are encountered, direct suggestions for hypermnesia are sometimes used, but with caution. Kolk and Mutalipassi (1982), working with narcotherapy, suggest using external stimuli to trigger the memory of the trauma, for example, the sound track of a battle for a war-traumatized patient. When the patient responds to uncovering with increased somatization, the therapist works more vigorously with imagery to help facilitate rechannelling of the conflictual affect away from the physiological processes and into fantasy productions. Each step toward uncovering is followed by additional integrative work.

Sometime during the uncovering process, specific split-off introjects become activated, such as a "killer-self, an immortal self, a bad self or a victim self" (Brende, 1984; Parson, 1984). These usually represent aspects of the traumatic situation that resonate with sadomasochistic impulses and contribute to the formation of new pathological representations in which the sadomasochistic impulses find an outlet. These impulses are not acceptable by conscious moral standards. The introjects are split off from conscious experience and typically remain inactive (except during flashbacks) at the expense of psychic integration. During the uncovering process, these introjects become activated. The veteran of a guerrilla war, for example, discovers the excitement and pleasure experienced during violent acts (Shatan, 1973). The task of the therapist is to help the patient integrate these dissociated aspects of the self (Brende & Benedict, 1980), while minimizing the potential acting out and somatization, which are high when the dissociated introjects become activated.

Hypnosis helps the patient gain access to these experiences and integrate them into the overall self-concept. Sometimes these introjects become activated spontaneously during guided imagery or during age regression. In such cases the therapist helps the patient accept and make sense out of these impulse derivatives in the overall context of the traumatic situation. Sometimes the therapist can intentionally direct the patient toward dissociated aspects of the self with ego state therapy. The therapist suggests, for example, that the aspect the patient associated with, say, the killing or badness should now speak. To facilitate integration, it is sometimes advisable for the patient to visualize the different aspects of the self coming together into a whole self.

The overall course of the uncovering phase of therapy is characterized by seemingly alternating forward and backward movement. It is not unusual for complicated PTSD patients to go through periods of intensification of symptoms (somatization, acting out, depression, substance abuse). They may be unable to produce any fantasy or affect, or they refuse outright to use hypnosis. The therapist who anticipates these periods as part of the typical course of working through complicated traumatization is less likely to become impatient. The traumatic memories, affects, and dissociated self-experiences must be continuously worked and reworked. Often the patient and the therapist together discover "layers" of traumatic events. Those that involve loss and grief become manifest early (Shatan, 1973; Spiegel, 1981); those involving threat to life or bodily harm, next; and those that involve moral conflicts, such as participation in atrocity or decisions about the life and death of others, manifest much later (Haley, 1985b).

A number of signs indicate when the uncovering process has reached completion. Symptoms diminish consistently. The emergence of new memories and fantasy productions associated with traumatic situations wind down. Sleep and dream life stabilize. Nightmares cease. Depression lifts. Many patients perceive themselves as "better" at this stage, and a number, unfortunately, terminate therapy.

The next phase of the therapy facilitates development of the self, which was arrested by the traumatization, and the integration of the traumatic events as a fact of one's life. The adolescent traumatized by war duty is not likely to have completed the normal process of identity formation (Haley, 1985b). The victim of childhood incest probably missed out on the normal playful explorations of childhood due to parentification (Gelinas, 1983). This phase of therapy if characterized by a playful therapeutic atmosphere in the context of which the patient explores dimensions of the self that were heretofore inhibited or kept private (Khan, 1963). In hypnosis the patient unleashes a wealth of fantasy productions not associated with the trauma and in daily life engages—albeit tentatively at first—in new activities. The therapist employs hypnotic imagery to help the patient discover new interests and activities. One goal is to help the patient overcome his restricted life style by actually engaging in new intersts and through them to achieve more pleasure as well as greater autonomy (Brende, 1984). Another goal is to help the patient become less passive, more healthily assertive with others with regard to his needs, or more sociable. Hypnotic rehearsal in fantasy and posthypnotic reinforcement of participation in new activities are the standard tools of this phase of treatment. For incest survivors, working through negative attitudes toward the body and correcting distortions in the body image may be indicated (Freytag, 1965). We also recommend the Ideal Self Technique for exploring new dimensions of the self.

It is especially important that the therapist function as an effective self-object (Kohut, 1971) for the patient during this phase of treatment. To provide the patient with an emotionally corrective experience, the therapist must show active support in and realistic praise for the patient's discoveries and accomplishments. The therapist must also be willing to participate in the playfulness of the relationship. Most of self-development is achieved not by specific hypnotic techniques, but through the quality of the relationship between the patient and the therapist. This is not to minimize the contribution of hypnosis. Ego strengthening suggestions, for example, should be used routinely at this stage of the therapy (Silver & Kelly, 1985).

During this phase patients begin to experience themselves and the traumatic events in a new way. They undergo a process by which they re-evaluate responsibility during the trauma. As they explore their own values and self-ideals, they achieve greater differentiation from the values (and lack of values) of those who participated in the traumatic event. Incest survivors lose their sense of badness. They may develop a conviction that the parent failed in responsibility as a parent, or they may come to see the wider context of the incest as a manifestation of family pathology or the repetition of transgenerational abuse. Vietnam veterans who participated in atrocities may come to view themselves as "dumb kids" who could not have been expected to challenge authority. They may come to hold the commanding officers and the government responsible (Haley, 1985b). The therapist helps the patient examine the total context of the decision making associated with the traumatic event (Silver & Kelly, 1985). As a consequence of the working through process, it is not uncommon for PTSD patients to show increased interest in political action and social advocacy during this phase of the treatment (Shatan, 1973). It is also common for the patient to discover positive consequences of traumatization (Scurfield, 1985), such as the strength of having survived, the depth of appreciation for human kindness, and the compassion that comes from having borne witness to dehumanizing destruction and greed.

The outcome of this self-development and integration phase is healthy self-esteem, autonomous pursuit of a range of work and recreational interests, and a reinvestment in relationships. Although the patient is considerably improved, residual problems in the regulation of drives may remain. The patient may still manifest the chronic irritability and propensity toward episodic rage attacks characteristic of complicated war traumatization (Kardiner, 1941; Kolb & Mutalipassi, 1982). Or the incest survivor may show some form of continuing sexual dysfunction. The therapist once again switches to an uncovering mode of therapy. At this stage, the patient typically presents in a neurotic-like manner. Using a dynamic treatment model, the therapist can help the patient actively to explore fantasy productions associated with the expression of aggression and sexual impulses in the context of the neurotic transference. To provide an emotionally corrective experience, the therapist avoids the extremes of giving permission to the expression of these impulses, on the one hand, while helping bring them to the patient's conscious awareness, on the other. Presumably the disregulation of impulses had occurred because of overstimulation during the traumatization. The therapist's neutral and consistent stance is now directed to the patient's reworking of impulse control in the context of the therapy. Sometimes behaviorally oriented assertiveness training or sex therapy serves as a useful adjunct.

Even where the patient successfully achieves the goals of each stage of the treatment, the biological sensitivity may endure. We have observed that the most successfully treated complicated PTSD patients retain some degree of hypersensitivity to stimuli. While trauma and sensation seeking may decrease, the vulnerability to startle and the autonomic hyperactivity remain. Behaviorally, desensitization has been strikingly ineffective in the treatment of the PTSD stress response (Kolb et al., 1984). Medications that block andrenergic response show some promise (Kolb et al., 1984; Van der Kolk et al., 1984). Learning voluntary control of physiological processes with biofeedback may also aid autonomic stabilization. (This is described in Brown & Fromm, 1986.) However, these techniques should not lead one to disregard the fact that the biological vulnerability may to some extent be permanent.

The treatment of complicated PTSD is one of the most challenging areas of hypnotherapy and hypnoanalysis. It usually takes years, and there are many pitfalls along the way. The therapist is required to adopt very different treatment models at different stages of the treatment. For example, a cognitive-behavioral model is useful in the earliest stabilization phase of the treatment; a dynamic-developmental model, during the uncovering phase; a self psychology model, during the self-development phase; a classical dynamic, conflict-defense model, during the drive integration stage; and a biological conditioning model, during the stress sensitivity phase. Table 8.3 summarizes these stages in the overall treatment.

Unfortunately, there are no systematic outcome studies of hypnotherapy in either simple or complicated PTSD yet. We hope this chapter and the next will stimulate further interest in this area.

9

A Long-Term Case of Hypnoanalysis: Child Abuse and Early Rape[1]

Most hypnoanalytic patients are seen once a week for a 50-minute hour and can be helped in 3 to 12 months. In chapter 7 and elsewhere (Eisen & Fromm, 1983; Fromm, 1981, 1984), we have discussed examples of short-term hypnotherapy. But some patients need more time: in particular, borderline and narcissistic patients, and those with posttraumatic stress disorders (PTSD). In this chapter we present such a long-term case.

ANAMNESIS

Jessica was a big, gawky, badly dressed 38-year-old woman, a psycho-analyst working in a large psychiatric teaching hospital. She had been in psychoanalysis three times. The first analysis lasted 3 years; the second, also 3 years; and the last she had broken off after 2 years. Her training analysis, the second of the three, had been very good, she felt. But she had never been able to develop a real relationship with her most recent analyst; he was "too rigid," she said.

Asked why she had gone into a third analysis when her second analysis had been so good, she said she felt the need to talk more about the severe child abuse she had been subjected to by both of her parents throughout her childhood. But the third analyst did not understand her, and now she wanted to try hypnoanalysis.

The patient had grown up in Montana in a Calvinist family to whom, according to her description, all pleasures were forbidden. Her father

---

[1] The patient's permission to publish her case was obtained beforehand, and informed consent was given again after she had read this chapter. The name "Jessica" is a pseudonym.

The reader is referred to Miller (1985) for a discussion of a case that is in many ways similar to this.

managed a small business; her mother was principal of a grammar school. Both parents were enormously strict. Jessica could never do anything that would please them and was beated by both of them, particularly by the mother, practically every day. Her mother conceived of all sexuality as bad and sinful and was always afraid the child was in danger of being sexually seduced either by her playmates or by adults. She therefore severely restricted Jessica's play with other children and being with adults outside the house, even her teachers. Throughout her childhood and later, Jessica thought that her parents' home was like a concentration camp and identified in her fantasy with concentration camp victims.

In childhood Jessica had had many respiratory illnesses, including allergies, during which she felt her mother had not taken care of her well enough. She said her mother had rejected her since birth (which statement the hypnotherapist later came to doubt as far as the first year of life was concerned, because Jessica herself was a very good and caring therapist).

The patient had a sister 7 years her junior. And until she was 11 years old, she said, she knew nothing of the existence of her half brother, 8 years her senior—the child of a previous marriage of her father. The half brother became a highly successful chemist and was the only member of her family with whom she has maintained a good relationship.

In her sophomore year in college, she went out with a man, held hands with him, and had a passionate sexual desire for him, which she could not stop. She thought having such intense feelings meant she was crazy and sinful. She prayed to God to take her sexual feelings away, but God did not. After the young man left her, she did not allow herself more than petting and necking with other men she fell in love with, even though she experienced intense sexual desire. At age 20, feeling she had "held out" against her sexual desires as long as she could, she had intercourse on alternate nights with two different young men she had dated simultaneously during the preceding 4 months. A few months later, she married one of them and had intercourse with him four or five times daily. Her grades in school improved as the inner sexual pressure was somewhat reduced, but the obsession with sexuality continued. She felt her sexual drive had been exceedingly strong. At first I saw this sexual obsession as counterphobic behavior; a month later, when I recognized the patient was a PTSD, I came to see it as an expression of the denial state in PTSDs, which we have described in chapter 8.

The patient was orgastic with her first husband, but the marriage deteriorated because, unlike the patient, the husband did not have any real intellectual or artistic interests. She divorced him and went to medical school, where her grades were excellent. She also went into her first psychoanalysis.

She met another man, "very handsome, very tall." They experimented with and enjoyed all forms of sexuality "except kinky, sadistic things." He was a "macho" male, who yelled and shouted at her for such things as walking barefoot at home. She enjoyed being yelled at, took the submissive role, and dressed and felt very feminine. After a while she felt the young man drank too much and hurt her physically with his "oversize penis," so she dropped him. The enormous and unremitting sexual drive that had bothered her so much continued unrelentingly.

She felt emotionally very ill, often suicidal, particularly when thinking of her parents. Her analyst advised her never to have anything to do with her parents again. For the next year she went to bed with many graduate students, tried to "control" her sexual drives, smoked pot occasionally, and "fell in love and went to bed with every man I met." During her residency, she went into her training analysis, which she felt was very good.

Eventually she met her current husband, an intellectual quite a bit older than she, and lived with him monogamously for a number of years before they got married. After 3 years of marriage and joyful sexual relations with him, suddenly, "after a D and C," she said, she found herself terribly frightened of getting "hurt" in intercourse. And while continuing to sleep in the same bed with her husband, she would no longer allow him to touch her except for giving her a goodnight kiss. She often felt as if she were fragmenting and went into panics.

As an adult, Jessica had a horseback riding accident in which her pelvis and femur were fractured. Since her father's death from a heart attack 5 years before she came to see me, she feared that she, too, would die of a heart attack. She was very hypochondriacal.

The patient was aware of being in a constant rage against her mother, against institutions of higher learning, against her superiors, and against her peers. She could not form any real relationships, she felt, except with her patients.

This was how things stood when the patient came for hypnoanalysis. She lived in a town some 300 miles away where there were no hypnotherapists, wanted to have a hypnoanalysis, and thus proposed to fly in to see me (E.F.) once a week. She diagnosed herself as a borderline but actually was a severely narcissistic personality with borderline features.

From a descriptive perspective, she met most of the diagnostic criteria for narcissistic personality disorders in DSM-III (American Psychiatric Association, 1980).

The criteria are:

1. Grandiosity.
2. Preoccupation with fantasies of unlimited success, power, brilliance,

beauty, or ideal love.

3. Exhibitionism (the person requires constant attention and admiration).

4. Cool indifference or marked feelings of rage, inferiority, shame, humiliation, or emptiness in response to criticism, indifference of others, or defeat.

5. At least two of the following characteristics of disturbance in interpersonal relationships: (a) entitlement (expectation of special favors without assuming reciprocal responsibility); (b) interpersonal exploitativeness; (c) relationships that characteristically oscillate between the extreme of overidealization and devaluation; and (d) lack of empathy (inability to recognize how others feel).

The patient certainly did not lack for empathy with her patients. She was very sensitive to how they felt. Grandiosity and fantasies of unlimited success were present to a minor degree. All the other diagnostic criteria were fully met, particularly rage in response to criticism, the need to have her self-esteem bolstered by constant support or admiration, the entitlement, the exploitativeness of taking advantage of others in order to indulge her own desires, and the lack of regard for the personal rights of others.

I (E.F.) considered hypnoanalysis with a developmental perspective to be the treatment of choice for this patient. Like Adler (1981, 1985), the authors do not view borderline and narcissistic personality disorders as totally separate entities. We conceive of them as being located along a continuum on the developmental line of the self, with the borderline patients at the lower end of the continuum and narcissists of more or less pathology distributed over the upper end. Borderline patients more easily split the (love) object into a good and a bad one, experience severe fragmentation of the self, or have serious difficulties in maintaining self-cohesiveness and stable "selfobject transferences" (Kohut, 1971). They fear annihilation and disintegration. Decompensation can proceed to psychosis.

In contrast, patients suffering from pathological narcissism have achieved a higher level along the developmental line of the self. Except for transient, but not seriously disintegrative, periods of fragmentation, they are able to maintain self-cohesiveness. Their selfobject transferences are relatively stable. Narcissistic patients have great difficulty with feelings of self-worth. They vascillate between severe lack of self-esteem on the one hand and feelings of grandiosity and entitlement on the other. They, too characteristically, have not fully reached the developmental stage of maintaining object constancy (Mahler et al., 1975), tend to see people as either "all-good" or "all-bad," and react to even slight frustrations, particularly to real or fancied abandonment or lack of recognition, with intense fury and anger—"narcissistic rage" (Kohut, 1972).

Phase 1 (November 1973–July 1974)
Screen Memories; Establishing the Hypnoanalyst as a Gratifying, "Good" Object

The patient showed excellent hypnotic ability. She achieved a score of ten on the Stanford Hypnotic Susceptibility Scale, Form C (Weitzenhoffer & Hilgard, 1962). In and out of hypnosis she talked endlessly about her "bad mother," who had abused her in childhood. Jessica's hatred for her parents was fierce. The only time she had gone home was for her father's funeral. She had had no contact with her mother or with her sister since the age of 20.

Within the first month of starting hypnoanalysis, she found herself at home "in a strange state, drawing feverishly." It was a spontaneous dissociative state.[2] She had had no intention to draw and did not know what she was drawing. It was as if her hand was drawing by itself (automatic writing). Very upset, she brought me the picture and told me that the picture showed her mother giving her an enema and holding her down. She said she never wanted to see this picture again. She could not bear to look at it. The picture (Fig. 9.1) showed a 3- or 4-year old little girl, lying on the bathroom floor, terrified, struggling and screaming, while a somewhat larger, half-nude person is kneeling over her in a coital position. All around the two figures were stabbing, sharply printed words: from the little girl, "No, no, no, no," emanated. "I don't understand; no words, no words; hot, wet; pain, pain, pain; throbbing, stabbing, hurt; rage, rage" seemed to belong to the girl too. The words "My will, my will; shut up; I'm your mother; do what I say; don't fight back; you'll get more" were placed closer to the other person. Above both of them one could decipher the words "silence, rushing, entering, gushing"; and "I'll help you, I'll help you."

Jessica said the picture showed her mother giving her enemas and her own terrible fear of the cruel mother and the enemas. On the side of the picture, in her own adult handwriting (deleted here for reasons of confidentiality), she had written, "There were no words; there were just

---

[2] The drawing shows symptomatically that the patient had moved toward the intrusive state of the PTSD (see chapter 8). However, she used the spontaneous dissociative state as a protective defense against the intrusive state and against the desire to confess and bring into the open the trauma that had happened to her. The trauma was so overwhelming and so deeply repressed that she could look at it only when in an altered state of consciousness, and even in that state only in the form of a screen memory.

The patient had not been taught self-hypnosis yet.

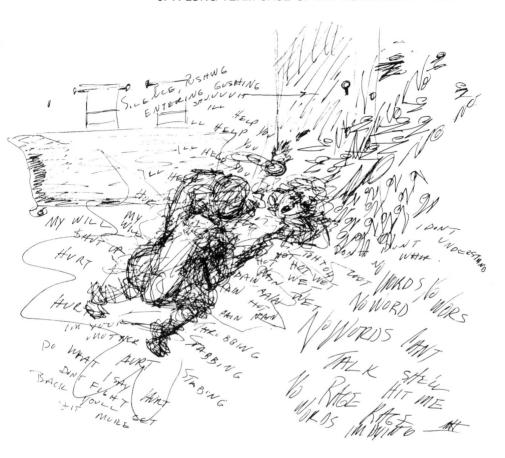

FIG. 9.1.

rushes of feeling—cold, naked on the floor—didn't dare kick her. She'd slap me again. I remember the cold, wet bathroom rug under me, and her indescribably ugly face—felt betrayed, isolated—what did I do to deserve this? Every cell, every inch of me shivered, trembled, and shook." As an afterthought the patient also had written in a corner of the picture, "I found myself doing the writing unexpectedly. Why, I don't know."

Mothers do not usually bare the lower parts of their own body when they give enemas to children. It seemed perfectly clear to me that the drawing Jessica called the "Enema Picture" represented a screen memory, and a covert hypnotic communication to me of a deeply repressed sexual attack by a male, which she must have suffered in childhood. But Jessica undoubtedly also had suffered much physical abuse from her parents, especially from her mother.

The patient spoke a great deal in the waking state about the weekly enemas and the beatings her mother had given her two to three times a week because the mother felt Jessica was stupid and bad. Because the internalized representations of the mother—and the father—were such bad internal objects, and because the patient at this stage seemed to be very close to being a borderline case, I decided to treat her as I would treat a borderline in hypnoanalysis, namely, according to the principles described by Baker (1981) and by Fromm (1984). (See chapter 8, this volume.) I had to become the "good mother" Jessica apparently had never had; then help her internalize that good object, so that she also could develop self-love; and subsequently assist her to achieve object constancy and self-cohesiveness and gain control over splitting. I hoped to help her progress from the near-borderline state of a severely narcissistic personality, through the less severe stages of narcissism to a neurosis, or perhaps even to full health.

In the first phase of hypnoanalysis, therefore, I took on the role of a totally accepting, gratifying, and nurturing mother figure, was always protective and soothing when Jessica began to be overwhelmed by affect, nearly always took her side when she complained about being treated "badly" by colleagues and supervisors, and always showed her, with "the gleam in the mother's eye" (Kohut, 1971, 1977), how proud I was of her when she achieved even minute successes in real life or any kind of gain in her therapy. I thus attempted to help the patient take the beginning steps towards object constancy and the acquisition of healthy self-esteem.

One day I induced an age regression in order to get more historical material. With strong affect, Jessica brought up the experience of a dog nibbling at her toes. She was a little girl. In great fear she pulled her feet up under herself while sitting on a couch in her parents' home. But her father laughingly egged on the dog to lick her feet. In the hypnotic experience, the mother walked out of the room without saying a word and did not protect her daughter from the father and the dog. I silently wondered about incest and the patient's defense against recognizing it by displacing the possible sexual molestation downward from the genitalia to the toes. I gently urged Jessica to give me more material about her father. She clammed up.

It become clear towards the end of Phase 1 that the patient had always had very lusty, heterosexual feelings and was afraid she would be overwhelmed by them.

Phase 2 (July 1974–September 1974)
Respecting for a While the Newly Developed Defense
Against Going Into Trance

For most of the first year of therapy (Phases 1–3), Jessica stormed into my office in the typical rage of the narcissist (Kohut, 1972), angry about something that had happened to her outside the therapy and that she experienced as an injury to her self-esteem. Occasionally she was furious because in the preceding hour I had given her only 5 or 10 minutes' overtime. She felt "entitled" to more.

For weeks, she avoided going into trance by filling up her hours with talk (in the waking state) about her anger about her colleagues and her teachers, who she thought did not treat her well. If we were to use hypnosis, she said, she would need double hours, the first one to talk about her daily life and the second for hypnoanalysis. She was given two consecutive hours but soon demanded very long inductions, and eventually she filled up even the second hour with talking in the waking state about her daily life. She talked about the troubles she had with her peers and older colleagues at the clinic, all of whom were "bad." Only her hypnoanalyst was "good." She could not write reports for the clinic at which she was working. Too much was "demanded" of her by the "bad" people. The "bad" people, she felt, in many ways were like her mother: they made constant demands. She thought she was a much better therapist than any of her colleagues and teachers.

I avoided pointing out the reality that Jessica was indeed quite a good therapist but not as good as in her narcissistic grandiosity she thought she was. Developmentally, Jessica was in the "splitting" period of the separation-individuation phase (Mahler et al., 1975), and seeing herself realistically as "Good-and-Bad-Me" was as yet not possible.

I decided to go slowly in the therapy. The patient had not as yet developed object constancy. I understood that she was: (a) afraid of losing the "good mother," the hypnoanalyst, if hypnoanalysis helped quickly; and (b) unconsciously afraid of going into deep states of trance because in them she might face the childhood rape or incest problem, which was still deeply repressed.

Jessica now took on a hobby of photography and became quite creative with it. I supported this, praised and encouraged her, and shared her pride in this new achievement. Thus, I was the "good mother," whom she needed to internalize. I even showed her that I did not mind her buying expensive photo equipment instead of paying her therapy bills on time. Photography symbolizes looking, and I hoped that the looking outside eventually would turn to looking in a more focused way inside. It did a year or two later.

Phase 3 (September 1974–November 1974)
Working Toward Internalization of the "Good Object"

Jessica continued to avoid hypnosis after she had had a nocturnal dream about having homosexual contact with me. In waking hours too such fears were voiced. I made it very clear to her that such feelings occur in many analyses and hypnoanalyses and that thoughts, fantasies, and dreams do not equal actions. I also told her very clearly that I would protect her from acting out homosexually with me and that I did not feel she was a homosexual. Her whole orientation had been heterosexual. I interpreted to her that the homosexual thoughts or dreams expressed her need to be held and hugged affectionately in the way she had wanted her mother to hold and hug her.

Jessica constantly tested—and exploited—the "good mother" figure by writing volumes of letters in between hours, which took me countless extra hours of unpaid reading. She still allowed hypnosis only rarely, and then only with much fuss: every crack in the venetian blinds behind her had to be shut carefully, and if someone was typing in the office above mine, she would refuse to go into trance.

She did tell me about her half brother, 8 years her senior, who was the only good love object she had had in the past. He had lived with his mother in another town. She remembered that when she was 11 years old she had found on her father's dresser a postcard written by someone who signed himself "Tim," announcing his impending arrival. She did not know who Tim was but was strangely agitated. When Tim did come and she met him, she felt great sexual excitement. He was so handsome in his ROTC uniform. He took her out on walks and played with her. They had had a warm interpersonal relationship ever since, even though they did not see each other more than a couple of times a year. She felt that without having this warm relationship with her half brother, she could never have survived emotionally. Without any connection being apparent to her, she then started to talk a good deal about her own interest in patients in whose family there was incest. She had developed this interest in the last few years and wondered why.

I began to wonder whether incest had occurred with the brother (rather than with the father) or whether the patient simply had had preadolescent sexual fantasies about the brother. Still, in order not to influence the patient's hypnoanalysis by my incest hypothesis, I was very careful not to mention a word about it to her. Hypnotherapists must be extremely cautious not to give overt or covert suggestions that might influence the patient to produce material that would confirm the therapist's hypothesis.

Phase 4 (November 1974–September 1975)
The Brother's Death; the Hypnoanalyst Providing a "Holding Environment"

At this critical point, during the months Jessica talked lovingly about her half brother, the brother died suddenly of a heart attack. Many of the therapy hours of the next few months were spent in my helping her—in the waking state and in trance (by means of imagery and free association)—

through the four phases of mourning (see Fromm & Eisen, 1982). In January 1975, Jessica produced a hypnotic fantasy in which her brother climbed over a high wall, came back, put a ladder against the wall, and asked her to climb up and jump down to the other side with him. She was ready to do so. I felt this was an unconscious suicidal fantasy, expressing a wish to join the brother in death. Thus, for once in an authoritarian voice (to prevent the possibility of suicide), I told her to turn around and come back down the ladder to the side where I was standing, waiting to take care of her and nurture her. At this point, to act as a permissive hypnotist would have been wrong.

A month later (February 1975), Jessica wrote me a letter, which, however, she did not give to me until a full year later, in February 1976. In this letter she said that the hypnotic hour with the ladder and her brother had been an extremely important one for her. My saying, "I am aware that you want me to take control of the choice" (between life and death) had been very important to her. She continued in the letter:

Freedom is sometimes an awful burden. You have recognized where I am and have made the choice for me. . . . Now I am in a safe emotional backwater, where things can more safely swim around and be looked at. You are a hovering Winnicottian presence that is providing a holding environment where things can grow. I trust that the pain will not become too great because you can tend to the carbon rods in the reactor pile and lower or raise the intensity of the atomic reactions within the uranium core. [The symbol of an atomic pile shows the tremendous fear the patient had that her affects would fragment her and lead to total annihilation of herself and others.] When there is an excess of neutrons, someone knows when to push the neutron-absorbing carbon rods in and the therapeutic energy is maintained, but at an optimum (not a maximum) level. It seems like the only chance I have ever had where I could relax and look without having to make things safe for myself. . . . I feel that the depressed child has been picked up, held, loved, and told we will look at the world. I do not mourn for something that should have been. It is probably more than a bit of merger, idealization, and twinship. I can have it if I want within a circumscribed sphere. And someday I will let go, look longingly at the therapy situation and go on, painfully say the last goodbye, but go on.[3] You and your husband got out from under the Nazis. I feel that you have made, of course, a contribution to "the field." But I feel, if for no other reason, you were saved for me. [This sentence shows the patient's enormous narcissistic need and grandiosity.] All I care about is what you mean in my life.

---

[3] The separation problem and the theme of termination of therapy after "growing up" played a large role throughout this hypnoanalysis. Jessica hoped for termination already towards the end of the first year, but dreaded it even more all along.

Toward the end of Phase 4, Jessica began to gain real object constancy. She could admit to herself that I, the overidealized mother figure, made mistakes sometimes and had my faults, and she could playfully tease me about my forgetfulness or my accent. She was able to tolerate a 5-week absence of mine without discomfort or fear of loss and abandonment. On rare occasions she would produce hypnotic imagery in which she saw and felt herself being an infant held in the arms of her mother, who looked at her fondly, and thus she would come to recognize that her mother was not an "all-bad" woman and had loved her as a baby.[4]

Phase 5 (September 1975–February 1976)
Return to Hypnosis and Careful Attempts to Let Repressed
Memory of Childhood Rape Rise Closer to Consciousness

While Jessica continued to fill the first three-quarters of her double hours with talking about her own patients, her supervisors, and so forth, she also became more willing again to use hypnosis. In fact, she pushed for it.

I frequently suggested now while she was in trance that some hypnotic imagery would come up that would give us a clue to understanding why for the last 2 years she had been so afraid of sexual arousal. But the hypnotic imagery she produced—defensively—always related to her mother's strictness and child abuse. Imagery produced by the patient herself rather than age regression induced by the hypnoanalyst was employed at this time, because the latter is more intrusive and confronting and I feared it would shatter her still quite weak ego structure.

Then one day in hypnosis Jessica herself produced a spontaneous, highly affect-laden regression, or hypermnesia, to age 3 or 4, in which a young soldier from a nearby army base stayed in her parents' home. He put her on his lap facing him, "felt" her "up with his long, narrow hands," made her "ride up and down," and caused her to be utterly overwhelmed with sexual excitement.

From the context in which this hypnotic material arose, I felt that the "soldier" probably was a screen memory for her half brother and that perhaps there had been some incestuous play between the two children. But my careful probing did not confirm this hypothesis. In and out of trance Jessica insisted the soldier was the soldier and no one else. She reiterated that she had not known her half brother—nor even known of his existence—until he came to visit them for the first time when she was 11 years old.

A few weeks later, in a self-hypnotic trance, she drew a picture of herself

---

[4] Had her mother rejected her as an infant, Jessica could never have become the excellent child analyst she already was when she came for therapy.

FIG. 9.2.

as a 3- or 4-year-old being held tightly on the soldier's lap. She emphasized her inability to escape by drawing next to it another picture of herself as the little girl being encased in a tight, metal drum.

Phase 6 (February 1976–August 1976)
Consolidating Object Constancy and Self-Constancy

This period was spent mainly in helping Jessica to consolidate object constancy as well as a cohesive, nonfragmented self (Kohut, 1971, 1977; Ornstein, 1974) and developing the insights that people, she and others, are neither "all-good" nor "all-bad" (Kernberg, 1975). Gaining control over splitting needed to be achieved before further uncovering of traumatic material could be attempted.

In late February 1976 Jessica gave me a letter in which with great shame—but with confidence that it would not make me turn away from her—she told me about sexual practices and fantasies she had had between ages 11 and 12, that is, in the year she said she had first met her half-brother and felt sexually exicted by him:

1. While playing on the floor with her dog, which butted against her and sniffed her crotch, she became sexually so excited and "swept away" that she pulled off her underwear, pulled the dog closer to herself, and let him lick her genitalia.
2. While babysitting with a 1½-year-old boy, she read *True Story* magazines lying around the house and was "utterly swept away" into sexual arousal. She lay down on the boy's parents' bed and fantasized pulling the little boy on top of herself, using his whole body for masturbatory purposes.

Jessica became aware of feeling a little more friendly lately towards her husband, though not able yet to really show him that. But there was less anger towards him and a greater desire to do things for him and with him.

When I asked her what was preventing her from resuming sexual relations with her husband, she said that she had abruptly terminated them when her husband asked her to take the superior position and insisted that she be more active and sometimes seduce him into having intercourse. She also complained that her husband would not cuddle her.

It was now clear why the patient had stopped having sexual relations with her husband. When he asked her to take the superior position, and to seduce him, the whole traumatic experience of sexual abuse in childhood was reactivated unconsciously and threw her into a sex phobia. The "soldier" had put the 3- or 4-year-old little girl on his lap, most likely opened his pants, penetrated her, and made her ride up and down on his penis. The attractive little girl had probably felt she had seduced him, and, in any case, felt torn up, damaged, abused. In addition, the child felt overwhelmed by her own sexual excitement. When Jessica was asked to assume the vertical position, it unconsciously to her was the equivalent of "sitting on the lap" of a man (the husband), and she again became terrified of being torn up and injured. But she did not know why. I interpreted the connection to her, and she accepted it.

Jessica, who for a long time had not been willing to do any self-hypnosis for fear of being overwhelmed by what might come up from her unconscious, now asked me to teach her self-hypnosis (again), so she could use it and bring more material into the therapy hour. Also, she now said she no longer needed lengthy induction techniques (on which she had insisted before and on which she later would insist again). She even said that she now expected soon to solve her sexual problem and end the therapy successfully. She knew she then could face life autonomously, without constant dependency on me, knowing I would always remain her friend and, as she said, "somehow inside of me." She was internalizing me as a person who appreciated her, and she was gaining healthy self-confidence.

At the start of the hypnoanalysis, Jessica has been close to being a borderline personality. By now she had improved greatly and had moved squarely into the developmental realm of narcissism. Because in any kind of therapy such patients frequently regress again under even minor stress, I continued to proceed slowly and carefully, never suggesting that as a child she had perhaps been raped by a member of the family. However, by pointing out that in and out of hypnosis she frequently talked about her father or her brother right after talking about the abuse by the soldier, I rather frequently gave her the chance to make that connection herself, if it existed and if and when she was ready to let it come into consciousness. She did not become aware of it . . . for more than a year, despite the fact that as a professionally trained psychoanalyst, Jessica of course knew that there often are important unconscious links between free associations given consecutively. The *incest* quality of the rape continued to be deeply repressed. I could not yet risk piercing the defense of repression because, at this stage, that most likely would have led to fragmentation of the self (Kohut, 1971). She was giving evidence that reliable self-functions (Kohut, 1977) were still missing: the ability to monitor affect and anxiety, to calm and soothe herself, and to regulate self-esteem. Further hypnoanalytic work was required for her to withstand the shock of possibly having to recognize an *incestuous* assault as a fact of her life.

We embarked on hypnotic experiences in which the patient could gain feelings of safety, inner enjoyment, and unity within herself. For instance, I induced trance with the image of a peaceful plastic sphere that surrounded Jessica and protected her from harm from anyone on the outside world as well as from being overwhelmed by her own affect. She could look out from that plastic sphere wherever she wanted to. She could also just float in it and allow feelings of relaxation, joy, and comfort to rise in her and sweep over her from her toes up through her legs, thighs, genitalia, torso, limbs, and neck into her head and all the way back down again, leisurely and pleasurably. Previously, when the Progressive Relaxation method was used for trance induction, I had always carefully avoided mention of the pelvis or the genitalia because Jessica had been so afraid of being over-whelmed, "driven out of her mind" by any sexual feelings. Now she could tolerate them.

And an interesting thing happened. At first in trance, and then later in the waking state, Jessica talked about the positive meaning of the child-hood bed and the room she had occupied until the age of 8. Lying on her bed, she could look out on a grove of trees and rose bushes, smell their fragrances, and fantasize beautiful things. Looking through the window into nature, she had found tranquility as a child. I interpreted to her that at these times she had created for herself her own "inner world" (Hartmann, 1958), a world in which imagery and the aesthetic enjoyment of nature provided her with the strength she needed to go on with life and not to despair at being treated so harshly by her parents. So, many hours were used to make the patient aware of her own inner resources, of fantasy, and the enjoyment of nature, which could serve her now and in the future even better than they had already in childhood. This was done for the purpose of ego strengthening and had an interesting effect half a year later. There arose in the patient a very strong desire to have a little farmhouse out in the country, surrounded by groves of trees into which she could look.

When Jessica was a child, her mother had tried to wean her away from her transitional object (Winnicott, 1953), a blanket, by cutting pieces off it day after day, until nothing was left. In childhood, it is important that the child keep his transitional object (blanket, teddy bear) for as long as he needs it to soothe himself when pained, lonely, or tired. Eventually the child is ready to give it up by himself. Jessica's mother forcefully tried to wean her away from her blanket before she was ready to give it up. So, in hypnosis it was given back to her. Sometimes, when she was very upset by reliving a childhood experience in hypnosis, I suggested that she imagine or hallucinate she had a blanket she could pull up and snuggle into. Or I put a real blanket over her. In trance, the adult part of the patient's ego felt deeply sad for the little girl, who was afraid that the blanket might be taken away from her. Jessica said that this fear had been much greater at night than during the day. At night, when she was asleep, anything could be taken away from her. She related to this the many months when she had been so afraid of hypnosis that she had not allowed me to use hypnosis with her. "I was afraid that you might take something away from me while

I was 'asleep'. That, of course, was a transference reaction. You are really not at all like my mother."

During Phase 6 I gave Jessica a little birthday present, a pin. She wrote me a note:

> Thank you so very much from a place that feels like the inside of a 4- or 5-year-old girl with blond curls and white shoes, who feels like a good child that without effort is recognized as that and has perhaps at last the feeling that her mother is proud of her. In my childhood home, birthday gifts and Christmas gifts were given only if you were good enough, and I always lived with the fear that I wouldn't be good enough and maybe would not get anything.

Perhaps in gratitude, in the next session she went into a very deep trance very quickly and had a spontaneous age regression, in which she voiced the wish for some pretty clothes. I suggested that some very pretty dresses for a little girl were lying "over there" on a chair; they were all for her. Could she see them (i.e., I "gave" them to her in trance)? One of the dresses, Jessica said, had a soft, velvety feeling both inside and outside and a beautiful purple color. Because her mother prematurely had taken her transitional object—the blanket—away from her, I wanted the patient to feel that she could "keep with her" and use whenever she wanted to this new transitional object, the velvet dress that made her feel so good. I told her that the dress would grow with her, and she could keep it forever.

Off and on, it helped her better tolerate the times of separation from me necessitated by my lecture tours. Another stone had been laid for the foundation of the patient's re-educational traversing of the separation-individuation period (Mahler et al., 1975), one of the most conflictful periods of her life. As Jessica said, "There is a lot of hope now. Eventually I will grow up and separate—and even look forward to it." But Jessica not infrequently fell back into angrily resenting my necessary absences or wanting to have me all to herself. Frequently she still felt that she wanted to, and was going to, force me to keep her in therapy "forever."

There was a short time during Phase 6 when Jessica began to feel some sympathy for her mother. She told me that her mother had always been overworked, holding a full-time job, and then being "abused" by the father, who made her work too hard at home.

Getting to the root of the sexual problem was not accomplished as quickly as I, as well as the adult part of Jessica, had hoped it would be.

During the summer of 1976, I found myself quite unwilling to use hypnosis with Jessica, partly because I was very overworked at that time (and hypnoanalysis puts more strain on the therapist than does psycho-analysis). The other reason I hesitated to use hypnosis at this time was that I wished to avoid the possibility of influencing the patient's recollections in hypnosis through my own hypothesis. I was fully aware that I still felt Jessica had been raped in childhood either by her father or, more likely, by her brother. But I also knew that this could be a wrong hypothesis. Perhaps the rapist had indeed been the soldier, or perhaps she had not been raped at all but only "felt up," as she said. Also, the rape or incest could have been purely a product of the patient's imagination, an oedipal fantasy. On the other hand, it was also possible that Jessica simply was not ready yet to face the incest question and thus resisted it for (valid) self-protective reasons.

In any case, I felt that if hypnosis were used at this time, the danger of the patient's accepting my hypothesis rather than coming to her own correct insight—whatever it might turn out to be—was too great. From my research I knew that hypnotic subjects like to oblige the researcher. When they know what the therapist's hypothesis is, they frequently produce the data that fit it. At this point it seemed safer to use waking-state therapy only, which we did for the next two months. But it also turned out to be less productive. Jessica spent the next 2 months obsessing again about her "bad," "rigid" teachers, her "malicious" peers, and, above all, her "bad" mother. I wondered why she had to hold on so tenaciously to what she felt had been bad experiences and to talk about them over and over again. The way Jessica talked about her mother and herself contained a great deal of self-pity and anger at the mother. For weeks it was like running the needle of a record player in the same groove. Only after 2 months did I realize that Jessica was also complaining about me, and with some good reason: like her mother—partly for selfish reasons (overwork)—I was "rigidly" with-holding hypnosis from her. To some degree I had acted like her ungiving, bad mother.

In between the (waking) psychotherapy sessions of the last few weeks, Jessica, apparently in self-hypnotic states, had been drawing bright red, round flowers with blue centers, from which black and brown lines emanated. She said these violent, flowerlike structures represented her genitalia. The black and brown lines were "lines of pain." The center of the flowers, she said, looked like targets. I had no doubt that these drawings represented defloration and penetration, and inasmuch as I felt that Jessica's ego was now strong enough to face more uncovering, it was time to agree to her request to reinstitute hypnosis. Jessica explained why she thought she could now get at deeply repressed and anxiety-arousing material in hypnosis better than in the waking state. She said, "In trance I now give the anxiety to you to hold. And then, with that security that you will hold the anxiety and will not let me be overwhelmed, I can proceed and get at the difficult material." I also agreed to see her for two double sessions a week instead of one. Jessica wanted to double the number of her therapy hours so she could terminate in 3 or 4 months. We used roughly one half of the hours for hypnosis, the others to work through in the waking state the material that had come up in hypnosis.

Phase 7 (September 1976–January 1977)
Further Uncovering of Repressed Material With Regard to
Rapes Suffered in Childhood

Jessica associated the violent flower drawings to masturbatory activities in which she was currently engaged. Up to this time she had masturbated exceedingly infrequently because, as she said, she felt it was sinful. As it turned out, however, the drawings really did not refer to masturbation. They referred to the traumatic rape experiences of her childhood that now began to come into sharper focus in the hypnotic sessions.

As an induction technique, we now used the Deep-Sea Diving Technique (see chapter 4) in which the patient was safely enclosed in a heavy, transparent capsule that could be lowered thousands of feet into the depths of the ocean. Jessica understood that the "depths of the ocean" symbolized the unconscious. She was not alone in this gondola. With her were oceanographers (symbolizing the therapist), who had taken similar trips with others many times before and who would assist her in exploring what was going on under the surface, perhaps even in making new discoveries. When Jessica was in at least medium-deep trance, I suggested that she could now look inside herself. Images and memories would come up that were connected with the sexual trauma that had happened to her in childhood.

Until then we knew with certainty only that the soldier had once "felt her up," when she was 3 or 4 years old. Perhaps he had also penetrated and deflorated her. At her very early age she had felt terrified and also overwhelmed by strong, pleasurable sexual feelings. Two other sexual traumata now emerged in the hypnosis sessions; both were clear-cut rape experiences.

In one of the hypnosis hours Jessica cried a good deal and saw a child, 3 or 4 years old, lying in bed, frightened, curled up to protect herself. When I asked where the child was afraid of getting hurt, Jessica tearfully said, "Up between the legs." I asked her what made the child fear that the area between the legs would get hurt. She said, "Somebody hit there." As the genital area certainly is a strange place to be hit, with some surprise in my voice I asked, "Hit there?" Jessica replied, "Oh, the child always got hit, always, everywhere. There, was the worst." After a while she said, "Something there is very bad. That's why the child got hit. I don't like to talk about this." And she clammed up. I empathized with her, saying I understood how difficult it was to talk about it, but urged her to face the problem. Supportively, I took the patient's hand in my own. Jessica then saw a shadow of a figure coming into her room, a figure that would hurt her. She felt like sliding down under the bed. I encouraged her in the hypnotic fantasy to do so, but to look up at the approaching figure and to see who it was. Jessica cried a good deal, pitifully, and in a child's voice said that she was curling her fingers and her toes into the metal springs under the bed so that nobody could pull her out or hurt her. She still only saw a shadow of a person, "so tall, very tall, almost as tall as the door," and said, "it feels like it is that soldier." Encouraged to look at the figure again, she looked, but all she could see were "black shoes, khaki pants." Although I encouraged her, she could not look up any higher than to see large feet and a strip of khaki pants above them. She still needed to defend herself against bringing the traumatic events into more than partial awareness—a defense that had to be respected. Therefore, I suggested that the person in the khaki pants was now walking out of the door of her room. Perhaps some other day she could look again and see who it was. Jessica calmed down a bit and then asked, "Why did they (her parents) let him into the house? Why did they not protect me?" After a while she said, "I don't know what happened, but I do know he had something to do with whatever happened." Again, she was told to let him go for now. Within the next few weeks what had happened would become clearer. The child could cry it all out here in therapy in the weeks to come and work it through. After a few minutes of silent crying, Jessica—still in trance—said, "The child is all right. She is sitting in bed reading. He is gone. She is bigger now. She is 7 years old. She is reading fairy tales." The patient also created a big, protective glass bubble, with the glass closed towards the door but open towards the window, from which she could look out and escape into her trees. In earlier hours she had made it clear that trees, like reading, to her represented her own inner world of fantasy, a world that was safe. But she said there was also the fear that the glass might shatter, and then she would be crazy. This hypnotic image clearly mirrored the patient's fear that under the impact of bringing the traumatic events into consciousness, she would fragment and become psychotic.

In this hypnotic hour Jessica also talked about not being able to get away from her mother when her mother beat her, because her mother's hands were so strong and she would hold her by the arms. But the mother usually beat her on the back of the calves. So the hitting in the genital area, in front, does not really refer to what the mother did to her. It does refer to the sexual assault. It refers directly to the "soldier." But, in some way, child abuse and sexual abuse were connected in the patient's mind.

During the next 2 weeks Jessica, in trance imagery, played with a protective fantasy, a shell in her childhood bed into which she could crawl when someone threatening would enter her room. The shell had magical qualities. With the patient in it, it could become so small that no one could find her, or it could vanish through an invisible trap door in her mattress, and she would be safe, curled up in it. She said the shell could read her mind and would come to her whenever she was anxious and needed it.

Jessica now had an added tool of self-protection at her disposal. I asked her to see herself again at "3 or 4 years." When she felt herself to be in her childhood bedroom, I said:

T: Now the door is opening and someone comes in. Let's see who it is. Perhaps it is a friendly person. Perhaps it is not. Let's see who it is.

P: I can't see the face. I can't see the face at all.

T: Can you see the figure?

P: Part of it.

T: Is it a man or a woman?

P: It's a man.

T: Can you see the trousers?

P: More than that. It makes me very cold. Scared. That's why I don't like to sit in chairs. [This is a hint of the penetration experience in childhood while she was sitting on the lap of the "soldier," who sat on a chair.]

T: [Backing off for a moment to use an ego-strengthening procedure]: Go back into your shell for a minute, gain strength, and then come out again and look him square in the face. Who is it?

P: It's a . . ., it's not a clear picture. It's something I'm aware of, but I don't see it as a picture.

T: Well. Whatever it is. Who is it?

P: [Blocks] . . . that soldier.

T: What is he doing?

P: I don't talk about it. I am afraid [said in the voice of a little girl]. I hate chairs [spoken in a reflective adult voice].

T: As the minutes go by, it will become easier and easier to talk about it.

P: I just want to run away [little girl's voice].

T: Go back in your shell and gain strength.

P: I just want to run away.

T: Gain new strength and come out again.

P: . . . pain all over and over [little girl's voice]; I don't want to do that! [adult voice.]

T: Once you can face it, things will fall into place and will become better.

P: It just can't be! [adult voice, unbelieving].

T: It can be. . . . And, unconsciously, you have known it all along. It is now trying to come into full consciousness. I am with you. I will not let it overwhelm you.

Two days later Jessica dropped me a note saying, "Don't worry. I am upset, but I can handle it."

The vacillation between little girl and adult voice indicated that while the patient during that hour was in a spontaneous age regression, in which she re-experienced one of the deeply traumatic events of her childhood, her adult ego, was not fully out of commission and simultaneously worked on recognizing and repressing or denying who the rapist really was.

During the week following the hour just reported, the patient again masturbated a good deal and found herself in a self-hypnotic state during the masturbations. She felt very frightened while masturbating and told herself that this probably had some connection with what she was working on in her hypnoanalysis. She decided to let imagery come up in her mind. An image of the lower part of a man's body in khaki pants came up, with his head hovering over his pubic region. In her next hour she reported:

What kept trying to come into my awareness during that self-hypnotic state was actually the image of . . . the bad image . . . [blocks] . . . the image of the phallus. And then I had a lot of questions about whether it (the rape) really had happened.[5] What then came into my awareness was a sharp feeling of pain in the vaginal area. I said to myself, "Well, maybe it really did happen." And then what came next was "Oh, this is why I am so afraid."

At the end of this waking hour, Jessica asked whether what she had brought up about the soldier in the heterohypnotic trance sessions and in

---

[5] The defensive functions of blocking and denial clearly can be discerned here. Even in self-hypnotic trance, some patients can defend themselves against letting unconscious, highly conflictful material come into full awareness.

self-hypnosis was a figment of her imagination or whether childhood rape really had happened. I told her I did not know for sure; only her unconscious knew. However, she would know the truth consciously when she was really ready to find it.

In the next hypnotic hour, Jessica saw the full figure of the soldier, who, she said, had raped her as a child. At first, she was very upset. Then, as a protective measure, she erected a glass wall between herself and the soldier, a wall of very strong glass through which, she said, he could not attack her. Eventually she changed the glass into a sort of one-way mirror through which she could see the soldier but the soldier could not see her. By the end of that session, I was more convinced that the soldier was not a screen memory but the real rapist.

A couple of weeks later, Jessica asked me to let her re-experience with their full force the affects she had had during the childhood rape(s). As I felt she was now strong enough to do so, I age-regressed her to "3 or 4 years." In trance she experienced great fear, coupled with a tense state of sexual arousal and a feeling that everything was frozen. She had the sense of sitting on someone's lap in her pretty pinafore, held tightly, facing him, and being moved up and down. She felt a piercing pain. There was blood on the floor. Everything went dark. She could not say who the "someone" was. She could not escape. He held her tightly. It was as if there were a fence around her. All she could do was kick him with the back of her shoe. But it also felt to her as if it were a game between her and whoever the "someone" was on whose lap she sat. The image of the fence crystallized into a feeling of being strapped by the arms of the person who was holding her on his lap.

I asked her who the person was on whose lap she sat. She couldn't say. I used a visual metaphor for communicating with her in primary process language, saying, "It's a puzzle. Let all the pieces of the puzzle fall together." She said: "I cannot. I am trapped. Why don't you let me get away?" I told her that the time had come when she needed to look at the person, to look at his face, in trance, and to recognize him, because I trusted she could do it now. Jessica did look, and said, "It's very confusing. I thought he was my friend." I agreed, "Very confusing, and very hard." Jessica cried and said, "My arms and legs don't work. I can't run away, I can't push him away." I empathized with her feeling helpless and— thinking that it was either the soldier or the father—said that was so because the patient was a little kid and he was a grownup. At that point in trance, Jessica shifted into a different ego state and put more accent on the adult ego. In a way she returned to the metaphor of the pieces of the puzzle, and said, "I cannot pull it all together. It's just all pieces." I gave her the posthypnotic suggestion that as the days of the following week proceeded, the puzzle would become clearer and clearer and the pieces would fall more and more together without her being overwhelmed. She shook her head and said, "No. The pressure is too much." She was told that we would end the trance in a few minutes and that she could bring up with herself as much of the repressed material as she would be able to face in the waking state. I also told her that as time went on and we continued to work with trance, she would be able to face more and more of it, both in the hypnotic and in the waking state.

After awakening, Jessica said the hour had been very difficult. In the trance her words had seemed to her to come from very far away, and a part of herself felt, when she listened to herself, that what she said wasn't so but that the words came anyway (cf. Fromm, 1965a). She felt as if she were two separate people, the child and the adult. Strangely, she said, the little child felt almost more real to her than the adult part, the part that was "trying to make sense out of it all."

In the waking state the patient reported that, throughout this session, she had had the feeling that in trance part of her had wanted to keep that experience repressed, to push it away, not to know about it.

> But it was like fog rolling in from under the door, anyhow; I could no longer keep it away. I didn't want to know about it. But it came into my consciousness in trance anyhow. Now it is foggy again. It's very, very confusing. In trance there were many me's: the person who was observing, the child who was experiencing, the person that is trying to listen, the person who doesn't want to hear it, and the voice of the foggy awareness that comes rolling in under the door.

The fog rolling in under the door shows the attempted "Return of the Repressed" (Freud, 1939/1964), while, with "Now it is foggy again," the patient also expressed the defense against it. The double use of the fog symbol is interesting.

In both of these heretofore repressed childhood experiences recovered in trance, the "soldier" who had "felt her up" was also the attacker. The session reported earlier, in which he had sexually attacked her on the floor and she had tried to hide under her bed, actually occurred somewhat later than the rape on the chair.

It now became clear emotionally to Jessica, too, why she panicked and stopped all sexual relations with her husband after the husband had asked her once to take the upper position in connubial intercourse. She could see now that deeply unconsciously it had stirred up the childhood experience of sitting on the soldier's lap and being deflorated and raped.

During the following week, Jessica stated that only within the last year had she begun to suspect that she had been raped as a child. I had suspected it for 3 years, practically since the beginning of the therapy—

that is, ever since the drawing of the "mother" giving her an enema—because what the patient had designated as the figure of the mother was a half-nude person, kneeling in a coital position over the child on the floor.

In another session, Jessica produced a hypnotic fantasy of a square box with razor-sharp edges that could cut anything coming near it. The box was whirling around in the air. Out of its sides extended metal arms with many bends and sharp claws that would cut deeply into the flesh, and streaks of blood of an invisible victim were running from the razor blades. She described her mother as having been like a hard box, with razor-sharp edges that persecuted her, hit her and hurt her, no matter where she was or what she would do. In the trance fantasy she tried to run into a closet, but the box followed her. She said she had never thought before of her mother as a box, but that was what the mother really was—a large box with razor-sharp edges. I suggested that she could take the box and put it on a shelf, where it would stay so she could look at it, but that the box needed no longer be part of her life and hurt her. At first she said that was impossible, the box was too heavy, she could not heave it up onto the shelf. But then suddenly she could. She filled in the holes from which the metal arms protruded and made them smaller and smaller till they finally became like pinholes. Then she saw the box shrinking, until it was no more than 6 inches long, 4 inches high, and 4 inches wide. It remained on the shelf where she had put it, and she could walk away from it. She heaved a sigh and said, "It's no longer dangerous; my mother is no longer dangerous to me." When I told her that now she could wake herself up, she grinned and said, "I started that already, before you told me. I was a naughty child today—I opposed you twice. First you told me to bring up the picture of the soldier, and I decided instead to bring up the picture of my mother. Then I decided to wake myself up before you even had told me. Are you angry at me?" (Said with a laughing face.) I said I wasn't angry at all; in fact, I appreciated her autonomy. That she could oppose me showed that she now had learned not all women were like her mother. And this was progress.

The next time, she drew a picture, which she entitled "Inside the Empty Box—Empty of a Real Mother." Inside it were a number of things: a large clock, which could activate a set of gears that could set in motion control and discipline, and a box with colored button handles, which, if pressed, would cause suffocation. Inside that box was another box labeled "trash box of mother," which contained things the patient felt her mother had disapproved of or robbed her of: her childhood blanket, torn into pieces; the face of a bright-eyed little girl; a fetus-like soft structure, near which the words "joy," "sex," and "softness" were written; and the torso of a woman with the word "good" written between her bare breasts. Although Jessica had been able to verbalize in the waking state that she understood her mother had her own severe neurosis to contend with and, on top of it, had been badly harassed by the father, the two box images she had in hypnosis certainly did not indicate any forgiveness. But perhaps a child who has been so abused and beaten by her mother can never really fully forgive her.

One of the characteristics of Jessica's trances was that she never could let the GRO fade. She would close her eyes and go into a medium trance—rarely as deeply as she was able to go—but she would hear every slight noise in the building. I pointed out to her now that perhaps she had developed this vigilance as a consequence of the childhood rape and that, in a way, she was still afraid the soldier might come into the room. Therefore, she had to listen for footsteps.

One week, in trance, the patient re-evoked in memory the traumatic event of the rape, but this time less as an image than as a feeling (hypermnestic recovery of affect). And while she felt the helplessness of the poor child who was held tightly by the soldier and could not escape, she also said that the child now was kicking and screaming. Thus, in hypnosis she tried to work through the trauma by taking the more ego-active role of fighting the aggressor than she had done in the real event in childhood. I encouraged her to kick, kick hard. Suddenly she brought up a third experience with the soldier. It had occurred at night in her room: the soldier, she felt, was sleeping on a cot in her room. He had gotten up from the cot in the middle of the night and had raped her again, in her bed. She became even angrier at her parents, particularly at her mother, than she had been before: How could the parents let the young man sleep in the same room with the little girl? How could they be unaware of the little girl's attractiveness? How could they fail to see that he might sexually attack her? How stupid they had been! By letting the soldier sleep in the same room with her, she felt, her parents had, stupidly though not intentionally, set her up for being raped.

She then also brought up another memory, namely, that since she was 5 or 6 years old, she had had the job of hanging up the laundry behind the house. She always felt a mixture of fear and revulsion when hanging her father's shorts on the laundry line. The rest of the laundry did not bother her. But she could hardly stand to touch the shorts. Again I thought: Perhaps the rapist was the father, but I said nothing to that effect to Jessica.

During the next month, Jessica began to see some positive characteristics in her parents, characteristics with which she had identified. For the first time, she began to talk about her father separately from her mother. She could see her father as an intelligent, able businessman, who, though he himself did not earn much, as an employee of his firm dealt with vast amounts of money in an efficient and able manner; and she felt that her mother had always displayed great generosity towards the neighbors. She felt she had identified with the attitudes of both parents in these respects.

She still was angry at both of her parents. They had beaten and abused her. To some degree her anger now also turned toward her former analyst, the one she had seen for 2 years prior to coming to me for hypnoanalysis. Why did he never discover that she had been raped? Why did this male psychoanalyst not fully believe her when she told him that she was physically and emotionally abused by her parents? I pointed out that sometimes deeply repressed, very traumatic material can be brought into waking consciousness only through hypnosis.

By this time Jessica had developed a mild desire to have a sexual relationship with her husband again. But still she could not tell him that, because she felt it would be "unfeminine." After inducing trance, I suggested to her that she picture herself in bed with her husband and reach out and touch his hand or shoulder. Jessica refused to imagine herself reaching out. She said that in any sexual relationship the man had to take the initiative. I pointed out that it was she who had rejected the husband for the last 4 years and refused to have intercourse with him; how could he fathom that now she wanted it? She freely admitted that she had not given him the slightest hint of her changed desires or feelings but expected him to sense, to divine, her change in attitude, "just as a caring mother senses a child's needs." I interpreted that she was demanding he be the "good mother" she never had had and that a husband could not be a mother.

I then gave Jessica a simple, purely relaxing hypnotic experience in order to help her when in bed with her husband to become more relaxed, less angry, less vigilant or fearful of attack (which I said was a transference from the soldier experience), and less demanding that he be omniscient. After a while, the patient angrily said that this was a waste of time. But, in the months that followed, she changed her appearance: she went on a diet, lost a good deal of weight, and dressed more femininely and with good taste.

One day Jessica reported that in a nocturnal dream she had seen blood on the floor. She wondered whether it had something to do with her first menstruation. I thought it referred to the defloration and told her again, in the waking state, that there could be more to the childhood molestation than we knew about. Immediately Jessica felt a painful rush of sexual feelings come up. I helped her into trance with the Deep-Sea Diving Technique, which she understood as being a technique that facilitates exploration of unconscious and repressed material. She saw two people swimming underwater effortlessly. Then she started to cry in trance and said, "I can't be involved with men. My father won't let me. He always takes the good things for himself." Again I felt some suspicion arise that perhaps the father, rather than the brother, had molested the child and committed the rape. But again I did not say anything.

Then, still in trance, Jessica talked about the time when she was about 13 and her mother went to work, on a 3–11 p.m. shift. She was alone with her father and baby sister and was frightened of her father. The fear clearly was related to her own oedipal wishes for the father. But I asked, "Frightened of what?" And Jessica defensively said, "Of his yelling at me or hitting me." She said that, as a child, for many years she desperately had wanted to run away from home, and she had wanted to kill her parents. She had no place to run to. Again, she compared her childhood to being in a concentration camp. Already, at age 7, she had wanted to get her father's pistol and shoot both parents. She had fantasies of killing them and then killing herself, but, even more, she just wanted to run away. But she never did. As the hour drew to a close, Jessica was still *extremely* upset. In order to help her reintegrate before leaving, I suggested that she see herself now as the child lying on her bed in her childhood home, looking out into the trees and creating again her own "inner world," wich had given her strength before. Jessica calmed down and left less upset. I told her she could call me anytime that day or in the following days if she needed me, an offer that had been made often at other times too.

Later that afternoon Jessica wrote me a note telling me she felt:

> . . . very whole. One thing I thought of as I left was that although I suffered deeply in trance today, I can now see that child not just as a victim or to be pitied. I see that child's experience as different from the experiences of concentration camp inmates. I also see her as a stronger child than I saw her before. Before, I saw me as a helpless victim in my family, crazy, depressed, distraught. Now, I see myself clearly as a child who helped herself and who must have had that capacity but did not recognize it. I also know now that I am an adult who probably won't regress again. And I realize the bed I had until I was seven was a primary soother for me. After seven, it became a secondary soother, and reading books became primary ones.

In the next hour Jessica speculated, in the waking state, that in her mind somehow the two diparate traumatic areas, child abuse and sexual abuse, had become connected with regard to the affect involved. But she stated that the rape had not been committed by the father, and the child abuse (beating) had been committed by both parents. As later developments in therapy revealed, she was right. The father had not raped her.

Because more uncovering was needed, some weeks later, after inducing trance, I again suggested to Jessica that an image would come up that related to the sexual trauma she had suffered in childhood. Jessica saw herself as a child, playing in an airy, roofless castle, running around with little boys. After being asked to go deeper in trance, she felt that the boys and she were running downstairs, deeper and deeper into the castle. The castle was very light, even in its deepest recesses. One could see into the bottom, the dungeons, which no longer were dark and scary, as she knew they had been in the past. There used to be monsters in the dungeons in that castle, but even the dungeons were fully light now. I interpreted to her while she was in trance that the castle represented her unconscious, which was no longer so frightening and full of monsters. The round, open, light castle also represented the childhood problem of being encircled, but no longer imprisoned by the "soldier's" arms.

Jessica's fantasy then changed: There was no longer any monster but only little boys with whom she could run and play. In most of the fantasy Jessica, too, was a little boy. At other times in the fantasy, she was the queen who lived in the castle. There was hardly any furniture in the castle, and she knew that she had to make the furniture for it. The stones from which the castle was built were so light and so clean. Even the straw in the dungeons was clean. It was springtime around the castle, warm and pleasant; birds were singing. Jessica commented that the new castle must have been built on the foundation of an older, constricting castle, the only remnants of which were the dungeons. But even the dungeons now were cleaned up, and the chains that had been used to manacle prisoners to the wall now were ropes, tying up no one any longer. The old castle either had been destroyed or had fallen down block by block. Suddenly she said, "It is as if I didn't want to know about the catacombs down there." I urged her to go down and look at them. The patient, in trance, went down and said, "That's where I killed the soldier."

What she referred to were recent hypnotic fantasies and three drawings executed in self-hypnosis, in which she had taken her revenge on the young man by cutting his heart out of his chest and castrating him on an Aztec altar; by manacling him and whipping him so he would bleed to death; and by letting him hang from his bound feet in an isolated tower in the desert, starving and dying of thirst. She let his body shrivel in the dry desert wind, which blew his ashes into oblivion. In these fantasies she also relived and brought into consciousness her terrible anger at the "soldier," an anger which until that time she had repressed. The patient felt that the rape experiences were "sort of like catacombs," and said she could bury these experiences now, get rid of them, and go up to the new castle, the light castle, in which she could run around and play.

Because I still believed that the brother, not the "soldier," had raped her, I urged her to let even more light shine into the catacombs and look at what was in there. Perhaps there was more in these catacombs, I said, than the rape and the soldier; or someone else; and perhaps that was all there was in it. Jessica saw a child in there who kicked and experienced the horror that she had gone through as a child when she was raped. She felt angry and sad. And betrayed. But she brought up the "soldier" again. As a small child, she had trusted the soldier, she said, and her trust had been betrayed. She saw the child crying, lying in a corner of a room all crumpled up. But she could not get really close to the child. I suggested the adult Jessica see herself, as a grownup, go over to that corner where the child was lying, crumpled up, and comfort the little girl. Jessica replied that she was picking up something that was frozen, cold as stone. It was the little girl. In the fantasy, the grown-up Jessica sat down in a chair and wrapped a blanket around little Jessica. She held the child gently in her "open arms," just rocking her. The child began to thaw and became alive again.

In the waking state, Jessica herself then interpreted that this is what the rape experience had done to her: It had turned her almost to stone. Right after making this interpretation, she said:

> Why can't I see fully what happened? Why can I only see a bit here and a bit there, but I can't see it all at one time and put it together? I can see the lone kid in the corner; I can see the kid that kicks and screams; I feel like the child that was torn apart inside, and I feel like the child for whom there was some pleasure. I also feel like the lonely child. There is a sliver of this and a sliver of that, but I can't put them all together.

I helped Jessica back into trance and suggested she take a strong magnet that would pull all of the slivers together. Instead, Jessica imagined a screen on which she saw a body pinned to a wall of ice and fire. It felt as if a thunderbolt had gone through that body. There was screaming, and fire, and shattering all at once. But she could see it only far, far away. To calm her and help her gain control over the frightening affects, I put my hand on her arm, a nonverbal hypnotic communication of emotional support. Then I suggested that she let the image get closer, so that she could see and feel it fully. After a very long pause, the patient said, "I can't. It's too scary." I suggested that "out in the woods" (which always had been a source of comfort to Jessica and now had become a symbol of her own good and comforting "inner world"), she could hear the woodpeckers; and as she heard the woodpeckers, the fragmented picture could come together, come closer, and not be so scary anymore. Jessica said, practically inaudibly, "Not today, not yet." So I asked her to return to the waking state.

But Jessica did not want to leave hypnosis and the airy, light part of the castle yet. She wanted to stay a while longer in the part of the castle where there was "good, eternal spring." I let her do that, even though it meant running overtime a good deal. In trance Jessica now remembered many good parts of her childhood, "wonderful things," such as making sand castles, stealing apples from trees, prowling around the stacks of the library.

Eventually she woke herself up. I asked her what she thought it meant that she could see light in the dungeons. She said it meant she was getting better. She also clarified another item: in the dungeons there had been only ropes lying on the ground, not chains. "Ropes can be cut, not chains. That, too, means that I am getting much better."

She felt that this was a very important hour. And while she remembered right after waking up all that had gone on in the hour, she was afraid that she soon would repress it, in a day or two, as she had done with many other important hours.

Phase 8 (September 1976–January 1977)
Who Was the Real Rapist?

Toward the end of the third year of hypnoanalysis, Jessica seriously wished to finish the hypnoanalysis soon. She asked to be given 4 hours instead of 2 during the next 3½ months in order to work through the loose ends of the therapy and to terminate. In particular, she wanted to do more work on the rape experiences and her feelings about them. It had been a long hypnoanalysis, but the patient had come a long way: she had moved from a narcissistic character disorder with borderline features to a neurosis (a sex phobia). She wanted to finish therapy within 3 to 4 months and buy herself a cabin on a wooded piece of land in the country. I felt her plan to terminate was feasible. The woods had personal significance for her as her private world of fantasy; trees had meant and given her inner strength in childhood.

However, Jessica was also ambivalent about termination. She vacillated between needing to show me that she was still ill and reproaching me for wanting to "push" her "out of therapy" on the one hand, and, on the other hand, really feeling much better and wanting to separate from the therapist-mother, be an autonomous adult, and go on with her life. That this patient had made enormous improvement was attested to by many outside sources: her husband, friends, and colleagues (even her former psychoanalyst, whom she had met at a party). In the summer of 1976, the patient wrote me the following note:

> Something different I have noticed lately—I have begun to be able to feel good about something I have done, within myself. When people responded well to the work I had done, when you said good things about me, and when my supervising analyst complimented me today on a particularly difficult piece of work I had done very well, I knew without a doubt they were right. It was a quiet, assured, solid feeling, no longer narcissistic grandiosity. I also do not fly into rages anymore.

Thus, in September 1976 a termination date for the end of the year was set, and I strongly urged Jessica to use self-hypnosis again in between hours. She did, but far less often than requested.

At the end of September, Jessica had a nocturnal dream she correctly related to re-experiencing in hypnosis the trauma of being raped by the "soldier" at the age of 3 or 4 and her fear that he would kill her in penetrating her. In addition, the dream contained the conviction that once this trauma was worked through, she would gain a full womanly identity, become an adult woman, and leave the hypnoanalyst's office. To leave me made her feel sad. She felt exhausted. But she said, "It is a good exhaustion."

During the next month, Jessica again relived in several age regressions in trance her lying under the bed as a child, trembling, because she knew someone was going to come in who would hurt her. I asked her to look up from under the bed to see who it was. Again she said she could see only his feet and the lower part of his trousers . . . khaki trousers, and she started to sob. I felt that she by now had gained enough ego strength to face the trauma fully.

Thus, over several sessions I encouraged Jessica to come forward from under the bed, look further up higher and higher, and eventually see the face of the intruder. I continued to vacillate between thinking that the rapist had been the brother or perhaps the father and believing that she really was right when she said it was the soldier. The khaki color of the uniform remained the same, and eventually the face turned up over and over again as that of the soldier. Still, I had doubts and thought it was the brother, because Jessica had been so agitated and sexually aroused when as an 11-year-old she found a postcard announcing the visit of "Tim," whom she supposedly did not know and had never heard of. I knew that Tim had worn a uniform, too: throughout his adolescent years, he had been in the ROTC; later he was in the Army. But whenever I probed about the brother's uniform, Jessica pointed out that the trousers of an ROTC uniform are not khaki but gray with a slightly pinkish overcast, and the jacket is olive drab. Up to January 1977, there also occasionally were indications that the incest could have been committed by the father. One such indication occurred when Jessica in hypnosis talked about what kind of person her father was and felt sexual excitement. She did not tell me this at the time, but only in the following hour, and said, "I feel like a mole that is quickly going underground, with you reaching after it but not being able to catch its tail or its feet. It is a form of an unharnessed, playful, wriggling away from 'mother.'" As a toddler, Jessica had been harnessed by her mother so she would not run away. She had always resented this harness, and, even when thinking about it as an adult, she had felt "badly abused." She was surprised her feelings had changed so much. The feeling of passively having to endure immobilization (as she had to during the rape on the soldier's lap) or restriction (in the harness the mother put on the toddler or the many prohibitions imposed on her throughout her childhood by her parents) now had changed to a feeling of ego activity and playfulness, in which she mischievously and playfully ran away from the transference figure of the mother-therapist, who was trying to catch her but did not succeed. The patient was intrigued and pleased when I said that these fantasies and behaviors indicated emotional growth and playful attempts at mastery and autonomy.

A few weeks later, Jessica was willing for the first time to look at the "Enema" picture again. I explained to her that this drawing and her panic-striken unwillingness to look at the drawing again, which had lasted for 3 years, had caused me from early on to suspect a deeply repressed child-hood rape in her background. A mother would not be lying bare-buttocked on top of her child when administering an enema! The patient could smile now . . . and agreed. She understood now that the drawing referred to the repressed childhood rape experiences she had wanted to keep repressed but also wanted to disclose in hypnoanalysis, so that she could free herself of the emotional burden of this trauma. And she said now that her mother had given her an enema only once in her whole life, not two or three times a week, as she had told me so often before. Jessica felt that the hours of the last 3 months, October–December 1976, had been the most important hours of all the 12 years she had spent in her four therapies (three psychoanalyses, one hypnoanalysis).

But even though the traumatic experiences with the soldier had been brought to consciousness, Jessica tenaciously held on to the fear that in intercourse with her husband she would become damaged, torn apart, hurt, a phobia she had developed 4 years earlier, when he asked her to take the upper position in intercourse. She continued to sleep in the same bed with him without allowing him to have intercourse with her. Jessica had shown a similar tenacity to hold on to bad experiences in her relationship to her mother earlier, during the 3-year hypnoanalysis period of enormous anger at the mother and self-pity.

I wanted her not to repress the childhood sexual traumata again, but to leave them behind and move on to a mature and happy sexual life. In a hypnotic session, remembering that Jessica herself had felt totally fenced in when the soldier grabbed her and held her so tightly, I used a fence symbol to help Jessica free herself from the emotional grasp of the two men who had abused her, the rapist "soldier" and the physically abusive father. I suggested that Jessica erect in her childhood home state a corral that would surround her father and the soldier, a high fence that would encircle them and from which they could not escape. She should padlock it, and then go eastward, to the state where she currently lived, to the place in the country where she had bought the house surrounded by woods. There, her husband or some other person she loved or could love was waiting for her tenderly, I said. To help her not to repress the sexual

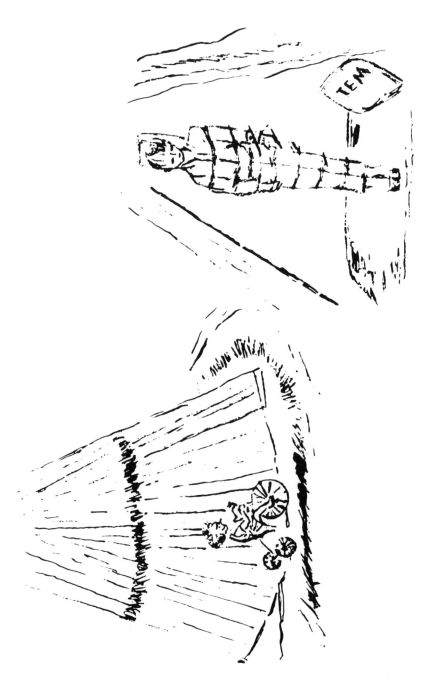

FIG. 9.3.

traumata again, I suggested that while walking away from the corral that enclosed her father and the soldier, Jessica could look back at them anytime, but they did not need to be part of her life any longer. She could leave them behind and turn to a better future, in her own "woods," her own inner, happier world. I asked Jessica to use this fantasy in self-hypnosis three times daily.

She called that evening to tell me that she had repressed the content of the fantasy she was supposed to use in self-hypnosis. On the telephone I encouraged her to think about it, and together we reconstructed the fantasy.

The next week, Jessica brought in some drawings she had made depicting the content of several self-hypnotic sessions during the preceding days. The most striking one (Fig. 9.3) showed on the left side a 3- or 4-year-old little girl riding on her tricycle around a closed tepee. Jessica had closed the open stockade of the corral I had suggested to her in the preceding hypnotic session, by leaning the vertical poles towards the middle of the structure so the corral now looked like a tepee. The child in that drawing is not able to get inside the tepee or to see what is in it. On the right hand side was the same "tepee" with what seemed to be an open flap, but Jessica described it as "what one could see through a small, keyhole-like opening in the wall" of the tepee. Inside this tepee-corral a young boy, about 12 years old, was strapped to a stake. Just outside the tent, on a stone, the initials of Jessica's half brother or father were carved. They had the same initials, she said. It was utterly clear now to me that the patient was saying her half brother had sexually attacked her when she was 3 or 4 years old and he was 12, that is, during his first visit, the memory of which she had totally repressed by the time of his second visit, when she was 11 years old.

Jessica said that she could not explain why she had put her brother's or father's initials on the stone. I probed by saying that the soldier had been older than 12, he had been 25 years old when he came to their house, and that Jessica had always drawn him with curly black hair. When I pointed out that the boy in the tepee had straight hair, Jessica flatly said, "I cannot draw curly hair." This was not true. She had always drawn both the soldier and herself with curly hair. I probed and probed, but Jessica could not make any connection between the letters and the boy at the stake. I was struck by this because the meaning was so obvious and the highly sophisticated patient, a psychoanalyst, could not see it. I began to feel that it would be cruel to lead or force Jessica to recognize that the soldier had been a screen memory and that the attacker had really been her brother. The brother, after all, had been the only person with whom she had had a positive, warm, and enduring relationship. He was her idol. Clearly, Jessica had indicated, over and over again, that she could not face losing this positive introject. I did not want to run the risk of destroying the one good family relationship Jessica had had. After agonizing about it for a few weeks, I decided to hold Jessica now to her desire to terminate, which she had expressed 5 months earlier. She would gain nothing, I felt, by realizing that the brother was the perpetrator of the crime, and the danger that she would fragment if she recognized it was disproportionately great. She had realized that she had been raped as a child. That was enough. A therapist must weigh advantages against disadvantages.

Phase 9 (February 1977–August 1977)
Beginning Termination

I reduced Jessica's hours again, to the original 2 hours per week, and told her termination within a few months was indicated. I also reminded her that I had agreed to let her delay all payments for the 2 additional weekly hours between September and December, if she would send me monthly payments for them right after she had terminated in December. It was now February, she had run up 6 months of unpaid bills with me, and I was not willing to let her increase this debt indefinitely. She had made no attempt to pay off her debt. Jessica said that she felt "entitled" to have 4 weekly hours of therapy, even if she paid for only 2, and that she would continue to use my money to pay for her new house. She became very angry every time I brought up the idea that she should set a termination date toward which we could then work. The mere word "termination" threw her into a narcissistic rage reminiscent of her earlier near-borderline state, a rage in which she threatened to destroy my property, throw her shoes through my window, and hurl a potted plant against the wall.

When I insisted on interpreting these rages on the transference level as the tantrums of a 2-year-old child in the separation-individuation period, Jessica brought up for the first time material that perhaps had been conscious to her, but which she had never divulged in the 3½ years of hypnoanalysis. At age 18, when she went to college (which ordinarily constitutes the final point in the adolescent's recapitulation of the separation-individuation process), she had felt that her parents had pushed her out of the nest and that she had not been ready to leave. At all other times, in the hypnotic state as well as in the waking state, she talked about so desolate and difficult a childhood that one would have expected her to be only too glad to leave the parental home and go to college. That she did not want to leave it strengthened my conviction that the parents—although certainly not "good"—in some ways must have satisfied some of her dependency needs, something the patient so far had only rarely been able to see.

Jessica angrily insisted over and over that she was not going to set a termination date, nor would she allow me to set one. She would remain in therapy for at least a dozen more years, or until my death. Thus, she tried to make therapy a "way of life." Jessica also was furious that I wanted her to deal with the transference issues of rage in the waking state in order to show her that her behavior was regressive and exploitative and her anger totally out of proportion. I interpreted that in the termination phase she was recapitulating early stages of her childhood development and of the therapy, namely, a wish to have a devoted mother serve her dependency needs forever and exclusively. That is an unrealistic wish healthy, normal children give up at the end of the separation-individuation period (Mahler, 1972; Mahler et al., 1975), at the age of 3.

Phase 9 was a very stormy and difficult period in the therapy. However, Jessica did pay back the money she owed me.

Phase 10 (May 1977–August 1977)
The Patient Recognizes That the Rapes Were Incestuous, But Is Now Strong Enough Not to Fragment Under the Impact of This Insight

Suddenly, on Mother's Day, Jessica called her mother and asked her questions about the soldier and her brother. The mother said that Jessica's half brother had spent 2 weeks at their house when he was 12 years old and that the soldier had visited only twice, both times accompanied by his girlfriend, and had never stayed overnight. The mother also told Jessica that the brother at age 12 already was extremely tall, taller than their father. Jessica suddenly recognized that, indeed, it had been her brother who had raped her when she was 4 years old and he was 12. Surprisingly, she managed to handle this insight calmly and coped with it by convincing herself that her brother must have been a very disturbed child; his mother had been an alcoholic. In fact, she said, he was a borderline, and from her experience with borderline children, she could understand that he wanted to be close to someone and sought closeness in that fashion. She felt he loved her and did it for that reason. In a beautiful and creatively written poem, the patient worked through the insight that it was her brother who had raped her.

I told her now what the main reason had been for my reducing her therapy hours since February, when I pressed for termination and no longer used hypnosis. Her "tepee" drawing with the straight-haired 12-year-old boy tied to a stake and her brother's initials on a stone next to him had shown to me clearly that unconsciously she knew her brother was the rapist. However, her refusal to recognize the so obvious meaning of the picture had convinced me that she really needed to protect herself—and be protected—from letting this knowledge rise into consciousness, ever. Jessica said I had made a mistake. Seeing how masterfully she had handled the insight of the incest committed by her beloved brother, I agreed that perhaps I had made a mistake. I explained that for 3 years the scientist in me, who wanted to get at the full truth, and the therapist, the caretaking, protective mother figure, had been in conflict about how far to press; that each time I had probed, the patient had reacted with utter denial, and that, therefore, I finally decided I had no right to press any further but must respect the patient's protective defense. I also explained that *some* defenses simply should never be lifted [such as the defense against bringing into consciousness mercifully repressed, unbearably horrible experiences from concentration camps (Wilson & Fromm, 1982)], and that, partly on the basis of that, I had decided to insist on termination. Jessica, who always compared what had happened to her in childhood to the concentration camps, understood that and said she appreciated my wanting to protect her from fragmenting under the impact of the insight that the rapist was her brother. Several months later she admitted that she had been able to accept this realization so calmly because she experienced "a tremendous sense of gratification" in feeling that she did, indeed, "possess" her brother in some way or had possessed him. No one could take that away from her. The memory of fusing with the beloved brother in the sexual acts, the symbiotic aspects of the relationship, was so important to her that it made up for the traumatic aspects. This, of course, was possible only because the patient had worked through her anger, hostility, and disappointment at the rapist-brother on the screen memory of the "soldier" in Phases 7 and 8.

Up to this point, Jessica had never been able to let the GRO fade, even when she went into very deep states of trance. In particular, she was always vigilant about footsteps out in the hall. As soon as she allowed herself to realize that the dead brother had been the childhood rapist, she experienced the fading of the GRO every time she went into trance. She no longer needed to guard herself against an (unknown) intruder who might force himself physically upon her or whose identity she might become aware of prematurely if she would fully let go in trance and not hold on in some ways to current reality.

Phase II (August 1977–December 1977)
Termination Proper

Termination had been indicated and worked at since February, but throughout the spring and most of the summer, Jessica refused to set a termination date towards which we would strive. She also clung to her sex phobia. But termination was overdue. So, in August I told her I would set a termination date for 3 months hence. I told her in the waking state that I felt she was engaging in a sit-down strike with me, preventing herself from making or improving object relationships with others (her husband, friends, and colleagues) by being able to hold on to me, the mother figure. I said I could no longer allow her to do that. A good mother lets her child go and become independent. Through hard and conscientious work in the hypnoanalysis, she had acquired the ego structures she did not have before, namely: the ability to regulate anxiety and affect, libidinal as well as angry and hostile affect, so they no longer overwhelmed her; the ability to soothe herself; and more realistic self-esteem. She also had shown that at her competent disposal she now had a tool for further growth: self-hypnosis. Her ego strength had increased so much and stabilized that I knew she could now use it autonomously without danger of fragmenting.

I told her the gains she had made in the work we had done together would not vanish; they were the basis from which she could and would continue to grow. This meant, I said, that it was up to her now to do her part in re-establishing a sexual relationship with her husband, whom she did not want to leave and who was trying to help her. She had to make the relationship one of *mutual* give and take. Above all, I said, I knew she now had enough ego strength to withdraw cathexis from me and invest it in the relationship with her husband and in making new and lasting friendships with other people or improve old friendships.

Jessica had come a long way. From a near-borderline, who was always afraid she would be overwhelmed by her affects and become psychotic, she had traversed successfully the vast terrain of preoedipal narcissistic development (Adler, 1981, 1985; Gedo & Goldberg, 1973), had achieved object constancy and healthy self-esteem, and had reached the developmental level of a neurosis (sex phobia). While working on her other problems, we had also continually worked on the sex phobia and uncovered its repressed, underlying cause, the childhood rape. For 2 years she had now consciously known that she had been raped in childhood and even had realized (without regressing into fragmentation!) that it was an incest. That she did not go to pieces when she realized it was an incest committed by her beloved brother, or within a few months after she had gained that insight, I told her, proved that she really had developed great ego strength and maturity. Yes, she still had not overcome the sexual phobia of the last 5 years. But when patients with phobic symptoms cling to their fear after all is analyzed, there comes a time when one cannot allow them to remain in the understanding analytic environment and go on talking about the symptom endlessly. One must force them to go out so they will confront their phobia and act.

Jessica obstinately fought to prolong the hypnoanalysis by 6 months, but I remained firm. She refused to let me help her with her mourning work and went into an angry depression for a month after termination. She came out of it feeling liberated and joyfully and creatively engaged in research and writing, which she always had insisted she simply could not do.

A year after termination she wrote me, "You did the right thing when you insisted on termination at the time you did," and detailed the internal posttherapy progress she had made. More of her narcissism, grandiosity, and especially her feelings of entitlement had "burnt away"; she had "practiced trying to listen to nonpatients and be interested in their point of view. If I can be the soul of tact with my patients, I can learn to be that with others, too." She could now give emotional warmth and understanding to her husband when he had problems that depressed him. She had made new friends, and old friends told her she had changed very favorably. Selflessly, she now began to be able to give to younger colleagues.

Furthermore, Jessica wrote:

> Now for the first time in my life, consistently day after day, I feel that my Self is my own, and no one else is responsible for it. And instead of this being an onerous burden, it is a quiet and fulfilling pleasure. I now have a cohesive sense of self.[6] For the first time in my life, without doubt I can say, "I am healthy." I know that no matter how bad the vicissitudes of life may be which I may have to face, there is a solid sense that I will hang together. Things have become something to master instead of to fear.

Since termination, the patient also has developed a new area of specialization for herself: the treatment of *perpetrators* of incest. She handles these patients with great skill and understanding.

SUMMARY AND CONCLUSIONS

This chapter has illustrated two clinical treatment issues: (a) hypnoanalysis with patients along the borderline-narcissistic continuum and (b) hypnoanalysis with post-traumatic stress disorders (PTSD). In addition, it has attempted to show the process, the flow, of hypnoanalysis in a difficult, long-term case.

The case study is an example of hypnoanalysis with severely disturbed patients. Hypnoanalysis with neurotic or psychosomatic problems usually takes somewhere between 3 months and a year. But hypnoanalysis with patients arrested at or regressed to preoedipal levels—the borderlines and the severely narcissistic patients—takes much longer. This case report exemplifies the use of hypnoanalysis to foster growth along the developmental line of the self, that is, along the continuum from borderline pathology to narcissism and eventually to neurosis or full health (Adler, 1981, 1985; Gedo & Goldberg, 1973). The chapter demonstrates the use of hypnoanalysis in effecting changes in the nature of the representational world, the world of internalized object and self-images. At first Jessica could see herself and other people only in black and white, either as "all

---

[6]May we remind the reader who wonders about the patient's use of highly technical psychoanalytic language that Jessica was a psychoanalyst.

good" or as "all bad." Her parents, her colleagues, and her current teachers were all "bad." She saw herself consciously as far superior to them, but unconsciously she felt she, too, was "all bad." Particularly during the first four phases, but actually even through Phase 9, I took on the role of the nurturing, always giving mother, and that of the mother who with great joy noted and talked about every tiny bit of progress, every little, and certainly all big, successes the patient had in real life or in therapy. This "gleam in the mother's eye" was emphasized so that the patient—whose mother had not been proud and fond of her during the separation-individuation period (and later)—could incorporate the hypnoanalyst as a good mother figure, internalize her, and gain self-esteem. The patient needed to feel that there must be good parts in herself, or else the hypnoanalyst—whom she esteemed and loved—would not love her. It was necessary for the patient to learn that not all people are like her bad mother and to bring together the split image of the "all good" and "all bad" self-representations so as to make for a more cohesive sense of self and for healthy self-esteem.

In the next few phases (the end of Phase 4 through Phase 6), we worked on object constancy. That is, I tried to get the patient to accept that people are not all good or all bad and that I was not that overidealized person, without any faults, that Jessica had made me into in the early phases of her therapy. I pointed out my typical forgetfulness, which had upset Jessica many a time, to show her that "good" people have a bad side too and that even though they have their faults, one can love them. Also they do not abandon you when they have to go on trips for a while.

And I showed the patient, for instance by teaching her self-hypnosis and by applauding every attempt at autonomy that she made, that I did not resent her striving for autonomy, but hoped to stimulate it as healthy progress on the way toward individuation and growing up.

The hypnotic techniques employed for achieving these goals were partly imagery and fantasy production and partly the nature of the hypnotic relationship. My own empathic mothering and mirroring stance served the patient as the basis for internalization and the building of psychic structure.

The case report also shows how to use hypnoanalysis to treat patients with post-traumatic stress disorders, in particular, patients who have suffered early incest and child abuse. As is characteristic of post-traumatic stress syndrome cases, the patient first produced a disguised presentation (the enema picture). This was followed by a screen memory (sexual abuse by the "soldier"), which was held on to and worked over and over before the incest component, that is, the full extent of the sexual trauma, finally could be recognized. Much of the working through of the trauma was done on the screen memory (the horror, the feeling of helplessness, the feeling of perhaps having contributed to the incest by being pretty, cute, and flirtatious; the fury against the perpetrator of the crime and the murderous rage against him). The screen memory of the soldier was needed for so long because the brother was a very beloved and admired figure, whom the patient, even after his death, could not afford to lose as an internalized love object and ego ideal, a stance with which the therapist agreed. By working through all these feelings on the screen memory of the "soldier," Jessica could be helped to retain that internalized good and beloved part of the brother that had given a family feeling of stability and warmth to her adolescence and adulthood, a feeling her rejecting and physically abusive parents had not been able to provide.

The case also demonstrates that with PTSDs, more than in any other emotional illness, it is necessary to respect the defenses, particularly the tenacity of the repression, and to understand the fear of being overwhelmed by affect. In many PTSDs there is an ever-present danger of acting out, which, however, in this case was not nearly as strong as the fear of being overwhelmed.

In the hypnoanalysis of post-traumatic stress disorders, intermittent resistance to trance characteristically occurs. Often material will come up for a while, and then the patient does not want to work with hypnosis any longer for either short or long periods of time. If one comes close to uncovering the actual trauma and the patient is not ready for it, hypnotizability and the willingness to work with hypnosis decrease markedly. When the patient again becomes willing to close in on the trauma, he or she will ask to use hypnosis again, and hypnotizability increases, often returning to its original level or exceeding it.

The case thus illustrates some of the special parameters and practical considerations of working with PTSDs and other traumatic neuroses. In such cases one must proceed much more slowly than in most hypnoanalyses. The case exemplifies some of the more difficult clinical cases one can handle with hypnoanalysis. Treatment of post-traumatic stress is technically one of the most difficult types of hypnotherapy or hypnoanalysis that one can undertake. It necessitates more symbolic handling of the material that comes up than do many other kinds of cases. The use of fantasy and age regression involving screen memories rather than the original trauma, the use of drawings and anagrams, and building in delays and not pushing are all techniques that can allow repressed material to unfold *at the patient's own speed*. Even when the hypnoanalyst for a very long time is aware of the trauma that the patient has gone through, he must not overwhelm the patient by confronting him with "the truth" or pushing him to become aware of the full truth.

In cases of repressed traumatic experiences, hypnoanalysis usually proceeds from the disguised presentation to the uncovering; first the uncovering in terms of screen memories (the "soldier" in the three childhood rape incidents) and then the uncovering in terms of the original trauma. If there is a danger of the patient's fragmenting under the impact of having to face the original trauma in all its starkness—that is, if the patient's ego is not strong enough to withstand such disclosure—the material is better worked out on the screen memory only. After the material has been uncovered and worked through, there follows a phase of liberation, increased self-development, and autonomy; and, after that, the working through of the sexual dysfunction, in or out of therapy.

This chapter also illustrates the ebb and flow of the process of hypnoanalysis, the working through of the material over and over again, which is characteristic of long-term cases in hypnoanalysis as well as in psychoanalysis. But note that with eight years of psychoanalysis, with very fine and competent psychoanalysts, the incest had remained so deeply repressed that none of the psychoanalysts even suspected it; in hypnosis, on the other hand, it rose so much closer to the surface and manifested itself in drawings, screen memories, and symbolic imagery so clearly that the hypnoanalyst could recognize it within the *first month* of the hypnoanalysis.

The hypnoanalytic methods employed in this therapy were: being a good, empathic mothering and proudly mirroring figure for the patient; working toward object constancy; working toward internalization of the "good" love object; integrating love and hate objects solidly and achieving separate self- and object constancy; gaining control over splitting as a defense; aiding the development of structure and realistic evaluation of the self and others; ego building and enhancing the patient's control over affect; careful, slow uncovering of the repressed trauma; and therapeutic alliance with the patient's adult ego.

The hypnoanalytic techniques employed for these purposes were: extensive imagery and fantasy production, free association, nonverbal communication, automatic drawing (done mostly in self-hypnosis), hypermnesia and age regression, hypnotic and posthypnotic suggestions, ego strengthening, dream interpretation, and transference analysis.

Appendix

TRAINING FOR HYPNOTHERAPY

Hypnotherapy done by lay practitioners lends itself to sensationalism. The history of hypnosis has been colored by periods in which hypnotherapists held out great promises to the public—boom times that were followed by periods of disenchantment when the miracles promised did not materialize.

Since the end of World War II, serious researchers all over the world, but particularly in the United States, have been conducting research into the nature of hypnosis and its phenomena and into its therapeutic uses and limitations. This growing group of devoted researchers and teachers has been trying to keep hypnosis on an even keel, out of the newspapers and away from sensationalism. Unfortunately, however, recent years have again seen a resurgence of teaching groups whose prerequisites for training in hypnosis are low and whose standards are questionable. Some may be able to provide adequate training in hypnotherapy, but many are not.

Prerequisites

Hypnotherapy requires far more than training in hypnosis alone. In fact, hypnotherapy should be taught only to physicians, dentists, psychologists with a Ph.D. (or advanced graduate students in accredited doctoral programs in psychology), and clinical social workers who have an advanced degree and certified clinical experience. Such eligibility requirements restrict the teaching of hypnotherapy only to those well trained in and experienced in the assessment of psychopathology and the practice of psychotherapy, with the exception of dentists, who are requested to use hypnosis for pain control only.

Persons who want to become hypnotherapists should obtain one of the prerequisite advanced degrees and either take courses given under the auspices of any of the following societies or check with them about the qualifications of a particular hypnotherapy teacher or advertised hypnosis courses. These four societies have reputable scientific, clinical, teaching, and ethical standards.

328

The Society for Clinical and Experimental Hypnosis
129-A Kings Park Drive
Liverpool, NY 13088

The American Society of Clinical Hypnosis
2250 E. Devon Avenue, Suite 218
Des Plaines, IL 60018

Division 30 (Psychological Hypnosis) of the American Psychological Association
1200 Seventeenth Street, NW
Washington, DC 20036

The International Society for Hypnosis
University of Melbourne
Austin Hospital
Heidelberg, Victoria, 3084,
Australia

All members of these hypnosis societies are also members in good standing of the recognized professional organization in their own field (e.g., American Medical Association, American Dental Association, American Psychological Association, National Register of Clinical Social Workers). Each is pledged to "limit his clinical and scientific use of hypnosis to the area of his competence as defined by the professional standards of his field" (Society for Clinical and Experimental Hypnosis, Code of Ethics, 1981), and not to offer professional services through the newspapers, radio, TV, or similar media.

Training Steps in Hypnotherapy

1. Unless the person who wants to learn hypnotherapy has already had university graduate training in hypnosis, he should take an introductory workshop in hypnosis given by one of the four aforementioned societies or from teachers designated by them. In these workshops, the novice in hypnosis learns about theories of hypnosis, induction and deepening techniques, sees them demonstrated, and practices them on his colleagues. Enrolment in these courses is limited, and practicing is conducted under careful supervision. A good introductory course meets throughout the academic semester or quarter or requires a *minimum* of 3 full days' (at least 21 hours) classroom attendance, of which at least 5 or 6 hours should be spent in supervised practice of induction and deepening techniques. The course should also cover at length goals of treatment and methods and procedures of the various forms of hypnotherapy.

2. After finishing the introductory course, the therapist should continue for a few months to practice induction and deepening techniques on experimental subjects or with acquaintances (but not on his family or his closest friends, because easily aroused transference feelings may lead to changes in their relationship). Then he can take on "easy" training cases for hypnotherapy, such as the brief symptomatic treatment of anxiety, phobias, headaches, or hypertension.

3. He should also try to get supervision from an experienced hypnotherapist where he lives. In metropolitan areas good supervisors can be found by consulting with the main offices of the Society for Clinical and Experimental Hypnosis or the American Society of Clinical Hypnosis. If no supervision is available, the candidate can take an advanced hypnotherapy workshop with case consultation format, in which he can present some of his own cases for supervision and consultation a year or two after the introductory workshop.

4. The next step is to take an intermediate or advanced workshop sponsored by one of the societies in the specialty area in which the therapist wants to work, for instance, hypnotherapy with children or pain.

5. After practicing hypnotherapy on "easy" cases for a year or two and taking a more advanced course or being supervised, the hypnotherapist is ready to take on more technically difficult cases, for instance, those requiring dynamic hypnotherapy or the use of hypnoanalysis.

6. Eventually, the hypnotherapist is ready to take on the highly difficult cases, such as post-traumatic stress syndromes, substance abuse, alcoholism, narcissistic character disorders, and borderline and psychotic conditions.

At any time after Step 4, and after reading the literature, the hypnotherapist should be able to aspire to Diplomate status in hypnosis. Each of the three professions of medicine, psychology, and dentistry has its own Board of Hypnosis: the American Board of Medical Hypnosis, the American Board of Psychological Hypnosis, and the American Board of Dental Hypnosis. Psychologists can take Board examinations either in Clinical Hypnosis or in Experimental Hypnosis, or in both. There is no Board for social workers yet.

Training Standards

Unfortunately, during the last few years a plethora of new groups of hypnosis "trainers" and hypnosis societies has sprung up that play on the public's desire for sensationalism and for quick and easy "remedies" for problems. Most of them have low standards and very few prerequisites of training and allow practically anybody into their courses indiscriminately.

Their curricula usually are narrow or idiosyncratic and not informed by the tradition of hypnosis research. They often allow unlimited enrolment— sometimes as many as 500 people in a workshop—and either have a high ratio of participants to supervisors or their practice sessions are not supervised at all. The duration of "workshops" often is no more than 3 hours, after which time the novice may be handed a diploma apparently "certifying" him to practice hypnosis. Groups or societies with such low standards are a great danger to the field of hypnosis and to the public. As has happened before, spurious training groups may propel the field into a boom-and-bust period; and their trainees, who have insufficient training in medicine and psychology, may seriously damage patients who suffer physical or emotional pain.

In contrast, the training standards of the four legitimate societies are high. All four have:

- Strict eligibility requirements.
- A consensual curriculum, informed by the research tradition.
- Limited course enrollment.
- Low ratio of workshop participants to supervisors.
- Highly trained workshop faculties
- And the high ethical standards of their societies.

References

Abraham, Hans A. (1968). Hypnosis used in the treatment of somatic manifestations of a psychiatric disorder. *American Journal of Clinical Hypnosis, 10*, 304–309.

Abrams, Stanley (1964a). The use of hypnotic technique with psychotics: A critical review. *American Journal of Psychotherapy, 18*, 79–94.

Adler, Alexander (1943). Neuropsychiatric complications in victims of Boston's Coconut Grove disaster. *Journal of the American Medical Association, 123*, 1098–1101.

Adler, Gerald (1981). The borderline-narcissistic personality disorder continuum. *American Journal of Psychiatry, 138*, 46–50.

Adler, Gerald (1985). *Borderline psychopathology and its treatment*. New York: Aronson.

Alexander, Franz, & French, Thomas M. (1946). *Psychoanalytic therapy: Principles and application*. New York: Ronald Press.

Allport, Gordon W. (1937). *Personality: A psychological interpretation*. New York: Holt, Rinehart & Winston.

American Psychiatric Association (1980). *Diagnostic and statistical manual* (3rd ed.) (DSM III). Washington, DC: American Psychiatric Association.

American Psychological Association (1981). Ethical principles of psychology. *American Psychologist, 36*, 633–638.

Anisman, Hymie (1978). Neurochemical changes elicited by stress: Behavioral correlates. In Hymie Anisman & Giorgio Bignami (Eds.) *Psychopharmacology of aversively motivated behavior* (pp. 119–172). New York: Plenum Press.

Arkema, Paul H. (1981). The borderline personality and transitional relatedness. *American Journal of Psychiatry, 138*, 172–177.

Ås, Arvid (1962a). A note on distractibility and hypnosis. *American Journal of Clinical Hypnosis, 5*, 135–137.

Ås, Arvid (1962b). Non-hypnotic experiences related to hypnotizability in male and female college students. *Scandinavian Journal of Psychology, 3*, 112–121.

Ås, Arvid (1967). Hypnosis as a subjective experience. In Jean Lassner (Ed.), *Hypnosis and psychosomatic medicine*. (pp. 1–6). New York: Springer-Verlag.

Ås, Arvid, & Ostvold, Siri (1968). Hypnosis as subjective experience. *Scandinavian Journal of Psychology, 9*, 33–38.

Bach, Sheldon. (1977). On the narcissistic state of consciousness. *International Journal of Psychoanalysis, 58*, 209–233.

Bakal, Peter A. (1981). Hypnotherapy for flight phobia. *American Journal of Clinical Hypnosis, 23*, 248–251.

Baker, Elgan L. (1981). An hypnotherapeutic approach to enhance object relatedness in psychotic patients. *International Journal of Clinical and Experimental Hypnosis, 124*, 136–147.

Balson, Paul M., & Dempster, Clifford R. (1980). Treatment of war neuroses from Vietnam. *Comprehensive Psychiatry, 21*, 167–175.

Bandura, Albert (1969). *Principles of behavior modification*. New York: Holt, Rinehart & Winston.

Bandura, Albert (1977). Self-efficacy: Toward a unifying theory of behavioral change. *Psychological Review, 84*, 191–215.

Bányai, Éva I., & Hilgard, Ernest R. (1976). A comparison of active-alert hypnosis with traditional relaxation induction. *Journal of Abnormal Psychology, 85,* 218–224.

Barber, Theodore X. (1961). Physiological effects of "hypnosis." *Psychological Bulletin, 58,* 390–419.

Barber, Theodore X. (1964). Hypnotizability, suggestibility, and personality: V. A critical review of research findings. *Psychological Reports, 14,* 299–320.

Barber, Theodore X., & Calverley, David S. (1962). "Hypnotic behavior" as a function of task motivation. *Journal of Psychology, 54,* 363–389.

Barber, Theodore X., & Calverley, David S. (1963). The relative effectiveness of task-motivating instructions and trance-induction procedure in the production of "hypnotic-like" behaviors. *Journal of Nervous & Mental Disease, 137,* 107–116.

Barber, Theodore X., & Calverley, David S. (1964). Toward a theory of "hypnotic" behavior: An experimental study of "hypnotic time distortion." *Archives of General Psychiatry, 10,* 209–216.

Barlow, David H., O'Brien, Gerald, Last, Cynthia G., & Holden, Arthur (1983). Couples treatment of agoraphobia: Initial outcome. In Kenneth D. Craig & Robert J. McMahon (Eds.), *Advances in clinical behavior therapy* (pp. 99–126). New York: Brunner/Mazel.

Barrett, Deirdre (1979). The hypnotic dream: Its relation to nocturnal dreams and waking fantasies. *Journal of Abnormal Psychology, 88,* 584–591.

Beck, Jacob, & Ambler, Bruce (1973). The effects of concentrated and distributed attention on peripheral acuity. *Perception and Psychophysics, 14,* 225–230.

Beebe, William (1954). A descent into perpetual night. In A.C. Spectorsky (Ed.), *The book of the sea* New York: Appleton-Century-Crofts, pp. 252–261.

Benson, Herbert (1975). *The relaxation response.* New York: William Morrow.

Bernheim, Hippolyte M. (1889). *Suggestive therapeutics: A treatise on the nature and uses of hypnotism.* C. A. Herter (Trans.). New York: G.P. Putnam's Sons.

Bernstein, Norman (1969). Psychogenic seizures in adolescent girls. *Behavioral Neuropsychiatry, 1,* 31–34.

Beutler, Larry E. (1979). Toward specific psychological therapies for specific conditions. *Journal of Consulting and Clinical Psychology, 47,* 882–897.

Blanck, Gertrude, & Blanck, Rubin (1974). *Ego psychology: Theory and practice.* New York: Columbia University Press.

Blatt, Sidney J., & Wild, Cynthia M. (1976). *Schizophrenia: A developmental analysis.* New York: Academic Press.

Blatt, Sidney J., Schimek, Jean G., & Brenneis, C. Brooks (1980). The nature of the psychotic experience and its implications for the therapeutic process. In John S. Strauss, Malcolm Bowers, T. Wayne Downey, Stephen Fleck, Stanley Jackson, & Ira LeVine (Eds.), *The psychotherapy of schizophrenia* (pp. 101–114). New York: Plenum Medical Books.

Bonny, Helen, & Savary, Louis M. (1973). *Music and your mind.* New York: Harper & Row.

Bourguignon, Erika (1973). *Religion, altered states of consciousness and social change.* Columbus: Ohio State University Press.

Boutin, Gerard E. (1978). Treatment of test anxiety by rational stage directed hypnotherapy: A case study. *American Journal of Clinical Hypnosis, 21,* 52–57.

Bowers, Kenneth S. (1966). Hypnotic behavior: The differentiation of trance and demand characteristic variables. *Journal of Abnormal Psychology, 71,* 42–51.

Bowers, Kenneth S. (1971). Sex and susceptibility as moderator variables in the relationship of creativity and hypnotic susceptibility. *Journal of Abnormal Psychology, 78,* 93–100.

Bowers, Kenneth S. (1976). *Hypnosis for the seriously curious.* New York: Norton.

Bowers, Kenneth S., & Brenneman, Heather A. (1979). Hypnosis and the perception of time. *International Journal of Clinical and Experimental Hypnosis, 27,* 29–41.

Bowers, Kenneth S., & Gilmore, J. Barnard (1969). Subjective report and credibility: An inquiry involving hypnotic hallucinations. *Journal of Abnormal Psychology, 74,* 443–451.

Bowers, Kenneth S., & van der Meulen, Sandra J. (1970). Effect of hypnotic susceptibility on creativity test performance. *Journal of Personality and Social Psychology, 14,* 247–256.

Bowers, Malcolm (1974). *Retreat from sanity: The structure of emerging psychosis.* New York: Human Sciences Press.

Bowers, Margaretta K. (1961). Theoretical considerations in the use of hypnosis in the treatment of schizophrenia. *International Journal of Clinical and Experimental Hypnosis, 9,* 39–46.

Bowers, Margaretta K., Brecher-Marer, Sylvia, Newton, Bernauer W., Piotrowski, Zygmund, Spyer, T. C., Taylor, William S. & Watkins, John G. (1971). Therapy of multiple personality. *International Journal of Clinical and Experimental Hypnosis, 19,* 57–65.

Bowers, Margaretta K., Brecher-Marer, Sylvia, & Polatin, Alvin H. (1961). Hypnosis in the study and treatment of schizophrenia—A case report. *International Journal of Clinical and Experimental Hypnosis, 9,* 119–138.

Bowers, Patricia (1982). The classic suggestion effect: Relationships with scales of hypnotizability, effortless experiencing, and imagery vividness. *International Journal of Clinical and Experimental Hypnosis, 30,* 270–279.

Bowers, Patricia G., & Bowers, Kenneth S. (1972). Hypnosis and creativity: A theoretical and empirical rapproachement. In Erika Fromm & Ronald E. Shor (Eds.), *Hypnosis: Research developments and perspectives* (pp. 255–291). Chicago: Aldine-Atherton.

Brady, John P., & Lind, Detlev L. (1961). Experimental analysis of hysterical blindness. *Archives of General Psychiatry, 4,* 331–339.

Braid, James (1843). *Neurypnology.* London: Churchill.

Braun, Bennett G. (1984). Uses of hypnosis with multiple personality. *Psychiatric Annals, 14,* 34–40.

Brende, Joel O. (1984). An educational-therapeutic group for drug and alcohol abusing combat veterans. *Journal of Contemporary Psychotherapy, 14,* 122–136.

Brende, Joel O., & Benedict, Bryce D. (1980). The Vietnam combat delayed stress syndrome: Hypnotherapy of "dissociative symptoms." *American Journal of Clinical Hypnosis, 23,* 34–40.

Brenman, Margaret (1949). Dreams and hypnosis. *Psychoanalytic Quarterly, 18,* 455–465.

Breuer, Josef & Freud, Sigmund (1955). Studies of hysteria. I: On physical mechanisms of hysterical phenomena: Preliminary communication. In J. Strachey (Ed.), *Standard Edition, 2,* pp. 1–181. London: Hogarth Press. (Original work published 1893–95.)

Brooks, J., & Scarano, T. (1982). Transcendental meditation in treatment of post-Vietnam veteran adjustment. Paper presented at the National Conference on the Treatment of Post-Vietnam Stress Disorder, Cincinnati, OH, Oct. 19.

Brown, Daniel P. (1985). Hypnosis as an adjunct to the psychotherapy of the severely disturbed patient: An affective development approach. *International Journal of Clinical and Experimental Hypnosis, 33,* 281–301.

Brown, Daniel, Forte, Michael, Rich, Philip, & Epstein, Gerald (1982–83). Phenomenological differences among self hypnosis, mindfulness meditation, and imaging. *Imagination, Cognition and Personality, 2,* 291–309.

Brown, Daniel, & Fromm, Erika (1987). *Hypnosis and behavioral medicine.* N.J.: Lawrence Erlbaum Associates.

Brown, Daniel, Sands, Stephen, & Jones, Stephanie (1985). *Hypnotic reconstruction of the body image in the severely disturbed patient.* Unpublished manuscript.

Brown, William (1920). The revival of emotional memories and its therapeutic value. *British Journal of Medical Psychology, 1,* 16–19.

Brunner, Jerome S. (1973). *Beyond the information given: Studies in the psychology of knowing.* Jeremy M. Anglin (Ed.), New York: Norton.

Bryan, Laurence L. (1961). Hypnotherapy of conversion hysteria. *American Journal of Clinical Hypnosis, 3,* 226–230.

Buchenholz, Bruce, & Frank, Richard (1949). The "concept of the self" in acute traumatic neurosis of war. *Journal of Nervous and Mental Disease, 107,* 55–60.

Buie, Dan H., & Adler, Gerald (1982). Definitive treatment of the borderline personality. *International Journal of Psychoanalytic Psychotherapy, 9,* 51–87.

Burgess, Ann W., & Holmstrom, Lynda L. (1974). Rape trauma syndrome. *American Journal of Psychiatry, 301,* 981–986.

Burglass, Dorothy, Clarke, J., Henderson, A. S., Kreitman, N., & Presley, A. S. (1977). A study of agoraphobic housewives. *Psychological Medicine, 7,* 73–86.

Burnham, Donald L., Gladstone, Arthur I., & Gibson, Robert W. (1969). *Schizophrenia and the need-fear dilemma.* New York: International Universities Press.

Bychowski, Gustav (1943). Disorders in the body-image in the clinical pictures of psychosis. *Journal of Nervous & Mental Disease, 97,* 310–334.

Bychowski, Gustav (1952). *Psychotherapy of psychosis.* New York: Grune & Stratton.

Bychowski, Gustav (1968). Permanent character changes as an aftereffect of persecution. In Henry Krystal (Ed.), *Massive psychic trauma* (pp. 75–85). New York: International Universities Press.

Caldwell, Troy A., & Stewart, Rege S. (1981). Hysterical seizures and hypnotherapy. *American Journal of Clinical Hypnosis, 23,* 294–298.

Campos, Joseph J., Hiatt, Susan, Ramsay, Douglas, Henderson, Charlotte, & Svejda, Marilyn (1978). The emergence of fear on the visual cliff. In Michael M. Lewis & Leonard Rosenblum (Eds.), *The development of affect* (pp. 149–182). New York: Plenum Press.

Carr, Daniel B., & Sheehan, David V. (1984). Panic anxiety: A new biological model. *Journal of Clinical Psychiatry, 45,* 323–330.

Caslant, E. (1921). *Méthode de développement des faculté supranormales.* Paris: Edition Rhea.

Cedercreutz, Claes, Lahteenmaki, Raimo, & Tullikoura, Jukka (1975). Hypnotic treatment of headache and vertigo in 120 patients with skull-injuries. In Lars-Eric Unestahl (Ed.), *Hypnosis in the seventies.* Orebrö, Sweden: Veje Förlag, 130–134.

Chambless, Dianne I. (1978). *The role of anxiety in flooding with agoraphobic clients.* Unpublished doctoral dissertation, Temple University.

Charcot, J. M. (1882). Essai d'une distinction nosographique des divers états compris sous le nom d'Hypnotisme. (Attempt to make a nosographic distinction of the different nervous states known under the name of hypnotism). *Comptes rendus de l'Academie des Sciences, 44,* Summarized in A. Binet and C. S. Féré, 1887, pp. 154–163.

Charcot, J. M. (1886). *Maladies du système nerveux. Oeuvres complètes, tôme premier.* Paris: Bureaux du Progrès Médical.

Cheek, David B., & LeCron, Leslie M. (1968). *Clinical hypnotherapy.* New York: Grune & Stratton.

Chiasson, Simon W. (1973). Chiasson's method. In *A syllabus on hypnosis and a handbook of therapeutic suggestions.* Des Plaines, IL: American Society of Clinical Hypnosis.

Clance, Pauline R., Mitchell, Michael, & Engelman, Suzanne R. (1980). Body cathexis in children as a function of awareness training and yoga. *Journal of Clinical Child Psychology, 9,* 82–85.

Clarke, J. Christopher, & Jackson, Arthur (1983). *Hypnosis and behavior therapy: The treatment of anxiety and phobias.* New York: Springer.

Cohen, Sheldon B. (1981). Phobia of bovine sounds. *American Journal of Clinical Hypnosis, 23,* 266–268.

Cooper, Leslie M., Banford, Suzanne A., Shubat, Errol, & Tart, Charles T. (1967). A further attempt to modify hypnotic susceptibility through repeated individualized experience. *International Journal of Clinical and Experimental Hypnosis, 15,* 118–124.

Cooper, Linn F., & Erickson, Milton H. (1959). *Time distortion in hypnosis: An experimental and clinical investigation* (2nd ed.). Baltimore: Williams & Wilkins. (Originally published 1954)

Copeland, Donna R. (1986). The application of object-relations theory to the hypnotherapy of developmental arrests: The borderline patient. *International Journal of Clinical and Experimental Hypnosis, 34,* 157–168.

Crasilneck, Harold B., & Hall, James A. (1975). *Clinical hypnosis: Principles and Applications.* New York: Grune & Stratton.

Crasilneck, Harold B., & Michael, Carmen M. (1957). Performance on the Bender under hypnotic age regression. *Journal of Abnormal and Social Psychology, 54,* 319–322.

Danieli, Yael (1985) The treatment and prevention of long-term effects and intergenerational transmission of victimization: A lesson from holocaust survivors and their children. In Charles R. Figley (Ed.), *Trauma and its wake: The study and treatment of post-traumatic stress disorder* (pp. 295–313). New York: Brunner/Mazel.

Daniels, Lloyd K. (1976). Rapid in-office and in-vivo desensitization of an injection phobia utilizing hypnosis. *American Journal of Clinical Hypnosis, 18,* 200–203.

Darby, Joel (1970). Alteration of some body image indexes in schizophrenics. *Journal of Consulting & Clinical Psychology, 35,* 116–121.

Davis, Robert C., & Friedman, Lucy N. (1985). The emotional aftermath of crime and violence. In Charles R. Figley (Ed.), *Trauma and its wake: The study and treatment of post-traumatic stress disorder* (pp. 90–112). New York: Brunner/Mazel.

DeFazio, Victor J., Rustin, Stanley, & Diamond, Arnold (1975). Symptom development in Vietnam era veterans. *American Journal of Orthopsychiatry, 45,* 158–163.

Deiker, Thomas E., & Pollack, Dan H. (1975). Integration of hypnotic and systematic desensitization techniques as in the treatment of phobias: A case report. *American Journal of Clinical Hypnosis, 17,* 170–174.

Deikman, Arthur J. (1971). Bimodal consciousness. *Archives of General Psychiatry, 25,* 481–489.

DePiano, Frank A., & Salzberg, Herman C. (1981). Hypnosis as an aid to recall of meaningful information presented under three types of arousal. *International Journal of Clinical and Experimental Hypnosis, 29,* 383–400.

Desoille, Robert (1966). *The directed daydream,* Frank Haronian (Trans.). New York: Psychosynthesis Research Foundation.

DeVoge, Susan (1975). A behavioral analysis of a group hypnosis treatment method. *American Journal of Clinical Hypnosis, 18,* 127–131.

Deyoub, Paul L., & Epstein, Seymour (1977). Short-term hypnotherapy for the treatment of flight phobia: A case report. *American Journal of Clinical Hypnosis, 19.* 251–254.

Dhanens, Thomas P. & Lundy, Richard M. (1975). Hypnotic and waking suggestions and recall. *International Journal of Clinical and Experimental Hypnosis, 23,* 68–79.

Diamond, Michael J. (1974). Modification of hypnotizability: A review. *Psychological Bulletin, 81,* 180–198.

Dobbs, D., & Wilson, W. P. (1960). Observations on persistance of war neurosis. *Diseases of the Nervous System, 21,* 686–694.

Domhoff, Bill (1964). Night dreams and hypnotic dreams: Is there evidence that they are different? *International Journal of Clinical and Experimental Hypnosis, 12,* 159–168.

Donaldson, Mary Ann, & Gardner, Russell (1985). Diagnosis and treatment of traumatic stress among women after childhood incest. In Charles R. Figley (Ed.), *Trauma and its wake: The study of post-traumatic stress disorder* (pp. 356–377). New York: Brunner/Mazel.

Doroff, David R. (1976). Developing and maintaining the therapeutic alliance with the narcissistic personality. *Journal of the American Academy of Psychoanalysis, 4,* 137–160.

Easton, Randolph, & Shor, Ronald E. (1975). Information processing analysis of the Chevreul Pendulum Illusion. *Journal of Experimental Psychology: Human Perception and Performance, 1,* 231–236.

Edelstien, M. Gerald (1981). *Trauma, trance, and transformation: A Clinical guide to hypnotherapy.* New York: Brunner/Mazel.

Edmondston, William E. (1977). Neutral hypnosis as relaxation. *American Journal of Clinical Hypnosis, 20,* 69–75.

Ehrenzweig, Anton (1953). *The psychoanalysis of artistic vision and hearing.* London: Routledge & Kegan Paul.

Ehrenzweig, Anton (1964). The undifferentiated matrix of artistic imagination. In Warner Muensterberger & Sidney Axelrad (Eds.), *The psychoanalytic study of society,* Vol. 3, pp. 373–398). New York: International Universities Press.

Eisen, Marlene R., & Fromm, Erika (1983). The clinical use of self-hypnosis in hypnotherapy: Tapping the functions of imagery and adaptive regression. *International Journal of Clinical and Experimental Hypnosis, 31,* 243–255.

Eissler, Kurt R. (1958). Remarks on some variations in psychoanalytic technique. *International Journal of Psycho-Analysis, 39,* 222–229.

Eliade, Mircea (1958). *Rites and symbols of initiation: The mysteries of birth and rebirth* (Willard R. Trask, Trans.). New York: Harper & Row.

Emde, Robert N., Kligman, David H., Reich, James H., & Wade, Ted D. (1978). Emotional expression in infancy: I. Initial studies of social signaling and an emergency model. In Michael Lewis & Leonard Rosenblum (Eds.), *The development of affect* (pp. 125–148). New York: Plenum Press.

Emmelkamp, Paul M. G. (1979). The behavioral study of clinical phobias. *Progress in Behavior Modification, 8,* 55–125.

Emmelkamp, Paul M. G., Kuipers, Antoinette C., & Eggeraat, Johan B. (1978). Cognitive modification versus prolonged exposure in vivo: A comparison with agoraphobics as subjects. *Behavior Research and Therapy, 16,* 33–41.

Emmelkamp, Paul M. G., & Kuipers, Antoinette C. (1979). Agoraphobia: A follow-up study four years after treatment. *British Journal of Psychiatry, 134,* 352–355.

Enneis, James M. (1950). The hypnodramatic technique. *Group Psychotherapy, 3,* 11–54.

Epstein, Gerald (1981). *Waking dream therapy: Dream process as imagination.* New York: Human Sciences Press.

Erickson, Milton H. (1939a). An experimental investigation of the possible anti-social use of hypnosis. *Psychiatry, 2,* 391–414.

Erickson, Milton H. (1939b). Experimental demonstrations of the psychopathology of everyday life. *Psychoanalytic Quarterly, 8,* 338–353.

Erickson, Milton H. (1941). The nature and character of post-hypnotic behavior. *Journal of General Psychology, 24,* 95–133.

Erickson, Milton H. (1954a). A clinical note on indirect hypnotic therapy. *Journal of Clinical and Experimental Hypnosis, 2,* 171–174.

Erickson, Milton H. (1954b). Pseudo-orientation in time as a hypnotherapeutic procedure. *Journal of Clinical and Experimental Hypnosis, 2,* 261–283.

Erickson, Milton H. (1954c). Special techniques of brief hypnotherapy. *Journal of Clinical and Experimental Hypnosis, 2,* 109–129.

Erickson, Milton H. (1959). Further techniques of hypnosis—Utilization techniques. *American Journal of Clinical Hypnosis, 2,* 3–21.

Erickson, Milton H. (1964a). An hypnotic technique for resistant patients: The patient, the technique and its rationale and field experiments. *American Journal of Clinical Hypnosis, 1,* 8–32.

Erickson, Milton H. (1964b). The confusion technique in hypnosis. *American Journal of Clinical Hypnosis, 6,* 183–207.

Erickson, Milton H. (1964c). The "surprise" and "my-friend-John" techniques of hypnosis: Minimal cues and natural field experimentation. *American Journal of Clinical Hypnosis, 6,* 293–307.

Erickson, Milton H. (1965). Deep hypnosis and its induction. In Leslie M. LeCron (Ed.), *Experimental Hypnosis* (pp. 70–112). New York: Citadel Press.

Erickson, Milton H., & Rossi, Ernest L. (1979). *Hypnotherapy: An exploratory casebook.* New York: Irvington.

Erikson, Kai T. (1976). Loss of community at Buffalo Creek. *American Journal of Psychiatry, 133,* 302–305.

Erikson, Erik H. (1950). *Childhood and society* (2nd ed.). New York: Norton.

Erikson, Erik H. (1968). *Identity: Youth and crisis.* New York: Norton.

Erikson, Erik H. (1984). Reflections on the last stage—and the first. In Albert J. Solnit, Ruth S. Eissler, & Peter B. Neubauer (Eds.), *The psychoanalytic study of the child, 39,* 155–165. New Haven: Yale University Press.

Evans, Frederick J. (1967). Suggestibility in the normal waking state. *Psychological Bulletin, 67,* 114–129.

Evans, Frederick J., & Kihlstrom, John F. (1973). Posthypnotic amnesia as disrupted retrieval. *Journal of Abnormal Psychology, 82,* 317–323.

Fairbairn, W. R. D. (1952). Endopsychic structure considered in terms of object-relationships. In W. R. D. Fairbairn, *An object-relations theory of the personality.* New York: Basic Books, 82–136. (Original work published 1944).

Fawcett, Jan, Leff, Melitta, & Bunney, William E., Jr. (1969). Suicide: Clues from interpersonal communication. *Archives of General Psychiatry, 21,* 129–137.

Federn, Paul (1952). *Ego psychology and the psychoses.* Eduardo Weiss (Ed.), New York: Basic Books.

Fehr, Fred S., & Stern, John A. (1967). The effect of hypnosis on attention to relevant and irrelevant stimuli. *International Journal of Clinical and Experimental Hypnosis, 15,* 134–143.

Fellows, Brian J., & Creamer, Mark (1978). An investigation of the role of "hypnosis," hypnotic susceptibility and hypnotic induction in the production of age regression. *British Journal of Social and Clinical Psychology, 17,* 165–171.

Fenichel, Otto (1945). *The psychoanalytic theory of the neuroses.* New York: Norton.

Ferenczi, Sándor (1926). On forced fantasies. In *Further contributions to the theory and technique of psychoanalysis,* (pp. 68–77). London: Hogarth Press.

Ferenczi, Sándor (1965). Comments on hypnosis. In Ronald E. Shor & Martin T. Orne (Eds.), *The nature of hypnosis: Selected basic readings* (pp. 177–182). New York: Holt, Rinehart & Winston.

Field, Peter B. (1966). Some self-rating measures related to hypnotizability. *Perceptual and Motor Skills, 23,* 1179–1187.

Field, Peter B., & Palmer, R. D. (1969). Factor analysis: Hypnosis Inventory. *International Journal of Clinical and Experimental Hypnosis, 17,* 50–61.

Figley, Charles R. (1978). *Stress disorders among Vietnam veterans: Theory, research and treatment.* New York: Brunner/Mazel.

Fischer, Roland (1971). A cartography of the ecstatic and meditative states. *Science, 174,* 897–904.

Fisher, Charles (1943). Hypnosis in treatment of neuroses due to war and to other causes. *War Medicine, 4,* 565–576.

Fisher, Seymour (1954). The role of expectation in the performance of posthypnotic behavior. *Journal of Abnormal and Social Psychology, 49,* 503–507.

Fogel, Sydney (1976). Psychogenic tremor and asomatognosia. *American Journal of Clinical Hypnosis, 19,* 57–61.

Fox, Jack (1960). The systematic use of hypnosis in individual and group psychotherapy. *International Journal of Clinical and Experimental Hypnosis, 8*, 109–114.

Fox, Richard P. (1974). Narcissistic rage and the problem of combat aggression. *Archives of General Psychiatry, 31*, 807–811.

Foy, D. W., Sipprelle, R. C., Reuger, D. B. & Carroll, E. M. (1984). Etiology of post-traumatic disorder in Vietnam veterans: Analysis of premilitary, military, and combat exposure influences. *Journal of Consulting and Clinical Psychology, 52*, 88–96.

Fraiberg, Selma (1969). Libidinal object constancy and mental representation. *The psycho-analytic study of the child, 24*, 9–47. New York: International Universities Press.

Frank, Jerome (1962). *Persuasion and healing.* New York: Schocken.

Frankel, Fred H. (1976). *Hypnosis: Trance as a coping mechanism.* New York: Plenum Medical Books.

Frankel, Fred H. (1982). Hypnosis and hypnotizability scales: A reply. *International Journal of Clinical and Experimental Hypnosis, 30*, 377–392.

Frankel, Fred H., Apfel, Roberta J., Kelly, Sean F., Benson, Herbert, Quinn, Thomas, Newmark, Justin, & Malmaud, Roslyn (1979). The use of hypnotizability scales in the clinic: A review after six years. *International Journal of Clinical and Experimental Hypnosis, 27*, 63–73.

Frankel, Fred H., & Orne, Martin T. (1976). Hypnotizability and phobic behavior. *Archives of General Psychiatry, 33*, 1259–1261.

French, Thomas M., & Fromm, Erika (1986). *Dream interpretation—A new approach.* Classics in Psychoanalysis. Monograph Series #5. New York: International Universities Press. (Originally published 1964, Basic Books)

Frétigny, K., & Virel, André (1968). *L'Imagerie mentale: introduction a L'oniro-therapie.* Geneva: Mont-Blanc.

Freud, Anna (1946). *The ego and the mechanisms of defense.* New York: International Universities Press. (Originally published 1926).

Freud, Anna (1965). The concept of developmental lines. In *The writings of Anna Freud: Vol. 6* (pp. 62–107). New York: International Universities Press.

Freud, Sigmund. (1933). *New introductory lectures on psychoanalysis.* New York: W.W. Norton.

Freud, Sigmund. (1953). The interpretation of dreams. In J. Strachey (Ed. and Trans.). *The standard edition of the complete psychological works of Sigmund Freud* (Vols. 4 & 5). London: Hogarth Press. (Original work published 1900)

Freud, Sigmund. (1955a). Analysis of a phobia in a five-year-old boy. In J. Strachey (Ed. and Trans.). *The standard edition of the complete psychological works of Sigmund Freud* (Vol. 10). London: Hogarth Press. (Original work published 1909)

Freud, Sigmund. (1955b). Lines of advance in psychoanalytic theory. In J. Strachey (Ed. and Trans.). *The standard edition of the complete psychological works of Sigmund Freud* (Vol. 17, pp. 157–168). London: Hogarth Press. (Original work published 1918).

Freud, Sigmund. (1959a). "Civilized" sexual morality and modern nervous illness. In J. Strachey (Ed. and Trans.). *The standard edition of the complete psychological works of Sigmund Freud* (Vol. 9, pp. 177–204). London: Hogarth Press (Original work published 1908).

Freud, Sigmund. (1959b). Inhibitions, symptoms, and anxiety. In J. Strachey (Ed. and Trans.). *The standard edition of the complete psychological works of Sigmund Freud* (Vol. 20, pp. 87–172). London: Hogarth Press. (Original work published 1926).

Freud, Sigmund. (1961). The ego and the id. In J. Strachey (Ed. and Trans.). *The standard edition of the complete psychological works of Sigmund Freud* (Vol. 16, p. 3–66). London: Hogarth Press. (Original work published 1923).

Freud, Sigmund. (1964). Moses and monotheism. In J. Strachey (Ed. and Trans.). *The standard edition of the complete psychological works of Sigmund Freud* (Vol. 23). London: Hogarth Press. (Original work published 1939).

Freytag, Fredericka (1965). The hallucinated unconscious body image. *American Journal of Clinical Hypnosis, 7,* 209–220.

Fromm, Erika (1965a). Hypnoanalysis: Theory and two case excerpts. *Psychotherapy: Theory, Research and Practice, 2,* 127–133.

Fromm, Erika (1965b). Spontaneous autohypnotic age-regression in a nocturnal dream. *International Journal of Clinical and Experimental Hypnosis, 13,* 119–131.

Fromm, Erika (1968). Transference and countertransference in hypnoanalysis. *International Journal of Clinical and Experimental Hypnosis, 16,* 77–84.

Fromm, Erika (1970). Age regression with unexpected reappearance of a repressed childhood language. *International Journal of Clinical and Experimental Hypnosis, 18,* 79–88.

Fromm, Erika (1972). Ego activity and ego passivity in hypnosis. *International Journal of Clinical and Experimental Hypnosis, 20,* 238–251.

Fromm, Erika (1976). Altered states of consciousness and ego psychology. *Social Service Review, 50,* 557–569.

Fromm, Erika (1977a). Altered states of consciousness and hypnosis: A discussion. *International Journal of Clinical and Experimental Hypnosis, 25,* 325–334.

Fromm, Erika. (1977b). An ego psychological theory of altered states of consciousness. *International Journal of Clinical and Experimental Hypnosis, 25,* 372–387.

Fromm, Erika. (1978–79). Primary and secondary process in waking and in altered states of consciousness. *Journal of Altered States of Consciousness, 4,* 115–128.

Fromm, Erika (1979). The nature of hypnosis and other altered states of consciousness: An ego-psychological theory. In Erika Fromm & Ronald E. Shor (Eds.), *Hypnosis: Developments in research and new perspectives,* 2nd ed., (pp. 81–103). New York: Aldine-Atherton.

Fromm, Erika. (1981). Ego-psychological parameters of hypnosis and their clinical applications. In Harold J. Wain (Ed.), *Clinical and theoretical aspects of hypnosis* (pp. 33–53). Symposia Specialists Medical Books.

Fromm, Erika. (1984). Theory and practice of hypnoanalysis. In William C. Wester II and Alexander Smith (Eds.), *Clinical hypnosis: A multidisciplinary approach.* New York: J. B. Lippincott.

Fromm, Erika (1984). Hypnoanalysis—with particular emphasis on the borderline patient. *Psychoanalytic Psychology, 1,* 61–76.

Fromm, Erika, Brown, Daniel P., Hurt, Stephen W., Oberlander, Joab Z., Boxer, Andrew M. & Pfeifer, Gary (1981). The phenomena and characteristics of self-hypnosis. *International Journal of Clinical and Experimental Hypnosis, 29,* 189–246.

Fromm, Erika, & Eisen, Marlene R. (1982). Self hypnosis as a therapeutic aid in the mourning process. *American Journal of Clinical Hypnosis, 25,* 3–14.

Fromm, Erika, & French, Thomas M. (1974). Formation and evaluation of hypotheses in dream interpretation. In Ralph E. Woods & Herbert B. Greenhouse (Eds.), *The new world of dreams* (pp. 271–283). New York: Macmillan.

Fromm, Erika, & Gardner, G. Gail (1979). Ego psychology and hypnoanalysis: An integration of theory and technique. *Bulletin of the Menninger Clinic, 43,* 413–423.

Fromm, Erika, & Hurt, Stephen W. (1980). Ego-psychological parameters of hypnosis and altered states of consciousness. In Graham D. Burrows & Lorraine Dennerstein (Eds.), *Handbook of hypnosis and psychosomatic medicine* (pp. 13–27). New York: Elsevier/ North Holland Biomedical Press.

Fromm, Erika, & Shor, Ronald E. (Eds.) (1979). *Hypnosis: Developments in research and new perspectives,* 2nd ed. New York: Aldine.

Fromm, Erika, & Skinner, Sarah, Lombard, Lisa, & Kahn, Stephen (in preparation). The modes of ego functioning in self-hypnosis.

Futterman, Samuel, & Pumpian-Mindlin, Eugene (1951). Traumatic war neuroses five years later. *American Journal of Psychiatry, 108,* 401–408.

Gardner, G. Gail (1973). Use of hypnosis for psychogenic epilepsy in a child. *American Journal of Clinical Hypnosis, 15,* 166–169.

Gardner, G. Gail (1976). Childhood, death, and human dignity: Hypnotherapy for David. *International Journal of Clinical and Experimental Hypnosis, 24,* 122–139.

Gardner, G. Gail, & Olness, Karen (1981). *Hypnosis and hypnotherapy with children.* New York: Grune & Stratton.

Gedo, John E., & Goldberg, Arnold (1973). *Models of the mind: A psychoanalytic theory.* Chicago: University of Chicago Press.

Gelinas, Denise J. (1983). The persisting negative effects of incest. *Psychiatry, 46,* 312–332.

Gibbons, Don E. (1979). *Applied hypnosis and hyperempiria.* New York & London: Plenum Press.

Gibbons, Don, Kilbourne, Leslie, Saunders, Alan, & Castles, Cheryl (1970). The cognitive control of behavior: A comparison of systematic desensitization and hypnotically induced "directed experience" techniques. *International Journal of Clinical and Experimental Hypnosis, 12,* 141–145.

Gidro-Frank, Lothar, & Bowersbush, Margarette K. (1948). A study of the plantar response in hypnotic age regression. *Journal of Nervous & Mental Disease, 107,* 443–458.

Gill, Merton M. (Ed.) (1967). *The collective papers of David Rapaport.* New York: Basic Books.

Gill, Merton M., & Brenman, Margaret M. (1959). *Hypnosis and related states: Psychoanalytic studies in regression.* New York: International Universities Press.

Giovacchini, Peter L. (1972). Technical difficulties in treating characterological disorders: Countertransference problems. *International Journal of Psychoanalytic Psychotherapy, 1,* 112–128.

Giovacchini, Peter L. (1979). *Treatment of primitive mental states.* New York: Aronson.

Glenn, T. J., & Simonds, J. F. (1977). Hypnotherapy of a psychogenic seizure disorder in an adolescent. *American Journal of Clinical Hypnosis, 19,* 245–249.

Gleser, Goldine C., Green, Bonnie L., & Winget, Carolynn N. (1981). *Prolonged psychosocial effects of disaster: A study of Buffalo Creek.* New York: Academic Press.

Glick, Burton S. (1970). Conditioning therapy with phobic patients: Success and failure. *American Journal of Psychotherapy, 24,* 92–101.

Goldstein, Alan J., & Chambless, Dianne I. (1978). A reanalysis of agoraphobia. *Behavior Therapy, 9,* 47–59.

Graham, Charles (1970). *The allocation of attention in a simultaneous audio-visual monitoring task in hypnotically susceptible and insusceptible subjects.* Unpublished doctoral dissertation, Pennsylvania State University, University Park.

Graham, Charles, & Evans, Frederick J. (1977). Hypnotizability and the deployment of waking attention. *Journal of Abnormal Psychology, 86,* 631–638.

Green, Bonnie L., Wilson, John P., & Lindy, Jacob D. (1985). Conceptualizing post-traumatic stress disorder: A psychosocial framework. In Charles R. Figley (Ed.), *Trauma and its Wake: The study and treatment of post-traumatic stress disorder* (pp. 53–69). New York: Brunner/Mazel.

Green, Elmer E., Green, Alyce M., & Walters, E. Dale (1970). Voluntary control of internal states: Psychological and physiological. *Journal of Transpersonal Psychology, 1,* 1–26.

Greenberg, Ira A. (1977). Hypnodrama and group hypnosis. In Ira A. Greenberg (Ed.) *Group hypnotherapy and hypnodrama.* Chicago: Nelson-Hall, 231–261.

Greenleaf, Eric (1969). Developmental-stage regression through hypnosis. *American Journal of Clinical Hypnosis, 12,* 20–36.

Greenleaf, Eric (1971). The red house: Hypnotherapy of hysterical blindness. *American Journal of Clinical Hypnosis, 13,* 155–161.

Greenspan, Stanley, & Lourie, Reginald S. (1981). Developmental structuralist approach to the classification of adaptive and pathologic personality organizations: Infancy and early childhood. *American Journal of Psychiatry, 138,* 725–735.

Grinker, Roy R., & Spiegel, John P. (1945). *Men under stress.* Philadelphia: Blakiston.

Gruenewald, Doris (1971a). Agoraphobia: A case study in hypnotherapy. *International Journal of Clinical and Experimental Hypnosis, 19,* 10–20.

Gruenewald, Doris (1971b) Transference and countertransference in hypnosis. *International Journal of Clinical and Experimental Hypnosis, 19,* 71–82.

Gruenewald, Doris (1982). Problems of relevance in the application of laboratory data to clinical situations. *International Journal of Clinical and Experimental Hypnosis, 30,* 345–353.

Gruenewald, Doris (1984). On the nature of multiple personality: Comparisons with hypnosis. *International Journal of Clinical and Experimental Hypnosis, 32,* 170–190.

Gruenewald, Doris, Fromm, Erika & Oberlander, Mark 1. (1979). Hypnosis and adaptive regression: An ego-psychological inquiry. In Erika Fromm & Ronald Shor (Eds.), *Hypnosis: Developments in research and new perspectives,* 2nd ed. (pp. 619–635). New York: Aldine.

Guntrip, Harry (1969). *Schizoid phenomena, object relations and the self* (2nd ed.). New York: International Universities Press.

Gustavson, John L., & Weight, David G. (1981). Hypnotherapy for a phobia of slugs: A case report. *American Journal of Clinical Hypnosis, 23,* 258–262.

Hagedorn, Judith (1970). The use of post-hypnotic suggestions for recall and amnesia to facilitate retention and to produce forgetting for previously learned materials in the classroom situation. (Doctoral dissertation, University of Tulsa, 1970) *Dissertation Abstracts International, 30,* 4275.

Haley, Sarah (1974). When the patient reports atrocities. *Archives of General Psychiatry, 30,* 191–196.

Haley, Sarah A. (1985a). Some of my best friends are dead: Treatment of the PTSD patient and his family. In William E. Kelly (Eds.), *Post-traumatic stress disorder and the war veteran patient* (pp. 54–70). New York: Brunner/Mazel.

Haley, Sarah A. (1985b). *I feel a little sad: The application of object relations theory to the hypnotherapy of post-traumatic stress disorders in Vietnam veterans.* Unpublished manuscript.

Hart, Henry (1961). A review of the psychoanalytic literature on passivity. *Psychiatric Quarterly, 35,* 331–352.

Hartland, John (1965). The value of "ego-strengthening" procedures prior to direct symptom removal under hypnosis. *American Journal of Clinical Hypnosis, 8,* 89–93.

Hartmann, Heinz (1958). *Ego psychology and the problem of adaptation* (David Rapaport, Trans.). New York: International Universities Press.

Herman, Judith & Schatzow, Emily (1984). Time-limited group therapy for women with a history of incest. *International Journal of Group Psychotherapy, 34,* 605–616.

Hilgard, Ernest R. (1965). *Hypnotic susceptibility.* New York: Harcourt, Brace & World.

Hilgard, Ernest R. (1969). Pain as a puzzle for psychology and physiology. *American Psychologist, 24,* 103–113.

Hilgard, Ernest R. (1973). The domain of hypnosis, with some comments on alternative paradigms. *American Psychologist, 28,* 972–982.

Hilgard, Ernest R. (1974). Toward a neo-dissociation theory: Multiple cognitive controls in human functioning. *Perspectives in Biology and Medicine, 17,* 301–316.

Hilgard, Ernest R. (1977). *Divided consciousness: Multiple controls in human thought and action.* New York: Wiley.

Hilgard, Ernest R., Crawford, Helen Joan, & Wert, Amy (1979). The Stanford Hypnotic Arm Levitation Induction and Test (SHALIT): A six-minute hypnotic induction and measurement scale. *International Journal of Clinical and Experimental Hypnosis, 27*, 111–124.

Hilgard, Ernest R., & Tart, Charles T. (1966). Responsiveness to suggestions following waking and imagination instructions and following induction of hypnosis. *Journal of Abnormal Psychology, 71*, 196–208.

Hilgard, Josephine R. (1970). *Personality and hypnosis: A study of imaginative involvement.* Chicago: University of Chicago Press.

Hilgard, Josephine R. (1974). Imaginative involvement: Some characteristics of the highly hypnotizable and nonhypnotizable. *International Journal of Clinical and Experimental Hypnosis, 22*, 138–156.

Hilgard, Josephine R. (1979). Imaginative and sensory-affective involvements in everyday life and in hypnosis. In Erika Fromm & Ronald Shor (Eds.), *Hypnosis: Developments in research and new perspectives* (2nd ed., pp. 483–517). New York: Aldine.

Hilgard, Josephine R. & Hilgard, Ernest R. (1979). Assessing hypnotic responsiveness in a clinical setting: A multi-item clinical scale and its advantages over single-item scales. *International Journal of Clinical and Experimental Hypnosis, 27*, 134–150.

Hodge, James R. (1976) Contractual aspects of hypnosis. *International Journal of Clinical and Experimental Hypnosis, 24*, 391–399.

Hodge, James R., & Wagner, Edwin E. (1964). The validity of hypnotically induced emotional states. *American Journal of Clinical Hypnosis, 7*, 37–41.

Hoppe, Klaus (1962) Persecution, depression and aggression. *Bulletin of the Menninger Clinic, 26*, 195–203.

Horner, Althea J. (1979). *Object relations and the developing ego in therapy.* New York: Aronson.

Horowitz, Mardi J. (1970) *Image formation and cognition.* New York: Appleton-Century-Crofts.

Horowitz, Mardi J. (1973). Phase oriented treatment of stress response syndromes. *American Journal of Psychotherapy, 27*, 506–515.

Horowitz, Mardi J. (1974). Stress response syndromes: Character style and dynamic psychotherapy. *Archives of General Psychiatry, 31*, 768–781.

Horowitz, Mardi J. (1976). *Stress response syndromes.* New York: Aronson.

Horowitz, Suzanne L. (1970). Strategies within hypnosis for reducing phobic behavior. *Journal of Abnormal Psychology, 75*, 104–112.

Horton, Paul, Lovy, J. William, & Coppolillo, Henry (1974). Personality disorders and transitional relatedness. *Archives of General Psychiatry, 30*, 618–622.

Hull, Clark L. (1933). *Hypnosis and suggestibility: An experimental approach.* New York: Appleton-Century-Crofts.

Hurst, Arthur. (1943). *Medical diseases of war* (3rd ed.). Baltimore: Williams & Wilkins.

Ingram, Rick E., Saccuzzo, Dennis P., McNeill, Brian W., & McDonald, Roy (1979). Speed of information processing in high and low susceptible subjects: A preliminary study. *International Journal of Clinical and Experimental Hypnosis, 27*, 42–47.

Insko, Chester A. (1967) *Theories of attitude change.* New York: Appleton-Century-Crofts.

Isaacs, Kenneth S. (1984). Feeling bad and feeling badly. *Psychoanalytic Psychology, 1*, 43–60.

Ivanov, N. V. (1977). Theory and practice of group hypnosis, or collective hypnosis, in the USSR. In Ira A. Greenberg (Ed.), *Group hypnotherapy and hypnodrama* (pp. 83–103). Chicago: Nelson-Hall.

Izard, Carroll E. (1977). *Human emotions.* New York: Plenum Press.

Jacobson, Edith (1971). *Depression: Comparative studies of normal, neurotic, and psychotic conditions. New York: International Universities Press.*

Jacobson, Edith. (1973). *The self and the object world.* New York: International Universities Press.

Jacobson, Edmond (1938). *Progressive relaxation.* Chicago: University of Chicago Press.

James, William (1961). *Psychology: The briefer course*. New York: Harper & Row. (Original work published 1892)

Janet, Pièrre (1889). *L'Automatisme psychologique*. Paris: Félix Alcan.

Janet, Pièrre (1924). *Principles of psychotherapy*. (H. M. Guthrie & E. R. Guthrie, Trans.). Freeport, New York: Books for Libraries Press.

Janet, Pièrre (1925). *Psychological healing: A historical and clinical study*. (Eden Paul & Cedar Paul, Trans.). New York: Macmillan. (Originally published 1919).

Janoff-Bulman, Ronnie (1985). The aftermath of victimization: Rebuilding shattered assumptions. In Charles R. Figley (Ed.), *Trauma and its Wake: The study and treatment of post-traumatic stress disorder* (pp. 15–35). New York: Brunner/Mazel.

Jellinek, Augusta (1949). Spontaneous imagery: A new psychotherapeutic approach. *American Journal of Psychotherapy, 3,* 372–391.

Jellinek, Elvin Morton (1960). *The disease concept of alcoholism*. New Haven, CT: Hillhouse Press.

Johnsgard, Keith W. (1969). Symbol confrontation in a recurrent nightmare. *Psychotherapy: Theory, Research and Practice, 6,* 177–187.

Johnson, Jean (1973). Effects of accurate expectations about sensations on the sensory and distress components of pain. *Journal of Personality and Social Psychology, 27,* 261–275.

Johnson, R. F. Q. (1976). Hypnotic time distortion and the enhancement of learning: New data pertinent to the Krauss-Katzell-Krauss experiment. *American Journal of Clinical Hypnosis, 19,* 98–102.

Jones, Ernest (1948). The nature of auto-suggestions. In *Papers on psychoanalysis*, 5th Ed. (pp. 273–293). Boston: Beacon Press. (Originally published 1923.)

Kahneman, Daniel (1973). *Attention and effort*. Englewood Cliffs, NJ: Prentice-Hall.

Kaplan, Jarett M., & Deabler, Herdis L. (1975). Hypnotherapy with a severe dissociative hysterical disorder. *American Journal of Clinical Hypnosis, 18,* 83–89.

Kardiner, Abram (1941). The traumatic neuroses of war. *Psychosomatic Medical Monograph*. New York: Paul Hoeber.

Kazdin, Alan E., & Wilcoxon, Linda A. (1976). Systematic desensitization and nonspecific treatment effects: A methodological evaluation. *Psychological Bulletin, 83,* 729–758.

Keane, Terence M., Fairbank, John A., Caddell, Juesta M., Zimering, Ross T., & Bender, Mary E. (1985) A behavioral approach to assessing and treating post-traumatic stress disorders in Vietnam veterans. In Charles R. Figley (Ed.), *Trauma and its wake: The study and treatment of post-traumatic stress disorder* (pp. 257–294). New York: Brunner/Mazel.

Kelman, Harold (1945). Character and the traumatic syndrome. *Journal of Nervous & Mental Disease, 102,* 121–153.

Kernberg, Otto F. (1968). The treatment of patients with borderline personality organization. *International Journal of Psycho-Analysis, 49,* 600–619.

Kernberg, Otto F. (1975). *Borderline conditions and pathological narcissism*. New York: Aronson.

Kernberg, Otto F. (1976). *Object relations theory and clinical psychoanalysis*. New York: Aronson.

Khan, M. Masud R. (1963). The concept of cumulative trauma. *The Psychoanalytic Study of the Child, 18,* 286–306. New York: International Universities Press.

Khantzian, Edward J. (1981). Some treatment implications of the ego and self disturbances in alcoholism. In Margaret H. Bean and Norman E. Zinberg (Eds.), *Dynamic approaches to the understanding and treatment of alcoholism* (pp. 163–188). New York: Free Press.

Kidder, Louise H. (1972). On becoming hypnotized: How skeptics become convinced: A case study of attitude change. *Journal of Abnormal Psychology, 80,* 317–322.

Kihlstrom, John F. (1977). Models of posthypnotic amnesia. *Annals of the New York Academy of Science, 296,* 284–301.

Kihlstrom, John F. (1978). Context and cognition in posthypnotic amnesia. *International Journal of Clinical and Experimental Hypnosis, 26,* 246–267.

Kilpatrick, Dean G., Véronen, Lois J., & Best, Connie L. (1985). Factors predicting psychological distress among rape victims. In Charles R. Figley (Ed.) *Trauma and its wake: The study and treatment of post-traumatic stress disorder* (pp. 113–141). New York: Brunner/Mazel.

Kinney, Jill M., & Sachs, Lewis B. (1974). Increasing hypnotic susceptibility. *Journal of Abnormal Psychology, 83,* 145–150.

Klein, George S. (1967). Peremptory ideation: Structure and force in motivated ideas. In Robert R. Holt (Ed.), *Motives and thought: Psychoanalytic essays in honor of David Rapaport.* New York: International Universities Press.

Klemperer, Edith (1965). Past ego states emerging in hypnoanalysis. *International Journal of Clinical and Experimental Hypnosis, 13,* 132–143.

Kline, Milton V. (1955). Theoretical and conceptual aspects of psychotherapy. In Milton V. Kline (Ed.), *Hypnodynamic psychology: An integrative approach to the behavior sciences* (pp. 75–203). New York: Julian Press.

Kline, Milton V. (1966). Hypnotic amnesia in psychotherapy. *International Journal of Clinical and Experimental Hypnosis, 14,* 112–120.

Kline, Milton V. (1970). The use of extended group hypnotherapy sessions in controlling cigarette habituation. *International Journal of Clinical and Experimental Hypnosis, 18,* 270–282.

Kodman, Frank, & Pattie, Frank A. (1958). Hypnotherapy of psychogenic hearing loss in children. *American Journal of Clinical Hypnosis, 1,* 9–13.

Kohut, Heinz (1966). Forms and transformations of narcissism. *Journal of the American Psychoanalytic Association, 14,* 243–272.

Kohut, Heinz (1971). *The analysis of the self.* New York: International Universities Press.

Kohut, Heinz (1972). Thoughts on narcissism and narcissistic rage. *The Psychoanalytic Study of the Child, 27,* 360–402. New Haven: Yale University Press.

Kohut, Heinz (1977). *The restoration of the self.* New York: International Universities Press.

Kolb, Lawrence C., Burris, B. Cullen, & Griffiths, Susan (1984). Propranolol and Clonidine in treatment of the chronic post-traumatic stress disorders of war. In Bessel A. van der Kolk (Ed.), *Post-traumatic stress disorder: Psychological and biological sequelae* (pp. 98–105). Washington, DC: American Psychiatric Press.

Kolb, Lawrence C., & Mutalipassi, Louis R. (1982). The conditioned emotional response: A subclass of the chronic and delayed post-traumatic stress disorder. *Psychiatric Annals, 12,* 979–987.

Kramer, Milton, Schoen, Lawrence, S., & Kinney, Lois (1984). The dream experience in dream-disturbed Vietnam veterans. In Bessel A. van der Kolk (Ed.), *Post-Traumatic stress disorder: Psychological and biological sequelae* (pp. 82–95). Washington, DC: American Psychiatric Press.

Krauss, Herbert H., Katzell, Raymond, & Krauss, Beatrice J. (1974). Effect of hypnotic time distortion upon free-recall learning. *Journal of Abnormal Psychology, 83,* 140–144.

Krippner, Stanley, & Bindler, Paul R. (1974). Hypnosis and attention: A review. *American Journal of Clinical Hypnosis, 16,* 166–177.

Kris, Ernst (1952). *Psychoanalytic explorations in art.* New York: International Universities Press. (Originally published 1936).

Kroger, William S., & Fezler, William D. (1976). *Hypnosis and behavior modification: Imagery conditioning.* Philadelphia: Lippincott.

Krystal, Henry (Ed.) (1968). *Massive psychic trauma.* New York: International Universities Press.

Krystal, Henry (1984). Psychoanalytic views on human emotional damages. In Bessel A. van der Kolk (Ed.), *Post-traumatic stress disorder: Psychological and biological sequelae* (pp. 2–28). Washington, DC: American Psychiatric Press.

Krystal, Henry, & Raskin, Herbert A. (1970) *Drug dependence: Aspects of ego functions.* Detroit: Wayne State University Press.

Kubie, Lawrence S. (1943a). Manual of emergency treatment for acute war neuroses. *War Medicine, 4,* 582–599.

Kubie, Lawrence S. (1943b). The use of induced hypnotic reveries in the recovery of repressed amnesic data. *Bulletin of the Menninger Clinic, 7,* 172–182.

Kubie, Lawrence S., & Margolin, Sydney (1944). The process of hypnotism and the nature of the hypnotic state. *American Journal of Psychiatry, 100,* 611–622.

Kunzendorf, Robert G. (1980). Imagery and consciousness: A scientific analysis of the mind-body problem. (Doctoral dissertation, University of Virginia). *Dissertation Abstracts International, 40,* 3448B–3449B.

LaBarbera, Joseph D., & Dozier, J. Emmett (1980). Hysterical seizures: The role of sexual exploitation. *Psychosomatics, 21,* 897–903.

Lacoursiere, Roy B., Godfrey, Kenneth E., & Ruby, Lorne (1980). Traumatic neurosis in the etiology of alcoholism: Vietnam combat and other trauma. *American Journal of Psychiatry, 137,* 966–968.

Lang, Peter J., Lazovik, A. David, & Reynolds, David J. (1965). Desensitization, suggestibility, and pseudotherapy. *Journal of Abnormal Psychology, 70,* 395–402.

Larkin, Anne R. (1979). The form and content of schizophrenic hallucinations. *American Journal of Psychiatry, 136,* 940–943.

Laufer, Robert S., Brett, Elizabeth, & Gallops, M. S. (1984). Post-traumatic stress disorder (PTSD) reconsidered: PTSD among Vietnam veterans. In Bessel A. van der Kolk (Ed.), *Post-traumatic stress disorder: Psychological and biological sequelae* (pp. 60–79). Washington, DC: American Psychiatric Press.

Laufer, Robert S., Frey-Wouters, Ellen, & Gallops, Mark S. (1985). Traumatic stressors in the Vietnam war and post-traumatic stress disorder. In Charles R. Figley (Ed.), *Trauma and its Wake: The study and treatment of post-traumatic stress disorder* (pp. 73–89). New York: Brunner/Mazel.

Laughlin, Henry P. (1967). *The neuroses.* Washington, DC: Butterworths.

Laurence, Jean-Roch R., & Perry, Campbell (1981). The "hidden observer" phenomenon in hypnosis: Some additional findings. *Journal of Abnormal Psychology, 90,* 334–344.

Lavoie, Germain, & Sabourin, Michel (1980). Hypnosis and schizophrenia: A review of experimental and clinical studies. In Graham D. Burrows & Lorraine Dennerstein (Eds.), *Handbook of hypnosis and psychosomatic medicine* (pp. 377–419). Amsterdam: Elsevier/North-Holland Biomedical Press.

Lavoie, Germain, Sabourin, Michel, & Langlois, Jacques (1973). Hypnotic susceptibility, amnesia and I.Q. in chronic schizophrenia. *International Journal of Clinical and Experimental Hypnosis, 21,* 157–168.

LeCron, Leslie M. (1948). A study of age regression under hypnosis. In Leslie M. Le Cron (Ed.), *Experimental hypnosis: A symposium of articles on research by many of the world's leading authorities* (pp. 155–174). New York: Macmillan.

LeCron, Leslie M. (1953). A method of measuring the depth of hypnosis. *Journal of Clinical and Experimental Hypnosis, 1,* 4–7.

Leahy, M. R. & Martin, I. C. A. (1967). Successful hypnotic abreaction after 20 years. *British Journal of Psychiatry, 113,* 383–385.

Leitenberg, Harold., Agras, W. Stewart, Thompson, Laurence E., & Wright, Dale E. (1968) Feedback in behavior modification: An experimental analysis in two phobic cases. *Journal of Applied Behavior Analysis, 1,* 131–137.

Leowald, Hans W. (1973). On internalization. *International Journal of Psychoanalysis, 54,* 9–17.

Leuba, Clarence (1960). Theories of hypnosis: A critique and a proposal. *American Journal of Clinical Hypnosis, 3,* 43–48.

Leuner, Hanscarl (1969). Guided affective imagery (GAI): A method of intensive psycho-
    therapy. *American Journal of Psychotherapy, 23,* 4–22.
Levendula, Dezso (1963). Principles of Gestalt therapy in relation to hypnotherapy. *American
    Journal of Clinical Hypnosis, 6,* 22–26.
Leventhal, Howard, & Everhart, Deborah (1979). Emotion, pain, and physical illness. In
    Carroll E. Izard (Ed.), *Emotions in personality and psychopathology.* New York: Plenum
    Press, 263–299.
Levin, Lois Ann, & Harrison, Robert (1976). Hypnosis and regression in the service of the
    ego. *International Journal of Clinical and Experimental Hypnosis, 24,* 400–418.
Levis, Donald J. & Hare, Nathan (1977). A review of the theoretical rationale and empirical
    support for the extinction approach of implosive (flooding) therapy. In Michel Hersen,
    Richard M. Eisler, & Peter M. Miller (Eds.), *Progress in behavior modification,* vol. 4.
    New York: Academic Press.
Lewis, Michael, Brooks, Jeanne, & Haviland, Jeannette (1978). Hearts and faces: A study in
    the measurement of emotion. In Michael Lewis & Leonard Rosenblum (Eds.), *The
    development of affect* (pp. 77–123). New York: Plenum Press.
Lichtenberg, Joseph D. (1975). The development of a sense of self. *Journal of the American
    Psychoanalytic Association, 23,* 453–483.
Lichtenberg, Joseph D. (1978). The testing of reality from the standpoint of the body self.
    Journal of the American Psychoanalytic Association, 26, 357–385.
Liébeault, Ambroise Auguste (1885). Anesthesie par suggestion. *Journal du Magnetisme,* 64–
    67.
Liébeault, Ambroise Auguste (1889). *Le sommeil provoqué et les états analogues.* Paris:
    Doin.
Liebert, Robert M., & Morris, Larry W. (1967). Cognitive and emotional components of test
    anxiety: A distinction and some initial data. *Psychological Reports, 20,* 975–978.
Lifton, Robert J. (1961). *Thought reform and the psychology of totalism.* New York: Norton.
Lifton, Robert J. (1967). *Death in life: Survivors of Hiroshima.* New York: Simon & Schuster.
Lifton, Robert J. (1968). Observations on Hiroshima survivors. In Henry Krystal (Ed.),
    Massive psychic trauma (pp. 168–189). New York: International Universities Press.
Lindner, Harold (1973). Psychogenic seizure states: A psychodynamic study. *International
    Journal of Clinical and Experimental Hypnosis, 21,* 261–271.
Lindy, Jacob D., Grace, Mary C., & Green, Bonnie L. (1984). Building a conceptual bridge
    between civilian trauma and war trauma: Preliminary psychological findings from a
    clinical sample of Vietnam veterans. In Bessel A. van der Kolk (Ed.), *Post-traumatic
    stress disorders: Psychological and biological sequelae,* (pp. 44–57). Washington, DC:
    American Psychiatric Press.
Lister, Eric D. (1982). Forced silence: A neglected dimension of trauma. *American Journal of
    Psychiatry, 139,* 872–875.
Little, Margaret I. (1960). On basic unity. *International Journal of Psychoanalysis, 41,* 377–
    384.
Logsdon, F. M. (1960). Age-regression in diagnosis and treatment of acrophobia. *American
    Journal of Clinical Hypnosis, 3,* 108–109.
Lombard, Lisa, Kahn, Stephen, & Fromm, Erika (in press). The role of imagery in self-
    hypnosis: Its relationship to personality characteristics and gender. *International Journal
    of Clinical and Experimental Hypnosis.*
London, Perry (1962). Hypnosis in children: An experimental approach. *International Jour-
    nal of Clinical and Experimental Hypnosis, 10,* 79–91.
London, Perry, Hart, Joseph, & Leibovitz, Morris (1968). EEG alpha rhythms and suscep-
    tibility to hypnosis. *Nature, 219,* 71–72.
Ludwig, Arnold M. (1966). Altered states of consciousness. *Archives of General Psychiatry,
    15,* 225–234.

Ludwig, Arnold M., Lyle, William H., & Miller, Jerome S. (1964). Group hypnotherapy techniques with drug addicts. *International Journal of Clinical and Experimental Hypnosis, 12,* 53–65.

Mahler, Margaret S. (1972). On the first three sub-phases of the separation-individuation process. *International Journal of Psychoanalysis, 53,* 333–338.

Mahler, Margaret S., & McDevitt, John B. (1982). Thoughts on the emergence of the sense of self, with particular emphasis on the body self. *Journal of the American Psychoanalytic Association, 30,* 827–848.

Mahler, Margaret S., Pine, Fred, & Bergman, Annie (1975). *The psychological birth of the human infant: Symbiosis and individuation.* New York: Basic Books.

Malmö, Robert B., Boag, Thomas J., & Raginsky, Bernard B. (1954). Electromyographic study of hypnotic deafness. *International Journal of Clinical and Experimental Hypnosis, 2,* 305–317.

Malmö, Robert B., Davis, John F., & Barza, Sidney. (1954). Total hysterical deafness: An experimental case study. *Journal of Personality, 21,* 188–204.

Maltsberger, John T., & Buie, Dan H. (1980). The devices of suicide: Revenge, riddance, and rebirth. *International Review of Psycho-Analysis, 7,* 61–72.

Marks, Isaac M. (1969). *Fears and phobias.* London: Heinemann.

Marks, Isaac M., Gelder, M. G., & Edwards, Griffith. (1968). Hypnosis and desensitization for phobias: A controlled prospective trial. *British Journal of Psychiatry, 114,* 1263–1274.

Mason, Russell E. (1961). *Internal perception and bodily functioning.* New York: International Universities Press.

Masterson, James F. (1976). *Psychotherapy of the borderline adult: A developmental approach.* New York: Brunner/Mazel.

Masterson, James F. (1981). *The narcissistic and borderline disorders: An integrated developmental approach.* New York: Brunner/Mazel.

Mavissakalian, Matig, & Barlow, David (1981). Phobia: An overview. In Matig Mavissakalian and David Barlow (Eds.), *Phobia: Psychological and pharmacological treatment.* New York: Guilford Press.

May, Philip R. A. (1968). *Treatment of schizophrenia: A comparative study of five treatment methods.* New York: Science House.

McCord, Hallack (1961). The "image" of the trance. *International Journal of Clinical and Experimental Hypnosis, 9,* 305–307.

McGuinness, Thomas P. (1984) Hypnosis in the treatment of phobias: A review of the literature. *American Journal of Clinical Hypnosis, 26,* 261–272.

Meerloo, Joost A. (1968) Delayed mourning in victims of extermination camps. In Henry Krystal (Ed.), *Massive psychic trauma* (pp. 72–75). New York: International Universities Press.

Meichenbaum, Donald H. (1972). Cognitive modification of test anxious college students. *Journal of Consulting and Clinical Psychology, 39,* 370–380.

Meissner, William W. (1981). *Internalization in psychoanalysis. Psychological Issues.* Monograph 50. New York: International Universities Press.

Melnick, Joseph, & Russell, Ronald (1976). Hypnosis versus systematic desensitization in the treatment of test anxiety. *Journal of Counseling Psychology, 23,* 291–295.

Mesmer, Franz Anton (1774). Memoire sur la découverte du magnetisme animal. Geneva. Avec le Precis historique écrite par M. Paradis en mars 1777. Paris: Didot, 1779. English version: Mesmerism by Doctor Mesmer: Dissertation on the discovery of animal magnetism. 1779. (V. R. Myers, trans.). Published with G. Frankau, Introductory monograph. London: Macdonald, 1948. Abridged version of Myer's translation in Jan Ehrenwald (Ed.), *From Medicine to Freud: An Anthology,* edited, with notes. New York: Dell, 1956, pp. 256–280. Second edition: *Memoir of F. A. Mesmer, doctor of medicine, on his discoveries,* (J. Eden, trans.) Mt. Vernon, NY: Eden Press, 1957.

Miller, Arnold (1985). Hypnotherapy in a case of dissociated incest. *International Journal of Clinical and Experimental Hypnosis, 34,* 1–6.

Mitchell, Meredith B. (1976). *Hypnotizability and distractibility. American Journal of Clinical Hypnosis, 13,* 35–45.

Modell, Arnold H. (1948). The theoretical implications of hallucinatory experience in schizophrenia. *Journal of the American Psychoanalytic Association, 6,* 442–480.

Modell, Arnold H. (1968). *Object love and reality.* New York: International Universities Press.

Mordey, Theobold (1965). Conditioning of appropriate behavior to anxiety producing stimuli: Hypnotherapy of a stage fright case. *American Journal of Clinical Hypnosis, 8,* 117–121.

Morgan, Arlene H., & Hilgard, Ernest R. (1973). Age differences in susceptibility to hypnosis. *International Journal of Clinical and Experimental Hypnosis, 21,* 78–85.

Morgan, Arlene H., & Hilgard, Josephine R. (1978–1979). The Stanford Hypnotic Clinical Scale for Children. *American Journal of Clinical Hypnosis, 21,* 148–155.

Morgan, Arlene H., Johnson, David L., & Hilgard, Ernest R. (1974). The stability of hypnotic susceptibility: A longitudinal study. *International Journal of Clinical and Experimental Hypnosis, 22,* 249–257.

Morrier, Edward J. (1984). Passivity as a sequel to combat trauma. *Journal of Contemporary Psychotherapy, 14,* 99–113.

Mosey, Anne C. (1969). Treatment of pathological distortion of body image. *American Journal of Occupational Therapy, 23,* 413–416.

Moskowitz, Arnold E. (1964). A clinical and experimental approach to the evaluation and treatment of a conversion reaction with hypnosis. *International Journal of Clinical and Experimental Hypnosis, 12,* 218–227.

Mühl, Anita (1952). Automatic writing and hypnosis. In Leslie M. LeCron (Ed.), *Experimental Hypnosis* (pp. 426–438). New York: Macmillan.

Murphy, Lois B. (1962). *The widening world of childhood.* New York: Basic Books.

Murray, Henry A. (1967) Dead to the World: Passions of Herman Melville. In Edwin S. Shneidman (Ed.), *Essays in self-destruction* (pp. 7–29). New York: Science House.

Nace, Edgar P., Meyers, Andrew L., O'Brien, Charles P., Ream, Norman, & Mintz, Jim (1977) Depression in veterans two years after Vietnam. *American Journal of Psychiatry, 134,* 167–170.

Naruse, Gosaku (1965). The hypnotic treatment of stage fright in champion athletes. *International Journal of Clinical and Experimental Hypnosis, 13,* 63–70.

Nash, Michael R., Johnson, Lynn S., & Tipton, Ronnie D. (1979) Hypnotic age regression and the occurrence of transitional object relationships. *Journal of Abnormal Psychology, 88,* 547–555.

Newman, C. Janet (1976). Children of disaster: Clinical observations at Buffalo Creek. *American Journal of Psychiatry, 133,* 306–310.

Niederland, William G. (1968). An interpretation of the psychological stresses and defenses in concentration-camp life and the late after-effects. In Henry Krystal (Ed.), *Massive psychic trauma* (pp. 60–72). New York: International Universities Press.

Novey, Samuel. (1959). A clinical view of affect theory in psychoanalysis. *International Journal of Psychoanalysis, 40,* 94–104.

O'Brien, Richard M., Cooley, Lewis E., Ciotti, Joseph, & Henninger, Kathleen M. (1981). Augmentation of systematic desensitization of snake phobia through posthypnotic dream suggestion. *American Journal of Clinical Hypnosis, 23,* 231–238.

O'Connell, Donald Neil (1964). An experimental comparison of hypnotic depth measured by self-ratings and by an objective scale. *International Journal of Clinical and Experimental Hypnosis, 12,* 34–46.

O'Donnell, John M. (1978). Implosive therapy with hypnosis in the treatment of cancer phobia: A case report. *Psychotherapy: Theory, Research and Practice, 15,* 8–12.

Orne, Martin T. (1959). The nature of hypnosis: Artifact and essence. *Journal of Abnormal and Social Psychology, 58,* 277–299.

Orne, Martin T. (1977). The construct of hypnosis: Implications of the definition for research and practice. *Annals of the New York Academy of Science, 296,* 14–33.

Orne, Martin T., & Evans, Frederick J. (1966). Inadvertent termination of hypnosis with hypnotized and simulating subjects. *International Journal of Clinical and Experimental Hypnosis, 14,* 61–78.

Orne, Martin T., Sheehan, Peter W., & Evans, Frederick J. (1968). Occurrence of posthypnotic behavior outside the experimental setting. *Journal of Personality and Social Psychology, 9,* 189–196.

Ornstein, Anna (1980–81). Transferences as differential diagnostic tools in psychoanalysis. *International Journal of Psychoanalytic Psychotherapy, 8,* 115–123.

Ornstein, Paul H. (1974). On narcissism: Beyond the introduction. *Annual Review of Psychoanalysis, 2,* 127–149.

Ornstein, Robert E. (1970). *On the experience of time.* Baltimore: Penguin Books.

Parson, Erwin R. (1984). The reparation of the self: Clinical and theoretical dimensions in the treatment of Vietnam combat veterans. *Journal of Contemporary Psychotherapy, 14,* 4–56.

Patterson, Richard B. (1980). Hypnotherapy of hysterical monocular blindness: A case report. *American Journal of Clinical Hypnosis, 23,* 119–121.

Pelletier, Aleid M. (1977). Hysterical aphonia: A case report. *American Journal of Clinical Hypnosis, 20,* 149–153.

Perry, Jalna (1980). Psychotherapy with schizophrenics. Unpublished manuscript, McLean Hospital, Belmont, MA.

Pettinati, Helen M. (1983). *Multiple measures of hypnotizability in hospitalized psychiatric patients.* Presented at the Annual Meeting, Society of Clinical and Experimental Hypnosis, Boston, Ma.

Piaget, Jean (1950). *The psychology of intelligence.* New York: Harcourt, Brace.

Piaget, Jean (1969). The construction of reality in the child. (M. Cook, trans.). New York: Basic Books.

Prince, Morton (1906). *The dissociation of a personality.* New York: Longmans Green.

Pynoos, Robert S. & Eth, Spencer (1985). Developmental perspective on psychic trauma in childhood. In Charles R. Figley (Ed.), *Trauma and its wake: The study and treatment of post-traumatic stress disorder* (pp. 36–52). New York: Brunner/Mazel.

Rachman, S., & Hodgson, R. (1974). I. Synchrony and desynchrony in fear and avoidance. *Behavior Research & Therapy, 12,* 311–318.

Raikov, Vladimir L. (1980). Age regression to infancy by adult subjects in deep hypnosis. *American Journal of Clinical Hypnosis, 22,* 156–163.

Raikov, Vladimir L. (1982). Hypnotic age regression to the neonatal period: Comparisons with role playing. *International Journal of Clinical and Experimental Hypnosis, 30,* 108–116.

Rapaport, David (1967). Some metapsychological considerations concerning activity and passivity. In Merton M. Gill (Ed.), *The Collected Papers of David Rapaport* (pp. 530–568). New York: Basic Books.

Reardon, William T. (1971). A new group hypnotherapy. *Journal of the American Society of Psychosomatic Dentistry and Medicine, 18,* 60–66.

Reyher, Joseph, & Pottinger, Josephine. (1976). The significance of the interpersonal relationship in the induction of hypnosis. *American Journal of Clinical Hypnosis, 19,* 103–107.

Reich, Annie (1973). Pathologic forms of self-esteem regulation. In *Annie Reich: Psychoanalytic contributions.* New York: International Universities Press.

Reiff, Robert, & Scheerer, Martin (1959). Memory and hypnotic age regression: *Developmental aspects of cognitive function explored through hypnosis*. New York: International Universities Press.

Reilley, Robert R., Parisher, Darrel W., Carona, Anthony, & Dobrovolsky, Nicholas W. (1980). Modifying hypnotic susceptibility by practice and instruction. *International Journal of Clinical and Experimental Hypnosis, 28*, 39–45.

Reyher, Joseph (1963). Free imagery: An uncovering procedure. *Journal of Clinical Psychology, 19*, 454–459.

Ritterman, Michele (1983). *Using hypnosis in family therapy*. San Francisco: Jossey-Bass.

Roberts, Alan H., & Tellegen, Auke (1973). Ratings of "trust" and hypnotic susceptibility. *International Journal of Clinical and Experimental Hypnosis, 21*, 289–297.

Rosen, Harold (1953). *Hypnotherapy in clinical psychiatry*. New York: Julian Press.

Rosen, Harold (1960, May 23). Hypnosis: Deep sleep and danger. *Newsweek*, p. 107A.

Rosenberg, Elizabeth (1949). Anxiety and the capacity to bear it. *International Journal of Psychoanalysis, 30*, 1–11.

Rosenberg, Milton J. (1959). A disconfirmation of the description of hypnosis as a dissociated state. *International Journal of Clinical and Experimental Hypnosis, 7*, 187–204.

Rosenhan, D. (1969). Hypnosis and personality: A moderator variable analysis. In Léon Chertok (Ed.), *Psychophysiological mechanisms of hypnosis*. New York: Springer Verlag.

Rosenthal, Ted L. (1967). Stimulus modality and aerophobia: Cautions for desensitization therapy. *American Journal of Clinical Hypnosis, 9*, 269–274.

Roth, Martin (1959). The phobic-anxiety-depersonalization syndrome. *Proceedings of the Royal Society of Medicine, 52*, 587–595.

Sacerdote, Paul (1978). *Induced dreams: About the theory and therapeutic applications of dreams hypnotically induced*. Brooklyn, NY: Theo Gaus.

Sacerdote, Paul (1982). A non-statistical dissertation about hypnotizability scales and clinical goals: Comparison with individualized induction and deepening procedures. *International Journal of Clinical and Experimental Hypnosis, 30*, 354–376.

Sachs, Lewis B. (1971). Construing hypnosis as modifiable behavior. In A. Jacobs & Lewis B. Sachs (Eds.), *The psychology of private events* (pp. 61–75). New York: Academic Press.

Sachs, Lewis B., & Anderson, Warren L. (1967). Modification of hypnotic susceptibility. *International Journal of Clinical and Experimental Hypnosis, 15*, 172–180.

Sanders, Raymond S., & Reyher, Joseph (1969). Sensory deprivation and the advancement of hypnotic susceptibility. *Journal of Abnormal Psychology, 74*, 375–381.

Sandler, Joseph, & Rosenblatt, Bernard (1962). The concept of the representational world. *The Psychoanalytic Study of the Child, 17*, 128–145. New York: International Universities Press.

Sarbin, Theodore R. (1950). Mental changes in experimental regression. *Journal of Personality, 19*, 221–228.

Sarbin, Theodore R. & Coe, William C. (1972). *Hypnosis: A social psychological analysis of influence communication*. New York: Holt, Rinehart & Winston.

Sarbin, Theodore R., & Slagle, Robert W. (1979). Hypnosis and psychophysiological outcomes. In Erika Fromm & Ronald E. Shor (Eds.), *Hypnosis: Developments in research and new perspectives*. 2nd ed. (pp. 273–303). New York: Aldine.

Scagnelli, Joan (1975) Therapy with eight schizophrenic and borderline patients: Summary of a therapy approach that employs a semi-symbiotic bond between patient and therapist. *Journal of Clinical Psychology, 31*, 519–525.

Scagnelli, Joan (1976). Hypnotherapy with schizophrenic and borderline patients: A summary of therapy with eight patients. *American Journal of Clinical Hypnosis, 19*, 33–38.

Scagnelli, Joan (1977). Hypnotic therapy with a borderline schizophrenic: A case of dream therapy. *American Journal of Clinical Hypnosis, 20,* 136–145.

Schafer, Donald W. & Hernandez, Abilio (1978). Hypnosis, pain and the context of therapy. *International Journal of Clinical and Experimental Hypnosis, 26,* 143–153.

Schneck, Jerome M. (1959). *Hypnosis in modern medicine.* Springfield, IL: Charles C. Thomas.

Schneck, Jerome M. (1966a). A study of alterations in body sensations during hypnoanalysis. *International Journal of Clinical and Experimental Hypnosis, 24,* 216–231.

Schneck, Jerome M. (1966b). Hypnoanalytic elucidation of a childhood germ phobia. *International Journal of Clinical and Experimental Hypnosis, 14,* 305–307.

Schroetter, Karl (1951). Experimental dreams. In David Rapaport (Ed.), *Organization and pathology of thought: Selected sources.* New York: Columbia University Press. pp. 234–248.

Schur, Max (1953), The ego in anxiety. In Rudolph M. Loewenstein (Ed.), *Drives, affects, behavior* (pp. 67–84). New York: International Universities Press.

Schur, Max (1955). Comments on the metapsychology of somatization. *The Psychoanalytic Study of the Child, 10,* 119–164. New York: International Universities Press.

Schwartz, Wynn (1978). Time and context during hypnotic involvement. *International Journal of Clinical and Experimental Hypnosis, 26,* 307–316.

Schwarz, Bert E., Bickford, Reginald, G., & Rasmussen, Waldemar (1955). Hypnotic phenomena, including hypnotically activated seizures, studied with the electroencephalogram. *Journal of Nervous & Mental Disease, 122,* 564–574.

Scott, David L. (1970). Treatment of a severe phobia for birds by hypnosis. *American Journal of Clinical Hypnosis, 12,* 146–149.

Scrignar, C. B. (1981). Rapid treatment of contamination phobia with handwashing compulsion by flooding with hypnosis. *American Journal of Clinical Hypnosis, 23,* 252–257.

Scurfield, Raymond M.. (1985) Post-trauma stress assessment and treatment: Overview and formulations. In Charles R. Figley (Ed.), *Trauma and its wake: The study and treatment of post-traumatic stress disorder* (pp. 219–256). New York: Brunner/Mazel,

Serlin, Florence Rhyn (1970). Techniques for the use of hypnosis in group therapy. *American Journal of Clinical Hypnosis, 12,* 177–202.

Shatan, Chaim F. (1973). The grief of soldiers: Vietnam combat veterans' self-help movement. *American Journal of Orthopsychiatry, 43,* 640–653.

Shatan, Chaim F. (1985). Have you hugged a Vietnam veteran today: The basic wound of catastrophic stress. In William E. Kelley (Ed.), *Post-traumatic stress disorder and the war veteran patient* (pp. 12–28). New York: Brunner/Mazel.

Shaw, H. L. (1977). A simple and effective treatment for flight phobia. *British Journal of Psychiatry, 130,* 229–232.

Sheehan, D. V., Latta, W. D., Regina, E. G., & Smith, G. M. (1979). Empirical assessment of Spiegel's Hypnotic Induction Profile and eye-roll hypothesis. *International Journal of Clinical and Experimental Hypnosis, 27,* 103–110.

Sheehan, Peter W. (1980). Factors influencing rapport in hypnosis. *Journal of Abnormal Psychology, 89,* 263–281.

Sheehan, Peter W. & McConkey, Kevin M. (1982) *Hypnosis and experience: The exploration of phenomena and process.* Hillsdale, NJ: Lawrence Erlbaum Associates.

Shor, Ronald E. (1959). Hypnosis and the concept of the generalized reality-orientation. *American Journal of Psychotherapy, 13,* 582–602.

Shor, Ronald E. (1960). The frequency of naturally occurring "hypnotic-like" experiences in the normal college population. *International Journal of Clinical and Experimental Hypnosis, 8,* 151–163.

Shor, Ronald E. (1962). Three dimensions of hypnotic depth. *International Journal of Clinical and Experimental Hypnosis, 10,* 23–38.

Shor, Ronald E. (1979). A phenomenological method for the measurement of variables important to an understanding of the nature of hypnosis. In Erika Fromm & Ronald E. Shor (Eds.), *Hypnosis: Research developments and new perspectives* (2nd ed., pp. 105–135). New York: Aldine.

Shor, Ronald E., & Easton, Randolph D. (1973). A preliminary report on research comparing self- and hetero-hypnosis. *American Journal of Clinical Hypnosis, 16,* 37–44.

Shor, Ronald E., & Orne, Emily C. (1962). *The Harvard Group Scale of Hypnotic Susceptibility, Form A.* Palo Alto, CA: Consulting Psychologists Press.

Shorr, Joseph E. (1972). *Psycho-imagination therapy.* New York: Intercontinental Medical Book.

Silberer, Herbert (1951). On symbol formation. In David Rapaport (Ed.) (pp. 208–223). *Organization and pathology of thought: Selected sources.* New York: Columbia University Press.

Silver, Steven M., & Kelly, William E. (1985). Hypnotherapy of post-traumatic stress disorder in combat veterans from WW II and Vietnam. In William E. Kelly (Ed.), *Post-Traumatic Stress Disorder and the War Veteran Patient* (pp. 211–233). New York: Brunner/Mazel.

Simmel, Ernst (1944). War neurosis. In Sándor Lorand (Ed.), *Psychoanalysis today* (pp. 227–248). New York: International Universities Press.

Singer, Jerome L. (1966). *Daydreaming.* New York: Random House.

Singer, Jerome L. (1979). Imagery and affect in psychotherapy: Elaborating private scripts and generating contexts. In Anees A. Sheikh & John T. Shaffer, (Eds.). *The potential of fantasy and imagination* (pp. 27–39). New York: Brandon House.

Sjoberg, B. M., Jr. & Hollister, L. E. (1965). The effects of psychotomimetic drugs on primary suggestibility. *Psychopharmacologia, 8,* 251–262.

Smith, Alexander H., Jr. (1984). Sources of efficacy in the hypnotic relationship—An object relations approach. In William C. Wester II & Alexander H. Smith, Jr., *Clinical hypnosis: A multidisciplinary approach.* Philadelphia: Lippincott.

Smith, Sydney (1977). The golden fantasy: A regressive reaction to separation anxiety. *International Journal of Psychoanalysis, 58,* 311–324.

Smyth, Larry D., & Lowy, Doug (1983). Auditory vigilance during hypnosis: A brief communication. *International Journal of Clinical and Experimental Hypnosis, 31,* 67–71.

Snaith, R. P. (1968). A clinical investigation of phobias: Part I. A critical examination of the existing literature. *British Journal of Psychiatry, 114,* 673–697.

Society for Clinical and Experimental Hypnosis. (1981). *Code of Ethics* (as amended October 9, 1980, New York, New York).

Sossi, Michael, Kahn, Stephen, & Fromm, Erika (in press). The relation of self-reports of hypnotic depth in self-hypnosis to hypnotic susceptibility and imagery production. *International Journal of Clinical and Experimental Hypnosis.*

Spanos, Nicholas P. (1971). Goal-directed fantasy and the performance of hypnotic test suggestions. *Psychiatry, 34,* 86–96.

Spanos, Nicholas P. (1982). Hypnotic behavior: A cognitive, social psychological perspective. *Research Communications in Psychology, Psychiatry and Behavior, 7,* 199–213.

Spanos, Nicholas P., & Bodorik, H. Lorraine (1977). Suggested amnesia and disorganized recall in hypnotic and task-motivated subjects. *Journal of Abnormal Psychology, 86,* 295–305.

Spanos, Nicholas P., Radtke-Bodorik, H. Lorraine & Stam, Henderikus J. (1980). Disorganized recall during suggested amnesia: Fact not artifact. *Journal of Abnormal Psychology, 89,* 1–19.

Spanos, Nicholas P., Rivers, Steven M. & Ross, Stewart (1977). Experienced involuntariness and response to hypnotic suggestions. In William E. Edmondston, Jr. (Ed.), Conceptual and investigative approaches to hypnosis and hypnotic phenomena. *Annals of The New York Academy of Science, 296,* 208–221.

Spanos, Nicholas P., Stam, Henderikus J., Rivers, Stephen M. & Radtke, H. Lorraine (1980) Meditation, expectation and performance on indices of nonanalytic attending. *International Journal of Clinical and Experimental Hypnosis, 28,* 244–251.

Spiegel, David (1981). Vietnam grief work using hypnosis. *American Journal of Clinical Hypnosis, 24,* 33–40.

Spiegel, David, Frischholz, Edward J., Maruffi, Brian, & Spiegel, Herbert (1981). Hypnotic responsivity and the treatment of flying phobia. *American Journal of Clinical Hypnosis, 23,* 239–247.

Spiegel, Herbert H., Shor, Joel, & Fishman, Sidney (1945). An hypnotic ablation technique for the study of personality development. *Psychosomatic Medicine, 7,* 272–278.

Spiegel, Herbert & Spiegel, David (1978). *Trance and treatment: Clinical uses of hypnosis.* New York: Basic Books.

Spiegel, Leo A. (1959). The self, the sense of self, and perception. *The Psychoanalytic Study of the Child, 14,* 81–109. New York: International Universities Press.

Spies, Gordon. (1979). Desensitization of test anxiety: Hypnosis compared with biofeedback. *American Journal of Clinical Hypnosis, 22,* 108–111.

Sroufe, L. Alan (1979). Socioemotional development. In Joy D. Osofsky (Ed.), *Handbook of infant development* (pp. 462–518). New York: Wiley.

Stein, Calvert (1963). The clenched fist technique as a hypnotic procedure in clinical psychotherapy. *American Journal of Clinical Hypnosis, 6,* 113–119.

Stern, Richard, & Marks, Isaac (1973). Brief and prolonged flooding: A comparison in agoraphobic patients. *Archives of General Psychiatry, 28,* 270–276.

Stolar, Donald S. (1975). The effect of positive social consequences upon hypnotic susceptibility and insusceptibility. (Doctoral dissertation. University of Chicago).

Stolar, Donald, & Fromm, Erika (1974). Activity and passivity of the ego in relation to the superego. *International Review of Psychoanalysis, 1,* 297–311.

Stolorow, Robert D., & Lachmann, Frank M. (1980). *Psychoanalysis of developmental arrests: Theory and treatment.* New York: International Universities Press.

Strayer, Richard, & Ellenhorn, Lewis (1975). Vietnam veterans: A study exploring adjustment patterns and attitudes. *Journal of Social Issues, 31,* 81–94.

Suinn, Richard M. (1981). Generalized anxiety disorder. In Samuel M. Turner (Ed.), *Behavioral theories and treatment of anxiety disorders* (pp. 279–320). New York: Plenum Press.

Suinn, Richard M., & Richardson, Frank (1971). Anxiety management training: A nonspecific behavior therapy program for anxiety control. *Behavior Therapy, 2,* 498–510.

Summit, Roland & Kryso, JoAnn (1978). Sexual abuse of children: A clinical spectrum. *American Journal of Orthopsychiatry, 48,* 237–251.

Surman, Owen S. (1979). Postnoxious desensitization: Some clinical notes on the combined use of hypnosis and systematic desensitization. *American Journal of Clinical Hypnosis, 22,* 54–60.

Sutcliffe, J. P., Perry, C. W., & Sheehan, Peter W. (1970). Relation of some aspects of imagery and fantasy to hypnotic susceptibility. *Journal of Abnormal Psychology, 76,* 279–287.

Tanay, Emanuel (1968). Initiation of psychotherapy with survivors of Nazi persecution. In Henry Krystal (Ed.), *Massive psychic trauma.* (pp. 219–233) New York: International Universities Press.

Tart, Charles T. (1963). Hypnotic depth and basal skin resistance. *International Journal of Clinical & Experimental Hypnosis, 11,* 81–92.

Tart, Charles T. (1966). Thought and imagery in the hypnotic state: Psychophysiological correlates. Paper presented at the American Psychological Association, New York.

Tart, Charles T. (Ed.) (1969). *Altered states of consciousness: A book of readings*. New York: Wiley.

Tart, Charles T. (1970a). Increases in hypnotizability resulting from a prolonged program for enhancing personal growth. *Journal of Abnormal Psychology, 75,* 260–266.

Tart, Charles T. (1970b). Self-report scales of hypnotic depth. *International Journal of Clinical and Experimental Hypnosis, 18,* 105–125.

Tart, Charles T. (1975). *States of consciousness*. New York: Dutton.

Tart, Charles T. (1979). Measuring the depth of an altered state of consciousness, with particular reference to self-report scales of hypnotic depth. In Erika Fromm & Ronald E. Shor, *Hypnosis: Developments in research and new perspectives* (2nd ed., pp. 567–601). New York: Aldine.

Taylor, A. J., & Frazer, A. G. (1982). The stress of post-disaster body handling and victim identification work. *Journal of Human Stress, 8,* 4–12.

Telch, Michael, Tearnan, Blake H., & Taylor, C. Barr (1983). Antidepressant medication in the treatment of agoraphobics: A critical review. *Behavior Research & Therapy, 21,* 505–518.

Tellegen, Auke, & Atkinson, Gilbert (1974). Openness to absorbing and self-altering experiences ("absorption"), a trait related to hypnotic susceptibility. *Journal of Abnormal Psychology, 83,* 268–277.

Thigpen, Corbett H., & Cleckley, Harvey M. (1957). *The three faces of Eve*. New York: McGraw-Hill.

Thorpe, Geoffrey L., & Burns, Laurence E. (1983). *The agoraphobic syndrome: Behavioral approaches to evaluation and treatment*. New York: Wiley.

Tilton, Peter (1983). Pseudo-orientation in time in the treatment of agoraphobia. *American Journal of Clinical Hypnosis, 25,* 267–269.

Titchener, James & Kapp, F. T. (1978). Post-traumatic decline. Paper presented at American Psychoanalytic Association Meeting, New York.

Tolpin, Marian. (1971). On the beginnings of a cohesive self: An application of the concept of transmuting internalization to the study of the transitional object and signal anxiety. *The Psychoanalytic Study of the Child, 26,* 316–353. New Haven: Yale University Press.

Tomkins, Silvan S. (1962–1963). *Affect, imagery, consciousness*. Vols. I & II. New York: Springer.

Trenerry, Max R., & Jackson, Thomas L. (1983). Hysterical dystonia successfully treated with post-hypnotic suggestion. *American Journal of Clinical Hypnosis, 26,* 42–44.

Tronick, Edward Z., Ricks, Margaret, & Cohn, Jeffrey M. (1982). Maternal and infant affective exchange: Patterns of adaptation. In Tiffany Field & Alan Fogel (Eds.), *Emotion and early interaction* (pp. 83–99). Hillsdale, NJ: Lawrence Erlbaum Associates.

True, Robert M. & Stephenson, Charles W. (1951). Controlled experiments correlating electro-encephalogram, pulse, and plantar reflexes with hypnotic age regression and induced emotional states. *Personality, 1,* 252–263.

Udolf, Roy (1981). *Handbook of hypnosis for professionals*. New York: Van Nostrand Reinhold Company.

Vaillant, George E. (1977). *Adaptation to life*. Boston: Little, Brown and Co.

Vaillant, George E. (1981). Dangers of psychotherapy in the treatment of alcoholism. In Margaret H. Bean and Norman E. Zinberg (Eds.) *Dynamic approaches to the understanding and treatment of alcoholism*. New York: The Free Press, A Division of Macmillan Publishing Co., Inc., 36–54.

Van der Hart, Onno (1981). Treatment of a phobia for dead birds: A case report. *The American Journal of Clinical Hypnosis, 23,* 263–265.

Van der Kolk, Bessel, Boyd, Helene., Krystal, John & Greenberg, Mark (1984). Post-traumatic stress disorder as a biologically based disorder: Implications of the animal model of inescapable shock. In Bessel A. van der Kolk (Ed.) *Post-traumatic stress disorder: Psychological and biological sequelae*. Washington, D.C.: American Psychiatric Press, Inc., 124–134.

Van Dyck, Richard, Spinhoven, Philip, & Commandeur, Jacques (1984a). Factoren van belang bij de werkzaamheid van toemkomstgerichte autohypnose bij fobische patienten (Important factors in future-oriented auto-hypnosis with phobic patients). *Kwartaalschrift voor directieve therapie en hypnose 4*, 26–41.

Van Dyck, Richard, Spinhoven, Philip, & Commandeur, Jacques (1984b). Klinische beschrijving en follow-up van de behandeling van vijf fobische patienten met toekomstgerichte zelfhypnose (Clinical description and follow-up of the treatment of five phobic patients with future-oriented self-hypnosis). *Kwartaalschrift voor directieve therapie en hypnose 4*, 131–154.

Van Nuys, David (1973). Meditation, attention, and hypnotic susceptibility: A correlational study. *International Journal of Clinical and Experimental Hypnosis, 21*, 59–69.

Venzlaff, Ulrich (1968). Forensic psychiatry of schizophrenia. In Henry Krystal (Ed.), *Massive psychic trauma* (pp. 110–125). New York: International Universities Press.

Volkan, Vamık (1976). *Primitive internalized object relations*. New York: International Universities Press.

Voth, Harold M. (1970). The analysis of metaphor. *Journal of the American Psychoanalytic Association, 18*, 599–621.

Wadden, Thomas A., & Anderton, Charles H. (1982). The clinical use of hypnosis. *Psychological Bulletin, 91*, 215–243.

Walk, Richard D. (1956). Self ratings of fear in a fear-invoking situation. *Journal of Abnormal and Social Psychology, 52*, 171–178.

Watkins, John G. (1947). Antisocial compulsions induced under hypnotic trance. *Journal of Abnormal and Social Psychology, 42*, 256–259.

Watkins, John G. (1949). *Hypnotherapy of war neurosis*. New York: Ronald Press.

Watkins, John G. (1971). The affect bridge: A hypnoanalytic technique. *International Journal of Clinical and Experimental Hypnosis, 19*, 21–27.

Watkins, John G. (1984). Multiple Personality. In Raymond Corsini & Bonie Ozaki (Eds.), *Encyclopedia of Psychology*. New York: Wiley.

Watkins, John G. & Watkins, Helen (1979). The theory and practice of ego state therapy. In Henry Grayson (Ed.), *Short-term approaches to psychotherapy* (pp. 176–220). New York: National Institute for the Psychotherapies and Human Sciences Press.

Watkins, Mary M. (1976). *Waking dreams*. New York: Gordon & Breach.

Watson, John B., & Raynor, Rosalie (1920). Conditioned emotional reactions. *Journal of Experimental Psychology, 3*, 1–14.

Weitzenhoffer, André M. (1957). *General techniques of hypnotism*. New York: Grune & Stratton.

Weitzenhoffer, André M. (1964). Explorations in hypnotic time distortion. I: Acquisitions of temporal reference frames under conditions of time distortion. *Journal of Nervous & Mental Disease, 138*, 354–366.

Weitzenhoffer, André M. (1974). When is an "instruction" an "instruction"? *International Journal of Clinical and Experimental Hypnosis, 22*, 258–269.

Weitzenhoffer, André M., & Hilgard, Ernest R. (1959). *Stanford Hypnotic Susceptibility Scale, Forms A & B*. Palo Alto, CA: Consulting Psychologists Press.

Weitzenhoffer, André M. & Hilgard, Ernest R. (1962). *Stanford Hypnotic Susceptibility Scale, Form C*. Palo Alto, CA: Consulting Psychologists Press.

Weitzenhoffer, André M., & Hilgard, Ernest R. (1963). *Stanford Profile Scales of Hypnotic Susceptibility, Forms I & II*. Palo Alto, CA: Consulting Psychologists Press.

Weitzenhoffer, André M., & Hilgard, Ernest R. (1967). *Stanford Profile Scales of Hypnotic Susceptibility, Forms I and II*. Palo Alto, CA: Consulting Psychologists Press.

Wexler, Milton. (1971). Schizophrenia: Conflict and deficiency. *Psychoanalytic Quarterly, 40,* 82–99.

White, Robert W. (1941). A preface to the theory of hypnotism. *Journal of Abnormal and Social Psychology, 36,* 477–505.

Wickramasekera, Ian (1973). Effects of electromyographic feedback on hypnotic susceptibility: More preliminary data. *Journal of Abnormal Psychology, 82,* 74–77.

Wilkins, Lee G., & Field, Peter B. (1968). Helpless under attack: Hypnotic abreaction in hysterical loss of vision. *American Journal of Clinical Hypnosis, 10,* 271–275.

Williamsen, John A., Johnson, Harold J. & Eriksen, Charles W. (1965). Some characteristics of posthypnotic amnesia. *Journal of Abnormal Psychology, 70,* 123–131.

Wilson, Arnold, & Fromm, Erika. (1982). Aftermath of the concentration camp: The second generation. *Journal of the American Academy of Psychoanalysis, 10,* 289–313.

Wilson, G. Terence (1984). Fear reduction methods and the treatment of anxiety disorders. In Cyril M. Franks, G. Terrance Wilson, Phillip C. Kendall, & Kelly D. Brownell (Eds.), *Annual review of behavior therapy: Vol. X* (pp. 87–122). New York: Guilford Press.

Wilson, John P., Smith, Wiken, & Johnson, Suzanne K. (1985). A comparative analysis of PTSD among various survivor groups. In Charles R. Figley (Ed.), *Trauma and its wake: The study and treatment of post-traumatic stress disorder* (pp. 142–172). New York: Brunner/Mazel.

Winnicott, Donald W. (1953). Transitional objects and transitional phenomena. *International Journal of Psychoanalysis, 34,* 89–99.

Winnicott, Donald W. (1958). *Collected papers.* New York: Basic Books.

Winnicott, Donald W. (1960). Ego distortion in terms of the true and false self. In *The maturational processes and the facilitating environment* (pp. 140–152). New York: International Universities Press.

Winnicott, Donald W. (1965). *The maturational processes and the facilitating environment: Studies in the theory of emotional development.* New York: International Universities Press.

Wolberg, Lewis R. (1945). *Hypnoanalysis.* (2nd ed.) New York: Grune & Stratton.

Wolberg, Lewis R. (1948). *Medical hypnosis. Vol I & II.* New York: Grune & Stratton.

Wolpe, Joseph (1958). *Psychotherapy by reciprocal inhibition.* Stanford, CA: Stanford University Press.

Woody, Robert H. (1973). Clinical suggestion and systematic desensitization. *The American Journal of Clinical Hypnosis, 15,* 250–257.

Zaccheo, Dominic, & Palmer, Michael B. (1980). Agorophobic-like behavior treated by recognition of and systematic desensitization to the theme, loss of control: A case report. *The Behavior Therapist, 3,* 7–8.

Zaretsky, Irving I., & Leone, Mark P. (1974). *Religious movements in contemporary America.* Princeton: Princeton University Press.

Ziegler, Frederick J., & Imboden, John B. (1962). Contemporary conversion reactions: II. A conceptual model. *Archives of General Psychiatry, 6,* 279–287.

Zilboorg, Gregory (1933). Anxiety without affect. *Psychoanalytic Quarterly, 2,* 48–67.

Zimbardo, Philip G., Marshall, Gary, & Maslach, Christina (1971). Liberating behavior from time-bound control: Expanding the present through hypnosis. *Journal of Applied Social Psychology, 1,* 305–323.

Zimbardo, Philip G., Marshall, Gary, White, Greg, & Maslach, Christina (1973). Objective assessment of hypnotically induced time distortion. *Science, 181,* 282–284.

Author Index

Subject Index